A SHORT HISTORY OF PARLIAMENT.

BY

B. C. SKOTTOWE, M.A.

NEW COLLEGE, OXFORD.

*Author of "Our Hanoverian Kings;" "Outlines of Constitutional History,"
etc., etc.*

ARDVA QVÆ PVLCRA

London:

SWAN SONNENSCHEIN, LOWREY & CO.,

PATERNOSTER SQUARE.

1886.

Butler & Tanner,
The Selwood Printing Works,
Frome, and London.

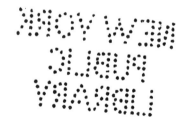

PREFACE.

THE idea of writing a short history of Parliament was first suggested to me by Mr. F. S. Pulling, of Exeter, who at one time I thought would have shared in the work. Circumstances, however, prevented this, and the book ultimately assumed a somewhat different form from that projected at first. The object with which it was written was the hope of imparting a certain amount of life to the dry bones which are strewn in the way of the constitutional student, and of combining instruction with a certain amount of amusement. Whether the effort has been successful or not the reader must judge for himself.

I must here take the opportunity to render my acknowledgments to Mr. F. York Powell, Mr. C. H. Carmichael, and Mr. A. B. Beaven for the kind assistance which they have rendered me—especially the latter, who undertook the laborious task of revising the whole of the MS. dealing with the period after 1660.

I am indebted to the kindness of Sir George Sitwell for a very early illustration of parliamentary corruption—an isolated evidence but sufficiently pregnant of meaning.

Extract from the will of Nicholas Stathum, Esq., of

Morley, co. Derby, dated 15 July, 1472, and proved on the fifth of August in the same year in the prerogative court Canterbury.

"*Item*, I received 10*s.* of . . . Bemont a worshippful Squier of the West Country by the hands of Page in the last Parleament. I did nothing there . . and if I did, it is against my conscience for so moche as I was one of the Parleament and should be indifferent in every matter of the Parleament, I will he have it ageyne."

OXFORD, 1886.

SHORT HISTORY OF PARLIAMENT.

CHAPTER I.

FORMATION OF PARLIAMENT.

SECTION 1.—*Folk-moots and Witena-gemôts.*

THE earliest form of National Assembly known to English History differed very considerably in character from the)dern Talking Machine which fills so many columns of the ily papers with its proceedings. Yet the connection between e Parliament and the Anglo-Saxon tribal meetings of freeholders olk-moot) is so intimate that the historian is justified in declar- ʒ that the former is but the latter transfigured and glorified nost beyond all recognition. Generations of different architects ve built, restored, improved on the original design with untiring rseverance and zeal, have reared a huge square keep in the ntre, have girdled it with successive circles of ramparts, bas- ins, and towers, have faced it with vast earthworks of the most proved modern construction, and dug deep ditches to bar the iset of the rude invader. Yet, though lost to sight, almost to emory, buried deeply amid the medley of later forms and styles, ere lies somewhere in the centre the solid Saxon masonry of the iginal foundation from which the completed structure has really rung.

The history of the British Parliament is in fact a record of ntinual growth, of wise and judicious pruning and training, of nstantly increasing energy and strength at each successive velopment.

B

It possesses therefore a curious interest, not merely for thos
who desire to study the most important and most interestin
branch of the history of their country, but also for the intelligen
historical student of every age and race.   For it is unique in th
annals of the nations.   Diets and Dietines, Things, States-General
Estates of every kind and tongue, which may be regarded a
foreign equivalents for some form of a Parliament, have existed a
different times in most of the European countries, and, springin
from the same origin as the Saxon Folk-moot, were graduall
dwarfed by the growth and stifled by the baleful shadow of des
potic monarchies or aristocracies, till they drooped and died pre
maturely, or survived ingloriously to draw on a wasted, shrunker
existence in an unhealthy atmosphere that was fatal to whole
some life.   The present century, it is true, has witnessed a grea
outburst or renaissance of constitutional forms and representative
assemblies on the Continent ; but they have sprung full-grown
from the heads of their creators, they are in no sense the result
of natural development, and in most cases they were directly
borrowed, with suitable or unsuitable modifications, from the
English Parliament itself.   The modern form of the English Parliament is, however, essentially the result of growth, and of growth
in a favourable atmosphere under natural conditions.   Its history
therefore possesses the unique attraction and advantage, that it
retraces its way step by step, without a single stop or break, right
back to the very origin of the English nation, and far beyond, till
it fades faintly away in the dim mists of prehistoric time.   It will
be enough, however, for the purpose at present in view if we
content ourselves with a very brief sketch of the earlier assemblies,
as a slight introduction to the more important chapters of parliamentary history which follow.

The Anglo-Saxon Witena-gemót, or Meeting of the Wise Men,
in its historical form, was an assembly of the important officials
of the kingdom, summoned by special invitation from the king
to meet at the place where he might happen to be staying.   Their
business was to advise him with regard to the government of the
kingdom ; and they probably expressed their opinions pretty freely
on all subjects, though it by no means follows that it produced
much effect.   It was an understood rule, that no new laws, and

nothing affecting a man's life or property, should be imposed without the consent of the people, which was obtained in later days by consulting a fairly large assembly of the freeholders; but, as a rule, the king's opinion had very considerable weight in the more ordinary administrative business, as perhaps was natural. Of course, all this must have varied considerably with the character and personal authority of individual kings; in the weak reign of Edward the Confessor, for instance, the king's opinion was not by any means so much thought of as that of powerful and popular nobles like Godwine, Leofric, and Siward. There was one right, however, which the Witan were always particular about—the appointment of the heir to the Crown. Sometimes this was done during the king's lifetime, at his special request; but the usual thing was to wait till his death, and then elect his eldest son, if of age and capable, or, if not, some one else from the royal family—generally the late king's younger brother.

The rights of the Witan tended to become pure formalism after the Conquest, for the Norman kings were practically absolute, and they legislated, taxed, and ruled at pleasure, unchecked by anything save the fear of rebellion. The forms of the Saxon Constitution were preserved, it is true, and during the Conqueror's reign the Witan met about three times a year. But they did not do much; they were far more like a court or levée, for purposes of display than a business-like affair, though they undoubtedly *did* transact business now and then.

The actual government of the country, however, was carried on by a much smaller body, which consisted roughly of the principal barons and bishops and some professional assistants, and was known by various names, such as the Ordinary Council, or the King's Court. But it is important to remember that under every form and title it was regarded simply as representing the Witan; the rights which it exercised were the rights of the Witan, its members were all members of the Witena-gemót as well, and its powers and existence merged wholly in those of the Witan when the latter assembled. The fiction, in short, was, that the Witan governed the country; the fact was, that this permanent commission did. The importance of this fiction was, however, unusually great, for it enabled the National Council to preserve powers which it must otherwise have infallibly lost, and to reassert its authority later without any difficulty when it became stronger.

After the death of the Conqueror, the regular yearly meetings of the Witan appear to have been dropped; but we really know very little on the subject till the reign of Henry II., when there was a great advance.

The Witan were frequently summoned, and were consulted on business of every kind; for Henry, conscious of his real power, and fully realizing the advantage he derived from the advice of prac tical men, never hesitated to ask for counsel when he required it. Their legislative powers, however, were still very shadowy; and the legal regulations or ordinances of Henry II. (Assizes) were as much due to the absolute will of the monarch solely, as the charters of the Norman kings were. The most decided advance is on the question of taxation, and this takes the form of an, as yet, extremely misty theory, that a man should not be taxed with out his own consent. It is true that the king still initiates all fresh taxation; that there is no record of a debate on finance till the reign of Richard I., and that individual opposition was no doubt, as a rule, overcome by force. But there are a few cases of distinct and successful refusal to contribute their share on the part of men high in office—such refusals being based simply on disapproval of. the nature or objects of the tax; but it seems probable that in such cases the only result of individual action was the exemption of the individual from the operation of the tax in question.

At the end of the twelfth century, therefore, the English Government was still practically a despotism, though its despotic character was considerably veiled by the constant use of con stitutional forms. The natural consequence, however, of the overwhelming strength of the Government, was the growth of a spirit of opposition, which as yet only manifested itself occa sionally in isolated instances; but might, under unusual pressure, develop into a powerful constitutional force. The misgovern ment of John supplied the necessary pressure, and united the whole nation in a stern determination to place some restrictions on the power which had been so grossly abused. John was compelled to set his seal to a declaration which implies throughout that the royal power was not absolute, but limited by custom and the rights of the people.   This document is known as Magna Carta.

The clauses dealing with the National Council were not, however, very extensive in scope.   One of them declared that the Great Council was to consist of all the tenants-in-chief, the greater tenants being summoned by special writs addressed to them personally, the lesser by general writs addressed to the sheriffs, thus fixing the widest form of the Council as the legal one.   The second clause prescribed that no aid or scutage,—a form of feudal taxation which hitherto had been levied purely at the pleasure of the king,—should be raised for the future without the consent of the National Council.   Certain special classes of aids, which were recognised as within the king's right, but could only be levied on three definite occasions in each reign, were ordered to be taken at a reasonable rate.   Scanty as these provisions were, they implied more than appeared on the surface ; and though they were *put in abeyance in the re-issues of the Charter*, the principles they embodied survived.   It was recognised that taxation was not a right exercised by the king, but a concession granted by the people ; and this view was confirmed by a clause in the re-issue of 1225, stating that the king granted the rights contained in the Charter on consideration of a gift of money.   Additional weight, moreover, was lent to this principle by the growth of taxation on movables, which affected all, and which could be based on no feudal fiction of an aid due to the lord.   Abundant evidence, moreover, exists of the reality of this principle in the frequent debates on taxation which occur during the reign of Henry III., and numerous positive refusals on the part of the barons to grant money, on the ground of extravagance and misgovernment.   The theory, however, that consent was necessary to taxation, stopped short as yet at the tenants-in-chief.   The feudal council still insisted on its right to bind the realm ; and if the king occasionally consulted the shire-courts on taxation, it was only in the hope of gaining more by private bargain with them than had been granted by the Council.

The reign of Henry III. was, in fact, one long struggle between the king and the barons, on the subject of taxation and the appointment and position of ministers—the former endeavouring to reassert the old view, that money could be raised at the royal pleasure, the latter striving to maintain the modern theory, that it could not be levied without the consent of the National Council, and yet yielding again and again to the insatiate demands of the king.   At last, however, continued misgovernment and over-taxation culminated in a crisis similar to that which had produced Magna Carta.   The barons in the Parliament of Oxford, 1258, under the leadership of the Earls of Leicester and Gloucester demanded from the king a long list of reforms, including the appointment of a small permanent ministerial council, to which was to be entrusted the entire management of the government and control of taxation.   To this demand the king was obliged to assent.

The new system, however, was bad in itself; it narrowed considerably the already too narrow limits of the legislative and financial council; it reduced the royal authority almost to a shadow; and it handed over almost all power to a small committee of a particular class, who .had had no experience as yet in government, and must infallibly quarrel among themselves. It is not singular, therefore, that it fell to pieces almost immediately.

Section 2.—*Simon de Montfort.*

Simon de Montfort, the second son of the Simon de Montfort renowned in the Albigensian Crusade, was by accident of birth a foreigner, though descended in the female line from English nobles.   The elder Simon had inherited from his mother certain claims to the English earldom of Leicester, which by special arrangement were transmitted to his second son.   During his early career the younger Simon gave little promise of fulfilling the part of patriot and statesman which he subsequently assumed. He was high in favour with Henry III.   He even incurred the resentment of the barons by a secret marriage with Henry's sister Eleanor.   But the king was fickle and changeable.   He quarrelled with Montfort as he had quarrelled with Hubert de Burgh before, equally without reason; only, however, to as sud-

enly and unaccountably restore him to favour in a very brief
pace of time, conferring on him the government of Gascony.
kill and severity combined enabled Simon to restore temporary
rder to this turbulent province; but, at the same time, created
or him many enemies, and gave Henry a fresh opportunity of
howing his ingratitude and folly. Giving ear to the complaints
f the Gascons—his own enemies and Simon's—he dismissed the
arl with bitter insult, only to find himself compelled shortly
fter to supplicate his assistance as the one hope of preserving
iascony to the English Crown.

From the return of Simon to England in 1254, he played an
mportant, though at first unconspicuous, part in the history of
his country. His merits were beginning to be recognised; and
is rise, though slow and almost unobserved, was steady and sure.
He had many claims to be ranked as a leader. In Gascony he
ad shown himself a statesman and general of no ordinary skill.
Past history proved that in the pursuit of right he would go far
nd fearlessly, even in defiance of the royal will. Above all, it
vas felt that he could be trusted, that he would remain firm to
he very death in the course he had chosen, that not all the
errors of this world or the next would turn him from his
lighted word. It was natural therefore that he should take a
prominent part in the crisis of 1258, though in the settlement
rranged at Oxford his views were overborne by the ambition
nd interest of the other barons. It seems impossible that he
could have approved of the oligarchy they proposed to establish;
t is even stated by one authority that he expressed his dis-
pproval with considerable vigour. When therefore it became
evident that the views of his colleagues were purely personal,
hat, satisfied with having obtained the government, they would
not proceed to reforms, that their incapacity and selfishness would
enable the king to reassert his old position, then Simon broke
vith them entirely, and stood forth as the champion of constitutional reform. This split in the baronial camp was followed
by a complete rearrangement of parties. Many of the barons
oined the king forthwith; some few only remained faithful to
Simon. His greatest strength, however, lay in the towns; and it
was their assistance alone which enabled him to resist the grow-

ing power of Henry, who was supported by the majority of the
baronage, the excommunications of the Pope, and the favour of
the King of France. Civil war broke out at last; but, overmatched as he was, Earl Simon contrived by superior generalship
to inflict a severe defeat on the royal army at Lewes, May 14,
1264, which gave the king into his hands as a prisoner, and
made him master of the kingdom.

A new scheme of government was at once drawn up, with the
assistance of a Parliament assembled at London, at which representatives of the counties were present. The supreme power was
still to reside in the king, but he was to exercise it only with the
consent of a Permanent Council of nine, nominated at first, and
to be supervised for a while, by Three Electors, of whom the Earl
of Leicester was naturally one. These councillors were to hold
office during good behaviour. In theory this form of government
was excellent, in practice it would have worked badly ; for the
electors were all partisans of Earl Simon, the councillors were
merely his nominees, and the government was thus committed
into the hands of a small party, to the exclusion of the great
majority of the realm. That part of the scheme, however, which
marks the most decided advance in constitutional principles was
the enlargement of the limits of the National Council. To the
Parliament of 1265, in addition to his baronial and ecclesiastical
partisans, Montfort summoned two knights from every shire
through the sheriffs, and two burgesses from every borough
through the officers of the borough, not merely for the grant of
taxation, but for the general discussion of public business. It
was no doubt the scanty numbers of his baronial supporters, and
the sturdy assistance furnished to him by the democracy, which
supplied the motive more than any definite plan of political
science ; but the fact invests the assembly of 1265 with unusual
importance as a broad landmark in constitutional and parliamentary history. Not that there was anything new in the idea
of representation ; the representative system had long been in
use in the local courts of the shires and hundreds for the
transaction of business, or in the calling of representatives to
the National Council ; they had occasionally been summoned
before during this century, though at long intervals, chiefly with

view to a grant of money. The importance of this assembly
es in the distinction definitely drawn between shire and borough
; political units, and in the recognition of the right of the people,
ot merely to be consulted on their own taxation, but also to
iare, however faintly, in the general government of the kingdom.
he first definite enunciation of this important constitutional
octrine is the real boon which England owes to Simon de
Iontfort; for it survived and proved fruitful in influence long
fter he and the Constitution he had sought to establish were
iined and destroyed. The fact, however, that this assembly was
ot a general convention of the tenants-in-chief or the three
states, destroys its title to be considered the first Parliament in
ie eyes of Dr. Stubbs

Events moved rapidly in 1265. Quarrels broke out among the
aronial leaders. Ambition, envy, personal hatred, returning
oyalty, discontent, treachery, and headstrong rashness, all
hirled together in a mad walpurgis dance, which ended in the
out at Evesham and the death of Earl Simon. Henry III.
eascended his throne in triumph, and for a while it seemed
s though the great patriot had lived and died in vain. Perhaps,
owever, it was best for his own fame, and best for England, that
e died when he did. He could not have ruled better than
Idward I., and he might have ruled far worse. He had all the
xperience which Edward brought in later years to the govern-
ient of the country, but he could never have ruled independently
f party, and he must in the long run have relied chiefly upon
orce to maintain his position against the royalists.

SECTION 3.—*The First Parliament.*

In the case of Earl Simon the good that he did lived after him,
he evil only was buried with his bones. The weaker parts of
iis Constitution fell to pieces at his death, the stronger alone
urvived him. He had set an example and fostered a growing
irinciple. They remained, working steadily and silently on the
xpectation of the people, and waiting for the new generation, to
vhose eyes they would come unsoiled by the passions and the
iloodshed of the civil war. It is scarcely rash to assert that, when

Edward I. ascended the throne, the principle was indisputably established that no man *ought* to be taxed without his own consent, though there were almost insuperable difficulties in the way of maintaining this right if the king chose to ignore it ; and that the most convenient and satisfactory way of obtaining the consent of the realm on the subject of taxation was by summoning some form of representative council on the model of that assembled by Earl Simon in 1265, though the exact form was as yet a matter of considerable uncertainty.   Thus it is evident that it depended in no small measure on the character of the king whether the principle would be allowed any active vitality.   It was therefore extremely fortunate that Edward I. was essentially a lawyer, with. a lawyer's respect for forms and precedents, a man utterly intolerant of any uncertainty or vagueness in legal matters, with a real delight in his necessary task of defining and fixing, and, so to speak, crystallizing the formless, almost half-liquid, institutions of which the administrative system was composed, preferring to act invariably in a regular and formal manner, and considering himself as much bound by his own acts as any modern judge of the Queen's Bench would be by his own decisions.   It is difficult to praise him much without really over-rating him, and yet to decry or depreciate him is to do him less than justice.   He intended undoubtedly to fix the Constitution on a firm basis, he intended to build up a strong and good government ; but he certainly did not intend the government he actually created, far less to impose so many restrictions on the royal power.   It seems almost as though he had a hobby for arranging things in boxes and pigeon-holes, with dockets and labels, hardly realizing that he was dealing, not with inert masses of matter, but with chemical bodies, which, if rashly brought together, would perhaps unite to form a new substance of unknown properties that might destroy its own creator, if incautiously handled.   Therefore, while fully crediting Edward with the great work that he actually completed—namely, the formation of a constitutional monarchy—it is impossible to admit that he intended to create more than an orderly despotism. Circumstances, however, were too strong for him.   Men and institutions refused alike to obey his will to the full ; sometimes they moved farther than he had designed, sometimes they stopped

1alf-way, and stood, like Atlas, unremoved, defiant cf coercion.
io in the end he found perhaps, with some faint tinge of the
eeling which oppressed the unhappy Frankenstein, that instead
f the mere machine he had projected, he had created an organic
1eing, instinct with vigorous life, which could act independently
f its creator's will with superhuman strength that mocked his
wn.

As might be expected, Edward did not long leave the National
Council in the uncertain, shapeless state in which he found it,
1alting undecidedly between the Constitutions of 1215 and 1265.
Like everything else which he handled, he soon impressed it
1ith a definite stamp, which, with slight modifications, it still
1ears at the present day. It is this which entitles Edward to the
redit of the formation of Parliament.

At first, however, matters are terribly vague. It is not till
282 that we can speak with any certainty, and then it becomes
lear that Edward has at last realized the convenience of sum-
noning representatives from the country to speak in the name
1f the people and grant him money. This tardy awakening was
lue to the large expenses of the Welsh war and the utterly in-
.dequate amount of the ordinary feudal revenue. It became
1ecessary to ask for a general grant on movable property, and
his could be best done in some really representative National
Council. The result was, that between 1282–94, Edward devised
. variety of experiments, none of which appear to have satisfied
1im so well as that which is recorded in the year 1295, the result
1eing that the latter ultimately formed the model on which future
Parliaments were moulded.

The first experiment was of an extremely singular nature. In
282 the National Council met in three divisions at three different
1laces; and each division acted, to all intents and purposes, inde-
1endently of the others. This expedient was prompted partly by
1ecessity, partly by convenience, partly no doubt by the hope of
essening the chances of resistance. The barons, in fact, were
1ith the king in Wales; it was therefore impossible for them to
1e present at a Parliament held in England; it was equally im-
1ossible to hold it at the seat of war. By appointing two meeting-
1laces for the rest of the realm, the king certainly lessened the

inconvenience and expense for those summoned to attend ; while by dividing the resistance, he undoubtedly diminished at once the probability and the strength of it. The towns appointed in the summons were York and Northampton; and to them were summoned the higher clergy, the representatives of the lower clergy, four knights from each shire, and two representatives from each borough and market town. In this Parliament we get a glimpse of an idea which was peculiarly Edward's own—the representation of the lower clergy in Parliament—but which was destined to failure owing to the stubborn opposition of the clergy themselves. In 1283 another anomalous assembly was summoned to Shrewsbury, including the barons, prelates, two knights from each shire, and two representatives apiece from twenty-one speci- fied cities and boroughs ; the representatives of the lower clergy were not summoned on this occasion. In 1290 a purely feudal assembly of bishops and barons was summoned to impose an aid which fell solely on the tenants-in-chief, and therefore might be supposed to lie within the competence of such a council. Later in the year, however, it was reinforced by the addition of two knights from each shire, no doubt in order that it might confer a more general grant of a fifteenth of all movables. There is no distinct record that representatives were present at the Parliaments of 1292, 1293, though they may have been. In 1294, however, to a great Parliament assembled in October at Westminster, Edward summoned, in addition to the magnates, four knights from each shire.

In 1295, however, he went further. Stating definitely as the grounds of his action that "what affected all should have the consent of all," he called together a complete representative assembly of all the estates of the realm, based primarily on the model of the Council of 1265. The barons and higher clergy were summoned individually by special writs addressed to each personally. The bishops' summons wound up with an injunction (the *premunientes* clause) that they should cause the lower clergy to elect proctors to represent them in Parliament. General writs, moreover, were addressed to the sheriffs, ordering them to pro- cure the election of two knights for their shire, and two citizens, or burgesses, for every city or borough within their shire. This ssembly differed materially from all that had preceded it; it ormed a model on which subsequent Parliaments were based; nd it is this fact which has earned for it the name of the Model 'arliament. For though many anomalous assemblies were held t intervals after this date, and the parliamentary representation f the lower clergy became in a very short time a dead letter; et the assembly of 1295 undoubtedly was a pattern to which the iter custom of Parliament conformed, as a rule, in all essential oints of summons, constitution, and forms of proceeding. In 1e opinion of Dr. Stubbs, that year established such a precedent 1at no assembly subsequent to that date can be regarded as a 'arliament at all unless it conforms in the minutest details to the ules then laid down.

It is as well to notice, however, that though the fiat of the 3ishop of Chester has fixed the date of the first Parliament at the ear 1295, yet the term "Parliament" itself is far older than that ate, and had no special technical meaning to contemporary his- orians. To them it simply meant a *palaver*, or talking assembly, nd was a word of Italian origin, used as the translation of *olloquium*. It was frequently employed by the chroniclers of the hirteenth century to designate assemblies far different in constitu- ion from a Parliament in the legal sense of the term, and among others it was applied to the council appointed by the barons at)xford, 1258. The earliest recorded use of the expression is in he year 1246. For the future, however, it will be used with the pecial significance ascribed to it by Dr. Stubbs, that of a repre- entative assembly modelled more or less exactly on the pattern of the Parliament of 1295.

CHAPTER II.

THE FORMATION OF PARLIAMENTARY GOVERNMENT. (1295-1460.)

SECTION 1.—*Historical Survey.*

ALMOST the first act of Parliament, when it was once definitely established on its present constitutional basis, was to assert its right to that control of the purse which was to prove its most irresistible instrument in the future. Unusual demands on the part of Edward I. for warlike purposes, in 1296, at last provoked the opposition of the barons, which was backed up by the support of the whole realm. Finally, Edward was compelled to grant in Parliament, 1297, a statute (the Confirmatio Cartarum)[1] which consisted of a reissue and confirmation of Magna Carta, and the Forest Charter, and some additional clauses intended to deprive the Crown of the power of arbitrary taxation which it had endeavoured to assume. The addition of these provisions was equivalent to a reinsertion in fuller detail of the constitutional clauses which had been omitted in the reissues of the Charter in the year 1216 and onwards. This statute forms an imperfect recognition of the great principle which was by this time thoroughly established and understood,,that no taxes ought to be levied without the consent of the nation expressed by the National Council. For nearly a century more, however, the fact was not fully comprehended by the king, and the imperfect nature of the prohibitions contained in the Confirmatio left ample room for raising money in ways which, though clearly against the spirit, did not exactly violate the letter of the law. For nearly a century, therefore, Parliament was occupied with remedial statutes, stopping up a loophole here, strengthening a weak place there, filling up with tireless patience the innumerable gaps and rents which the sword of the prerogative continually made in their

---

[1] The knights of the shire represented the Commons in this Parliament.

inancial armour. This tedious and disheartening process was, as it happened, considerably facilitated by the foreign wars of Edward III., which obliged him continually to apply to Parliament for large supplies of money, and enabled it to exact in return some legislative plug, or plate, or rivet, to help on the work. It was also facilitated considerably by the haughty character and imperious views of Edward, who had not much intention of being bound by his promises against his will, and therefore had little objection to make them, provided his financial necessities were supplied for the time. Parliament, in fact, bought with hard cash a long series of statutes confirming, or conferring, a number of important rights, concessions, and privileges, the very frequency of which shows that they were perhaps not very effective individually and immediately, but which, taken collectively, formed a strong constitutional barrier against the undue exercise of prerogative in the future. By the end of Edward's reign precise declarations had been entered on the statute roll of the illegality of the various expedients by which the king had evaded the letter of the Charters, and in addition Parliament had established on a satisfactory basis the right to appropriate[1] to particular purposes the sums which it granted, and to appoint auditors[2] to examine the accounts of the expenditure of the appropriated money with the view of insuring its proper application to its destined end.

The right of the Commons to be consulted on taxation might seem to spring naturally from the fact that they were originally summoned for the express and sole purpose of voting money. The difficulties of the weak Edward II., and the necessities of the strong Edward III., and the consequent desire of both to conciliate their help in the hour of need, enabled them to make good their position as a body of equal power with the Lords:— with an equal right to share in legislation, to advise and criticise the policy of the king, and to rebuke and, if need be, punish not only the lower but even the highest personalities of the executive. Their right to concur in legislation was declared by statute in

---

[1] First instance of appropriation occurs in 1353, when a subsidy on wool was appropriated to the purposes of the French war.

[2] First instance occurs in 1340.

1322, and their assent is invariably mentioned during the century ; in fact, the statutes of the period are really the king's answers to the petitions of the Commons for redress of grievances, and are more or less drawn up on the lines of the petitions themselves. The king and Lords still retained some powers of issuing administrative laws in the shape of Ordinances, but these powers were only exercised for temporary needs or during the absence of Parliament.   On several occasions the Commons are reported to have advised Edward III. on the subject of his wars with France and Scotland, and especially with regard to the conclusion of the Treaty of Brétigni.   They interfered, moreover, in ecclesiastical matters, complaining bitterly of the conduct of the Papacy, and recommending remedial legislation.   They also, at different times, severely criticised unpopular administrations, unsuccessful courses of policy, illegal proceedings at parliamentary elections, and a host of other dissimilar subjects, with almost the same restless activity which characterizes the House of Commons at the present day, with the important difference, however, as Sir Erskine May points out, that in the fourteenth century they had no means of *enforcing* their advice—at the utmost they could only purchase compliance.

It was no doubt with the view of obtaining some indirect control over the actions of the king that the Commons insisted at intervals on their right to elect, or at least to share in the election of, the Privy Council, and further invented the powerful weapon of Impeachment as a punishment and warning to evil counsellors. It was during the unscrupulous and unsuccessful administration of John of Gaunt, at the close of his father's reign, that this engine was first brought into use.   When Parliament met in 1376, the Commons, instigated and supported by the Black Prince, attacked the Government with a long list of complaints, demanded a reorganization of the Privy Council, and presented at the bar of the House of Lords articles of impeachment for high crimes and misdemeanours against Lords Nevill and Latimer, both members of the Government, and several other offenders.   The accused were thereupon tried by the Lords, and condemned. ` vigorous measures of reform earned for its authors the "The Good Parliament."

The reign of Richard II. is the turning-point in the struggle
etween Parliament and the prerogative. All through the earlier
ears the Commons, aided by the weakness of his minority, con-
nued to labour at the edifice of constitutional government. By
equent reassertion they secured, on a firm basis of precedent
nd custom, the rights established under Edward III., and
btained such an amount of control over the Privy Council that
or some years, in the words of Hallam, "the whole executive
overnment was transferred to the two Houses." At the close of
ie reign, however, an important crisis arose. Richard, relying
n the help and acquiescence of a packed Parliament, established
imself in a position of practical absolutism, and entered on a
areer of tyranny and extortion which soon alienated all classes
f the nation. They rose in revolt, pulled down the pinchbeck
espotism, and by the mouth of a full Parliament solemnly
eposed the would-be despot, transferring the crown to Henry
f Lancaster as the most suitable man of the Royal Family.

It was natural that a king whose sole title was that of election
y Parliament, and whose earlier years were troubled by continual
iot and insurrection, should be compelled to assume to a very
arge extent the position of constitutional monarch, marked out
or him by the Commons. The old rights, therefore, were asserted
nd exercised with the regularity of routine, and completed by a
ew fresh improvements. The entire control of taxation was
nally assured to the Commons by their successful assertion, in
407, of the axiom that all money-bills must originate in the
ower House. Their right to concur in legislation was placed on
firmer footing by the practice introduced under Henry VI., of
ringing in their petitions in the form of complete statutes, under
he name of Bills, with the view of insuring that, for the future,
he laws entered on the rolls of Parliament should correspond
xactly to their desires. Shortly after the origin of this practice,
he House of Lords also began to bring in Bills, which they after-
ards sent to the Commons. The kings, however, claimed the
ight of interfering with the full legislative powers of Parliament
y means of the prerogative of dispensation. They claimed, in
act, the right of declaring that the law should not apply in par-
icular cases; and though this power was in itself useful and

C

almost necessary, it was of course subject to great abuses, and
was naturally viewed with some jealousy by the Commons. Under
the first two kings of the House of Lancaster, however, the powers
of the two Houses were fully and frankly recognised, and there is
no trace of even the slightest dissension between Henry V. and
his Parliaments. Henry VI., during the earlier and happier part
of his reign, was ruled by a council which, to a great extent,
represented the Parliament, though the character of Parliament
itself was changing, the Commons were ceasing to be really representative of the country, and all power was falling into the hands
of a few great barons, who struggled for the supremacy in the
council, just as later they were to struggle in the field. The
intimate connection and real confidence existing between the
House of Lancaster and their Parliaments was, perhaps, most
conclusively shown by the creation of a permanent royal revenue
in the shape of grants of the customs and of tunnage and poundage for life.

During this period, the constitutional theory of government by
Parliament was established on so firm a foundation that it was
able to last unimpaired amid the rude shocks to which it was
later subjected.

SECTION 2.—*Internal Details.*

The first difficulty which confronts us is to account satisfactorily for the preference obviously given to Westminster, from
the time of Edward I., as the meeting-place of Parliament, and
still more to explain the cause of its gradual restriction to Westminster alone. Whether there were any legends attaching to the
marshy village which had risen round the palace and church of
the Confessor, connecting it with the lost Clovesho, or the Tot-
hill meeting-place of early English Witena-gemóts, whether it was
due to the sanctity ascribed to the residence of the saintly king
himself, or to mere propinquity to the capital, it is impossible
to say. At first, moreover, Westminster was but one of three
 ̇oal cities in which the Conqueror year by year assembled
 ̇ Witan. Clarendon, Northampton, Woodstock, Oxford,
ns, have at least as good a title under the Plantagenets to
d the meeting-place of Parliament. Statutes of Win-

chester, Gloucester, Acton Burnell, Rhuddlan, vie with statutes of Westminster under the first Edward. York, Northampton, Lincoln, Winchester, Bury St. Edmunds, were all distinguished by sessions of Parliament under his successors. The reign of Edward I., however, says Dr. Stubbs, "saw the whole of the administrative machinery permanently settled in and around the palace (of Westminster) ; and thus from the very first introduction of representative members, the National Council had its regular home there. There, with a few casual exceptions, all the properly constituted Parliaments of England have been held."

The exact date of the separation of the two Houses cannot be fixed exactly, but it was completely effected by the middle of the fourteenth century. At first there appeared some possibility that the Lords and knights of the shire might unite into one Upper House, leaving the burgesses to form a Lower House by themselves. The distinctions, however, between the Lords and knights were broad and deep. Not only were the former far greater in wealth and power, but they enjoyed the privilege of being summoned to Parliament by a writ addressed to them personally, whereas the knights were assembled by a general summons sent to the sheriff. The Lords, moreover, paid larger sums in the way of feudal dues. There were also strong resemblances between the knights and burgesses in the way of similarity of summons, representative character, and local connection. It was natural, therefore, that when the division was finally made, the Lords should draw off into an Upper House, the two branches of the Commons uniting to form the Lower. This separation was complete by the year 1339. The union of the knights and burgesses was, as it happened, highly important, for the presence of the seventy-four knights[1] gave to the House of Commons the weight, permanency, and respect which an assembly of mere burgesses would certainly have never commanded. Edward I. had further contemplated the presence of another element in the shape of representatives (proctors) of the

---

[1] Monmouth was enfranchised 1536, and the Welsh counties in the same year were given *one* knight each. Cheshire was enfranchised in 1543 ; Durham in 1673.

lower clergy in Parliament. Whether these latter would ultimately have coalesced with the knights and burgesses, or split off into a third House of their own, it is only possible to vaguely conjecture, for from the very first they objected to attend at all, and persisted in preferring to vote taxation in their own assembly, Convocation. When, therefore, it was found that their grants were sufficiently liberal, they were at last allowed to please themselves, with the result that they entirely lost all share in the government of the country.[1]

The House of Lords, therefore, consisted of the Lords Spiritual—the two archbishops, the bishops, and a varying number of mitred abbots; and the Lords Temporal—including at first the barons, earls, and a duke or two, later more dukes, and marquises and viscounts as well. These were the Peers;[2] the rest of the realm were Commoners, represented in the Commons by the knights or burgesses, or, if clergymen, totally unrepresented in Parliament. It was this sharp division between the two classes which caused the eldest sons of peers to be regarded as Commoners, in spite of their courtesy titles, and admitted them to the House of Commons.[3] It may be as well to note that the judges were summoned regularly after 1295 to attend the sittings of the House of Lords, but were not regarded as peers, and, as a rule, had no right of voting.

The House of Commons consisted at first strictly of knights of the shire and burgesses. The difficulty, however, of obtaining a sufficient number of knights to serve rendered it soon necessary to be content with esquires instead; but a property qualification was established in 1430, which excluded all but knights or esquires possessed of landed estates to the annual value of £20. That the knights and esquires in question did not regard their privilege as a valuable one is shown by the fact that in the early days it was the custom for those elected to serve in Parliament to be paid by their constituents at the rate of 4s. a day during

---

[1] In 1664 they began to vote at parliamentary elections. *v.* p. 113.
[2] No woman was ever summoned to the House of Lords.
First case was that of the eldest son of the Earl of Bedford, temp. y VIII.

the sitting of Parliament. The burgesses, it may be added, were accustomed to receive 2*s.* per day for their parliamentary services. The increasing value of a seat may be historically traced by the frequent occurrence of bargains to do the work for less than the legal wages,—gradually even of agreements to forego them altogether,—and this practice, which becomes noticeable even as early as the reign of Edward IV., developes into the rule, with but few exceptions, under the later Tudors [1] and their successors.

The complete representative assembly planned out by Edward I. tended gradually to lose its full representative character. First there was the defection of the lower clergy. Then the borough elections in time fell into the hands of a few men, whether official persons, or members of some particular association, or merely owners of certain ancient tenements. The county elections, moreover, which at first were conducted by all the members of the shire-courts, gradually became a matter of arrangement among the principal landowners ; and the exclusion of the lower ranks of the people was rendered complete by the statute of 1430, which disfranchised all but the forty-shilling freeholders. From the earliest times there are records of troubles connected with the elections, the undue exercise of the sheriff's influence being especially conspicuous. Attempts were made to remedy this by various statutes, prescribing penalties of various kinds, insisting on residence as a qualification for candidature, and, above all, disqualifying the sheriffs from election themselves. The elections, however, tended to become less and less free, and the more valuable a seat became, the greater the inducement to adopt all methods to secure it ; the restrictions with regard to residence became a dead letter almost directly ; the disqualification of the sheriffs did not destroy their power of abusing their great local influence. The jurisdiction over election disputes was exercised at first by the Chancery, which had issued the summons to the sheriff, and though this may have at first secured an impartial trial, it placed a very

---

[1] The last case occurred in 1681, when Thomas King, member for Harwich, demanded and obtained his statutable wages. The custom is obsolete, but has never been actually abolished by statute.

dangerous weapon in the hands of the Crown, which might be used with fatal effect against the independence of Parliament. No doubt it was in view of this that a statute in 1410 vested it in the Justices of Assize.

Most of the officers of Parliament must have existed in some form or other from the earliest days. The Chancellor naturally presided over the House of Lords as over the Magnum Concilium. The position and title of Speaker was, however, first given in 1377 to Thomas Hungerford. The first Clerk of Parliament [1] was William Ayremin, 1315. The first allusion to a Clerk of the House of Commons occurs in 1388 with reference to John Scardesburgh; but the office was obviously not a new one at that date. The existence, moreover, of the Clerk of the Crown, the Serjeant-at-Arms of each House, and the two Ushers, is shown, says Dr. Stubbs, by occasional references on the rolls of Parliament, but the development of their functions is of later growth. The same statement will almost apply to most of the forms of the two Houses, the origin of which is extremely uncertain, though their early use is well attested.

The business of the session usually began with the election of the Speaker, which was then submitted to the king's approval and sanction. The Speaker, once confirmed in his place, proceeded to claim the usual privileges of the Commons in a short speech. The Chancellor next explained to the whole Parliament the purposes for which they had been called together. Afterwards the two Houses withdrew to their separate chambers and proceeded to business. Even in the earliest times there is to be observed the germ of the later distinction between money-bills, public bills, and private bills. Legislation founded on private petitions is not dealt with with much formality, and the result is not inscribed on the Statute Roll. Grants of money are always the special province of the Commons. The principal business of the session was then, as now, the full discussion of petitions (later, Bills) for redress of national grievances—including a first and second reading for the examination of the general principle of the proposed law, a debate in Committee over the details, and a third

---

[1] Or Clerk of the House of Lords.

reading, or final summing up. The same forms were observed in the Lords, and the petition or bill was then laid before the king for his approval, which he signified in the old Norman-French phrase, "*Le roy le veut ;*" intimating his dissent by the polite evasion, "*Le roy s'avisera.*"[1] The session was usually ended by dissolution, as soon as the business for which Parliament had been summoned was terminated. Therefore it was quite possible, and usual, for several Parliaments to meet in one year; nor was it till the sessions increased in duration that the demand for annual Parliaments arose.

The principal privileges claimed by both Houses were the right of debating freely and in secret on any subject which might interest them, and also personal freedom from liability to arrest and imprisonment. Both these rights were extremely ancient, and seem inherent in the nature of any deliberative assembly, in order to insure that its opinions may be expressed fearlessly, and that its numbers may not be liable to sudden diminutions. As a rule, these privileges were claimed by the Commons in each Parliament, and with few exceptions were rigidly enforced. The Lords, in addition, exercised the special rights of voting by proxy, of recording their protest or dissent on the rolls of their House when voting in the minority, of personal access to the king, and several other privileges of an honorary character, of which the most important was the right of being tried by their peers, that is, the House of Lords. It may also be important to note that the Lords alone exercised the judicial powers of the old Witenagemót, and that the Commons in the first year of Henry IV. expressly disclaimed any right to share in them. The Commons, on the other hand, asserted their exclusive right to the control of all financial questions.

---

[1] The forms of assent for private bills and money-bills were different. All these phrases have survived to the present day.

CHAPTER III.

PERSONAL GOVERNMENT. (1460–1529.)

SECTION 1.—*The New Monarchy* (1460–1509).

THE close of the Lancastrian period was followed by an almost complete suspension of parliamentary life. A detailed account of the causes must be sought in more general history. It must suffice for our purposes to briefly note that the accession of the House of York implied the triumph of legitimist over parliamentary rules of succession ; and the almost complete extinction of the baronage in the wars left the Commons to bear the full weight of opposition alone, a task for which they were as yet totally unfitted. A singular period of arbitrary government therefore follows hard on the epoch of formation ; the absolute will of the king almost entirely takes the place of the formalities of parliamentary government. Parliament itself meets only on very rare occasions, and the object with which it is summoned is either to grant the king a permanent revenue, or to provide him at will with supplementary additional grants. " During the twenty-five years of the York dynasty, the country was only seven times called upon to elect a new Parliament," says Dr. Stubbs ; " the sessions of those Parliaments which really met extended over a very few months ; and the records of the sessions are so barren as to silence any regrets at their infrequency." The reign of Edward IV. was a period of pure despotism, during which Parliament entirely lost all control over the government, and its own existence seemed perilously near its close. The reign of Richard III. was more fertile in promises of constitutional government than in actual results, owing to its abrupt termination. Circumstances obliged Henry VII. to base his claim to the throne on a parliamentary title ; but his real claim in right of conquest was abundantly testified to by his principles of government, which rendered his reign a reproduction of that of Edward IV., and

dded another quarter of a century to the long sleep of Parlia-
ient. Throughout his whole reign Henry summoned Parliament
nly seven times, and during the last thirteen years only once, in
504. Money was invariably the object of its summons.

The extraordinary servility of Parliament—especially shown in
ie regularity with which they rendered each successive monarch
t his accession partially independent of their help, by granting
im a revenue for life [1]—can be best accounted for by a brief
xamination of its constitution and character. The long wars,
nd the attainders and executions which followed the alternate
iumphs of each party, had swept off nearly all the old nobility
ho had been accustomed to act as leaders of the Opposition,
nd had served as powerful checks on the ambition of the Crown.
he old race of haughty, independent Churchmen had died out as
ell, and were succeeded by men who looked to the royal favour
ir advancement and protection from the hatred of the nation.
/hen Henry VII. therefore summoned the Lords to the Parlia-
ient of 1485, it is scarcely singular that there appeared only
venty-nine temporal peers, several of whom were new creations.
here was, therefore, a permanent royal majority of ecclesiastics
lready existing; and the new nobility who grew up under the
'udors were more likely to buy safety and advancement by
dhering to the ranks of this majority, than to take up the useless
nd dangerous part of opposition. The Lords, in consequence,
ntirely ceased to exercise any check on the Crown, and became
istead its ready instrument. The Commons had not yet
cquired self-importance and self-reliance enough to act alone.
)eprived of their leaders they were helpless; nor was it till they
:arned to follow the lead of the king that they emerged again
om the pathless slough in which they were plunged.

SECTION 2.—*Early Years of Henry VIII* (1509–29).

The parliamentary history of the reign of Henry VIII. is
ivided into three very distinct periods. During the first (1509–
515), Parliament was assembled at intervals chiefly to vote

---

[1] The customs, and tunnage and poundage, were granted in this way to each
ing until the accession of Charles I.

money for carrying on the continental war. During the second
(1515-1529), Parliament again suffered an almost total eclipse,
and, with a single exception in 1523, was not summoned to share
in the government of the country, or even to vote supplies for the
maintenance of the administration. The third (1529-1547) is
remarkable for a great parliamentary revival. Parliament meets
continually, with but very slight intermissions, is constantly employed in transacting business of the most varied and opposite
description, and displays a legislative activity which makes this
period one of the most remarkable and most fertile in the legal
annals of this country.

The early period was at first uneventful, save for repeated grants
of taxation for war. The case of Richard Strode, however, in
1512, forms an important epoch in the history of privilege.

Richard Strode, member for the borough of Plympton, in
Devonshire, proposed certain Bills in Parliament for the regula-
tion of the Cornish mines. He was in consequence prosecuted
by the Stannary Courts[1] for an infringement of their privileges,
and imprisoned in a dungeon in Lidford Castle, where he remained for three weeks, until delivered by a writ of privilege.
Attention had been attracted to his case by the non-performance
of his duties as one of the collectors appointed to raise the
fifteenth voted in Parliament in consequence of his arrest. The
case was carefully inquired into by the Commons and decided
to be a gross violation of their rights of freedom of debate and
liberty of the person. It was determined to proceed by Act of
Parliament, in order that a definite decision of the whole Legislature might be recorded on the subject of privilege. Henry made
it a rule not to interfere with his Parliaments so long as their
proceedings did not trench on his authority; he readily signified
his assent, therefore, to the statute which is usually described as
the "Statute anent Richard Strode" (4 Henry VIII. c. 8). It
declared the action of the Stannary Courts against Strode illegal
and void; and added that all similar actions, condemnations, and
punishments instituted and enforced in the future for any words
spoken in Parliament or any bill brought forward in Parliament

---

[1] These Courts had special jurisdiction over the Duchy of Cornwall.

ould be utterly illegal and void as well. This is the first statute
1ich deals with the question of freedom of debate.

During the second period (1515–1529), the ruling genius of the
overnment was the great minister-ecclesiastic, Cardinal Wolsey.
aturally of despotic views himself, he desired to release his
aster from the trammels of the Constitution and render him
preme in uncontrolled despotism.   With the keen eye of a
1tesman, he realized at once that the strongest check on the
)wer of the monarch lay in the free traditions of the Parliament,
1d these he determined to remove.   Active measures of repression
1d coercion, however, formed no part of his plan.   Parliament
1s not to be forced, or even bribed, to submit unquestioningly
the views of the Government.   It was simply to be deprived
all power of expressing any opinion at all.   It was to dream
7ay in numbing inactivity, lapped in a long, long sleep, which is
nearly akin to death, until at last—like the Dodo and other
1achronisms—it should have the good taste to become decently
tinct.   A great gap therefore ensues in the history of Parliament.
etween the years 1515–1523 no summons was issued to the
tates of the realm; and again between the years 1523–1529
1other blank occurs in the parliamentary annals.   But for the
1gle exception of the Parliament summoned in 1523, the period
the great Cardinal might be described as an epoch of undiluted
ersonal government.

Eight long years of peace and ordinary expenditure had facili-
ted the execution of Wolsey's plan, and then the outbreak of
ar involved him in unusual expenses, which drove him to his
it's end to find the necessary cash.   All attempts to raise money
' extra-parliamentary means having failed, he decided once
ore to assemble the representatives of the people in order to
)tain a general grant.   In April, therefore, Parliament met at
e Black Friars, and Sir Thomas More, a member of the Council,
1s chosen Speaker of the Commons by the influence of the
)urt.   The influence of the Court, in fact, was very great in this
1rliament, owing to the presence of a large number of Crown
)minees and placeholders who voted solidly together for their
1tron on all occasions; the resistance, therefore, which the Com-
ons offered to the unprecedented demands of the Government

really betokens a courage and independence on the part of the
country members—if we may antedate an expression—which must
relieve them entirely from the charge of blind subservience to the
views of the Crown and disregard of the feelings of the country.
On April 29, Wolsey in person demanded from the House a vote
of one-fifth of every man's goods and land, which he calculated
would amount to £800,000.   The Commons made no reply
whatever to this speech, though he repeatedly called on various
members to give him a reasonable answer.   At last, Sir Thomas
More, bending the knee, replied that the Commons were accustomed to return answer only by the mouth of their Speaker; that
it was impossible for him to convey their reply until he had their
instructions, which they could not give until they had debated
the question, and this they claimed the right of doing in private,
in accordance with their privileges.   So Wolsey was obliged to
withdraw.   A long discussion ensued, in which the Commons
displayed gross ignorance of the real condition of England in
estimating the number of parishes at 40,000, whereas they really
did not amount to 15,000.   Even with this over-estimate, they
considered the royal demands utterly outrageous.   Wolsey therefore attempted a little brow-beating, in the hopes of producing
the desired effect.   He appeared in all his pomp, with "his
maces, his pillers, his poleaxes, his crosse, his belt, and the great
seale too."   But all these trappings of authority were as inefficacious as his arguments.   The Commons listened to him again
in absolute silence, unconvinced, and positively refused to discuss
the question in his presence.   On his departure, the debate was
continued for sixteen days with the utmost vehemence; but the
solid ranks of the king's party were utterly inaccessible to argument, and they eventually carried the day in favour of a heavy tax.
Wolsey was so disgusted with the independence of Parliament,
that he determined for the future to raise money by unconstitutional and unpopular means, rather than again assemble a body
he so heartily distrusted.

CHAPTER IV.

PERSONAL GOVERNMENT WITH PARLIAMENT.
(1529–1588.)

SECTION 1.—*Later Years of Henry VIII. Management*
(1529–47).

THE re-assembling of the two Houses in 1529 marked the fall of Wolsey and Wolsey's system, and is the great turning-point of the reign. Henry suddenly awoke to the fact that in Parliament there lay ready to his hand an engine of almost incalculable power and the utmost facility, which, if properly handled and guided, might be employed to carry out his most arbitrary views, and to render his personal government more supremely absolute than before. Circumstances rendered it probable that their own privileges were not infringed, and constitutional forms were strictly observed, Parliament would follow the lead of the king, as they had in earlier times followed the barons and bishops. The chances of resistance, moreover, could be minimised by a judicious distribution of places among the members, by additions at intervals to the list of boroughs, and by active interference, if necessary, to secure the election of members who were not likely to prove troublesome. The result of this new policy was a very considerable change in the principles of government. The system of the New Monarchy, which had hitherto been based on personal government without Parliament, assumed the form of personal government by means of Parliament, which commonly, though incorrectly, known as the Tudor Despotism. The mode of government, in fact, is no whit less arbitrary than before. Cruel and bloody laws are enforced as rigorously, outrageous acts of tyranny are perpetrated on individuals as recklessly ; but it is no longer the king who is the sole instrument of violence,—the blame is now shared with the ministers who propose, and the Parliament who assent, if indeed it is not entirely shifted on to their shoulders. This system of parliament-

29

ary tyranny, of absolutism hiding behind a constitutional mask, is so essentially a peculiarity of the Tudor period; and the great Reformation Parliament, which met in 1529, is so thoroughly a typical Parliament of this epoch, that it seems only fitting to deal with it in some detail,—especially as the work that it effected was really of incalculable importance in the history of the nation. It was also a remarkable fact that it sat for seven years (1529–36), being adjourned from time to time by prorogations, which were quite new in parliamentary practice. The custom hitherto had been to summon Parliaments whenever they were required to transact particular business, and dissolve them as soon as it was completed. The business laid before them was usually mainly connected with taxation, and the expense of the session was so very unwillingly borne by the constituencies, the inconvenience by the representatives, that it was therefore only to be expected that it should not be prolonged beyond the barest necessity. Now, however, that Parliament became of more importance, and was admitted to a share in the government of the country, the position of members became more desirable and more honourable, and they ceased in consequence to demand the payment of their wages from the constituencies. As an epoch therefore of development, both of the nation and of parliamentary practice, the Parliament of 1529 is worthy of more than a passing notice.

"According to the summons," says Hall, "the King of England began his Parliament November 3rd, on which day he came by water to his palace of Bridewell; and there he and his nobles put on their robes of Parliament, and so came to the Black Friar Church, where a mass of the Holy Ghost was solemnly sung by the king's chaplain; and after the mass the king, with all his Lords and Commons, came into the Parliament. The king sat on his throne, and Sir Thomas More, his Chancellor, made an eloquent oration, setting forth the causes why the king had so summoned them." After this the Commons adjourned to their own House to elect their Speaker and discuss their plans. It is highly probable that an intimation was given to them that an attack on the Church would not be disagreeable to the king's wishes, and this was so exactly in accordance with the public
ᵗnion of the country, that a formal Act of Accusation against the

iole body of the clergy was soon drawn up.   At the same time
is a remarkable fact that for the first time the king's ministers
tempted no open interference, and the Commons were left to
itiate and discuss whatever might please them.

The Act of Accusation declared the clergy guilty of innumerable
)uses, vices, injustices, and tyrannies, and petitioned for their
dress.   The bishops returned an arrogant answer, which the
ng handed to the Commons with the brief commentary, "We
ink their answer will smally please you, for it seemeth to us
ry slender."   The Parliament replied to this defiance by pass-
g three statutes, which reduced all ecclesiastical fees to fixed and
asonable rates, and prohibited pluralities, non-residence, and
ading on the part of clergymen.   During the debate in the
ouse of Lords, the Bishop of Rochester had made himself the
)okesman of the ecclesiastics, and hinted angrily that the Com-
ons were losing their faith.   The Commons by the mouth of
ieir Speaker, Sir Thomas Audeley, declared their resentment to
ie king, and the bishop was forced to humbly apologise and
2clare that he had not meant to accuse them of want of faith.
hus triumphantly ended the first session of this Parliament,
)ecember 17th, 1529.

During the second session, the House of Commons confined
iemselves mainly to secular business.   Early in the year 1531,
owever, they were called upon to pass the Act pardoning the
lergy from the liability to outlawry and forfeiture which the
itter had incurred under the Statute of Premunire by submitting
) Wolsey's legatine authority; and this forms a very remarkable
dmission on the part of the most despotic of kings that the
ionarch has no power to suspend the operation of a statute gen-
rally, though he may dispense its action in particular cases.   The
)ommons, however, insisted on passing a general act of pardon
or the whole nation, who they declared were equally guilty with
he clergy ; and the somewhat singular result followed, that Par-
iament not only pardoned the nation, but solemnly and gravely
orgave themselves as well for their own breach of their own laws.
['his session was longer than the first; it had opened on January
:6th, 1531.   It lasted altogether for ten weeks.

On January 15th, 1532, Parliament met for the third session,

and proceeded steadily on its task of reforming the Church.   The
privilege of benefit of clergy was considerably restricted.   Men
were no longer to travel out of their own dioceses for trial at the
bidding of the ecclesiastical courts, except for some few special
causes, such as heresy.   A direct step towards a breach with
Rome was hinted at in a statute forbidding the payment of
annates (or first-fruits) to the Pope, which, however, was not to
become law till the king should so will.   The explanation of this
extraordinary provision is to be found in the political history.
Henry was now engaged in his great contest with Clement VII.
over the divorce from Catherine of Aragon, and this provisional
statute was simply designed as a menace to Rome.   The business
of the session concluded with an Act embodying a declaration on
the part of the bishops that no constitution should for the future
be enacted by them without the king's licence.   This Act completed the great revolution begun in 1529, and reduced the
clergy once more to their rightful position as an estate of the
realm.   There was a greater revolution, however, to follow.

When Parliament met again, on the 4th of February, 1533, a
great change had occurred.   Henry, furious at the Pope's delays
over the divorce, had decided to do without him, and obtain a
divorce in his own courts.   Parliament was to be the instrument
which should enable him to break the tie between the English
Church and Rome, and render any further interference by the
Pope in the matter of none effect.   As evidence, however, that the
Parliament did not proceed to their work inspired by blind furious
hatred of either the Pope or the Church, it is sufficient to mention
that the business which first received their consideration was of
an economic and industrial nature solely.   Then they proceeded
calmly and judicially to declare in the Act of Appeals what they
considered the legal relations between the Pope and the realm of
England had been and ought to be.   They stated in so many
words that England was an independent Empire; that the
English Church had never been subject to the interference of any
exterior person; that statutes had frequently been passed at
intervals in the history of the nation to prevent any such interference on the part of the Pope or other foreign potentates; that
as, in spite of this, the Pope had interfered repeatedly, they now

acted that no appeals should be carried to Rome for the future.

legal theory they were undoubtedly right in their historical sertions, but the practice had differed very considerably, and doubtedly in thus breaking entirely free from the supremacy of me the Parliament accomplished a revolution which far ex-ded in importance and daring even the boldest and most eeping of its previous acts.

The session of 1534 produced a series of fresh statutes against : Pope. Parliament re-assembled January 15th to complete the rk of the last session. The Annates Act was first made abso-e. Then the king's assent was declared to be necessary to the lidity of any canons enacted in Convocation, and so the legisla-e power of the clergy passed from them. The carrying of any peals to Rome was rendered unlawful under any circumstances, d a court of appeal for spiritual cases was created, which was own in later days as the High Court of Delegates. It was ther provided that archbishops and bishops should be nomi-ted by the sovereign in the form at present in force. The yment of Peter's pence to Rome was to be discontinued, and a st of other minor exactions of different kinds were similarly ped off. The important question of the succession then gaged the attention of Parliament. Owing to the king's orce and re-marriage, it was now in rather an uncertain state. Succession Act was therefore passed, declaring the nullity of : marriage with Catherine, and the validity of the marriage h Anne. The crown was entailed on the king's heirs by this rriage, and all persons were required to take an oath to their lief in the truth of the statements contained in the Act. ally, Parliament considered it necessary to place on record a tement that in their various measures directed against Rome y were separating from the Papacy only, not from the Church Christ, which is in itself conclusive evidence that it were re rightly called "the Reforming" than "the Reformation rliament."

The opposition, however, which these changes excited among tain sections of the people, determined the Government to nplete their list of measures with a high hand; and Parlia-nt was summoned again for this purpose on Nov. 3rd, 1534.

D

The king was declared to be "Supreme Head of the Church,"
and the spiritual body was thus subordinated to the Crown.
This famous Act of Supremacy, moreover, empowered the king
to inquire into heresies and correct them; and it was on the
basis of the power thus conferred that the Court of High Commission, later in the century, built up its terrible jurisdiction. A
second Act vested all first-fruits and tenths in the Crown. A
third affixed the penalties of high treason to the crime of casting
any doubt on the orthodoxy of the king, and allowed the inter-
rogation of suspected persons, with the view of ascertaining their
true opinions : this was, perhaps, the most dangerously oppressive power that could have been entrusted to a despotic government.

The guiding spirit in all these sweeping measures was a man
of humble, almost unknown, birth. The annals of the great
Revolution are but a portion of the life of Thomas Cromwell.
A servant of Wolsey, he had been employed by the latter in the
work of suppressing some of the small monasteries. Later, he
was the only man of all the Cardinal's numerous dependants who
had the courage to defend the fallen minister on his impeachment, and the ability to do it successfully. With singular daring
he even sought the king's presence, and advised him to settle
the question of the divorce by the exercise of his own supremacy.
Henry was struck at once by the boldness of the counsel and the
ability of its author; and though he naturally shrank at first
from carrying it into execution till the negotiations with the Pope
had entirely failed, he took Cromwell at once into his service,
and did not forget his words. Cromwell became Secretary of
State, representing the Government in the House of Commons,
which followed his lead with blind obedience. His policy was
to exalt the power of the monarchy at the expense of all com-
petitors, so that there should be but one ruler in England, and
that ruler absolute in all things. The pretensions, the power
and the wealth of the Church had survived the shock of the Civil
Wars, though they had prostrated the strength of the baronage.
They were now attacked by the medium of Parliament, and their
power crumbled away at once to powder. Later in the crisis of
the divorce, his words in the bygone time became instinct with

tive vitality, and it was really the hand of Cromwell which
t through alike the chains of Rome and the marriage with
therine of Aragon. To guarantee the existence of the system
iich he had reared, he created a reign of terror, in which not
ly deeds but words, and even thoughts, which could be con-
ued into opposition of even the most trivial kind, were
nished with ruthless severity. True, however, to his original
ins, in all his most tyrannical and unconstitutional deeds
: acted with the help of Parliament. It was Parliament
iich attacked the liberty of the person ; which forced men to
criminate themselves on pain of their silence being deemed a
oof of guilt; which sent the highest and most illustrious of
nglish nobles, churchmen, scholars to the scaffold in crowds ;
iich invented the crowning injustice of condemning men unheard,
r the Bill of Attainder. Yet there was no man in England but
iew that the puppets only danced as their master pulled the
rings; that it was the cold, cruel, calculating brain of Cromwell
hich prompted these "bloody laws," his merciless hand which
rought such terrible energy to their execution.

The work of Parliament was not yet complete; another
ission must be accomplished before they could be dismissed to
ieir homes. The monasteries were as yet untouched, and were
: once the most vulnerable and dangerous part of the Church
rganization. The monks, the preachers, the confessors were
ie hottest opponents of the new system; their influence was
aturally widespread among the ignorant rustics, and was exer-
ised with unrelenting hostility against the minister and his policy.
Ie determined, therefore, to deal these secret sowers of sedition
blow which should paralyse their enmity for the future ; the
ideous immorality and abuses in which most of them were
redeemably sunk supplied a ready pretext for stringent measures.
commission was therefore appointed to inquire and reform.
t declared the smaller monasteries utterly irreformable, and in
onsequence Parliament in the session of 1536 decreed the
bolition of all whose incomes amounted to less than £200 a
ear, their property passing to the Crown. With this important
vork ended the great Parliament, which was dissolved April 4th,
1536.

All through the progress of the Revolution it is in the Commons that the interest of the narrative is centred. The Lords
had ceased to be the leaders of the English nation ; the king and
his ministers had taken their place, and worked wholly by means
of the Commons. The Peers saw measures pass into law again
and again which they would have gladly rejected had they dared.
They were forced to submit to disrespectful criticism, to endure
unpalatable innovations in constitutional custom, to receive with
as good a grace as they could command undisguised dictation
from a body which they had been accustomed to regard as their
inferiors. It is not the least among the changes effected by the
Parliament of 1529–36, that in it the Commons, who had hitherto
confined themselves to voting supplies and passing measures, now
took upon themselves for the first time to interfere with a high
hand in every branch of public business; and this sudden leap
into political activity must be ascribed mainly to the prompting
and leadership of Thomas Cromwell.

The policy thus inaugurated, of using Parliament as the
instrument of despotism, was preserved consistently all through
the reign, and the result was an unprecedented increase of the
power of the Crown, and a most extraordinary submission to
its most extravagant whims. The authority of Parliament was
invoked to unloose the marriages with Anne Boleyn and Anne of
Cleves, to declare Mary and Elizabeth alike illegitimate, to dissolve the large monasteries and exclude the mitred abbots from
the House of Lords, thereby reducing the ecclesiastical peers to
a minority which was totally unable to resist the progress of the
Reformation. The right of settling the succession, even by his
last will, was conferred on Henry. A large portion of the
legislative power was surrendered to him by a statute, which
gave him the right of issuing Proclamations in Council, touching all save life and land, which should be as binding on the
subject as if they were regular statutes. Twice was he released
from repaying moneys which he had raised by loan. The religion
of the country was arranged in accordance with his wishes, by a
statute known as the Six Articles. Perhaps, however, the most
extraordinary infringement on the Constitution perpetrated by the
' of Parliament, was the practice of condemning political offenders

)y Act of Parliament (Bill of Attainder), without hearing them in
heir own defence. This iniquitous invention was devised by
'romwell as a convenient mode of despatching political opponents
gainst whom no legal charge could be brought. He inquired,
herefore, of the judges whether, if Parliament should by a regular
:gislative Act attaint a man of treason and condemn him to death
,ithout hearing him, the attainder could ever be questioned. The
udges, however,—and to their credit be it recorded,—answered that
his was a very dangerous question, and that Parliament should
ather set the example to inferior courts by proceeding according
o justice. Being charged, however, on their loyalty to answer
ruly, they replied that an Act of Attainder, like any other Act of
'arliament could never be disputed in any court of law, even
hough the attainted person were not heard in his own defence
iefore the Act was passed—in other words, that the legislative
iody had the absolute power of formally decreeing anything
,hich might strike its fancy. By the irony of Nemesis, how-
:ver, it was Cromwell himself who was first condemned in this
niquitous manner for an offence not punishable by the ordinary
aw; but he headed a long list of illustrious victims whose real
:rime consisted in their unwillingness to submit unquestioningly
o the despotic commands of the monarch.

What strikes a modern reader as so remarkable in the history
if this period is that Parliament should have allowed itself so
eadily to become the instrument of Henry's will, nor is it pos-
ible to attribute its subservience simply to the loss of its natural
eaders, the nobles and clergy, nor yet to the unlimited pack-
ng of boroughs and bribing of members, which Mr. Friedmann
:ndeavours to render solely responsible for it. Henry certainly
:annot have been merely an unpopular tyrannical sovereign,
orcing hateful laws down the throats of his subjects by the help
if a packed Parliament of nominees, the fifty yeomen of the guard,
ind the scanty company of artillerymen,—the London Trained
3ands alone could have turned such a preposterous despotism
nside out in a very short time, and the Pilgrimage of Grace
vould have ended far differently. In fact, though undoubtedly
races are found that the Government thought very little of inter-
ering with the elections where any distinctly obnoxious member

was elected, and that in the General Election of 1539, after the suppression of the rebellion, every nerve was strained to destroy any chance of opposition, still, in the absence of any proof to the contrary, we are justified in supposing that Henry relied mainly on his own great popularity, on the complete accord existing between him, his Parliaments, and the mass of the nation, and the thorough trust which the middle classes reposed in him as the one man able to steer the country safely through the dangers and difficulties of the troublous time. "When the waves roll mountains high," they would have said, "and the hurricane rages round the devoted vessel, it is no time to bind the captain on whom our safety depends, by the forms and regulations intended for fair weather." They committed their liberties into the hands of the king as the sole hope of preservation from the bloodshed and the anarchy of a fresh civil war.

It was only natural under the circumstances that Henry should maintain to the utmost the rights and privileges of a body which was so useful to him ; was it not a cheap and easy way of repaying them for the solid support which they rendered to his government ? He had allowed them to assert their right of freedom of speech in 1512 ; in 1541 the Speaker formally claimed it as an undoubted right at the opening of Parliament, and it has invariably been similarly claimed at the opening of every fresh Parliament. In 1543 a case arose which enabled them to introduce an improvement in the mode of effecting the release of members when subjected to arrest. George Ferrers, member for Plymouth, was arrested as surety for another by the officers of the city of London, and sent to prison. Sir Thomas Moyle, the Speaker, laid the matter before the House of Commons, and the House indignantly ordered their Serjeant-at-Arms to demand the release of the prisoner. In fact, they now undertook for the first time to release their members by their own officer, the Serjeant-at-Arms. The City officers, however, loudly maintained that no extraneous officials had any right or jurisdiction within their liberties ; and a regular pitched battle ensued over this difference of opinion between the myrmidons of the prison and those of the Parliament, in which the Serjeant, with great ingenuity of invention, if a slight lack of reverence, made use of the "mace" as a

ub, and plied it with great zeal and energy. The Commons
ere much disgusted; they pronounced the City officials guilty of
eat contempt. The Chancellor suggested proceeding for the
lease of Ferrers by writ in the ordinary way, but the Commons
ould not hear of it—they were determined that the release
iould be effected by the Serjeant and mace. The second
ppearance of the Serjeant was more successful; for the City
ficials were thoroughly alarmed, and so Ferrers was promptly
leased. The Commons now proceeded to vengeance. The
ieriffs, the creditor, the clerk of the prison, and five constables
ere sent to prison, and incarcerated for three days, when they
ere set at liberty, after humble apologies. So ended that part
f the matter. Henry, however, on receiving a formal commu-
ication, expressed his thorough approbation of the whole course
f action on the part of the House of Commons. "I understand,"
e added in words which deserve to be quoted, "that you, not
nly for your own persons, but also for your necessary servants,
ven to your cooks and housekeepers, enjoy the said privilege;
isomuch as my Lord Chancellor here present hath informed us
iat, he being Speaker of Parliament, the cook of the Temple was
rrested in London, and in execution upon a statute of the staple;
nd forsomuch as during all the Parliament the said cook served
ie Speaker in that office, he was taken out of execution by
rivilege of Parliament. And further, we be informed by our
idges, that we at no time stand so highly in our estate royal as
i the time of the Parliament, wherein we as head and you as
iembers are conjoined and knit together in one body politic, so
s whatsoever offence or injury during that time is offered to the
ieanest member of the House is to be judged as done against
ur person and the whole court of Parliament; which prerogative
f the court is so great, as all acts and processes coming out of
ny inferior courts must for the time cease and give place to the
ighest."

"The despotism of Henry," sums up a modern historian, "was
ideed splendidly veiled, when he could applaud so resolved an
ssertion of the liberties of the House of Commons, and could
cknowledge that any portion of his own power was dependent
in their presence and their aid."

SECTION 2.—*Edward VI. and Mary. Packing*
(1547–58).

To outward appearance the government of Henry's children was no whit less despotic than that of their father ; but there are many signs that they did not preserve his absolute dominion over Parliament. In the first place, most of the sanguinary and arbitrary laws of Henry VIII. were repealed by the first Parliament of Edward VI. The statute of proclamations, the new treasons and felonies, were all swept away, the royal power was reduced to its original dimensions in the eye of the law, and an additional safeguard was provided for persons accused of treason by an enactment that two witnesses should be necessary to establish the offence.

Secondly, though Somerset and Northumberland were able to make use of Parliament to force the reformed religion on the reluctant nation, and Mary in turn, with equal ease, restored the supremacy of Catholicism and the Pope by the same potent assistance, still there is ample evidence that Parliament did not yield that blind, slavish obedience to the commands of the regents or the queen that had attended the behests of Henry. There are numerous instances when the Commons rejected bills coming down from the Upper House. They refused to attaint Tunstal, Bishop of Durham, for misprision of treason in 1553. They debated long in the same session before they would grant a subsidy at all to the unpopular Northumberland. They refused to interfere in the very slightest degree, in spite of Mary's behest, with the lands of the monasteries which had been distributed among laymen. Later in the year, in the same Parliament, they showed conclusively that the only terms on which they would re-establish the Catholic religion were that these lands should not be restored to the Church ; and altogether they showed a most impenitent preference for heresy, coupled with the retention of their ill-gotten acquisitions, rather than orthodoxy if it involved a surrender of the latter. On this point, in fact, they proved utterly impracticable ; and at last the Spanish Court advised Mary to accept the restoration of Catholicism on these terms, as there appeared no chance of any better. Moreover, they obstinately resisted the Spanish match, and they steadily refused to exclude Elizabeth from the succession.   There is no doubt, however, that this opposition offered to the proposals of the Crown was prompted mainly by self-interest, religious feeling, and the personal unpopularity of the ruler, rather than any great constitutional awakening ; for it must be borne in mind that Northumberland and Mary must be regarded as partisans in the great religious question of the day, whereas Henry, as a rule, preserved an impartiality in religious questions, which was as pitiless in its action as original in its conception.

Thirdly, abundant evidence is forthcoming that frequent attempts were made to counteract, or indeed to stifle, this opposition in Parliament by active interference in the existing constituencies and a lavish creation of new ones.   Bribery, corruption, intimidation, took the place of the lofty supremacy and the consistent confidence which marked the relations between Henry VIII. and his Parliament.   Twenty-two boroughs were created in Edward's reign, avowedly for electioneering purposes, of which no less than seven were small villages in Cornwall, a county peculiarly susceptible to royal influence.   Mary added fourteen more of the same type, with no apparent object except to secure a parliamentary majority.   Moreover, the Parliament of January, 1553, the last of Edward's reign, was almost a nomination Parliament.   Circulars were, in some instances, addressed to the sheriffs of counties or mayors of towns naming the persons who were to be chosen, and commanding the electors to vote for them.   In other cases, the Crown ordered particular individuals, by a personal letter, to offer themselves for election, hinting, not obscurely, that the influence of the Crown would insure their return.   Concessions, moreover, were promised to the city of London to procure its support.   These strenuous efforts were, however, not attended with any startling success, for the Parliament assembled in this way offered more opposition than any of its predecessors—a fact which no doubt gave Northumberland reason to congratulate himself that he had not committed the imprudence of allowing the constituencies to choose freely for themselves.   Again, in 1554, after Wyatt's rebellion, Mary issued a circular to the mayors and sheriffs, requiring them to admonish the voters to choose "such as, being eligible by order of the laws, were of a wise, grave, and Catholic sort"; and the citizens of London were sufficiently tractable to elect four members satisfactory to the Court as an example to the rest of the realm. The Earl of Sussex, moreover, wrote to the electors of Norfolk and Yarmouth, requesting them to vote for a person whom he would name, and who, we may be sure, was not deficient in affection for the queen. And yet this very Parliament showed as much dislike for the Spanish match, and the restoration of the Church lands, as if it had been composed entirely of Protestants freely elected.

If further evidence were necessary to prove that Parliament was growing restive, it is to be found in the history of privilege. No record of its violation on the part of the Crown breaks the steady monotony of parliamentary eloquence under Henry VIII. Henry was strong enough to disregard the opposition of individual members; he was even strong enough to allow Parliament to enforce its privileges against all offenders with a high hand. With the reign of Mary began the system of suppressing freedom of speech by force, which is such a sure sign of incipient weakness. During her third Parliament she even committed some knights to the Tower for their speeches in Parliament.

The result of this growing independence of Parliament was an attempt to return to the old system of personal government without the help of Parliament. Numerous illegal proclamations were issued, which were enforced as laws, both by Edward and Mary. Martial law was occasionally used as more favourable to prerogative than the ordinary law. Mary even ventured to anticipate the consent of Parliament in deposing the Protestant bishops and altering the established worship. She raised money at intervals by benevolences; she imposed a duty on cloth without consent of Parliament; and her reign is especially remarkable for the fact that torture and other illegal modes of punishment were more frequently used than in all the preceding history of the realm. In 1557 an ecclesiastical commission was appointed of her authority solely, empowering the bishops to punish "devilish and clamorous persons," which practically meant the Protestants. The germs of parliamentary opposition were, in fact, already making themselves dimly perceptible, though as yet in such an embryonic condition as to be of very slight importance as an obstacle to the will of the Crown.

SECTION 3.—*Elizabeth. Interference* (1558–88).

Elizabeth succeeded to the throne under circumstances of great difficulty and danger. Her title was a purely parliamentary one, resting on the will of Henry VIII., made in accordance with powers conferred on him by statute, and was naturally disputed by the adherents of Mary Stuart of Scotland. Among her enemies were several powerful foreign states, and a certain number of her own subjects even, all of whom were really inspired by religious animosity, and who would have undoubtedly found Elizabeth's title sufficiently valid if she had happened to be a Catholic. In times of such danger it was only natural that extraordinary powers should be committed to the Crown, and should be exercised with the utmost stringency on all who were suspected of hostility to the Government. It was also unfortunately inevitable that much that was really prompted by sincere, conscientious scruples, and an honest desire to advance the welfare of the nation, should be mistaken for obstinate obstruction and presumptuous interference. This is especially noticeable in the history of Parliament. Elizabeth, in fact, inherited the despotic temper of her father and his arbitrary traditions of government. She regarded the Parliament as an useful supplement to the royal power, an efficient instrument in the royal hands, but by no means as an organic body capable of action without the royal initiative. Any such attempt she considered a mere perversion of the regular order of things arising from the heady reasonings of dangerous men, perhaps even the malicious promptings of secret foes, which called for instant suppression ere the results became serious. Parliament, however, had passed through a severe training in the preceding Tudor reigns. Under Edward VI. it had become restive; it had several times offered a steady resistance to the most cherished plans of Queen Mary. Under Elizabeth it asserted itself still more boldly. It began to take upon itself the function of discussing matters of

pressing import, and laying its advice before the Crown with con
siderable earnestness and persistency, wholly unasked—in many
cases even in direct defiance of a royal prohibition. The chief
lines on which these, to Elizabeth, unwelcome discussions ran,
were the question of the succession, which was very unsettled,
and the ecclesiastical organization and ritual, which, in the opinion
of many, was in an equally unsatisfactory state. This boldness
was no doubt due, in a great measure, to the presence of a large
number of Puritans, who wished both to reform the Church on a
severer basis, and exclude all chance of a Catholic heir succeed-
ing to the throne ; but it was also partly prompted by honest
patriotism, and a desire to diminish the perils which surrounded
the queen's life, and found expression in the numerous plots of
the reign. These discussions, however, Elizabeth was determined
to prevent, and the modes which she adopted were extremely
various and equally inefficacious. The creation of new boroughs
was carried to an unprecedented extent—*sixty-two* altogether
were added to the existing constituencies, solely with the view
of increasing the numbers of the supporters of the Government.
Parliament itself was very seldom summoned at all during the
early years of the reign, and the queen practised the utmost
economy in order to avoid any necessity for its presence. When,
moreover, it actually met, it was usually ordered to confine itself
strictly to the business on hand; the Speakers were instructed
to stop any discussion of unwelcome subjects : there were always
a Secretary and several Privy Councillors present among the
members, whose duty it was to expound the royal wishes and to
support the prerogative, while their presence and close relation to
the Crown would naturally act as a check on all but the boldest
spirits; those members, moreover, who, in spite of the queen's prohibition, insisted on their right to debate on any matter of public
interest, were, in many cases, sharply censured by the Council and
committed as a further warning to prison. Elizabeth interfered
more frequently and deliberately with the rights of freedom of
speech than any of her predecessors, and during the early part of
the reign, her tactics were usually marked with a certain amount of
success. We have now, in fact, got beyond the period when
Parliament could be "managed" or even "packed," so as to

)e utterly quiescent. Nothing but the sharp chastisement of im-
)risonment will stop the tongues of the bold spirits who oppose
he Crown single-handed and maintain the privileges of Parlia-
nent ; nor is imprisonment itself altogether a successful remedy,
or in each case it merely staves off the question of right for a
ew years. Still, on the whole, during the early part of the reign,
vith the exception of occasional ebullitions of resistance, Eliza-
)eth's Parliaments accepted all her acts as inevitable and right
mder the circumstances, and frequently testified their thorough
rust in her by grants which rendered her independent of them
or some time.

The first Parliament was occupied mainly with the restoration
)f the ecclesiastical system of Henry VIII. By 1563, however,
he importance of the succession question had become so pressing
:hat it was decided to bring forward an address to the queen in
ipite of her known repugnance to any discussion of the subject.
The address, however, produced no result, except a determination
on her part not to summon them again till it seemed absolutely
necessary. This session was remarkable for a law which excluded Catholics from the House of Commons, by requiring all
members to take the oath of supremacy, which the Catholics
were unable to do, as it implied an abjuration of the authority of
the Pope.

On the 30th September, 1566, Elizabeth's third Parliament
assembled. The House of Commons was the same which had
been elected at the beginning of the reign in the strength of the
Protestant reaction. Their first act was to remove all doubts
as to the validity of the consecration of the bishops at the
beginning of the reign ; their second to discuss the succession.
In fact, on October 18th, Mr. Molyneux proposed that the subsidy and the succession should be considered together, in order
to secure the arrangement of the latter. Sir Ralph Sadler, in
the hope of stopping the discussion, stated that he had heard
the queen say she intended to marry; and this statement was
formally confirmed next day by Cecil, Sir Francis Knowles, and
Sir Ambrose Cave. The Commons, however, were determined
on something more definite, and they proposed a conference
with the Lords to discuss the question. After sitting in con-

ference for a fortnight, an address was got ready to be presented. The queen now instructed the Marquis of Winchester, one of the oldest peers, to move that the address be not presented; and as his interference was ineffectual, she sent for the leading peers, and rated them rudely and sharply for daring to suggest that she should marry. On November 2nd, however, the address was presented and read by Bacon. The Commons prayed that she would marry as soon as possible, and further, to guard against all risks, that she would name a successor. Elizabeth was furious at this. She reprimanded them for their presumption, declared that she was not surprised at the Commons, for they had small experience, and acted like boys; but she wondered that the Lords should have gone along with them, and roundly asserted that if she named a successor, the realm would never more be free from civil war. Then her temper burst all bounds, and turning on the unlucky bishops, she abandoned all her notes, and addressed them with extempore eloquence. She bade them go home and amend their own lives, and set an honest example in their families. She told them that if the Peers did their duty, it would be to reduce them to their proper places, and that she would not forget hers, whatever the Peers might do. She vowed that it was only her great clemency which prevented her making an example of the whole set of them, and that she was determined now to marry that her husband might make them bitterly regret that they ever dared to thwart and cross their queen. And in this tragi-comic manner the interview ended abruptly and unproductively. The Commons, however, were as determined as the queen was obstinate, and though Cecil solemnly assured them that the queen intended to marry, another wrangling debate began again on Friday, November 8th. On Saturday, Elizabeth sent down a peremptory message that the succession was not to be touched on again, on pain of her displeasure. This attempt to stifle the freedom of debate only poured oil on the fire by raising a new and dangerous question of privilege. On Monday, Mr. Paul Wentworth inquired whether the queen's order was not a violation of their privileges, and a tremendous wrangle of five hours' duration followed, which was only ended by an adjournment—in itself an almost unprecedented occurrence. Elizabeth, more angry than ever, ordered that there should be no further argument. The Commons, in reply, presented an address, in which they regretted that the succession question should be delayed, and declared it their "ancient and audable custom, by her Majesty always confirmed, to treat and devise all matters honourable to her Majesty and profitable to the Crown." The storm, however, might possibly have been averted by Elizabeth's remarkable tact but for a new bone of contention. Mr. Dalton, on November 21st, entered into a general attack on the Queen of Scots and her claims, and gradually plunged deeply into the forbidden subject of the succession. Elizabeth promptly ordered him into custody. The Commons, however, protested firmly and decidedly, and the queen had the good sense to see that she could not treat them like so many mutinous school-boys. Dalton was released, and Parliament, to prove their real loyalty and affection for her, gave her an unusually large subsidy. They voted her an income-tax for two years, and it was only her own positive refusal to accept more which prevented them making the grant a larger one. They took the advantage, however, of the address at the dissolution, which was read by Mr. Speaker Onslow, to thank the queen in such a pointed manner for her promise to marry, that she rose from the throne in considerable anger, and lectured them severely in return before ordering the Lord Keeper to dissolve Parliament.

Five years elapsed before Parliament was summoned again, for Elizabeth was equally unwilling to marry or to arrange a definite order of succession. She dreaded a renewal of the wrangles, the insulting debates on her age and likelihood of bearing children, the frequent addresses beseeching her to marry, or at least declare her successor—all of which were no doubt extremely disagreeable. It was not, therefore, till the emptiness of her treasury positively compelled her, that she again summoned the two Houses of Parliament.

The Parliament which met on April 2nd, 1571, was fiercely Protestant. The plots of the Catholics, the massacres in the Netherlands, the fear of Spain, had produced a blind hatred of the Catholics, of Mary Stuart, and of any leanings towards

Catholicism. Parliament soon incurred the anger of the queen by proposing various reforms in the ritual and service of the Church of a decidedly Puritan tendency, by passing stringent laws directed against the Catholics, and especially by protesting against many things which Elizabeth regarded as entirely outside their province. In fact, there is little doubt that Elizabeth considered their interference in ecclesiastical matters, and the freedom with 'which they discussed ecclesiastical questions, as an intolerable impertinence. At last Mr. Strickland brought about a climax by introducing a bill for the reform of the Prayer-book. He was at once sent for, reprimanded, and forbidden to return to Parliament, but the Commons supported his cause so energetically that the queen was obliged to give in. The rest of the session was spent in passing severe laws against the supporters of Mary and the Pope; a subsidy of £100,000 was voted without any opposition; and Parliament was dismissed May 29th, after a long lecture from the throne on their arrogance, presumption, and folly. Most of Elizabeth's Parliaments ended in this ungracious way, which bears a very marked resemblance to a feminine desire to have the last word.

The Parliament of 1572, which met May 8th, was remarkable for a most determined attack on Mary Stuart, in consequence of universal indignation at the discovery of the Ridolphi Plot. The Council had made up their minds to introduce a Bill of Attainder against the Scotch queen, and the Commons so thoroughly sympathised with the views of the Council, that by the 19th they had determined to attaint her, and so "touch her in life as well as in title." Elizabeth, however, was firmly opposed to this measure, and the most conclusive arguments were in vain laid before her by the bishops, Lord Burleigh, and the Commons, in favour of the measure which they regarded as necessary to the safety of the queen and the realm. She allowed them to wreak their vengeance on the Duke of Norfolk, one of the prime movers in the plot, but when they endeavoured at least to disable Mary effectually from the succession, she interposed all sorts of difficulties and delays, finally proroguing them till October, thus effectually staving off the unwelcome question.

In the next session, which began February, 1576, a fresh
quarrel arose on the religious question. Elizabeth peremptorily
forbade the Commons to interfere with the established organization or worship in any way, and this interference was strongly
resented by the Protestant, and especially the Puritan members,
who regarded it as an outrageous violation of their privilege of
freedom of debate. Peter Wentworth, member for Tregony,
in Cornwall, a brother of Paul Wentworth, who had already
championed the cause of privilege, delivered a speech of great
boldness in defence of the liberties of the Commons. He complained "that not only were they forbidden to speak of religion,
but now they were to be silent on matters touching the interests
of every tradesman in the realm." "The customs duties were
suspended in favour of noblemen and courtiers; honest men
were robbed in thousands that three or four persons connected
with the palace might be enriched; and yet Parliament was
expected to be silent." "In the last Parliament he saw the liberty
of free speech so much and so many ways infringed, and so
many abuses offered to this honourable Council as had much
grieved him." "Either a rumour was spread about the House
that her Majesty was offended, or a message would come down
desiring that this or that complaint should not be mentioned.
He wished such rumours and messages were buried with the
other of them in hell." "None is without fault; no, not their
noble queen, but had committed great and dangerous faults to
herself." A rough, blunt speech, loyal enough in the main, but
decidedly unparliamentary, and containing reflections on the
queen's government which would have been considered indecent
in far less disturbed times. As it was, the Commons were
alarmed at his boldness, and they anticipated any action on the
part of the Government by sequestering him themselves. On
the report of a Committee of the House he was sent to the
Tower, where he remained a month, and then was reinstated by
the queen's order, after apologising on his knees to the Speaker
for his fault.

The session of 1576 was also remarkable for a case arising on
the subject of privilege. Smalley, a member's servant, was
arrested for debt. The Commons journals inform us that "after

E

sundry reasons, arguments, and disputations, and, what was more, after rescinding a previous resolution that they could find no precedents for setting at liberty any one in arrest, except by writ of privilege," they decided to repeat the process, which had not been made use of since the case of Ferrers.   The Serjeant-at-Arms was sent to release Smalley, February, 1575/6, but on its being subsequently discovered that he had procured this arrest with the view of defrauding his creditor of the debt, he was sent to prison for a month, and ordered to pay £100 to the plaintiff.

The next session began on January 16th, 1581.   It was understood that the session was to be a short one ; and the queen had intimated that she would not allow any interference with the Church on their part.   Sir John Popham, the Speaker, in compliance with her view, recommended them to be " discrete and brief."   Paul Wentworth, however, followed him with a recommendation that they should open proceedings by appointing a " fast of the House," and that business should commence every morning with a sermon at seven o'clock.   The House agreed, and though Sir F. Knowles, representing the queen, protested against it, the motion was carried.   Sunday the 25th was named for the fast.   Next day Elizabeth sent for Popham, and on his return he informed the House that her Majesty was much displeased with them, and required them to recall their resolutions.   Knowles spoke after him, stating that the queen did not object to fasting in itself, but thought it an affair outside their province, and especially considered it ungrateful of Wentworth, after her lenity to his brother.   Sir Nicholas St. Leger advised them to yield on the ground of their great affection for the queen, and they accepted his advice.   Sir Walter Mildmay then made a speech on the dangers which beset them, which they had only escaped through the ability of the queen, who had carried on the government at her own cost, without asking for subsidies.   He dilated on her virtues and talents, and finally proposed that measures should be taken to protect the realm against the Jesuit missionaries.   An Act was passed affixing the penalties of high treason to all conversions effected by Catholic priests, while aiding and abetting such acts was to be punished as isprision. A large subsidy was voted, and after a few more measures, Parliament was prorogued March 18th, by the queen in person. She thanked them for their services, but specially exempted from her thanks "those members of the Commons House as had during the season dealt more rashly in some things than was fit for them to do."

In this session occurred the leading precedent for the expulsion of a member from the House of Commons. Arthur Hall, member for Grantham, was charged with having published a slanderous book reflecting on the House of Commons generally, and also on individual members. He had several times previously incurred the anger of the House, but had escaped on apologising. Now, however, they determined to make an example of him. He was therefore expelled the House, fined 500 marks, and sent to the Tower, where he remained in confinement till released by the dissolution of Parliament.

A General Election was ordered for a new Parliament at the end of 1584—the Parliament of 1572 having been at last dissolved. The House met on November 23rd, in a perfect frenzy of terror and fury at the daring invasion of the Jesuits, and the plots directed against Elizabeth's life. After much consideration, a bill was brought in to render all Jesuits and seminary priests liable to the punishment of high treason if found within the realm after forty days. It was opposed by Dr. Parry, member for Queenborough, who denounced it as "cruel and bloody." He was committed instantly to the custody of the Serjeant, who placed him on his knees at the bar. Being required to explain his words, he declared that he had not meant to offend, and that he would reserve his reasons. Elizabeth interposed in his behalf, and after acknowledging his fault, he was allowed to resume his seat. The real loyalty and affection of the House towards the queen was strikingly shown on the adjournment, December 21st. Sir Christopher Hatton, who notified Elizabeth's pleasure, proposed to the House that before they separated, they should join him in a prayer for the queen's continued preservation, which they did with the greatest fervour, all on their knees, on the floor of the House. When they assembled again, the discovery of a fresh plot against Elizabeth's life roused them to such fury that they passed a statute for the queen's security, under which Mary Stuart was shortly executed.

The session of 1586 came hard on the discovery of the Babington Plot, and the Houses, after considering and debating the matter with great care, advised the execution of Mary as a traitress under the statute of 1585. During this session two important cases of privilege arose. A poor currier, named Bland, was accused of uttering contemptuous words against the Commons. He was cited to the bar of the House, and only discharged after making a humble submission, and paying a fine of 20*s*. The second case affected the jurisdiction over contested elections, which had been first claimed under Mary. Some irregularity occurred with regard to the returns for the county of Norfolk. The Chancellor, therefore, issued a fresh writ, and another member was elected. The Commons took the matter up, and, in spite of a peremptory order from the queen not to meddle with matters which did not concern them, appointed a committee to inquire into and settle the matter.

The queen, in spite of her lectures to her Commons on their presumption, had not really met with any opposition since 1576. In February, 1588, however, zeal for ecclesiastical reformation inspired one Mr. Cope to bring forward a Bill annulling all the laws affecting ecclesiastical government then existing, and introducing a new form of common prayer in the shape of a new Prayer-book, a copy of which he submitted to the House with the Bill. The Speaker, Serjeant Pickering, tried to prevent the Bill being read, and in consequence Peter Wentworth demanded to know whether the House had or had not the full right of discussing any laws they liked, and whether the Sovereign, or Speaker, had any right to prevent them. The Speaker declined to read out these questions, and showed them to a courtier, who procured the committal of Wentworth, Cope, and all who had supported them, to the Tower, where they remained three weeks, till the dissolution released them.

CHAPTER V.

RISE OF THE OPPOSITION. (1588–1640.)

SECTION 1.—*Last Years of Elizabeth* (1588–1603).

THE destruction of the Spanish Armada, 1588, marks the beginning of a new period in the history of the Parliament, hich may be described as the rise of the Opposition and the efeasance of the Tudor despotism. The Tudors had played ieir part in the history of the country successfully. Their strong ands had steered England through the difficult and dangerous :isis of the early Reformation period, at a time when no class as strong enough to assume the government of the country, when ie people had lost their old leaders, and knew not as yet where) look for fresh ones. Exceptional dangers and panic thereby iduced enabled the Tudor dynasty to grasp exceptional powers ith the full consent of the people, who saw in the exercise f these powers the sole hope of safety. Unusual stretches of uthority and outrageous acts of oppression were winked at, nay, ven condoned, in order that the hands of the Government might ot be weakened. Opposition of any kind was rarely offered, was onciliated by the slightest concession, was willing to be cajoled 'ith extraordinary facility. The Tudors, moreover, were possessed f wonderful tact ; they always knew how to trim their sails to the opular blast, to yield at the right time with a grace that disarmed pposition at once, and enabled them to resume the old course at 'ill, unfettered by any fears of the consequences. Even under :lizabeth, the strictures of the Wentworths and other parlia- ientary critics were not directed against Elizabeth's principle of overnment in general—that was recognised to be as yet the only ine possible.

With the destruction of the Armada, however, this exceptional tate of things came to an end, and it was felt that the exceptional node of government should terminate as well. The crisis had been successfully tided over, the danger of a Spanish invasion and a Catholic league against England was averted, the "state of siege" was concluded, and a return to constitutional and ordinary methods seemed the natural result. This, however, neither Elizabeth nor her successors understood, nor was it unnatural that they should not. Elizabeth's wonderful feminine tact, however, enabled her to avoid any direct quarrel with the growing forces of the opposition; but the utterly impracticable character of the first two Stuarts fostered the rising discontent, and fanned the smouldering embers to angry flames, till the whole realm took fire.

The change was apparent almost directly in the Parliament of 1588–89. It was still more so in the Parliament of 1593. For though the Crown assumed in the latter a higher tone than it had ever done before on the subject of freedom of speech, this did not prevent the succession question from being mooted with great determination by Peter Wentworth, nor reforms of the ecclesiastical courts being proposed by Mr. Morice. Wentworth and Morice were both imprisoned, but this was the last victory which Elizabeth was to win in Parliament by the old violent tactics. This session was also remarkable for a contest in which the Commons successfully maintained against the Crown and the Lords their sole right to the initiation of money-bills.

It was in the Parliament of 1601 that the first great battle of the Opposition was fought and its victory won. The struggle arose on the question of monopolies, which had become a great abuse. Attempts had been made in previous Parliaments to deal with the question, but without success. In 1597 they were protested against unsuccessfully. In 1601, however, a list was made out, and it was proposed to abolish them by law. An eager debate followed. Robert Cecil, the Secretary, and Francis Bacon strongly upheld prerogative, in language dimly foreshadowing the absurd hyperbole of later days. Mr. Davis declared that "God hath given that power to absolute princes which He attributes to Himself." Serjeant Heyle roundly asserted that the queen could take what she pleased from the subject, of right. The opponents of the monopolies, however, were firm, and Elizabeth at last wisely ended the question by voluntarily offering to surrender them.

In minor matters, moreover, the Commons showed their determination to maintain their privileges. They complained to the Lords in 1597 that they had received a message from the Commons at their bar without rising from their place or uncovering. This, however, the Lords proved from precedents to be the proper procedure in the case of messages. The Commons also remonstrated against amendments being sent down on paper instead of parchment, though this would be hardly worth recording but for the growing determination which it shows on their part to resist all encroachments on their rights.

Section 2.—*James I* (1603-1625).

James I. came to the throne at a very critical period of our history. The Puritan opposition was now organized and powerful, and though Elizabeth's tact and popularity had postponed till her death the impending struggle between liberty and prerogative, the advent of her successor was naturally looked forward to with considerable eagerness. Voluntary concessions were expected at his hands ; or, in default, there was a settled determination to resist all attempted infringements of the privileges of Parliament and the liberties of the subject. Much therefore depended on James's character and policy. Skilful management and a gracious demeanour might have averted the contest. Unfortunately, or perhaps we should rather say fortunately, James was imbued with the mistaken notion that the crown of the Tudors descended to him by " divine right," that their powers and prerogatives came to him as part of an indefeasible inheritance, and that resistance to his divinely-gifted authority was little short of impiety. By the side of such majestic claims, the privileges of Parliament and the liberties of the subject were dwarfed to nothingness, and the whole body of the common law itself was but so many acres of discoloured parchment when subjected to the overruling influence of the extraordinary prerogative which James asserted to reside in the Crown. There was no hope of concession, no chance of compromise, no possibility of agreement. The triumph of either side, moreover, was not compatible with anything short of a complete surrender on the part of the other. Parliament must either acknowledge to the full that the king's power was twofold, ordinary and extraordinary—the former being subject to the restrictions of the common law; and the latter, the exercise of which would be left wholly to the king's discretion, being entirely uncontrolled : or else Parliament must resist to the uttermost, must maintain every tittle of their own claims, must resent the smallest infringement of their privileges, must refurbish up all the old weapons in the constitutional arsenal, and must even venture on the dangerous task of forging new ones. The whole tendency of parliamentary history during the preceding century was in the direction of unqualified resistance, and there was no longer any imminent danger which had made men fear to weaken the government, even when they disapproved of its action. The constitutional path lay broad and white before the feet of the Commons, and if its end were lost as yet in the dim mists of the future, the marks by the wayside were drawn clear and distinct enough at starting.

The House of Commons was divided at the accession of James into two distinct parties—the Government and the Opposition. The former included a number of officials and a large body of Crown nominees; the latter consisted of two classes—country gentlemen of wealth and local influence sent by the freeholders of their counties to represent them in Parliament; and men of ability, who supplied their lack of local influence by the favour and help of some great landed proprietor, or the recommendation of a knot of influential men, or the admiration or corruption of some small constituency. Among the last class of members was a considerable body of lawyers, who became known to the electors by their talents displayed at the bar, and whose entrance into Parliament was rendered possible by the defeasance of the restrictions which had insisted on residence as a qualification for membership.[1] "The services which this class of men rendered to the cause of freedom were," says Professor Gardiner, "incalculable. The learning of the ablest lawyers in the sixteenth century may have been small in comparison with the stores of knowledge which may be acquired in our own day; but relatively to the general level of education, it stood far higher. A few years later

---

[1] *v.* p. 21.

race of parliamentary statesmen would arise among the country
entlemen ; but as yet almost all pretension to statesmanship
as confined to the council-table and its supporters. For the
resent, the burden of the conflict in the Commons lay upon the
wyers, who at once gave to the struggle against the Crown that
rong legal character which it never afterwards lost."

" Between the Crown and the House of Commons," continues
rofessor Gardiner, "the House of Lords could only play a sub-
rdinate part. It had no longer sufficient power to act indepen-
ently of both." It was at present entirely in sympathy with the
ng and the prerogative. There is no trace of any opposition in
s ranks in the first years of James I.

The first note of battle was sounded by the king. In January,
504, a proclamation was issued calling upon the constituencies
) send up members to Parliament, declaring that the elections
ould be made freely, and recommending the choice of suitable
en. The proclamation further ordered that all returns should
e made to the Chancery, where, if "any should be found to be
ade contrary to the proclamation," they were to be rejected as
nlawful and insufficient. This last clause, involving an infringe-
ent of a much-cherished privilege, was sure to provoke the most
iolent opposition.

On March 19th, Parliament met, and it was noticed that there
as an unusually full attendance. It might also have been
emarked, as a sign of the times, that the Crown was only repre-
ented in the Commons by inferior men. There were no Privy
Councillors, no Secretary as in Elizabeth's days ; only an under-
ecretary and some other minor officials. Evidently the new
ing did not attach much importance to the difficult task of con-
iliating the good-will of the House of Commons.

The leading man in Parliament at the commencement of the
ession was Sir Francis Bacon. Two boroughs had elected him
s their representative. His name occurred on nearly every
ommittee of any weight—generally in the important capacity of
eporter (chairman). He was invariably selected as one of the
eaders in conferences with the House of Lords. He was now,
n fact, in the full tide of his parliamentary success. Next to
3acon the most influential man was Sir Edwin Sandys. After

these may be mentioned Nicholas Fuller, Hakewill, Thomas Wentworth—the son of Elizabeth's old enemy, the two Hydes, and some others; but there are few who deserve special attention.

It was felt from the first that a struggle with the Crown was at hand, and this feeling was expressed by the Speaker, Sir Edward Philips, when, in reply to an address from the throne, he reminded the king that the royal power was limited, and that the privileges of Parliament were as undoubted as the rights of the prerogative.

It was on the question of privilege of Parliament that the quarrel began. The Commons found almost as soon as they had assembled that the Chancery had, in accordance with the king's proclamation, inquired into the Buckinghamshire election, and rejected the elected member, Sir Francis Goodwin, as an outlaw and an unsuitable person. A new election was therefore held, and Sir John Fortescue elected in his place. The subject was raised in the House, the action of Chancery deliberately ignored, and Goodwin summoned to take his seat in the ordinary way, just as if nothing had happened. A long dispute with the Crown naturally ensued. James struck at once at the root of the matter, by denying that the House had any jurisdiction over elections at all. The House as firmly maintained their sole right. In the end a compromise was effected. The king acknowledged that he was mistaken, and that the Commons were in the right on the question of privilege, but he requested as a personal favour that they would set aside both parties, and issue a writ for a new election ; this the Commons assented to without any difficulty. "That the substantial advantage remained with the Commons," says Professor Gardiner, "is evident from the fact that they at once proceeded without any opposition to investigate two other cases of contested elections." It may be as well to add that their right to decide all matters connected with their own elections was never again disputed.

There was another question of privilege also to be dealt with. Sir Thomas Shirley, member for Steyning, had been arrested for debt shortly after his election, but before the meeting of Parliament, and imprisoned in the Fleet. The Commons sent their

Serjeant to demand his release. The Warden of the Fleet, however, refused to surrender him, for fear of becoming personally answerable for the debt in his place. The Commons found themselves in a dilemma. They committed the warden to the Tower, and further to a filthy dungeon called the Little Ease; but it was not until the king interposed at their special request, and ordered the warden to submit, that Shirley was enabled to take his seat in Parliament. In order, however to definitely settle the law of privilege for the future, and to provide for certain hardships arising out of it, a statute was immediately passed, which declared the privilege of freedom from arrest, the right of either House to free a privileged person from arrest, and the right to punish all who make or procure arrests, to be already existing law; and further added, that a jailer who delivered up a privileged person at the order of either House should not be liable to any action at law in consequence, and that the creditor of the privileged person might bring a fresh suit against the latter at the expiration of his privilege. This statute was the *first legislative recognition of this privilege.*

A long and stormy session followed, occupied chiefly with complaints with regard to the burdens of feudalism, which still fell heavily on the subject, though the feudal system itself had long been obsolete; recriminations over ecclesiastical matters, and the proposed Union of England and Scotland; besides other disputes of various kinds. In the end the Commons drew up an elaborate Apology, with the view of explaining to the king their true constitutional position and privileges, of which, in their opinion, he appeared to have a very inadequate conception. They began by informing him that they had selected him as king of choice, not of necessity; that their privileges did not depend on his will, but were theirs of right; that they had complete and sole jurisdiction over their own elections. They further claimed the full right of freedom of speech, and begged that for the future he would only listen to official accounts of their proceedings, and not to private and malicious misrepresentations. This apology formed the constitutional manifesto of the Commons, to which they adhered steadily during the whole of the struggle. "They did not ask for anything which was not in accordance with justice. They did not demand a single privilege which was not necessary for the good of the nation as well as for their own dignity." This apology was never actually presented to the king, but it is highly probable that he must have seen a copy of it.

Fresh subjects of dispute were continually arising : the Commons attacked the great trading companies ; the Crown supported them. The Commons desired to maintain the old unfriendly relations with Spain ; James wished for peace and a Spanish alliance. The Commons were disposed to extend toleration to the Puritans ; James put the Puritan leaders in prison. James intended to relax the operation of the penal laws against the Catholics ; the Commons were bent on a more rigorous enforce-men of the existing laws and the addition of new ones. In many cases the king's proposed policy was by far the more enlightened and reasonable of the two, but his methods were invariably unwise, and his demeanour exasperating almost to imbecility.

The rising importance of Parliament was most strongly testified to by the Gunpowder Plot—a conspiracy devised by a few desperate men, Catholics by religion, who were ready for any wild and daring scheme that gave hope of relief from the cruel and unjust oppression of the penal laws. The plots of Elizabeth's reign had all been directed against the life of the queen alone ; that once taken away, the whole framework of government would have fallen into disorder. But now the Catholics began to realize that their true oppressors were the Parliament, and that any stroke would be wanting in completeness if it left Parliament uninjured. The details of the plot,—the names of the conspirators, the cellar under the Houses of Parliament, the sacks of coal and barrels of gunpowder which were hidden in it, the comings and goings of Mr. Guido Fawkes with the lantern and conical hat, well-known and beloved by the youth of England, the leaking out of the plot through the tenderness and timidity of one of the conspirators, the last grand sensational tableau of the arrest of Mr. Fawkes and the discovery of the gunpowder,—all these belong to more general history.

The next session of Parliament lasted from January 21, 1605/6, to May 27, 1606. Constant recriminations arose between the

ing and the Commons on various subjects, but there was no
ery decided action on either side. The rule, however, that a
ill cannot be proposed twice in the session was established,
robably for the first time, by the action of the Lords, who
eremptorily rejected one which the Commons sent up to them
iortly after they had thrown out a previous bill to the same
ffect.

In the session of November 18, 1606—June 4, 1607, the same
iscord prevailed. The principal cause of dispute was the king's
roject of the Union. During the debates on this subject, Sir
'hristopher Pigott, member for Bucks, described the Scots as
eggars, rebels, traitors; declared that there had not been a
ingle king of Scotland who had not been murdered by his
ibjects; and roundly asserted that it was as reasonable to unite
ingland and Scotland as it would be to place a prisoner at the
ar on an equality with a judge upon the bench. The Commons
stened in silence; no doubt in secret sympathy as well. The
ing, however, was furious, and his anger obliged them to take
ome notice of Pigott's unnecessary and indecent violence.
They resolved first that Pigott, being a member of the House,
ras not liable to be called in question elsewhere; and then, in
irder to satisfy the king, they decreed his expulsion and imprison-
nent.

During another debate Mr. Fuller drew a doleful picture of
he results which would flow to England from the union—im-
ioverishment, depression of trade, oppression under the heel of
he foreigner. Bacon replied at length, and supported the
inion enthusiastically, denying Fuller's statements, and drawing
i counter-picture in glowing colours. But in spite of his argu-
nents, and the well-known wishes of the king, the Commons
vould have none of it.

Their obstinacy, their complaints, and their bold assertion of
:heir privileges, so offended James that he allowed a year and a
half to elapse before he summoned them again. During this
period he made his first essay at arbitrary government, and inaugurated the policy, which was to be so characteristic of this
dynasty, of employing the judges as a means of superseding the
Legislature, and deciding all disputed points of law in favour of

the Crown.   When, therefore, his financial difficulties compelled him once more to summon Parliament, February 9, 1609, there were a long list of grievances waiting to be redressed.   Special efforts were made to secure a majority for the Crown.   Wherever a vacancy had occurred during the prorogation, letters were sent to people of influence requesting that royal nominees might be elected.   In some cases the answers were favourable ; in others, the constituency, while refusing the candidate proffered by the Crown, guaranteed that their members should vote entirely according to the wishes of the Government.

The session opened, however, with a tremendous skirmish over the decision in Bates' case, which had affirmed, in defiance of common law, statutes, and precedents, that the king could of his own prerogative increase the amount of the customs without referring the matter to Parliament.   For four days the question was debated, in spite of the king's prohibition ; Whitelocke, Hakewill, and Yelverton, being especially conspicuous in their denunciations of the illegality of the decision.   The House was nearly unanimous against the Crown, and in the end they presented a strong remonstrance, both with regard to the illegality of the increase of the customs and the king's attempt to stifle discussion. They complained, moreover, in succession, of a long list of grievances, and showed themselves altogether so intractable, and so reluctant to grant money, until their grievances were redressed, that James at last, in a huff, dissolved them, February 9, 1611.

A second period of arbitrary government now ensued, and once more James had to face the difficulty of making two ends meet without the help of Parliament.   His financial expedients, however, were highly unsuccessful, and at the end of three years he was glad to listen to a project communicated to him by Sir Henry Nevile, Bacon, and some others.   They proposed to influence the elections, to win over the leaders of the opposition by royal favours, to buy votes by flattery, force desertions by intimidation, conciliate many by small concessions, and then Parliament, thus happily converted from its evil ways, would of course vote unlimited supplies.   The scheme of these "Undertakers," however, leaked out, and caused general indignation, with the result that

ie Court candidates were rejected on all sides; that the Govern-
ent found themselves in a small minority; that when Parlia-
ent met at last, April 5, 1614, the Commons proved to be no
ore ready to be cajoled out of their money in return for nothing
ian their predecessors had been; and that James endured them
r barely two months, and then dissolved them in a rage. From
ie circumstance of its not having passed a single bill, this
isembly was nicknamed " the Addled Parliament."

James now committed himself still more deeply to the struggle
ith the House of Commons, by imprisoning four of the members,
hose language had been unusually warm. The importance of
iis step it is impossible to overrate. It was a declaration of war
) the death, and it must inevitably provoke reprisals. By it
imes asserted his right to control the representatives of the
eople; and the latter would inevitably bethink themselves of
ie days when they had controlled the executive.

For seven years James governed without Parliament, badly
nd unsuccessfully, plunging more deeply into arbitrary methods,
nd yet totally unable to supply himself with enough money to
arry on the government with any rag of credit. The outbreak
f the Thirty Years' war, however, obliged him once more to
ummon Parliament, and lay before them the hopeless state-
ient of his financial difficulties.

The Parliament which met January 30, 1620/1, was remarkable
1 many ways. First, most of the men who became prominent in
he impending struggle were returned to it. Secondly, we find
or the first time a small Liberal minority in the House of Lords
ympathising with the aims of the Commons, consisting of the
iarls of Essex, Southampton, Warwick, Oxford, Saye and Sele,
nd Lord Spencer. Thirdly, that far from being inspired from
he first with any formed hostility to the king, the Commons were
)ossessed with a most conciliatory spirit; and, if James would
inly have consented to reform abuses at home and to defend
?rotestantism abroad, they were prepared to follow him with un-
juestioning fidelity. From the first they showed their desire for
:onciliation. They complained, it is true, that the laws were not
)roperly enforced against the Catholics, and also that their privi-
eges had been violated by the arrests at the end of the preceding

Parliament ; but they readily accepted the king's assurances that
it should not occur again, and they voted two subsidies with great
alacrity.

On the motion of Sir Edward Coke, who, disgraced by the
Court, now took up the position of popular leader, the Commons
appointed a committee to inquire into grievances; and the
revelations which followed provoked such an outcry that nothing
short of stringent measures would satisfy them.   They therefore
revived the old weapon of impeachment, which had fallen into
disuse since 1449, owing to the preference which the Tudor
dynasty had displayed for Bills of Attainder, as the surest mode
of attacking political offenders, while their own weakness and
subservience during that period had prevented their acting on
their own initiative.   Articles of impeachment were drawn up
against some holders of royal monopolies who had grossly abused
their powers, against judges who had turned justice into injustice,
and, lastly, against Lord Chancellor Bacon himself, for receiving
bribes from the suitors in his own court.   The indictment in
the latter case was laid before the House of Peers while Bacon
was actually presiding on the woolsack.   He was found guilty,
and condemned in heavy penalties.   The proceedings in this
case are of particular importance, for Bacon was a royal minister,—
nay one of the highest,—and the action of the Commons was
undoubtedly as much inspired by resentment at the systematic
way in which he had upheld the prerogative at the Chancery as
by the love of judicial purity.   In the midst of these wise and
necessary measures, however, they brought disgrace on themselves, and became involved in a quarrel with the Lords, by
ordering that one Mr. Floyd, a Roman Catholic barrister, should
be punished with inhuman severity for the crime of exulting in
the misfortunes of James's son-in-law, the unlucky Frederick
Count Palatine.   The Lords declared that the judicial rights of
Parliament belonged to them alone, and that the Commons had
the power of accusation only, quoting in support of this statement a declaration to the same effect made by the Commons in
the first year of Henry IV.[1]   The Commons, not feeling them-

----

[1] *v.* p. 23.

lves in a position to deny their own words, assented to the
aim of the Lords, and transferred to them the privilege of
indemning the miserable wretch to an altogether monstrous
inishment.

The harmony between the king and his Parliament did not
st long. He offended them by a sudden prorogation; still more
ι prosecutions instituted during the recess against their principal
aders—Sir Edward Coke and Sir Edwin Sandys; still more by
s manifest leanings to a Spanish alliance and a Spanish marriage
r his son Charles. James, in reply to their complaints, only
ld them not to interfere with foreign policy, which was no
isiness of theirs. They sent up at once an energetic protesta-
on, claiming the full right of discussing freely any subject they
ight select without censure from any outside power. James's
iswer was sharp and short. Sending for the Journals of the
[ouse, he tore out the protestation with his own hands, in the
resence of the Privy Council, and immediately afterwards dis-
)lved Parliament. His principal opponents—Coke, Philips,
elden, Pym, Mallory, and the Earl of Oxford were com-
iitted to prison. And so James returned once more to his old
ays.

The last Parliament of the reign, summoned in February, 1623/4,
as chiefly remarkable for an effort on the part of Prince Charles
nd the Duke of Buckingham to recover their lost popularity by
ipporting the Commons in their desire for a Spanish war, and
y hounding them on to impeach Lord High Treasurer Middlesex,
staunch supporter of the Spanish alliance, on the nominal ground
f bribery and malversation of public money. The accusation
as a mere blind to hide their personal feeling, but the case was
f the utmost importance. It confirmed for ever to the Commons
ieir right of impeaching the royal ministers, which the single
ase of Bacon might have been insufficient to establish. It also
efinitely enunciated the constitutional doctrine, that ministers
re responsible to Parliament for their conduct. "Steenie,
teenie," said the old king in disgust at the suicidal folly of his
ivourite, "you are a fool. You are making a rod, and you will
e scourged well with it yourself." Then turning to Charles, he
varned him that he would soon have his "bellyful of impeach-

F

ments." It is worth noting that this Parliament was the only one in the reign which did not terminate in passion and anger on both sides, and that this unusual circumstance was mainly due to the satisfaction of the Commons at that event which had caused James the bitterest chagrin—the total failure of his efforts to bring about the Spanish marriage.

CHAPTER VI.

THE EARLY STRUGGLES WITH CHARLES I.

(1625-1640.)

THE popularity which Charles and his favourite had gained by their conduct in the Parliament of 1624 was but short-ived, and it had almost entirely vanished by the meeting of the irst Parliament of the new reign. The grievances under which he people laboured were too numerous and real to be easily for-;otten ; the state of the royal finances was far too embarrassed ; he open favour accorded by the Court to the Arminian clergy and the preachers of passive obedience was too alarming ; the French marriage and the toleration conceded to the Catholics were too exasperating ; the part which Charles and Buckingham had really played in the Spanish negotiations was too dishonest and equivocal, for it to be possible for the nation to retain very long any confidence in the new king, or in the man to whose malign influence they attributed all their evils.

The General Election of 1625 was an exciting time. Never had the competition for seats been so keen within the memory of man. Never had the meeting of Parliament been so numerously attended—and this though the plague was raging in London. Sir Edward Coke, Sir John Eliot, Sir Dudley Digges, Mr. Pym, Mr. Mallory, Sir Thomas Wentworth, Sir Edward Philips, and many others who had been prominent in preceding Parliaments, or were destined to come to the front in future ones, were all returned to Westminster. The speech from the throne was con-ciliatory, but vague. The Commons were reminded of the king's necessities, and that the breach with Spain was mainly their own work. Money was urgently asked for, but no sum was named and no details given. The Commons were anxious and distrust-ful. They feared to make the king independent of them too soon, and they determined to be sparing of the supplies. It

was this feeling which prompted them to offer Charles only two
subsidies, and to limit the usual grant of tunnage and poundage
to one year only.   They were resolved not to grant more until
grievances had been redressed, and their determination was
strengthened by the news that English ships had been lent by
the Government to France for the ruin of the Huguenots of La
Rochelle.   This occurred during a prorogation brought about by
the alarming increase of the plague.   When the two Houses
reassembled at Oxford, Aug. 1, Sir Edward Philips definitely took
the lead in denouncing the disasters and failures of the royal
policy : there was a general outcry against misgovernment and
mismanagement; and at last Sir Francis Seymour spoke out
what was in the mind of all.   " Let us lay the fault where it is," he
said.   " The Duke of Buckingham is trusted, and it must needs
be either in him or his agents."   Furious at this attack on his
favourite, Charles immediately dissolved them, and thus definitely
committed himself to the downward path which led to destruction.

The failure of another expedition against Cadiz obliged the
king to summon a Parliament again very shortly.   In the hope
of lessening the chances of opposition, sheriffdoms were very
unwisely conferred on Coke, Seymour, Philips, Wentworth, and
two others, with the object of disqualifying them for Parliament.
Coke, however, declared that the disqualification applied only to
his own county, and secured his election for another ; but still
the move was so far successful that none of the six appear to
have sat in this Parliament.   This trivial success, however, was
amply counterbalanced by the exasperation which it excited
among the popular party, and especially the devolving of the
leadership on Sir John Eliot.   The name of Eliot is in fact as
much identified with this Parliament as those of Coke and Philips
with the two preceding ones.

Eliot, however, was not yet committed to opposition.   In the
last Parliament he had even defended Buckingham's integrity.
Nothing but dire experience would have thrown him over to the
other side.   Had Charles met his Parliament in a different spirit,
had he courted inquiry in the slightest, instead of merely demanding money, Eliot might not have broken loose from the
Court.   But the Court stood firm in its old unbending position,

ınd Eliot's first words were to declare, in impassioned language, hat the country had been brought to the verge of ruin, and to lemand a committee of inquiry into the causes. Till this ıad been done, nothing should be said about the king's supply.

Three great committees were quickly appointed, one for eligion, one for grievances, and the third for evils and their emedies. An extraordinary number of abuses and illegalities vere immediately revealed, and it soon became apparent that the ırimary cause of the mismanagement and failure of the war, the lisordered state of the finances, and the peculations in the public ;ervice, was to be found in the all-controlling influence of the Duke of Buckingham. In vain the king demanded money : ıe was presented instead with a long list of grievances requiring .nstant remedy. In vain he warned them angrily that they had better not aim at any of his servants in their search after griev-ınces—still less at the Duke of Buckingham : in repiy, Dr. Turner rose and told the House openly, that the cause of all their grievances was " that great man, the Duke of Buckingham," and in a series of six questions denounced the chief crimes of the duke as a matter of common fame. Then Eliot again assumed the leadership of the House, and formally proposed the impeach-ment of Buckingham. After a debate whether common fame were a sufficient ground, which was decided in the affirmative, the Commons resolved upon the impeachment, and determined "to proceed to the great affair of Buckingham morning and after-noon till it was done, to the end that they might proceed to con-sider his Majesty's demand for supply."

Charles did not dare let the impeachment be carried to its close, for he could not even rely on the Lords, owing to his unwise interference with their privileges. The Earl of Bristol, late ambassador to Spain, could have explained Buckingham's exact share in the Spanish business with most undesirable accuracy : he was, therefore, first refused his summons, and then ordered to abstain from appearing in Parliament. The Earl of Arundel was Buckingham's principal enemy and the holder of six proxies : his hostility had been stifled by imprisonment. In each case, how-ever, the king had to give in, and the Lords successfully placed on record a protest of the right of a peer to receive his special

summons, and that the privilege of freedom of the person availed
in all cases but those of treason, felony, and refusing to give
securities against breach of the peace.   In despair, Charles
brought a prosecution for high treason against Bristol in order
to stop his tongue, but the Commons frustrated this move by
permitting him to be heard by counsel. The impeachment opened
on May 8, the principal leaders among the managers being
Sir John Eliot and Sir Dudley Digges.

Digges began by stating the doctrine of ministerial responsibility on the broadest lines.   Mr. Selden then dilated on the
inefficiency of the navy under Buckingham's *régime*.   Serjeant
Glanville denounced the exactions wrung from the East India
Company, and the treacherous loan of ships to France to be
used against the Protestants of Rochelle.   Mr. Herbert protested
that the accumulation of so many offices in one hand was hurtful
to the dearest interests of the realm.   Mr. Pym spoke of the
nepotism which had disgraced Buckingham's career.   Others
added each their quota to the whole.   Lastly, Eliot summed up
in a speech of extraordinary power and virulence.   He denied
most emphatically that any man could shelter himself under the
king's commands from the consequences of his own evil deeds.
He denounced Buckingham as a second Sejanus, a bold, proud,
and slanderous man.   He pointed to Buckingham where he sat
with his costly robes glittering with priceless jewels, and a contemptuous smile wreathing his handsome features, "My lords,
you *see* the man.   What have been his actions, whom he is like,
you know.   I leave him to your judgment."   Eliot and Digges
even ventured to hint that Buckingham was directly or indirectly
responsible for James's death by poison.

For the boldness of their speeches, and more especially for the
last insinuation, Eliot and Digges were committed to the Tower,
only to be released again almost immediately, when it was found
that the Commons absolutely refused to do any business without
them.   Ungracious apologies for violence were offered on both
sides. Eliot and Digges reappeared in the Commons, and the impeachment continued.   At last, Charles perceiving plainly that
there was no hope of an acquittal or a breakdown, peremptorily
demanded a subsidy, and on receiving in answer only a most

energetic remonstrance, dissolved Parliament the very next day, June 15, 1626.

These hasty and premature dissolutions of Parliament under the specious appearance of staving them off for awhile, served but to aggravate the embarrassments of the Crown. The same men were, for the most part, returned again and again, and they came back to Westminster more irritated and desperate of reconciliation with the sovereign than before. Even Clarendon, writing in exile under the Commonwealth, declares that " no man can show a source from whence these waters of bitterness we now taste have more probably flowed, than from these unseasonable, unskilful, and precipitate dissolutions of Parliament." If, moreover, the king intended to prevent all attacks on his Government by dissolving Parliament, the time must eventually come when he must endeavour to rule without a Parliament, and commit himself more deeply than ever to the perilous venture on which he had started. For twenty-one months, therefore, he endeavoured to carry on the government without Parliament, and succeeded, at the cost of alienating the majority of the nation by his financial experiments. Then the absolute necessity of procuring a large sum to repair the deficit in the exchequer, caused by the miserable failure of the expedition to the Isle of Rhé, obliged him once more to risk the unwelcome prospect of meeting another Parliament.

The elections went dead against the Crown. All who had taken any part in resisting Charles's arbitrary exactions of money were welcomed by the electors with the utmost enthusiasm, and it is curious to note that among them was Sir Thomas Wentworth, afterwards the principal instrument of Charles's policy, and " damned to everlasting fame " under the name of Strafford. Parliament did not meet till March 17, 1628; but a few days before, the principal leaders had assembled at the house of Sir Robert Cotton, and decided not to renew the impeachment of Buckingham—Coke, Philips, Wentworth, Selden, Eliot, all concurring in the view that it was far more necessary, nay vital, to vindicate first the rights of the subject which had been violated so unsparingly during the late period of personal government.

The speech from the throne was not conciliatory. Charles

"scorned to threaten them," but only "because they were not his equals." The ministers and courtiers demanded an immediate supply. In reply, Wentworth denounced the illegalities of the last year. "They have taken from us!" he cried, "What shall I say? Indeed, what have they left us?" Then he demanded signal retribution on the guilty instruments. In the debates which ensued, grievances were discussed unsparingly—illegal imprisonments, illegal taxation, martial law, illegal billeting of soldiers were all passed in review, with every now and then a fling at the illegal toleration permitted to the Catholics. Meanwhile the king was at his wit's end for his supply, for though the Commons proposed to give him five subsidies, this was to be conditional on redress of grievances. Conspicuous among the popular leaders during these debates were Eliot and Wentworth—Eliot now, as ever, commanding the reverence of the House by his unflinching integrity, his patriotic earnestness, his stern adherence to constitutional precedent; Wentworth, however, coming more and more to the front, and assuming definitely the foremost place in right of his superior daring and self-confidence. Selden, Coke, Littleton, Digges, Noy, and other eminent lawyers lent the weight of their eloquence and learning to the popular cause. The Attorney-General Heath, Serjeant Ashley and others supported the interests of the Crown.

A series of petitions against grievances were sent up to the king. Ultimately they were incorporated in a grand whole which is known as the Petition of Right. The wrongs complained of were—(1) Illegal levying of taxation without consent of Parliament in defiance of statute law; (2) Illegal imprisonment of men without cause, in defiance of statute law; (3) Illegal billeting of soldiers on the people against their will; (4) Illegal use of martial law. The whole wound up with a demand that these illegalities should not be repeated. This Petition was mainly the work of Coke, though it undoubtedly sprang primarily from the initiative of Wentworth.

Wentworth's leadership was, however, drawing nigh to its close. All through he had based his conduct on the theory that the king really meant well, and that the blame lay with the agents, above all with Buckingham. The king, however, returned an vasive reply to the Petition, which was tantamount to a refusal: ie fallacy of Wentworth's views was thereby revealed; the ommons were plunged once more in hopeless despair. Their eling of utter helplessness produced a strange scene. Strong, earded men broke into sobs and tears like frightened children. hilips at last rose, and in a broken voice, told the House that ɔ good could come of their remaining there. Let them ask leave ɩ go home. Eliot, once more taking up the position that /entworth had abdicated, declared that the king was misin- ɔrmed as to their conduct, and especially with regard to any spersions on ministers. He was proceeding further, when Finch, ie Speaker, rose and interrupted him. "There is a command ɩd on me," he said, with tears in his eyes, "to interrupt any ɩat should go about to lay an aspersion on the ministers of state." liot at once sat down—since he could not speak freely, he ould not speak at all; and Digges expressed the sense of the [ouse, when he declared that if they might not discuss these ɩings in Parliament, it were best for them to begone to their ɔmes.

The House resolved itself into Committee, and Finch, thus :leased from his duties, hurried to the king. Meanwhile Coke ttacked Buckingham, and referred with unmistakable meaning ɩ the impeachment of Middlesex in 1624, which Charles himself ad approved of. Selden advised the House to continue what ie last Parliament had begun. Altogether the ferment was so reat, and the representations of Finch were so alarming, that ɩharles withdrew from his original position, and the royal assent as at last affixed to the Petition of Right, June 9. The Com- ɩons expressed their gratitude by granting the five subsidies.

The Petition, however, was clearly intended to be a dead letter, ɔr when the Commons proceeded to act upon it, to examine rievances, and to punish evil-doers,—especially to declare Buck- ɩgham the primary cause of all, and to forbid the illegal collec- ɩon of tunnage and poundage,—the quarrel at once broke out gain, and Charles, returning to his old suicidal policy, suddenly ɩrorogued them.

The recess was full of stirring events. The assassination of Buckingham removed the screen which had hidden the true extent of the king's share in the events of the reign, and brought him at last face to face with the people, soon to be recognised as the true and sole cause of their misfortunes.   Saville, Noy, Little- ton, and, greatest of all, Wentworth, lured by the prospect of royal favour and a great career, deserted what seemed a losing cause, and became the strongest supporters of the Court.   The illegal practices, moreover, complained of in the Petition of Rights, had been continued, and by the time that Parliament reassembled, January 20, 1628/9, there was quite a fresh crop of grievances waiting to be remedied.   The greatest cause of distrust lay in the promotion and favour accorded to the Arminian clergy, especially to those who had by their violent speeches and writings incurred the censure of Parliament.

When Parliament assembled therefore, the House of Commons, under the leadership of Eliot, proceeded to take measures for preserving the religion of the country, and vindicating the liberty of the subject.   The king met their efforts by repeated adjourn- ments, during which several attempts were made in vain to come to some arrangement with the popular leaders.   When the House was at last allowed to meet again, March 2, it was expected that it would assemble only to be once more adjourned, and Eliot determined that before this was effected he would move a great protest which should serve as an appeal to the people against the king.   For this design Eliot was alone responsible ; and of the principal leaders Selden alone supported him.   Digges, Philips, Pym, would have nothing to do with it.   It was easy, however, to find assistance among members less distinguished, and a curious scene ensued.

Sir John Finch, the Speaker, in accordance with what was usually an empty formality, put the question, "That this House do now adjourn."   To his astonishment a chorus of "Noes" followed, and Eliot at once rose to address the House.   Finch, however, stopped him, declaring that he had the absolute com- mand of the king to leave the chair if any member attempted to speak.   As he moved to leave the chair, Denzil Holles and Ben- jamin Valentine seized him by the arms, thrust him back into the seat, and endeavoured to hold him down.   The Privy Council- lors at once rushed to the rescue, and a skirmish ensued, during

·hich Finch broke at last from his captors. Crowds of members,
owever, surrounded him; he was dragged back and forced into
ιe chair. "God's wounds!" cried Holles, "you shall sit till we
lease to rise."

The door was now locked, and Eliot began to speak. When,
owever, he wished to put the question that his protest be
arried, Finch refused to read the protest, or put the question.
ι tremendous wrangle now ensued. Member after member
poke, and threatened Finch with the direst penalties if he held
ɔ his refusal. Finch, with tears in his voice, steadily persisted,
nd implored the House not to force him to his ruin. At last
elden moved that Finch by his refusal to act had abdicated his
ffice, and that Eliot do now take the chair and read the protest
imself. An unexpected obstacle, however, arose. It was found
hat Eliot, despairing of success, had thrown the paper into the
ιre.

Whatever was to be done must be done quickly, for Maxwell,
he Usher of the Black Rod, was even now knocking at the door
ɲith a message from the king, nor could there be much doubt as
ɔ its purport. Holles came forward without a moment's delay,
ecited what he could remember of the protest, and put the
ɾuestion to the House himself. A chorus of "Ay, ay," followed.
Γhe House then voted its own adjournment, and the doors were
ǀung open just as the king's guards arrived with orders to break
hem down.

The king at once hastened to take vengeance on the "vipers"
ɲho had opposed him. Eliot, Holles, Selden, Long, Valentine,
ǂtrode, and a number of others were committed to prison in de-
ιance of 4 Hen. VIII.[1], which the judges declared to be a special
ǀtatute affecting Richard Strode only, and not a general statute,
ǀeclaratory of a general privilege. Eliot, Holles, and Valentine,
ιs the principal offenders, were sent to the Tower, where Eliot
ǀhortly afterwards ended his life, and Holles and Valentine remained till 1640.

From 1629 to 1640, Charles ruled without Parliament, raising
ταxes by prerogative, legislating by royal proclamations, carrying

---

[1] *z.* p. 26.

on the government solely at his own discretion. He gathered strength, however, from no element in the kingdom. Unstable as water, he did not excel, and his most arbitrary acts were dictated, not by any settled and far-reaching scheme of despotism, but the temporary necessities of his Exchequer. In the end he was foolish enough to attack the religion of the Scots, provoked them to rebellion, and was reduced to financial ruin by their success.

In despair he summoned another Parliament, with some vague hope of frightening or cajoling them into granting money. He had now an unrivalled opportunity for effecting a reconciliation, for the new Parliament was inspired by the most moderate sentiments. Hyde declared that its loyal and conciliatory feeling was marvellous, and this even when his reforming theories had become obscured in the royalist views of Clarendon. Falkland said that its conduct made him in love with the very name of Parliament. St. John and the more determined patriots thought that its moderation was carried too far, and that the times required sharper and more decided treatment. Conciliation might have effected much ; an opposite policy could only produce a fresh quarrel ; a sudden dissolution must lead to financial ruin.

Charles had, however, no intention of conciliation. If Parliament would grant money, well ; if not, he would do without them. Parliament proposed indeed to grant money, but they also proceeded to discuss grievances. Pym and Hampden were of no mind to make the king independent of them till the wrongs endured during the last eleven years had been righted. Impatient at the delay, Charles persuaded the Peers to vote that supply should be taken first. The Commons, however, resented this breach of their financial privilege so warmly that the Lords were frightened, and apologised. Very shortly after, Charles became convinced that the Commons were neither to be frightened nor cajoled, and he dissolved Parliament in a rage, when it was only three weeks old. The brevity of the session earned for this assembly the name of the Short Parliament.

Fate, however, was against the king, and the period of his arbitrary government was nigh to its close. Worsted ignominiously by the Scots, without money, with a mutinous army, and an

ıgry people around him clamouring for a Parliament, no expe-
ent seemed open to him but to summon another Parliament.
he Scots demanded it, the Peers advised it, the country peti
ɔned eagerly for it ; the only alternative was violence, and that
ıs impossible in the face of the victorious Scottish army. Un-
illingly, therefore, Charles surrendered to the inevitable, and
rits were issued for a new Parliament.

CHAPTER VII.

THE LONG PARLIAMENT.

(1640–1660.)

Section 1.—*Constitutional Reforms.*

THE General Election of 1640 was held amid the wildest excitement. Both parties had exerted their utmost efforts to secure the choice of their own candidates. Hampden and the other popular leaders had gone from shire to shire to address the electors, and exhort them to be true to themselves and the Constitution. The result was that the Court candidates were rejected on all sides, and a large constitutional majority returned to Westminster. When Parliament met, November 3, the popular party were confident of success, relying on their own numbers, on the sympathy of the people, and the support of the Scotch army. To Charles, no doubt, it seemed that they were assembled simply to vote money for the payment of the Scots: but the parliamentary leaders regarded their summons as the prelude to sweeping reforms, which should restore the old balance of the Constitution, and create fresh guarantees for its future security. The presence of the Scotch army in the North of England and the demands of the Scots for money, were important elements in the political crisis, for they constituted a powerful check on the king's prerogative of dissolution; but the days had gone by when Parliament could be treated as a mere tax-raising machine. At the same time they were as yet resolved to do nothing new. Their work was to be based on old laws and old precedents, the rights they would claim were rights which they believed to be inherent in the Constitution.

An important sign of the times was to be found in the nomination of William Lenthall to be Speaker. Charles would have preferred one of his own adherents, but the turn of the elections had rendered this impossible. The nomination, however, was acceptable to the leading men of the Commons, and Lenthall

ought to the Chair a very fair knowledge of precedent, and,
ove all, an impartiality of conduct during political controversy
1ich enabled him to fulfil his duties with a fuller appreciation of
e true position of a Speaker than had characterized any of his
edecessors.

The most prominent man among the Commons was, un-
)ubtedly, Pym : not yet their recognised leader, and not to be
1til some months of conflict and terror had brought the strongest
the front by abasing all others ; but the directing influence of
small body of men "who constituted the inspiring force of the
irliamentary opposition." The Earl of Bedford and Hampden,
1e wisest and most temperate of the opposition in Lords and
ommons, regarded him as their chief. Strode, St. John, Holles,
rle, and Fiennes, the strong men of Parliament, were content to
1llow his lead.

The debate of November 7 was a long outburst of suppressed
)mplaint. Member after member presented petitions of griev-
1ces. At the end, Pym rose to direct the attention of Parliament
) the root of the matter. "The distempers of the time," he said,
are well known. They need not repetition, for though we have
ood laws yet they want their execution, or if they are executed,
is in the wrong sense. . . . There is a design to alter law
nd religion." He ran over quickly a long catalogue of evidence
1 support of his assertion, and moved that a committee be
ppointed to inquire into the danger of the kingdom.

On November 10, in view of a plot which had come to the
ars of several members, Pym rose and moved that the doors
hould be locked. After a long discussion, during which Pym
lenounced Strafford as "an apostate from the cause of liberty
)ecome the greatest enemy to liberty," it was resolved by the
1niversal consent of the whole House to impeach him ; and Pym,
ollowed by a crowd of members, carried up the message at once
:o the Lords.

The news was taken to Strafford himself. " I will go," he said
vith haughty indignation, "and look my accusers in the face."
He entered the House with the imperious air and scowling brow
of an angry dictator. But the spell of his influence was broken,
and his appearance was greeted by loud shouts of "Withdraw,

withdraw." He was compelled to retire in confusion; but in a few minutes was summoned back to the House to hear on his knees the order of his committal to the custody of the Usher of the Black Rod. The House of Commons at once proceeded to draw up the grounds of his accusation. It was completed and carried up to the Lords by the 25th, and the Lords immediately committed Strafford to the Tower pending his trial.

This vigorous action, which can only be regarded as a measure of self-preservation, was followed by the impeachment of Archbishop Laud, Lord Keeper Finch, Secretary Windebank, and several of the judges, for their conduct during the period of Charles's arbitrary government. One of the judges, Berkeley, was actually presiding in the Court of King's Bench when Maxwell, the Usher of the Black Rod, entered with the order for his arrest. Maxwell ordered him to come down from the bench, and there was nothing for it but to obey. This arrest of a judge on the bench itself was perhaps a more striking proof of the power of Parliament than even the impeachment of Strafford.

A number of remedial statutes were gradually passed. The irregular and arbitrary jurisdiction of the Court of High Commission, the Court of Star Chamber, and all the Courts depending on the latter, were swept away, the principal victims of oppression released, and their condemnation and punishment denounced as illegal. The raising of ship-money, and the judgment delivered against Mr. John Hampden on his disputing its legality, were both declared to be utterly illegal. A final declaration was registered against the practice of levying money unconstitutionally by a statute which enacted "that no custom or other charge whatsoever may be laid on any merchandise exported or imported without common consent of Parliament." Most important of all, perhaps, from our point of view, was the Triennial Act, the first attempt to regulate the intermission and duration of Parliament by statute. It enacted that Parliament should last for three years, and should not be intermitted for more than three:—complicated provisions being added to admit of its being summoned by the Lord Chancellor, or the Peers, or of its assembling on the sole initiative of the people in default of regular summons. Various other statutes completed the work, and, without depriving the

ionarchy of anything which it had anciently possessed, stamped
ith the brand of illegality most of the instruments of govern-
ient and devices for raising money which Charles and James
ad made use of to support their arbitrary rule.

It is important to notice that Mr. Hyde and Lord Falkland,
ho became subsequently the leaders of the royalist party, were
; convinced of the necessity of passing these highly constitu-
onal measures as Mr. Pym and Mr. Hampden, or even
[r. Cromwell, who was already beginning to be known as a man
ho would go far and fearlessly. There was as yet no division
i Parliament : all were earnestly intent on reform and the
:storation of constitutional government ; the later divisions into
.oyalists, Parliamentarians, and the Root and Branch party,
ere not apparent. Culpepper, the third of the later moderate
io, was loudest in his denunciation of the illegal practices of the
)yal monopolists. Falkland contributed more than any other
ian to the passing of the resolutions against ship-money. The
iscussion on the impeachment of Finch elicited the assertion
om Hyde that if it were treason to kill a judge, it was much
iore so to slay justice itself by illegal decisions. The earnest-
ess of Parliament could not have been more conclusively shown
ian by their only allowing themselves four days' vacation at
:hristmas, 1640, and the zeal with which they worked for ten
ionths at the work of reform.

The first faint mutterings of discord were, however, heard even
i 1640, over the ecclesiastical questions. The debate on
piscopacy, February 8, 1641, brought out the strong divergence
etween the views of the two parties : the advocates of a
emocratic church, who were headed by Pym, Hampden, St.
)hn, Holles, Fiennes, and the defenders of episcopacy, Falkland,
[yde, Culpepper, Selden, Hopton, and Waller, who followed
ie lead of Digby. Lord Digby, however, really stood on a
:ry different basis to his companions : he secretly represented
ie Court, or rather the queen, to whose blandishments he had
y now succumbed. His companions were merely inspired by an
onest belief that ecclesiastical reform might be best effected with-
ut the use of extreme measures : they had no leanings as yet to
ie Court or the queen. The efforts of the moderate party, after

G

a long debate and a further discussion by a committee, success-fully shelved the dangerous question of Episcopacy for the time.

Charles's policy appears to have been to yield on all disputed topics, simply in order to lull his enemies to a false security until such time when he had gathered sufficient strength to exact heavy vengeance. He no doubt hoped that a quarrel would soon break out between Parliament and the Scotch army, which would prove the ruin of both ; but the Parliamentarians, scenting the danger, exerted their powers and resources to pay the wages of the Scots, and in addition voted them a present of £300,000, which secured their friendship and assistance on the firmest basis for the future. His assent was granted in pure duplicity, or, as he would have termed it, diplomacy, to the various unwelcome statutes presented to him, and without the slightest intention of observing them a day longer than necessity compelled. It was, moreover, most certainly with the same view of allaying suspicion that he con-sented to the impeachment of Strafford.

After a long delay, spent by both sides in procuring evi-dence, the trial of the Earl of Strafford began, March 22, 1641. Westminster Hall was fitted up for the occasion with a bar, a witness-box, seats for the Peers, the managers, the Lower House, and even for spectators. At the west end a throne had been erected, but it was empty, and the face of the king might have been seen peering anxiously from a box which had been specially arranged for him and the queen. With the view of preserving a certain effect of *incognito*, a lattice had been erected in front of it, but Charles's first act was to tear down the obstacle and exhibit himself to the full view of the managers.

On the 23rd, Pym opened the case against Strafford with the charges relating to his government in Ireland. He accused him of tyranny and oppression, and deduced the inference that he was ready to violate the laws of England as he had violated the laws of Ireland. Granted, however, that the charges were true, they did not constitute the offence of treason under the Treason Acts ; and however desirable it might be to chastise this arch-offender against the Constitution, it was impossible to punish him under the strict letter of the law. Pym, indeed, advanced the theory that a settled design to subvert the Constitution was treason in the

ghest and most heinous degree; but he quoted no law or pre-
:dent in support of his view, and the doctrine was dangerously
rtile in its possible application.

Strafford was therefore able to make a vigorous defence. He
:nied that he had violated the Constitution in Ireland; he
sserted that he had acted with the best intentions all through,
d that in no case had he exceeded the licence allowed to his
redecessors. There was so much obvious truth in his statements
at he aroused considerable sympathy. The ladies who had
ntrived to obtain entrance, influenced chiefly by commisera-
on for the man who was struggling for his life against such des-
erate odds with so much courage and proud humility, declared
rongly in his favour. The Peers gradually veered over to the
nviction that, whatever punishment his offences might deserve,
would be the height of injustice to treat them as treason. In
roportion as the impression which Strafford created became more
vourable on the general mass of the audience, the Commons
ecame more and more exasperated, more disposed to break
rough the slow formalities of the law, and fix their teeth venge-
lly in the throat of the prey. Sir Symonds d'Ewes, to whose
iary we are indebted for most of our knowledge of the proceed-
igs of this Parliament, records that one member even insisted
at the Peers should be requested to stop the prisoner's mouth
hen he spoke too long.

The disclosure of a plot to use the army of the North against
'arliament made Pym more determined than ever to exact the
ttermost penalty from Strafford; and, with this view, he hurried
apidly over the Irish charges, which had obviously missed fire,
nd handed on the task of further accusation to Bulstrode White-
ocke.

On April 5, Whitelocke charged Strafford with raising an army
f Irish Papists; with "conspiring for the ruin and destruction
f the kingdom of England and of his Majesty's subjects, and
.ltering and subverting the fundamental laws and established
overnment of this kingdom"; with advising the king that if Par-
iament failed to supply him, he "might use his prerogative as he
leased to levy what he needed, and that he should be acquitted
f God and man if he took some courses to supply himself,

though it were against the will of his subjects"; finally, with having procured the dissolution of the Short Parliament, and given the king the pernicious counsel that, "having tried the affections of his people, he was to do everything that power would admit, and that he had an army in Ireland which he might employ to reduce *this kingdom.*"

The whole question turned on the meaning of the last words. They had been spoken at a meeting of the Council during a discussion on the Scotch war, and *primâ facie* they could only apply to rebellious Scotland. Sir Harry Vane the elder, a member of the Council, was summoned to testify to the utterance of the words, but he firmly declined to say whether "this kingdom" meant England or Scotland; and the Lord Steward at last interposed with the ruling that it was not the business of a witness to interpret the facts: whereat Maynard, one of the managers, sarcastically exclaimed that Vane was being questioned "whether this kingdom be this kingdom."

In reply, Strafford strenuously denied that the words were susceptible of any interpretation but the obvious one, Scotland; and then once more he took his stand on the letter of the law. If it were treason, he argued, with a vivid appreciation of the position of his judges, for a man to deliver an honest opinion under an oath of secrecy, with regard to such a state of danger as when an enemy is either actually entered, or ready to enter, the kingdom, he did not think that "any wise and noble person of fortune would, in the future, upon such perilous and unsafe terms, adventure to be a councillor to the king." There was little doubt at the close of his speech that he had hit the right nail on the head. D'Ewes records that even from the benches on which the Commons were grouped, there arose a murmur of admiration when Strafford resumed his seat. To the minds of his judges he had satisfactorily disproved the charge of treason under this head, and on several other points, raised successively by Whitelocke, Erle, and Glyn, he was equally successful. There appeared to be no prospect of a condemnation, and the strict legal impartiality which the Lords persisted in preserving, told so manifestly to the advantage of the accused, that at last the Commons gave vent to their rage in shouts and disorder. The sitting broke up in great con-

sion ; and amid the laughter of the king, and the scarcely con-
:aled joy of the prisoner, the two Houses hurried indignantly
om the Hall.

Outside events were mainly responsible for this violence.
resh disclosures had been made respecting the continuance of
ie army plot. The House, at once furious and frightened, and
etermined to sacrifice Strafford as a warning to those who might
e disposed to imitate him, were ready to listen to the violent
>unsels of the extreme party. It was during these troubled days
iat on Saturday, April 12, at the end of the third week of the
ial, in spite of the advice of Pym and Hampden, extreme views
revailed, and a Bill of Attainder was brought in and read a first
me. Strangely enough, among the list of its most earnest
dvocates are the names of Hyde and Falkland. Still the
npeachment was not yet definitely abandoned.

The Peers, however, were furious at the mere idea of the
ttainder. " It is an unnatural motion," they exclaimed, " for
ie head to be governed by the tail. We will never suffer our-
elves to be suppressed by a popular faction. They determined
> ignore it entirely, and on April 13 they called on Strafford to
nake his defence.

He asked them to say whether his acts amounted to treason.
Vo man had been condemned in this way for 240 years. Was it
afe to add so weightily to the difficulties of the king's ministers?
Ie appealed to their feelings as fathers by a timely burst of
ears, as he referred to his children who would be left orphans
>ehind him, and with the words of the *Te Deum* on his lips he
at down. In reply, Glyn reiterated the charge against him that
ie was the " evil spirit that hath moved among us for many years,
ind hath been the author and ground of all our distractions."
?ym rose next to declare that Strafford had debased the character
>f the nation, and destroyed the harmony between the king and
iis people : surely this were greater treason than the debasing of
he king's coin—a more heinous offence than the inadequate list
n the Treason Act. "Nothing can be more equal than that he
should perish by the justice of that law which he would have
subverted ; neither will this be a new way of blood. There are
narks enough to trace this law to the very original of this kingdom ;

and if it hath not been put in execution, as he allegeth, these 240 years, it was not for want of law, but that all that time hath not bred a man bold enough to commit such crimes as these, which is a circumstance much aggravating his offence, and making him no whit less liable to punishment, because he is the only man that in so long a time had ventured upon such a treason as this." Strafford's arguments, however, were unanswerable from the legal point of view; it became only too evident that the Lords must acquit. The Commons were all the more determined that he should die as a warning to great and cunning offenders in the future.

The Bill of Attainder was therefore read a second time and sent into committee April 14. The discussion was conducted very rapidly; for though Strafford's friends did their best to urge again his own arguments against the charge of treason, they were but a scanty band, and were no doubt considerably influenced by the intolerance of their opponents, who had hardly patience to listen or to answer. By the 19th, in spite of the strenuous exertions of Selden and Holborne, the committee voted by three to one that Strafford was a traitor.

The third reading (April 21) was principally remarkable for an impassioned speech from Lord Digby, who had openly gone over to the Court, but his efforts were of no avail. The bill passed by a majority of 204 to 59—Pym, Hyde, Falkland all voting for it; Digby, Selden, Holborne being the only names of note in the minority.

It was arranged with the Lords that the forms of the impeachment should continue, but the question to be argued should be the legality of the Bill of Attainder. The Lords were rapidly forsaking their attitude of impartiality. The air was full of rumours of plots and foreign alliances, all intended to supply weapons against the Parliament. The change of feeling was expressed by St. John on the 29th, when arguing before the Lords. He broke away suddenly from law and precedent, and took his stand upon the broad ground of necessity and self-preservation. "We give law," he said, " to hares and deer, because they be beasts of chase; but it was never accounted cruelty or foul play to knock foxes and wolves on the head as soon as they can be found, because hey be beasts of prey." Nor was his argument repugnant to his earers. The feeling that there could be no safety for any of hem if Strafford escaped was beginning to produce its inevitable ffect.

A season of wild panic and its natural attendant, insane rage, vas setting in. The doors of the House of Lords were beset very day by frantic mobs from the City, shrieking and yelling for ustice on Strafford. A placard was posted up on the door of the Commons containing the names of the fifty-nine " Straffordians, etrayers of their country." The knock of the Usher of the 3lack Rod, when he came to summon the Commons to the House of Lords to hear a speech from the throne, was sufficient o send a terrified rumour round the benches of instant dissolution ind violence to follow. The creaking of a board under the veight of two stout members during a debate sent the House into convulsions of alarm as at a new Gunpowder Plot, and brought he trained bands down from the City to the rescue. Sir Symonds l'Ewes records that one morning they met with their minds so urdened with the solemnity of their position, that they remained ilently regarding one another as men looking for counsel and inding none. Then the Clerk began to read the order of the day. The first bill was for regulating the trade of wire-drawing. The subject seemed so ludicrously inappropriate to the electric state of their feelings, that they broke into a shout of hysterical laughter, ind then again there was a long silence.

It was, no doubt, the feeling that the king could be no longer trusted, which turned the scale against Strafford. A further proof of it was given by the introduction of the bill that Parliament should not be dissolved without its own consent, which was approved not only by Pym and Hampden, but also by Hyde and Falkland. On May 8, both bills passed the Upper House, and after some delay Charles assented to them, May 10.

The attainder of Strafford and the Permanency Act definitely mark the departure of the Commons from the strict path of constitutional reform. Of the latter statute, Mr. Hallam remarks that "it was ostensibly grounded on the necessity of

---

i "Const. Hist." ii. p. 112.

speedily raising money for the relief of the army in the northern part of the realm, and the impossibility of borrowing on the authority of resolutions of Parliament unless some security was furnished to the creditors that the assembly would not be dissolved before sufficient provision had been made for repayment of moneys to be raised. But the chief motive was no doubt a just apprehension of the king's intention to overthrow the Parliament, and of personal danger to the popular leaders after a dissolution." The discovery of the Army Plot and the king's share in it was as much the cause of the Permanency Act as of the execution of Strafford. The utter duplicity of Charles, the feeling that he could not be trusted in the smallest thing, was here, as always, the chief cause of his disasters.

During the debates in May, on the Bill for the Exclusion of the Bishops from the House of Lords, the divergence between the subsequent parties became more apparent. Hyde and Falkland both defended the bishops, and opposed the bill to the utmost. Digby also warmly attacked the bill, but Digby was the queen's henchman, soon to be raised to the peerage as a reward for his faithful services, and especially his speech and vote against the attainder of Strafford. The extreme party, already beginning to be known as the Root and Branch, brought in by way of retaliation to this opposition a bill for the total abolition of episcopacy, and it was only the common fear of the king's designs, and the alarm aroused by the discovery of the second Army Plot, which produced an agreement and a compromise, by which the question was once more shelved for a time.

The departure of Charles for Scotland, August 10, was productive of an important innovation. Parliament began, almost from necessity, to issue ordinances without the king, and it was almost inevitable that this power should grow at the expense of the king's prerogative. On September 8, Parliament adjourned for six weeks, and the first period of its sessions was at an end. "It was the last time," says Professor Gardiner, "in which the two parties into which the House of Commons was divided, loyally co-operated with one another. Whatever had been done so far by the Long Parliament stood the test of time, and was accepted as the starting-point of the restored

onarchical constitution in 1660. Yet from that moment of
parent unanimity dates the beginning of embittered strife,"
hich entirely frustrated all future efforts to create durable insti-
tions during the revolutionary period.

SECTION 2.—*Unconstitutional Violence.*

"The rock of offence," continues Professor Gardiner, "lay
. the proposed ecclesiastical legislation of Parliament for the
moval of the bishops from the House of Lords." One party
as resolutely opposed to the continuance of the misrule of the
piscopate in any shape; the other was outraged and alarmed
y the fanaticism of the Presbyterians and the indecent violence
: other sectaries. Each party considered that the welfare of
ιe Church and the country was inseparably connected with the
iumph of their own opinion: compromise on the subject was
npossible for any length of time; only the gravest alarm had
:ndered it possible hitherto. It was natural, therefore, that on
ιe renewal of the question, shortly after the reassembling of
arliament, the two parties of Episcopalians and anti-Episco-
alians divided definitely from one another.

Moreover, the concessions which the king had made were
onsidered by many to be sufficient. Further restrictions on the
)yal power, they imagined, were unnecessary; the demand for
ιem was ungenerous. Charles's ready and reckless compliance
'ith all demands had even inspired many with a feeling of
onfidence and compassion. Natural repulsion to all extreme
ιeasures and religious hostility to the extreme party drew the
Ξpiscopalians imperceptibly into sympathy with the king. They
)ndly believed in the return of the prodigal to constitutional
'ays; they refused to suppose that he was actuated solely by
he desire of gaining time. The excessive taxation, moreover,
'hich Parliament had been obliged to levy for the payment of
he two armies, contributed in no small measure to diminish the
)opularity of the popular leaders, and to provoke unfavourable
:omparisons between the existing state and the rule of the king.

The popular chiefs knew too well that Charles could not be
rusted. They had proofs of designs for their own destruction,
o which he had consented. He was openly suspected by the

Scots of an attempt to seize the Scotch leaders. What was there to prevent his repeating the attempt in England? Pym and Hampden feared that his easy surrender was but a mask to hide his secret purposes. His false and deceitful character was too well known to them for them to believe that he would hold to his word a moment longer than necessity compelled. Fresh guarantees were necessary, the royal prerogative must submit to fresh limitations, its powers of offence must be considerably reduced, before any confidence could be reposed in the durability of the restored Constitution.

The news of the outbreak of the Irish Rebellion (November 1) seemed to them the confirmation of their fears. They saw in it the secret hand of the king. With the view of arresting the reaction in favour of the king, and preventing any possibility of violence in England, Pym and Hampden determined to bring forward a great appeal to the people, which was intended to warn them to beware of what they were doing by stating in full the whole record of the past perfidy and tyranny of the king, and to exhort their assistance in order to insure the continuance of better government in the future (November 8). It was inevitable that this Grand Remonstrance should be stained by considerable exaggeration, but there was a broad vein of truth running through it all. It began by roundly declaring that the king's evil counsellors had designed to subvert "the fundamental laws and principles of government upon which the religion and justice of the kingdom were firmly established." It recited in order a long list of enormities, beginning with the disasters of Buckingham's government, and going through the reign down to the hasty dissolution of the Short Parliament. Finally, it enumerated the good deeds of the existing Parliament, and demanded reform in the Church, reform in the government, and the total suppression of Papacy.

The debate began on November 8, and the House resolved itself into Committee for a closer discussion November 9. No opposition was offered to the paragraphs reciting the king's past misgovernment, nor are there any divisions reported during the first two days. Bad news from Ireland, however, compelled the House to turn their attention entirely to the vital question of the uppression of the Irish Rebellion, nor was it till the 15th and 6th that the Remonstrance finally passed through committee,—lmost unimpaired, though Hyde and his friends turned definitely oyalist on this question, and offered the most strenuous oppo-ition, especially to the clauses which dealt with the question of cclesiastical reform. The final reading was fixed for the 20th, ut the actual debate was further adjourned under strong ressure to the 22nd. In the interval, however, between the 6th and 20th, the temper of the House was not improved by he discovery of another plot to overawe them by means of the rmy.

The supporters of the Remonstrance were now hopeful and onfident. "Why would you have it put off?" inquired Cromwell f Falkland, who had most strenuously resisted the proposal to egin the debate on the 20th. "There would not have been ime enough," replied the latter; "for sure there will be some lebate." "A very sorry one," returned Cromwell, with undue contempt.

The discussion opened at noon on the 22nd, and it was fully understood that now the question of the acceptance or rejection of the Remonstrance as a whole was laid before the House. A great debate began, which was sustained for fourteen hours with the utmost warmth. Falkland and Dering complained of the attacks on the bishops and Arminians. Culpepper roundly asserted that the Commons had no right to draw up such a Remonstrance without the Lords, still less to send it out among the people. Hyde strangely enough assented to the truth of the paragraphs dealing with the misgovernment of the king.

On the parliamentary side, Pym, as usual, was conspicuous. "The honour of the king," he said, "lies in the safety of the people, and we must tell the truth. The plots have been very near the king, all driven home to the Court and the popish party." Turning then to the ecclesiastical question, he denounced the popish lords and bishops, who hindered them and the king; he declared roundly that altar-worship was idolatry, and that many of the separatists had been driven from the Church by an obstinate resistance of the Church dignitaries on points which were only important to tender consciences. Finally, he asserted that the king's evil counsellors were the cause of all the troubles of the reign, and that Parliament had a right to demand their removal, and to advise on the appointment of new ones.

As the debate rolled on, the shades of night fell darkly over the eager assembly. Candles were brought in, and at last, by this uncertain light, at the midnight hour, the division was taken. One hundred and fifty-nine voted that the Remonstrance do pass; one hundred and forty-eight voted against it.

Mr. Peard, the member for Barnstaple, moved at once that the Remonstrance be printed, in order that it might be scattered far and wide among the people and act as an appeal to them from the king. Hyde and Culpepper opposed the design, and asked the leave of the House to protest. Other voices cried out their protest, and Mr. Geoffrey Palmer rose in a great state of excitement, and declared that he protested, "in the name of himself and the rest." Instantly a loud tumult and confusion arose. A number of voices shouted "All, all." Some waved their hats; others snatched their swords, scabbards and all, from their belts, and held them out by the hilt with the point to the ground. " I thought," says an eye-witness, " we had all sat in the valley of the shadow of death; for we, like Joab's and Abner's young men, had catched at each other's locks, and sheathed our swords in each other's bowels, had not the sagacity and calmness of Mr. Hampden, by a short speech, prevented it." Further discussion was wisely postponed, and at four in the morning the House rose.

As Falkland and Cromwell left the house together, Cromwell told his companion: "If the Remonstrance had been rejected, I would have sold all I had the next morning, and never seen England any more; and I know there are many other honest men of this same resolution."

Mr. Palmer's conduct, however, had raised an important question which required immediate settlement. The right of protesting in the minority had never been recognised in the Commons. It had always been exclusively confined to the Lords. This right, once acknowledged in the Commons, would have diminished the importance and weight of their decisions by destroying the appearance of unanimity which the jealously guarded privilege of secrecy f debate tended so greatly to preserve. On the 24th, Palmer as summoned before the House to answer for his unwarrantable ehaviour, was committed to the Tower, and was only released fter twelve days' imprisonment on making a humble apology nd retractation. The question of the right of protest was definitely ettled in this rough and ready way.

On December 1 the Remonstrance was presented to the king t Hampton Court. He received it almost as if it were unworthy f serious consideration, and said that he would think it over. 'he retort of the Commons came quick and sharp. On December 15, by 135 votes to 83, they resolved to print the Remonstrance nd appeal to the people.

When the king thought fit to return a reply, he first rated the lommons severely for their disrespect in venturing to print their omplaints, and then gave the lie almost *in toto* to the whole. Ie professed himself the champion of the ancient Constitution nd the ancient Church, only admitting the necessity for the very lightest changes. More significant still was his attempt to get he Tower into the hands of one of his most reckless followers. The result was, that the Commons, in a sudden access of panic, efused the guard they had previously demanded so earnestly, inless it might be commanded by the Earl of Essex, and even velcomed the presence of the riotous rabble which came daily lown from the City, intent on mischief, for at least they were more riendly to the parliamentary leaders than to the king. It was luring these turbulent days, when skirmishes occurred almost laily in and about Westminster and Whitehall, between the high-nettled royalist gentlemen and the close-cropped apprentices who ormed the majority of the City mob, that the terms "Cavaliers" ind "Roundheads" were first flung from one side to the other n equal scorn and contempt. It was in consequence of this violence, that twelve of the bishops, in real terror of the fury of he populace which was directed chiefly against them, absented hemselves from the House of Lords, and were even foolish enough to sign a protest declaring that Parliament was no longer ree, the immediate result being their impeachment and imprisonment by the House of Commons.

The debates on the Grand Remonstrance had drawn the line

hard and fast between the party of conservation and the party of change, and had moreover inspired a belief in the mind of Charles that the two parties were evenly balanced. He now called to office the leaders of the opposition to that measure. Falkland was made Secretary of State and Culpepper Chancellor of the Exchequer. Hyde, though he became the principal adviser of the king, preferred to remain an unofficial member of the House of Commons, no doubt with the view that he could do better service to his royal master in that capacity.

It was, however, the chief cause of Charles's troubles that he never could remain long in a constitutional course. The simpler process of cutting the knot had always greater attractions for him. It only required a rumour of a threatened impeachment levelled against the queen to reverse all his good resolutions, to upset the influence of Hyde, Falkland, and Culpepper, and to precipitate him into the ill-advised scheme of impeaching the six principal leaders of the Opposition with the view of taking the parliamentary bull by the horns. The intended victims were—Pym, Hampden, Holles, Hazelrig and Strode in the Commons, and Viscount Mandeville [1] in the Lords.

When the Lords met, January 3, the Attorney-General, Sir Edward Herbert, appeared, recited the charge of treason against the six persons, and demanded their arrest. The news was received with considerable excitement in the House of Commons, which increased tenfold when Pym rose in his place to inform them that his study, as well as those of Holles and Hampden, had been sealed up by the king's directions. They voted this a breach of privilege, and were proceeding to ask the concurrence of the Lords, when the Serjeant-at-Arms entered the House with the king's warrant for the arrest of the five members. The Commons refused to give them up, and returned a reply to the king that the matter concerned their privileges, and required consideration, but added that they would be themselves responsible for the appearance of the accused to answer any legal charge. This precipitate action on the part of the king threw the Lords, almost in a body, on the side of the Commons. He could count no

---

[1] Formerly Lord Kimbolton, afterwards Earl of Manchester.

nger upon them; he determined to take the matter decidedly to his own hands.

On January 4, when the Commons met, the five members protested their innocence in turn to the House. In the afternoon, ord was sent by the Earl of Essex that the king was coming in erson to arrest them. Shortly afterwards Mr. Nathaniel Fiennes mounced to the House that a Frenchman, named Langres, had me in hot haste to say that the king was on the road to Westinster with over three hundred armed men at his heels. The ve members were at once requested to retire. Strode alone sisted on remaining to face the worst, and his friends were bliged to drag him out by his cloak before he would consent to company Pym and the rest. Once out of the House, they astened to the riverside, and were rowed swiftly down to the ity.

Meanwhile the king was entering New Palace Yard, and a essage actually arrived informing the Commons of his arrival. he great majority of his followers remained outside in the hall; nt, no doubt in obedience to previous orders, about eighty ressed after him into the lobby, among whom were "divers fficers of the late army of the North and other desperate iffians," besides "some of his pensioners." As he entered with ie young Elector Palatine, he charged them all "on their lives ot to come in"; but it was obvious that he wished the House to e aware that he was prepared to use force if it were necessary. he Earl of Roxburgh stood just within the door, leaning against , keeping it open, so that Sir Symonds d'Ewes and Sir Ralph erney, who were in the House, could see through the open door ie truculent figure of Captain David Hyde, one of the greatest coundrels in England, standing by Roxburgh's side, holding his word upright in its scabbard, and beyond them the savage and ienacing forms of the desperadoes and officers who thronged the bby, armed to the teeth with swords and pistols—many of them aving left their cloaks in the hall for greater freedom in the xpected fray.

The Commons rose bareheaded as the king entered, and the ing also removed his hat. Then he moved forward, and his glance almost instinctively travelled along the line of sullen scowling faces to the seat on the right hand near the bar where Pym usually sat. It was empty. It would not have been easy, says Rushworth, to discern any of the five members had they been there, among so many faces packed together; but Charles would have known Pym—King Pym, his rival—anywhere. Pym was not there, and so, perhaps, without any definitely formed purpose in his mind the king moved up the House towards the Speaker's chair. Lenthall came out to meet him. "By your leave, Mr. Speaker," said Charles, "I must borrow your chair a little." Then, standing in front of it, he cast his eyes round the house in search of his prey.

After a while he addressed the House—"Gentlemen," he said, "I am sorry for this occasion of coming unto you. Yester-day I sent a Serjeant-at-Arms upon a very important occasion to apprehend some that by my command were accused of high treason, whereunto I did expect obedience and not a message; and I must declare unto you here, that, albeit no king that ever was in England shall be more careful of your privileges to maintain them to the uttermost of his power than I shall be, yet you must know that in cases of treason no person hath a privilege; and therefore I am come to know if any of these persons that were accused are here."

A further searching glance from face to face must have con-vinced him that they were not—that the great plot had failed, and he had now to deal with the consequences. "I do not see any of them," he muttered angrily; "I think I should know them,"—and it is easy to imagine the significance of the last sentence. "For I must tell you," he continued after another pause, "that so long as those 'persons that I have accused—for no slight crime, but for treason—are here, I cannot expect that this House can be in the right way that I do heartily wish it. Therefore, I am come to tell you that I must have them where-soever I find them. Is Mr. Pym here?" he demanded. But there was no reply. "Is Mr. Holles here?" and the same dead silence followed. He turned to Lenthall, "Are any of these persons in the House? Do you see any of them? Where are they?"

Lenthall fell on his knee and humbly declared the true position f the Speaker. "May it please your Majesty, I have neither yes to see nor tongue to speak in this place, but as this House ; pleased to direct me, whose servant I am here; and I umbly beg your Majesty's pardon that I cannot give any ther answer than this to what your Majesty is pleased to demand f me."

"Well, well," replied Charles, "'tis no matter. I think my yes are as good as another's." Once more there was a "dreadil silence," while the king scrutinized the faces on both sides of he House—but in vain. The game of brag had failed. He ad played for the highest stake, and turned up zero. "Well," e concluded, "I see all the birds are flown. I do expect rom you that you shall send them unto me as soon as they eturn hither. If not, I will seek them myself, for their treason ; foul, and such a one as you will thank me to discover. But assure you, *on the word of a king*, that I never did intend any ɔrce, but shall proceed against them in a legal and fair way, ɔr I never meant any other. I see I cannot do what I came ɔr. I think this is no unfit occasion to repeat what I have said ɔrmerly, that whatsoever I have done in favour, and to the ood of my subjects, I do mean to maintain it."

A strange commentary on his speech was furnished by the onduct of his followers waiting outside. "I warrant you," cried ne, cocking his pistol, "I am a good marksman, I will hit ure." "A pox take the House of Commons," growled another. 'Let them be hanged if they will." But perhaps the most onclusive of all, were the exclamations of disappointment which ailed the news of the disappearance of the five. "Zounds!" tormed one of them in wrath, "they are gone, and now we re never the better for our coming."

As the king passed down the House, sullen murmurs of disontent muttered threateningly along the crowded benches, ɹhich, almost before he had departed, broke out into loud cries f "Privilege, privilege." With these cries ringing in his ears, nd amid the shouts and execrations of the disappointed desperdoes, he passed along to Whitehall. And so ended the parliaɹentary contest between the king and his subjects.

"The arrest of the five members," observes Mr. Forster, "was

H

the final stage of the struggle against the Grand Remonstrance.
It was a violent effort to reverse the eleven votes by which the
victory was achieved, and to constitute the leaders of the minority
masters of the House of Commons." The immediate question
on which the outbreak of the civil war ultimately turned, was the
demand of Parliament that to them should be transferred the
full control of the militia ; but this demand was prompted by the
inveterate distrust and fear of the king, which the attempt on the
five members had fanned to an extraordinary height, and " when
Charles and his armed attendants passed through the lobby of
the House of Commons on the 4th of January, the civil war
had substantially begun."

The Commons' Committee appointed to inquire into the
matter, decidedly declared that the attempted arrest was a breach
of privilege. Treason, they argued, must have been committed
in the House or out of it. If the former, only the House (under
the privilege of secrecy) could bear witness of it. If the latter,
the House must be convinced of the truth of the charge before
surrendering its members. In either case it was definitely laid
down that no member of the House could be arrested without
the consent of the House ; and that the only legal mode of trying a member of the House for treason was by the ordinary
common law procedure of a true bill of a grand jury, and subsequent trial by a petty jury.

On January 10, the king departed from Whitehall, never to
enter it again save as a prisoner. The next day saw the triumphant return of the five members to Westminster, accompanied by
the trained bands of the City, and a host of boats manned by the
seamen and watermen of the Thames. Pym was now the acknowledged chief of the nation. The parliamentary struggle was
practically at an end ; the outbreak of the civil war was a mere
question of time.

SECTION 3.—*The Revolutionary Period.*

The Commons at once acted vigorously and decidedly. They
announced to the Lords that they would be glad of their help,
but if it were refused they would do their best to save the kingdom alone. This bold announcement scared the Lords from

their policy of obstruction, and bills were rapidly passed, excluding the bishops from the Upper House, and transferring to Parliament the control of the army and navy. A long paper war ensued between king and Parliament on these subjects, during the progress of which Hyde, Falkland, and the Royalists, amounting to thirty-two peers and sixty members of the House of Commons, withdrew from Westminster and joined the king at York. The demands of the Parliament rose continually higher, and in the end Charles determined to settle the disputed questions by force of arms. The parliamentary leaders at once declared the full capacity of the two Houses to act with sovereign power without the king. An executive committee of the principal men was appointed, and a parliamentary army raised.

On the revolutionary period which follows, it is impossible to do more than touch briefly, owing to its absence of constitutional value, save in ultimate result. It was this mutilated Parliament, no longer fully representative of the realm, which carried on the war to its successful close. It was this same Parliament, or rather its Presbyterian majority, headed by Holles, who quarrelled with their victorious army, and the generals, Cromwell, Fairfax, and Ireton. It was this Parliament, still further reduced by Colonel Pride's forcible purge of forty members, and a later expulsion of one hundred more, which, under the title of the Rump, earned for itself undying fame by the execution of Charles, and the abolition of monarchy and the House of Lords. Their greed of power, however, led them to endeavour to perpetuate their own individual existence in the new Parliament, which was now urgently demanded. This attempt brought them into collision with Cromwell and the army, and after vain efforts at an accommodation, the general called in the aid of a company of musketeers, drove the members out of the Commons' House by force, and locked the door. "We have heard," said John Bradshaw, one of the executive committee, "what you have done this morning at the House, but you mistake, sir, if you think this Parliament dissolved. No power on earth can dissolve this Parliament but itself."

These words sound the key-note of the difficulties which beset Cromwell's efforts to restore parliamentary government. There was a strong republican party, headed by Vane and Ludlow, who were alienated by the expulsion of the Rump just as the Presbyterians had been thrown into opposition by the removal of Holles and their other leaders. These two parties were far more difficult to deal with than the Royalists and the Anabaptists, who confined their efforts to secret plots of insurrection and assassination; for they contrived invariably to secure a very strong position in Cromwell's Parliaments, and by systematic obstruction and open hostility rendered all effectual action out of the question. The imposition of oaths to support the existing Government produced little good, for the oath was taken with the lips, and rejected immediately by the heart. The natural result was the total failure and early dissolution of the Parliaments of 1654 and 1657.

The Parliament of 1654, however, will always form a memorable date in our parliamentary annals as the first Parliament which was representative of the United Kingdom, and as the first step in the direction of a reform of the representative system. Its numbers were 460 in all, of whom 400 sat for England, 30 for Scotland, 30 for Ireland. A number of rotten boroughs were disfranchised, and their members given to the counties. A number of large towns, among which was Birmingham, were enfranchised. A partial redistribution of the county seats was made so as to establish some sort of equality between population and representation, a uniform qualification of £200 being fixed for both electors and members. With the dissolution of this Parliament ended all hope of a restoration of constitutional government, for Cromwell did not dare to trust to freedom of election again.

His death plunged the country into a series of disputes between the military leaders, amid which the survivors of the Rump, declaring that their dissolution was invalid as having been effected without their consent, reassembled and endeavoured to grasp into their hands again the reins of power, only to be once more dissolved by General Monk as the first step in the direction of the restoration of the monarchy. Overtures were immediately made to Charles II., and a Convention Parliament summoned to treat for his return.

The lawyers of the Restoration declared of course that the legal constitution had been only suspended during this period, hat it revived again at its close, and that the work of Cromwell ied with him. But this, however true in law, was false in eality. The monarchies of Charles I. and of his son stood on vo sides of a gulf which no legal formula could successfully oan ; the cause of absolute monarchy was lost for ever, and the redominant influence of the House of Commons in the govern- ient of the nation was successfully established. Cromwell's ynasty indeed died with him, but the spirit which had animated ie men of the Great Rebellion lived on.

CHAPTER VIII.

PARLIAMENTS OF THE RESTORATION.
(1660–88.)

SECTION I.—*The Convention of* 1660.

PARLIAMENT met the 25th of April, 1660. The Commons proceeded at once to choose a Speaker, and their choice fell on Sir Harbottle Grimston, a Presbyterian, who was very favourable to the king's return. The Peers met in the House of Lords, and elected the Earl of Manchester to be their president. Their number, moreover, having by the 27th risen to thirty-six, they signalised that day by the first public use of a privilege long proscribed, and desired a conference with the Commons on the affairs of the kingdom. The Commons meanwhile had acted strictly according to the ancient forms. Committees of Privilege had been appointed. Solemn votes of thanks had been decreed to Monk and Ingoldsby for their great and manifold services. It is highly probable that the question of imposing some limitations on the royal power would have been discussed at the conference, but when the day came the whole subject was adroitly evaded by a stroke of management. Mr. Annesley reported to the Commons, by order, that the Council of State had received letters from the king. Sir John Grenville, the bearer, was thereupon called in, and the king's letter to the Speaker was recited to the House. The royal missives to the Lord Mayor and General Monk, for the City and army, were next read, amid manifestations of the utmost loyalty and enthusiasm.

A similar scene was shortly afterwards enacted in the Lords. Loyal answers were immediately prepared by both Houses; Grenville was publicly thanked and rewarded by the Commons; and resolutions were hastily carried in favour of the re-establishment of monarchy. The Commons voted the king a present of £50,000 for his immediate necessities. The Lords ordered

1at all statues of the parliamentary leaders and generals should
e destroyed, and the arms of the Commonwealth taken down
r defaced. A committee was appointed to prepare a settle-
1ent for the principal difficulties, such as the indemnity for those
ho had acted under the late Government, the abolition of the
1ilitary tenures, and a provision for the royal revenue in re-
1rn for the contemplated abolition of the feudal dues. Orders
ere issued that the king should be publicly prayed for in all
:ligious services. The new-born loyalty of Parliament reached
s climax in an attempt to obliterate the very remembrance of
1e Great Rebellion by a preposterous decree that the king should
2 held to have succeeded to the throne from the date of his
.ther's death, with the ridiculous result that the first year of his
:tual reign (1660) is regarded for all legal purposes as the twelfth
f Charles II.

Having thus surpassed all previous efforts, the Convention
ppointed commissioners to entreat the king's return. Some
1tempt was made by Mr. Hale, afterwards the celebrated
'hief Justice, to insist that some limitations, based on the offers
1ade to Charles I. during the revolutionary period, should be
1laced on the royal power as the conditions of the Restoration ;
1ut in reply Monk argued that the danger of any further delay
'as great and imminent, and that the king was far more likely to
onsent to limitations in the future if he were received with un-
uestioning loyalty at first. His view in the end prevailed ; the
nthusiasm of the moment overwhelmed the prudent counsels
f cooler-headed men. The king was proclaimed on .the 8th
t Temple Bar, outside Whitehall, and in Palace Yard ; and
n the 29th he made his entry into the capital, amid a tumult
f wild, unreasonable joy. Who would have imagined that
ll these exaggerated rejoicings would so soon be changed to
uspicion, almost to hate? A number of bills, in fact, were
egun without any very clear prospect of completion ; but save
or this the king returned to the throne of his ancestors un-
rammelled by any conditions, and to this cause Bishop Burnet,
omewhat hastily, attributes all the errors of the reign. The sole
1recaution, in fact, that the Convention took against an absolute
eturn to the old purely personal government of Charles I. was in

the form of a bill embodying a request for the confirmation of Magna Carta, the Petition of Right, and various other statutes and privileges of Parliament which had been asserted in 1641. To this statute the king gave his assent almost at the moment of his arrival. It is difficult, however, to condemn them for their inaction. There was an almost irresistible disinclination on the part of the majority for any further delay, and no little danger in-volved in it, as well not only of a rupture of the negotiations, but of a fresh outbreak on the part of the military party. There was, moreover, an almost insuperable obstacle in the way of treaty-making with the king. The recognition of his title involved the condemnation of the Convention as an illegal, because self-con-stituted body. How then could such an assembly conclude any binding agreement? No conditions, in fact, made before the king's return could have stood sound in law unless they were confirmed by Act of Parliament after the Restoration. There is little doubt, moreover, that Charles would have agreed to almost any conditions, in the firm belief that "the next free Parliament summoned by his own order would undo all this work of stipula-tion, and restore him to an unfettered prerogative"; and in all human probability he would have been fully justified by the event. It was more likely that a gracious and generous reception might induce him to consent to subsequent limitations by Act of Parlia-ment, than that, in the hour of triumph, he would consider himself bound by a treaty void in law, and imposed on him solely by stern necessity.

It may be urged that the most prudent course would have been to have declared a vacancy of the throne during the period of the Commonwealth, and to have offered the crown to Charles as an elected king, as in the famous case of William of Orange. The circumstances, however, were very different, and the difference rendered such a course of action impossible. Charles II. was restored by an outbreak of returning loyalty, stimulated almost to frenzy by disgust at the anarchy which had prevailed since the death of Cromwell. The nation attributed to their rebellion against the king all the evils which had befallen them of late; they were determined both to restore the ancient ꞯnasty and to treat as an usurpation, not an interregnum, the

hole period of the Commonwealth. The men of the Restoration
ere too powerfully swayed by the passions of the moment to be
ble to coolly deliberate the burning question of the king's return,
r to discuss in a business-like manner the surest mode of effect-
ıg the re-establishment of the royal power with those limitations
hich experience had proved to be necessary. They were unable
ı act solely with a view to expediency at a time when they were
overned wholly by enthusiasm. Moreover, it would have been
xtremely difficult in the then imperfect state of political science,
nd the undeveloped or ruined condition of political institutions,
ı draw up an ideal constitution on the spur of the moment.
'here must have been errors on the one side or the other—the
ıost probable result being to reduce the power of the Crown and
.ords to a shadow. It would have been still more difficult for
ıis to be effected by a large popular assembly which had no
xperience in constitution making, and which, with their eyes
linded by the total failure alike of the governments of Charles I.,
he Long Parliament, and Cromwell, would certainly have been
nfitted to select from the ruined fragments of all three systems
he few sound portions as a foundation for a new one. It was
asiest to return to the old *régime*, suspending the work of reform
or the present; and it seemed wiser to wait for a more judicial
ein before commencing the difficult task of excision. The men
ıf the Convention Parliament, moreover, knew not that the flood
ıf awakened loyalty would sweep them away, and with them the
:ounsels of the prudent party, long before a quarter of their pro-
ected work was accomplished; nor did they imagine for an
nstant that by deferring conditions until after the king's return
hey were practically depriving themselves of the power of making
hem at all. Plausible therefore as Burnet's verdict may seem by
he light of subsequent history, it seems, after a more thoughtful
:onsideration of the circumstances, that a satisfactory settlement
:ould not possibly have been arranged, and that further delay
vould only have embittered the king against the Presbyterian
eaders, and facilitated the designs of the republican party.

It had been originally intended that the Parliament should do
nothing more than formally acknowledge the king; then it should
be dissolved and a fresh one summoned. It was, however, con-

sidered a dangerous experiment to commit the country in its then excited state to a General Election ; and there were, moreover, a number of points which required immediate settlement. The king therefore recognised the Lower House as a lawfully elected body ;—many, however, held that it was still an illegal assembly, its legality being tainted from the outset by its election without the necessary formality of the royal writs. Such as it was, however, it continued to sit, and busied itself at once with the settlement of pressing questions.

The king in his declaration from Breda had endeavoured to allay the apprehensions of his subjects by laying down certain views of a conciliatory nature. He advised that a general pardon should be issued to all but those excepted by Parliament ; that liberty of conscience should be granted to all whose ideas were not subversive of the peace of the realm ; that all claims to landed property should be equitably settled in Parliament ; and that Monk's army should be paid their arrears in full. These four points therefore, and a contribution of their own in the shape of the abolition of the feudal system, and re-settlement of the revenue which was the natural result, were the ostensible motive of the continued existence of the Convention.

The indemnity was first dealt with ; in fact, it had been discussed to some extent already. The general opinion was unanimous, that some of the regicides should be excepted. Monk would have limited the exceptions to four ; the ultra-loyalists clamoured for all. Eventually, by Monk's advice, it was resolved on the 14th May that only seven names should be excluded from the Act of Indemnity. The exuberant ebullition of loyalty which burst out on the return of the king caused the question to be reopened again later on with great acrimony ; and after numerous long debates the Commons finally voted that those regicides who had not surrendered themselves in accordance with a proclamation dated June 8, should be deprived of all the benefits of the Act of Indemnity ; eleven, moreover, being specially mentioned by name. The bill was now sent up to the Lords, who were decidedly more cavalier in feeling, and consequently less lenient in tone. By the end of July they had determined to exclude all the regicide judges and five others,—Vane, Lambert, Haselrig,

Axtel, and Hacker. In August they even proceeded to an odious measure for the satisfaction of private revenge. The nearest relatives of the Duke of Hamilton, Lords Holland, Capel, and Derby, who had been executed under the Commonwealth, were each empowered to select for exception one of the persons who had taken part in the condemnation of those noblemen. Lord Denbigh, the brother-in-law of the Duke of Hamilton, confined himself to naming a person who was dead; but the relatives of the three other peers were not so humane. By the 9th of August the Lords had resolved to inflict heavy penalties on all those who had sat in any illegal high court of justice. This severity and delay were very unwelcome to the king and his advisers, both because they desired that the expectations of lenity held out at Breda should not be disappointed, and also because the discussion of this subject blocked the progress of all other business. On the 27th of August, therefore, the king personally recommended haste, a compromise was rapidly effected between the moderate and extreme parties, and it was arranged that the regicides who surrendered should be tried for their lives, but should not be executed except by order of Parliament. The bill in its final form was a general pardon for all offences committed since the year 1637, with the exception of fifty-one persons who were concerned in the death of Charles I., and some other exceptions.

Next came the settlement of the revenue. It was desirable to provide the Crown with an adequate income for ordinary expenses without depriving Parliament of its control over extraordinary expenditure. A committee was appointed to inquire into the subject, and in the end it was decided to settle on the king a fixed revenue of £1,200,000 per annum, by a grant of tunnage and poundage for life, and a hereditary excise. The latter grant was intended as a compensation for the surrender of the feudal dues which was arranged by Act of Parliament. The sum, however, fixed for the revenue was utterly inadequate to the expenses ; the funds assigned to supply it were insufficient for that purpose. Unfortunately, too, the private expenses of the Crown and those of the public service were included under the same head, and this afforded opportunities for starving the

public service in order to gratify personal extravagance. The
settlement, therefore, was unsatisfactory from the very first : all
inducement to economy was destroyed by the hopelessness of
attempting to balance the two sides of the account ; repeated
applications to Parliament were necessary to carry on the government at all.

The next step was perhaps the most difficult and dangerous ;
yet it was effected with startling facility, affording the strongest
testimony of the order-loving instincts of the nation. The soldiers
of the old Cromwellian army were naturally not pleased with the
destruction of the military *régime*; their continued existence was
a standing threat to the new Government. Vigilance, conciliation, the prompt payment of arrears, and a judicious method of
disbanding averted the danger. The Lord Chancellor, at the
adjournment of Parliament, September 13, 1660, made a speech
with reference to the army which was highly calculated to soothe
their feelings, and by the end of the year the complete dissolution
of this formidable force was quietly accomplished—two regiments
being alone retained.

The resettlement of the landed property of the realm was by
no means such an easy matter. The Crown lands, Church lands,
and those of many distinguished Royalists, had been sold by the
late Government: in some cases at very high prices. The House
of Commons itself contained many who had profited by these
sales, and were naturally unwilling to disgorge their acquisitions
without compensation. They therefore brought in a bill to
confirm the sales or give indemnity to the purchasers. The
Royalists soon inserted a clause of exception in favour of the
Crown lands, though the principle of composition for ecclesiastical property was steadily adhered to. The bill got on but
slowly, and had not advanced far when it was stifled by the
dissolution, and the matter practically left to the decisions of the
courts of law in individual cases.

No great change had attended the restoration of the old system
of government in temporal matters ; but the question of the
ecclesiastical constitution and government involved more difficulty in consequence of the sweeping expulsion of those clergy
who had refused to take the Covenant, and though the Presby-

erian discipline and government had been only partially intro-
luced, yet the Episcopalian system had been entirely uprooted.
The Presbyterian clergy had co-operated in the Restoration ; it
was only natural that they should expect some countenance,
hough it was inevitable that the Episcopalian system should be
estored. A compromise was therefore proposed by the moderate
arty : to restore the old clergy ejected under the Commonwealth
without giving them any title to the intermediate profits, and to
onfirm the rights of those actual incumbents whose claims were
ot disputed. The measure made no provision for freedom of
onscience, which would have been seriously affected by the
estoration of the old ecclesiastical organization, and the consequent revival of the Acts of Uniformity and Supremacy. All
oncession on this head, however, the bishops decidedly refused
o grant, and the king was not desirous of incurring the hostility
f his friends for the benefit of his father's foes. Negotiations
were actually set on foot, and Charles even ventured to issue a
leclaration of liberty of conscience in points of ritual, but the
egotiations were ineffectual, and when the declaration was
rought forward in Parliament to be confirmed by statute, it was
pposed by the whole strength of the Court party and rejected.
Shortly afterwards, on the 24th of December, the Convention was
lissolved by the king in person, on which occasion the Speaker
ook the opportunity to deliver an address, in which exaggerated
oyalty struggled with the most servile adulation to express itself
n suitable phrases.

SECTION 2.—*The Long or Pension Parliament* (1661-79).

The royalist lawyers maintained that the Acts of this Parliament
were invalid unless confirmed by the next, because it had not been
properly summoned by royal writ. It was therefore really of vital
importance to assemble another as soon as possible, to obtain the
confirmation so necessary to the safety of the kingdom. The
new Parliament, however, was elected in the flood-tide of loyalty,
swollen to unusual height by the failure of a republican outbreak,
and in consequence the Cavalier element predominated largely.
The Presbyterian members numbered no more than fifty, a nucleus

round which the opposition was to gather later on ; but the marvel really was, under the circumstances of the General Election, that their numbers were not even smaller.

The new Parliament met on the 8th of May, and was opened by the king in a speech announcing his intended marriage with the Princess of Portugal. Clarendon, the Chancellor, followed, and reminded the Commons that their first duty was to confirm the Acts of the last Parliament, hinting obscurely at some scheme of comprehension in Church matters for the benefit of tender consciences. The temper of the Commons, however, was soon shown. They elected as their Speaker Edward Turnour, a strong adherent of the Duke of York. Motions were carried that the Solemn League and Covenant should be burned by the common hangman ; and the Acts for creating a High Court to try Charles I., for declaring the Commonwealth, and a number of others, were ordered to be treated with the same indignity. A special law of treason was passed for the protection of Charles's life and government. It was solemnly declared that the legislative power could not be exercised by Parliament alone ; the militia was restored to the king ; and, no doubt in vindictive memory of the stormy sessions and debates of the Long Parliament, it was decided that no petition or address should be presented to king or Parliament by more than ten persons, and that no petition for alteration of matters established by law in Church and State should be signed by more than twenty persons, unless its contents were sanctioned by three justices, or the majority of the grand jury, or the Lord Mayor, aldermen, and Common Council in London. So far from devising any scheme of comprehension, they next proceeded to exclude the Dissenters entirely from corporations, where their chief strength hitherto lay. The bill was brought into the Commons on June 19, and was stoutly opposed, but it eventually passed, December 20, 1661. It required all members of corporations to take the oaths of allegiance and supremacy, and the sacrament in the English form ; to solemnly renounce the Covenant, and declare their abhorrence of "that traitorous position, that the subject could lawfully take up arms against the king or his servants." This Parliament, in fact, deliberately renewed the attempt to render the Church a state engine, and suppress all Dissent by a rigorous

ᵣstem of exclusion. The Corporation Act was only the first of a
ᵣries of statutes of similar tendency. It was followed by an Act
ᵣr restoring the bishops to the House of Lords, which was hurried
ᵣrough both Houses in June, 1662, with singular ease. An Act of
ᵢniformity moreover was introduced in the Lords, to compel all
ᵢergymen, on pain of deprivation, to declare their full assent to
ᵢe Book of Common Prayer, and to make episcopal ordination
ᵢecessary for all ministers. Intolerant however as it was, this bill
ᵢas considered far too liberal by the Commons. Accordingly
ᵣesh clauses of exclusion were added; and all provision for
ᵢose of the clergy who should refuse the tests was peremptorily
ᵤt off. The Lords, who now by a strange whirl of fortune's
ᵣheel were by far the most tolerant of the two Houses, tried in
ᵥain to soften these effects of religious animosity; but the Com-
ᵢons remained firm, and at last the Lords were obliged to
ᵢve way on all points. Thus, in spite of the declaration from
ᵦreda, religious persecution was introduced into the law; and
ᵢ consequence of the provisions of the Act of Uniformity,
ᵦbout 2,000 ministers were ejected from their livings on St.
ᵦartholomew's Day (August 24), 1662.

An effort was even made in this Parliament to revive the extinct
ᵤrisdiction of the Star Chamber, and to repeal the Triennial Act :
ᵢt met, however, with failure, nor did the Parliament manifest any
ᵢesire to confirm the Acts of the Convention. A bill was indeed
ᵦrought in early in the session for that purpose, but the Royalists
ᵣhowed such open dislike to the measure—above all because it
ᵢncluded the Act of Indemnity—that little progress was made
ᵥith it. Charles and Clarendon, however, considered themselves
ᵦound in honour to secure its success; and, by dint of exercis-
ng some considerable pressure on the Commons, the bill was
ᵢt last sent up, and on the 8th July received the royal assent.
Parliament, however, was able to satisfy its desire for vengeance
ᵢn those excepted from the benefits of the Act—especially by the
ᵢxecution of Vane and the imprisonment of Lambert.

When therefore it was adjourned at the end of July, a great
ᵢeal had been effected. The old system of government was
ᵣestored with fresh safeguards against any attempts of enemies;
the Acts of the Commonwealth were stamped with thᵣ

indelible brand of illegality and treason; the Church was re-established, now confessedly no longer co-extensive with the nation, but a body in a peculiar relation to the State.   Parliament had moreover gone considerably beyond the limits which prudence should have dictated, and manifested a subserviency and a hankering after obsolete principles of despotism which were really far more due to temporary enthusiasm than to any permanent retrogression in public spirit.

During the recess, however, Charles, mainly actuated no doubt by the desire to relieve the Catholics, to whose religion he was secretly attached, issued a Declaration of Indulgence to tender consciences; and promised to obtain in the next session an Act which would enable him to exercise the dispensing power of the Crown to grant relief in individual cases.   At the opening of Parliament, February 18, 1663, he urged the adoption of his Declaration, but it was rejected by Parliament, who declared that the dispensing power could not be applied to whole statutes.   A bill was brought in in the Upper House to give effect to the king's promise, but it was also rejected, and with it vanished all chance of conciliation.

The session of 1663 was remarkable for an extraordinary scene. This was the impeachment of Clarendon, the Chancellor, by Lord Bristol.   Clarendon had become extremely distasteful to the king, the royal favourite (Lady Castlemaine), and all the Court set generally.   He was also odious to the Catholics for his opposition to the king's plan of toleration.   Bristol, their leader, hoped to revive his own declining reputation, and to secure the king's favour, by attacking the unpopular minister. He accused him of truckling to Rome, of endeavouring to alienate the affections of the people from the king, and of high treason generally.   The Duke of York promptly rose and informed the Lords that the king highly disapproved of this impeachment—as no doubt he did, for it would have been extremely inconvenient for him if the grounds of these accusations had been examined too narrowly. Bristol thereupon with a theatrical gesture tore open his doublet, and exclaimed that he received this blow from the king's brother with uncovered breast; there in Parliament, as a peer of the realm, he was his equal.   Clarendon now plunged into the fray

l attacked him with bitter irony :—how was it that he, a Catholic
r, had suddenly become such an active defender of Protestant·
? Bristol retorted angrily that he was a Catholic, but not an
ierent of the Romish court ; nor as a good patriot did he desire
nce more to gain a footing in England. Flaws, however, were
covered in the form of the impeachment, and as the king was
mly opposed to it, it was found advisable to let the question
p.

The rest of the acts of this remarkable Parliament can be only
efly referred to. Perhaps the most important event in its after
ory was the surrender by the clergy of their right of separate
ation. By a private agreement to that effect, concluded in
54 between Clarendon and Archbishop Sheldon, grants in
liament became binding on the whole people. Since then the
rgy have claimed the right of voting for parliamentary elections
respect of their ecclesiastical freeholds. The same year was
nalised by the repeal of the Triennial Act, and disgraced by a
nventicle Act, which punished as a seditious assembly any
eting for religious purposes of more than five persons except
se held in accordance with the practice of the Church of
gland—the result being to fill the gaols with Nonconformists.
1665 the same spirit of bigotry dictated a Five Mile Act,
ich forbade any clergyman to teach in schools or come within
e miles of any corporate town or borough, unless he would
oscribe the Act of Uniformity and declare on oath his adhesion
the doctrine of passive obedience. This year was also
nalised by the renewal of an important constitutional principle
the appropriation of supplies voted in Parliament. Sir George
wning proposed that the money granted for the Dutch war
ould be specially appropriated to that purpose ; and though
arendon strongly opposed the motion, Charles exercised all his
luence to secure its passage through Parliament. Probably he
lized that it would be easier to obtain advances from bankers
on such a guarantee. In the next year, 1666, when the large
st and small success of the war gave birth to grave suspicions,
e House appointed a committee to audit the accounts of the
pplies. Once more they were opposed by Clarendon, and on
is occasion by the king as well. He had no desire for the

I

Commons to discover his misapplication of the public money,
and he supported his minister even to the extent of proroguing
Parliament to stave off the unwelcome question.   In the ensuing
session, however, the matter was taken up again, and a regular
commission appointed with full powers of auditing the public
accounts.   Parliament also proceeded to set another ancient
right on its former constitutional footing, by passing a resolution
that the law of Richard Strode (4 Hen. VIII. c. 8), was a general
law, and that the proceedings in Eliot's case (5 Car. I.) were
illegal.   They also showed their rising distrust of the king by
loud protests and petitions against a standing army, when a force
of 20,000 men were hastily levied to defend the coast from the
Dutch.   The event of the year, however, was the fall of
Clarendon, who, now thoroughly unpopular, was gladly abandoned
by the king to his enemies in Parliament.   They impeached him
for mismanaging the Dutch war and general misgovernment.
He fled to escape the penalty.

The results of Clarendon's administration were threefold: the
rise of the Cabinet system, the complete restoration of parliamentary government, and the formation of a strong opposition.
The first of these was the natural result of an enormous enlargement of the ranks of the Privy Council by the admission of all the
leading men of the time—men of the most opposite views.   It
was impossible to govern by means of such an unwieldy body;
and the king fell into the habit of consulting his own immediate
friends in private on questions of importance before submitting
them to the Council.   The government was really, therefore,
carried on by Clarendon and three others: and the Commons, by
impeaching him for his official conduct, went a long way towards
establishing the doctrine that a minister must rely on the
excellence and success of his measures, not on the favour of
the king.   Still, at the same time, it was pretty obvious that
the king's favour had been entirely withdrawn from Clarendon,
and that his overthrow was as much due to Charles's own desire
for revenge as the minister's misgovernment.   The complete
restoration of parliamentary government had been effected piece
by piece; for though the repeal of the Triennial Act entrusted a
dangerous discretion to the king with regard to the summoning

Parliament, yet his revenue was so inadequate that it was possible for him to intermit the sessions for very long, even with ⸱ help of the large subsidies which he continually received from ⸱nce. Parliament, therefore, had recovered its ancient right of ⸱it and appropriation; it had reasserted the privilege of free⸱ ⸱m of discussion; it had resisted the attempt of the king to ⸱pense the laws; it had re-established the principle that ⸱nisters should be answerable to the representatives of the ⸱ion; and it had expressly insisted on Clarendon's arbitrary ⸱ringements of the liberty of the subject as a principal ground ⸱ his impeachment. The growth of the opposition was due to ⸱eral causes. The old Royalists considered themselves neglected ⸱ the Indemnity question, and were consequently discontented: ⸱sonal liberty had been frequently violated by Clarendon: ⸱rendon himself had never been really a favourite with the ⸱ple: the heavy taxation for the Dutch war and the ill-success ⸱ich attended it increased his unpopularity: the sale of Dunkirk ⸱s regarded by many as a blot on the national honour: Charles ⸱nself was too profligate in life to command much esteem when ⸱ce the first effervescence of the Restoration had subsided, and ⸱ had exposed himself to grave suspicions with regard to the ⸱blic money, which were calculated to alienate many: the Non- ⸱nformists, moreover, had been persecuted with a ferocity that ⸱used considerable sympathy among all who were not led away ⸱ bigoted Anglicanism. There were therefore very powerful ⸱ments of opposition roused through the country against the ⸱vernment and the king, which gathered naturally round the ⸱ginal Presbyterian nucleus in the Parliament, and required very ⸱eful handling during the rest of the reign. The sacrifice of ⸱rendon and of a defaulting officer, Sir George Carteret, the ⸱easurer of the Navy (1669), conciliated the Commons in no ⸱all measure, and staved off for some time any open quarrel ⸱h the king and his administration.

The crisis was averted till 1672/3—chiefly by the receipt of ⸱avy sums from France which rendered Charles independent ⸱ parliamentary grants, and by the practice of proroguing Parlia- ⸱nt for lengthy periods. This latter policy told heavily against ⸱ king, however, in the long run, for " the growing discontents and suspicions of the people acquired strength by the stoppage of the regular channel of complaint." This was especially the case after the long prorogation between April, 1671, and Feb., 1672/3, during which so many outrageous assertions of prerogative were made that "the Court so lost the confidence of the House of Commons that with all the lavish corruption of the following period it could never regain a secure majority on any important question."

During the period between 1667–73, usually known as that of the Cabal, two important disputes arose between the two Houses on very different subjects. The first was the case of *Skinner v. the East India Company*. Skinner complained to the Lords that he had been robbed and ill-treated by the servants of the Company in the maintenance of their monopoly of the Indian trade. The Company denied that the Lords had any right to interfere. The Lords, however, took no notice of this, and condemned them to pay a fine of £5,000. They thereupon petitioned the Commons against the decision of the Lords. The Commons resolved that the Lords had no business in the matter at all. The Lords replied with an angry vote "that the House of Commons, entertaining the scandalous petition of the East India Company against the Lords' House of Parliament, and their proceedings, examinations, and votes thereupon had and made, are a breach of the privileges of the House of Peers;" adding that their own proceedings were quite in accordance with law and precedent. An attempt was made to settle the question by a conference, but it failed, and both sides proceeded to violence, which of course fell on the heads of third parties. Skinner was arrested by order of the Commons, the chairman of the Company by order of the Lords. The king at last endeavoured to stop the quarrel by a succession of adjournments and prorogations; but it broke out again and again at each fresh meeting of Parliament, until at last he recommended both parties to end the matter by erasing all records of the question from the journals and letting it drop. This expedient was gladly adopted to remove the deadlock;—but from that date the Lords have never claimed any right to exercise original jurisdiction. The second dispute arose in April, 1671, over a money-bill. The Lords reduced the amount of a sugar-

ill. It was in consequence resolved by the Commons, "that in
ll aids given to the king by the Commons the rate or tax ought
ot to be altered by the Lords." Several conferences were held
n the subject without any conclusion being arrived at, for pre-
edent seemed undoubtedly to be in favour of the Lords. The
ractice, however, has been since that date, that when the Lords
ntroduce any amendment which the Commons desire to adopt,
ne latter throw out the old bill and the amendment, and bring
n a new one with the amendment incorporated in it. Practically,
nerefore, the Lords have lost the power of amending money-
ills.

The rising opposition in Parliament was brought to a head by
ne events of the long prorogation from April, 1671, to February,
672/3. The declaration of war with Holland, the ill-success
nhich followed it, and the fraudulent stoppage of payment by the
Exchequer, were capped by a fresh attempt to assert the king's
ight of granting dispensation from the requirements of the law, in
nrder to remit the penalties incurred by Catholics and Dissenters.
When Parliament first assembled, however, in February, 1672/3,
hey did not seem to fully realize the danger of this claim on the
nart of prerogative ; but the feeling against it gradually grew more
general, and the storm at last rose to such a height that Charles
nas afraid to resist any longer. Even the Dissenters, whom it
nould have benefited, were opposed to obtaining toleration by
llegal modes. So in the end it was withdrawn, amid loud com-
nlaints of the king against the conduct of the Commons. The
nuestion, however, did not end there, for grave suspicions were
aroused among the leaders of the Opposition, or Country party, as
hey were called. A schism occurred even in the ranks of the
Ministry, and Shaftesbury and Buckingham behaved more as
hough they were enemies, than members of the Government. A
nery widespread belief was growing up that the king meditated
the restoration of Catholicism, and that the Declaration of Indulgence was but the prelude to far more dangerous and daring
attempts.

If it be true, as the French ambassador stated, that Shaftesbury
had been incautiously informed of the conclusion of the secret
treaty with France without his advice or even knowledge, one of

the provisions of which was that every effort was to be made to re-establish Catholicism in England, a ready explanation is furnished, both of his present ambiguous conduct and subsequent active opposition. He had supported the Declaration for the benefit of the Dissenters; but he would be no party to a popish plot. The general feeling that there was a popish plot on foot produced an Act for preventing the increase of Catholicism, which is commonly known as the Test Act. It required all persons holding office under the Crown to take the Sacrament in the English form, in addition to the oaths of supremacy and allegiance, and to make a solemn declaration that they did not believe in the doctrine of transubstantiation. The latter point, involving a denial of a vital doctrine of the Roman Catholic Church, would effectually exclude all Catholics. The Act was double-edged—it attacked the Dissenters equally. The Dissenters, however, supported it zealously. Their views were expressed very clearly by Alderman Love, who declared that his party had no desire to claim admission to the Church; all that they wanted was freedom of worship, which could be granted by the indulgence of Parliament. The Act passed rapidly through the Commons, with hardly the slightest opposition. In the Lords it was attacked severely by Lord Clifford, the Catholic leader of the Government, but it passed easily, owing to the open support of Buckingham and Shaftesbury. The results were very sweeping. Clifford, the Lord High Treasurer, was obliged to resign his post: the Duke of York gave up the Admiralty: the Catholics were hopelessly excluded from all offices whatever.

Encouraged by this triumph, Parliament went still further, and impeached Buckingham, Arlington, and Lauderdale, three members of the fallen Ministry. It protested most energetically against the maintenance of a standing army. It brought such an amount of pressure to bear on the king with regard to his foreign policy, and criticised it so adversely and unsparingly in the debates on Supply of 1673/4, that he was compelled to break his engagements with France and conclude peace, in February, 1673/4. Finally it drew up a plan of a Habeas Corpus Act for the better security of the liberty of the subject, which was, however, rejected by the Lords. The result of the sessions was that, though none

these constitutional claims had been fought out, yet Parliament
d given to the English Administration an entirely Protestant
aracter, and had shown that it could interfere almost inde-
ndently in the complications of Europe.

Clifford was succeeded by the Earl of Danby, who endeavoured
 neutralize opposition in Parliament by an elaborate system of
ibery, the idea of which he had borrowed from his predecessors.
1e period of his government presents a very singular appearance
 the historical student. Danby himself was opposed to the
ng's French policy; at the same time, regarding himself as the
ng's minister, he would not resist his commands directly, though
: did all he could to thwart these projects indirectly. The
ountry party were anxious for war with France; at the same
ne they distrusted the king so heartily, that they were afraid to
ant him supplies to raise troops for the war, for fear he should
e them to make himself supreme in the realm by military force;
any of them too were undoubtedly in direct receipt of sums of
oney from Louis XIV. as an encouragement to continue this
opposition, which was so useful to him. Charles himself had no
al desire for war, and in fact was heavily paid for his neutrality;
it he kept up a pretence of preparation in order to satisfy
anby and the Opposition. The result of this extraordinary
osition was that, after maintaining his majority with some diffi-
ilty for a short time by dint of profuse bribery, Danby at last
ll a victim to his mistaken views of his duty to his sovereign.
he Commons were furnished with conclusive evidence that he
ad been instrumental in concluding a treaty of neutrality with
rance at a time when he was openly advocating war, and they
romptly impeached him. Their violence was no doubt mainly
ue to their fears with regard to the designs of the Catholics, and
1ey were goaded to frenzy by the disclosures known as the
opish Plot. This panic of rage and terror had already been pro-
uctive (during the year 1678) of an Act requiring all members
f Parliament to take the declaration against transubstantiation,
hus excluding the Catholic peers from the House of Lords for
he first time in English history, an exception in favour of the
Duke of York being only secured by two votes. The importance
of Danby's impeachment was great, for it struck at the king

through him.   There was no doubt that he acted under the
king's direct order, and he produced the king's pardon for his
deed.   It was decided, however, that neither the king's order nor
the king's pardon could be pleaded in bar of an impeachment.
Custom and precedent were undoubtedly in favour of Danby ; but
the Commons were able to maintain the Whig theory—that a
minister is directly responsible to the nation for all acts done in
his official capacity, and can no longer shelter himself from the
consequences by pleading the will of the sovereign.   During the
preliminary stages of the impeachment, the Commons endeavoured
to exclude the bishops from sitting in judgment, but without
success ; the Lords maintained their right, which was undoubtedly
good in law.   In the hope of saving Danby, Charles at last took
the extreme measure of dissolving this Parliament.   So ended
the second Long Parliament, which had now sat for nearly eighteen
years, and which had witnessed so many changes of feeling, from
the fervid loyalty of the Restoration to the clamorous hostility
during the Popish Plot.

Section 3.—*Last Parliaments of Charles* II. (1679–85).

The elections went dead against the Court.   The Country
party returned with a large majority, and immediately resumed
the proceedings against Danby, declaring that an impeachment
was not affected by a dissolution—an entirely new, though highly
practical doctrine.   Moreover, convinced that the only way of
securing the liberties of the country was to shut out the Duke of
York from the succession, an Exclusion Bill was brought in to
render a Catholic incapable of ascending the throne.   An attempt
was made by the Court to interpose a barrier between the king
and the Commons, by reviving the power of the Privy Council,
and re-establishing it on a sound basis.   The scheme, however,
failed entirely, and in order to avert the passing of the Exclusion
Bill by the Commons, the king was obliged to prorogue and
subsequently dissolve Parliament.   In spite, however, of the
violence which disgraced it, this Parliament of 1679 deserves an
honourable remembrance for the securities which it provided
against arbitrary infringements on the liberty of the subject, by

assing the Habeas Corpus Act. A new Parliament was summoned to meet in October, 1679, but it assembled merely to be prorogued till January, 1679/80. All through the recess, the Opposition kept up the most violent agitation against the Government; and as the year drew near to its close, a large number of petitions, numerously signed, were sent up to the king, praying that Parliament might meet on the appointed day. The king's party, on the other hand, were not idle; and there was still deep-rooted in the hearts of the people a strong feeling of loyalty to the Crown, which was shocked by this unusual attempt to control its actions. In consequence, numerous other petitions were sent up to the king, expressing the utmost horror of the first petitions.

When Parliament at last met in October, it divided at once into two definite parties, who taunted their enemies as "Petitioners" and "Abhorrers." Later these names were exchanged for the more modern ones of "Whigs" and "Tories"—the former drawn from the nickname given to the wildest and most uncompromising republican party in Scotland; the latter identifying the Royalists with the roughest and most uncivilized remnants of the old Irish, who clung obstinately to their ancient habits and laws, strongly resisting any attempts to force on them the English Constitution in Church and State: the point of the insult lying in each case in the fact that these extreme opinions were, of course, regarded by both parties with equal abhorrence. At the opening of Parliament the Exclusion Bill was introduced once more, passed rapidly through the Commons, and sent up to the Lords. It was brought in by Lord Russell, who was accompanied by a number of members of the Lower House, the Lord Mayor, and other officials of the City. Many of the Peers were decidedly in favour of it: Shaftesbury, Essex, and Sunderland all spoke strongly in support of it. The bishops were at their wits' end, for they had been informed that the king particularly wished that a dispute between the two Houses should be averted. The discussion dragged slowly on in committee, and then Lord Halifax rose to speak—an old enemy of the Duke of York, and a strong opponent of the Papacy, but an equally firm upholder of hereditary right. The debate became a brilliant combat of eloquence between him and Shaftesbury; a rhetorical battle, the like of which was not to be seen again in the century. "Ah," said the old men, shaking their heads, when later generations marvelled at the eloquence of some rising statesman of the day, "but you should have heard Lord Halifax on the Exclusion Bill." In the end he prevailed, and the bill was rejected ; but the Commons showed their rage and disappointment with so much violence that the king, in self-defence, was obliged to dissolve them, January 18, 1680/1. Their extravagant conduct, in fact, put them entirely in the wrong, and gave Charles the handle against them which he desired. The turn of the tide was really reached when the action of the " Petitioners " aroused the angry protests of the " Abhorrers." The loyalty of the country was rudely awakened and gathered steadily round the king. The rash attempt to deprive the Duke of York of his right, in favour of the illegitimate Monmouth, roused the most active enthusiasm for the royal house, and when Charles dismissed his Parliament the game was practically in his hands. After a last unsuccessful attempt at a compromise with a fresh Parliament at Oxford in March, he determined to rule without one, and so powerful was the royalist reaction in favour of indefeasible right, that, after he had avenged himself on his enemies, he found himself able to dispense with Parliament during the last four years of his reign.

SECTION 4.—*James* II (1685–88).

The strength of this royalist reaction enabled James II. to succeed to the throne unopposed in 1685, and gave him a Parliament the like of which for subservience had never been heard of before in England. And yet appearances were very deceptive. Most of the enthusiasm which had gathered round the throne at the end of the preceding reign had been purely personal to Charles. He was always a favourite with the people himself, even when his ministers were most thoroughly unpopular ; and his pleasure-loving, selfish character was too accurately gauged by his subjects for them to imagine that he could really be the dark and terrible being who figured so conspicuously in the angry denunciations of Shaftesbury and his followers. Moreover, the chief supporters of the Crown were the clergy : they were

ot likely to agree to any attacks on the established religion.
ames himself was regarded with distrust as a Papist; his morose,
loomy nature, made men ready to believe any ill of him without
nuch effort; and he was married to a Papist.   The grovelling
omage with which he was treated by the Tory party at his acces-
ion was very deceptive : they would be the first to oppose any
chemes for restoring Catholicism.   The cry that the Church was
1 danger would be quite enough to turn their skin-deep passive
bedience, into active hostility of an almost Whig type.

James probably intended to rule without a Parliament, for he
ully realized that in order to keep this body in a state of subervience, it was necessary to adopt a system of " management "
hich was very distasteful to his despotic principles.   No doubt
e summoned them, in the first instance, merely as an experiment to see what they would do; for all his actions point to a
ettled plan of personal government, in spite of his early promises
f constitutional rule.   He began by levying and using the
ustoms without waiting for a parliamentary grant; he openly
nformed his Parliament that there were a number of officers
erving in the militia who had not qualified according to the Test
Act, and in whose favour he had dispensed with the requirements
f the law; he announced his intention of granting toleration to
he Catholics, and on the smallest signs of opposition prorogued
Parliament at once.   Yet he could hardly complain of over
oldness on the part of that body.   It had accepted most of his
leeds with the meekness of a lamb.   It had granted him such a
ermanent revenue as almost to render him independent of it.
t had passed a new treason law for the better protection of his
erson.   On the suppression of Monmouth's rebellion, he an-
ounced that he intended to maintain a standing army; but far
rom offering any opposition, it proceeded to bring in a bill for
a grant of £700,000 to provide the pay—in fact, by dismiss-
ng it so suddenly James sacrificed this liberal grant entirely.
But he saw clearly that the experiment had failed; subservient
as the Commons were, there was *one* topic on which he could
ot hope for unquestioning obedience, and so he determined to
ule without it.

For nearly three years he was allowed to govern as he liked;

during which period he laboured with all his strength to make himself absolute and to restore the Roman Catholic religion. His measures, however, were attended by little success, for very few indeed were sincerely anxious for such a restoration. Nor did he even excite much alarm, for his reign was regarded but as an interlude—all would return to the good old state when Princess Mary came to the throne. The birth of the young Prince of Wales, however, changed the current of ideas. There seemed now considerable danger of the perpetuation of these obnoxious changes under a dynasty of Catholic kings. The danger called for prompt and decisive action, and the Revolution of 1688 swept down at one blow the frail fabric which James had striven so hard to rear.

CHAPTER IX.

THE REVOLUTION OF 1688-9.

THE difficulties created by the second flight of James and the loss of the great seal were met by prompt yet constitutional action. An assembly was summoned, consisting of the Lords and all those gentlemen who had sat in Parliament during the reign of Charles II. After discussing the state of the nation at length, they decided that William should issue writs in his own name for the election of a Convention Parliament on the model of that of 1660, and that to this body should be entrusted the task of settling the government of the country.

Parliament met on the 22nd of January, 1688/9. Henry Powle and Lord Halifax were elected to preside in the two Houses, and an address was at once drawn up describing the Prince of Orange as the glorious instrument in God's hands for the freedom of the kingdom from Popery and arbitrary power, and expressing their gratitude both for the promptitude with which he had assumed the charge of the administration and the care which he had devoted to the fulfilment of the trust. They further begged him to continue to retain it until they should have decided on some course of action.

January 28 was fixed on as the day for discussing the state of the nation, and on the suggestion of Sir Edward Seymour it was decided that the House should resolve itself into a grand committee in order that every member should be able to speak as often as appeared necessary—it was felt that on such an important subject the fullest expression of opinion was desirable, and yet there was a strong objection to breaking through the rule which prohibited members from speaking more than once during an ordinary debate.

The discussion was begun by Gilbert Dolben, a lawyer of some eminence, who laid down the view adopted by the Tories—that

James's voluntary withdrawal from the Crown involved a laying down of it which amounted to civil death, and that therefore it devolved by hereditary right on the next heir.   Dolben was followed by Sir Richard Temple, a thorough Whig.   He maintained that James had attempted to violate the existing constitution, and had forfeited his right to the throne in consequence.   "If King James has left the Government," he concluded forcibly, "and there be not a vacancy, what do we here?"   It was so obvious that he was advising James's deposition, that Sir Christopher Musgrave invited the lawyers to declare whether Parliament had the power of deposing a king.   Sir Robert Howard in reply denied the Divine right of kings, and advanced the new theory that the Government was grounded on a compact with the people, the breach of which was naturally followed by the dissolution of James's Government.   The lawyers, however, strongly opposed this view.   Sir Robert Sawyer denied that the Commons possessed any power over the king.   "How could there be?" he asked, "when only the propertied classes of the nation were represented in them?"   Heneage Finch followed with a warning of the danger of appealing to the state of nature—that were to destroy all rights of property.   How was it possible, he asked, for the people to have control over the Crown, or for James to forfeit it?   He might forfeit the personal exercise of the government, no doubt, but that was all.

On the other side the sanctity of hereditary right was as vigorously impeached.   Sir George Treby argued that the throne was actually vacant, and that there was no choice left but to supply the vacancy.   It mattered little that the Convention did not represent the whole of England ; they represented the most valuable portion and all who deserved a share in the government. The general opinion concurred with him.   Sir William Williams declared that the king's flight was conclusive in itself ; there was no need to depose him.   "We come," said Pulteney, "to supply what the king has taken from us."

Eventually a compromise was effected.   The resolution finally carried put aside entirely the questions of forfeiture and hereditary right, and confined itself to the statement "that King James II., having endeavoured to subvert the Constitution of the kingdom

y breaking the original contract between king and people, and
aving by the advice of Jesuits and other wicked persons violated
ie fundamental laws and withdrawn himself out of the kingdom,
as abdicated the government, and the throne is thereby vacant."
his was followed by a second resolution, added at the instance
f Colonel Birch :—" That it hath been found by experience in-
onsistent with the safety and welfare of this Protestant kingdom
) be governed by a popish prince."

These resolutions were sent up to the Lords. The second was
ccepted at once, but the first provoked a warm debate. There
as a long discussion at the outset whether there should be a
egency, and there was only a majority of two against it. The
riginal contract did not find many more supporters. The state-
ent with regard to James's misgovernment was accepted readily
nough, but the word " deserted " was substituted for " abdi-
ated," and the final—perhaps the most important—clause "that
ie throne was thereby vacant," was rejected altogether.

The prince now considered that the moment had come when
e ought to explain his own views decidedly in order to strengthen
he hands of the Whigs in the Upper House. He declared that
ie would be neither regent nor prince consort; he would be
ing, or would return to Holland. This statement produced
he desired impression. After a long conference with the Com-
nons, in which the questions were fully discussed, the Lords at
ast gave way, and resolved not to press their amendments to
he resolutions of the Commons. Nay, more, they proposed and
arried without a division that the Prince and Princess of Orange
)e declared King and Queen of England. This total surrender
)f the Tories was mainly due to a speech delivered by Lord
Halifax on February 6. He declared himself for the prince ex-
lusively ; he rejected at once the idea of declaring Mary Queen
vith William as Prince Consort, or of giving them equal powers.
He demanded the Crown in fact for William alone, and his
)pinion ultimately triumphed.

The Commons, however, proceeded more deliberately. They
were determined not to settle the government until they had
made some provision for the security of religion and the maintenance of the laws and liberties of England. A committee had

been nominated consisting of the leaders of all parties, to whom was entrusted the duty of drawing up a draft of a solemn declaration of the rights claimed by the people. The draft was laid before the Commons on February 2. It enumerated all the acts which had set James II. at variance with the nation, and declared them to be illegal. Suspensions, dispensations, and even the execution of the law by royal prerogative without consent of, Parliament, the establishment of a new Ecclesiastical Court, the disarming of Protestant subjects, the maintenance of a standing army in time of peace without consent of Parliament, were all branded as illegal. The questions which had arisen during the Stuart era with regard to the power of the prerogative and of the rights of Parliament were all decided in favour of the latter, before the accession of a new sovereign. Further the committee declared that the militia in its present condition was burdensome to the people ; the judges must be made more independent ; the procedure on trials for high treason must be altered in favour of the subject ; security must be provided for the privileges and frequent sessions of Parliament, and that it should not be dissolved till the business before it was transacted. They resolved in addition that royal pardons should not be pleadable with regard to parliamentary impeachments. They recommended further, for the protection of religion, that no member of the royal family should be allowed to marry a Catholic, and that the king and queen should be required to bind themselves in a specially prepared coronation oath to maintain the Protestant establishment.

Taken as they stood, the articles would have reduced the power of the monarch to a shadow; so William was obliged to interfere again with decision. "He had come to England," he said, "to restore its laws and liberties, but not to rob the Crown of its rights; he would not accept any limitation which was not prescribed by the existing laws ; and he would not allow the prerogative to be destroyed." He had the advantage in the contest, for Parliament could not do without him—that was universally felt—and so they again yielded, and consented to considerably revise the obnoxious articles. The clause with regard to the militia and the provisions for the independence of the judges rere omitted; the privileges of Parliament were secured, but here was no further question of a limitation of the prerogative f dissolution; and the most offensive innovation of all—the ;gulation with regard to the right of pardon—was expressly renounced. Still, in its final form the Declaration confirmed to 'arliament the principal rights which they had so long asserted gainst the royal power, and formed a strong foundation for arliamentary government in the future.

The Lower House next voted that the administration should est exclusively in the hands of William in spite of the nominal quality of Mary's title; nor would they even admit a proposal nat the queen should be regent by law during the king's absence n Holland. They were determined that the stability of the overnment should not be shaken by the diverse action of two ndependent wills. They added, moreover, under the advice f Serjeant Holt, that the throne should be continued to the urvivor of the two. In conclusion, they decided that the full 'lantagenet title, " King of England, France, and Ireland," hould be maintained.

On the 18th February, the Lords and Commons assembled n the Banqueting House. The Settlement and the Declaration f Rights were read, and the crown was solemnly offered to Villiam and Mary on the agreed conditions. The prince declared that he accepted the crown in his wife's name and his wn, and that he would protect the rights, privileges, and religion f the country.

The Declaration of Rights in its final form as presented to Villiam consists of three parts: a short summary of the illegal nd arbitrary acts of James II., which had induced the Parliament to declare the throne vacant; a solemn declaration of their llegality; and a number of clauses offering the crown to William nd Mary with the arranged limitations. It was turned into . statute some months later, October 25, 1689, by Act of Parliament, under the name of the Bill of Rights (1 W. and M.), with ome slight modifications and additions, in the shape of a new rticle incapacitating all Catholics, or persons married to Catholics, rom ascending the throne, and transferring the crown under nuch circumstances to the next heir, and a toning down of the

K

provision with regard to the dispensing power to a mere declaration of the illegality of its use "as it hath been exercised of late."

The contents of the Bill of Rights briefly summarised are as
follows :—

That whereas. James II., by the advice of evil persons,
endeavoured to subvert the laws and religion by—

   (1) dispensing and suspending the laws ;
   (2) violating the right of petitioning ;
   (3) erecting an Ecclesiastical Commission by prerogative ;
   (4) raising taxes without consent of Parliament;
   (5) keeping up a standing army ;
   (6) disarming Protestants and permitting Papists to be armed;
   (7) interfering with parliamentary elections ;
   (8) obtaining illegal judicial decisions ;
   (9) tampering with the formation of juries ;
  (10) demanding excessive bail ;
  (11) inflicting excessive fines;

which acts are illegal :

And whereas James II. has abdicated the government, and the
throne is thereby vacant, the Prince of Orange assembled the
Lords and Commons, who declared that—

I. (1) the suspending power is illegal ;
    (2) the dispensing power as it hath been exercised of late
       is illegal ;
    (3) the Ecclesiastical Commission and all similar courts
       are illegal ;
    (4) raising money without consent of Parliament is illegal;
    (5) petitioning is lawful;
    (6) keeping a standing army in time of peace without con-
       sent of Parliament is illegal ;
    (7) Protestants may carry lawful arms;
    (8) Parliamentary elections ought to be free ;
    (9) freedom of speech in Parliament should not be inter-
       fered with ;
   (10) excessive bail should not be required, nor excessive
        fines imposed;
   (11) jurors should be freeholders ;
   (12) Parliaments should be summoned frequently.

hese rights the Lords and Commons claimed and insisted on as
ieir undoubted rights and liberties.

II.   They resolved, also, that the Prince and Princess of
range be declared King and Queen ; the royal power to go
, the survivor ; the government to be exercised during the joint
:ign by the prince solely.   After their death the crown to go to
ieir joint issue ; then to the Princess Anne and her issue ; then
, the Prince's issue by any subsequent marriage.

III.   They declared that no Papist, or any person married to
Papist, shall be capable of inheriting or enjoying the crown ;
iat such persons shall be therefore regarded as civilly dead, and
ie realm be released from all duty of allegiance to them.

Thus was accomplished the great Revolution of 1688.   " It
nally decided," says Macaulay (Hist. ii. p. 396), " the great
uestion whether the popular element, which had ever since
ie age of Fitz Walter and De Montfort been found in the
:nglish polity, should be destroyed by the monarchical element,
r should be suffered to develop itself freely and to become
ominant.   The strife between the two principles had been long,
erce, and doubtful.   It had lasted through four reigns.   It had
roduced seditions, impeachments, rebellions, battles, sieges,
roscriptions, judicial massacres.   Sometimes liberty, sometimes
)yalty had seemed on the point of perishing.   During many
ears one half of the energy of England had. been employed in
ounteracting the other half.   The executive power and the
:gislative power had so effectually impeded each other, that
ie State had been of no account in Europe.   The King-at-Arms,
'ho proclaimed William and Mary before Whitehall Gate, did,
1 truth, announce that this great struggle was over ; that there
'as entire union between the throne and Parliament ; and that
:ngland, long dependent and degraded, was again a power of
ie first rank ; that the ancient laws by which prerogative was
ounded would thenceforth be held as sacred as the prerogative
:self ; that the executive administration would be conducted
1 conformity with the sense of the representatives of the nation ;
nd that no reform, which the two Houses should after mature-
leliberation propose, would be obstinately withstood by the
overeign.   The Declaration of Right, though it made nothing

law which had not been law before, contained the germ of every good law which has been passed during more than a century and a half, of every good law which may hereafter, in the course of ages, be found necessary to promote the public weal and to satisfy the demands of public opinion."

The greatest change, however, effected by the Revolution was undoubtedly the change of feeling in the nation. The fundamental maxims of the Constitution, both as they regard king and subject, may seem nearly the same; but the disposition with which they were received and interpreted was entirely different. The doctrine of passive obedience would have been obnoxious and absurd with regard to a dynasty created by Parliament, and the Revolution really swept away all the old royalist views with regard to the prerogative and the wickedness of resistance. William was in fact too obviously the creature of the Parliament, and the result of the worst form of resistance; the rights of the reigning family, and of the actual monarch, too unmistakably rested solely on the convention with the Parliament and people, for the spell of indefeasible right to maintain its hold any longer on the nation. "The great advantage, therefore," says Mr. Hallam, " of the Revolution, consists in that which was reckoned its reproach by many and its misfortune by more—that it broke the line of succession. No other remedy could have been found, according to the temper and prejudices of those times, against the unceasing conspiracy of power. But when the very tenure of power was conditional, when the Crown, as we may say, gave recognisances for its good behaviour, when any violent and concerted aggressions on public liberty would have ruined those who could only resist an inveterate faction by the arms which liberty put in their hands, the several parts of the Constitution were kept in cohesion by a tie far stronger than statutes, that of a common interest in its preservation."

CHAPTER X.

THE FORMATION OF THE CABINET SYSTEM.
(1689-1719.)

SECTION 1.— *William III* (1689-1702).

THE Convention was continued as a Parliament—its new life dating from February 18. To prevent accidents it ᴣgan by enacting that the previous proceedings were to be held good and valid as if the two Houses had been summoned in e usual way. A special clause required that members should ke the oath of allegiance to William and Mary before arch on pain of disqualification. A Toleration Act was passed lieving the Dissenters from penalties though not allowing em any political privileges. Shortly afterwards, two important onstitutional principles were initiated by the limitation of the upplies to the period of the ensuing year, and the passing of the rst Mutiny Act. The Commons did not interfere with the ereditary revenue, but they introduced an important change of roceeding with regard to the votes for the public expenditure. n exact estimate was brought forward of the expenses of the ear, and the sums required to cover them—this is known as the ppropriation Act: the sums were voted in detail, and strictly ppropriated to the purpose mentioned: commissioners were ppointed to take charge of the money raised from the country : uditors were also appointed to see that the public accounts were orrect. This principle, which became grafted permanently on he Constitution, ended at a blow the old financial struggles etween the Crown and the Parliament, and proved an efficient ecurity against the encroachments of the former and a powerful veapon in the hands of the latter for the coercion of a minister vho is out of harmony with them. The first Mutiny Act was necessary consequence of the clause in the Bill of Rights which leclared the illegality of the maintenance of a standing army without the consent of Parliament, and therefore rendered it impossible and illegal to enforce discipline without special parliamentary provision. The mutiny of a Scotch regiment in 1689 revealed the necessity for some such measure, and the Act passed in consequence to meet the temporary need became the regular mode by which Parliament consented annually to the maintenance of the army and the artificial restrictions of military law and discipline. The power of withholding this assent from a would-be despotic monarch or minister constitutes the second great check on arbitrary power which arose purely from parliamentary practice after the Revolution.

The true result of the Revolution had been to transfer the supreme authority from the Crown to the Parliament. The king entirely lost his old attribute of indefeasible right: he was now king by Act of Parliament. The natural consequence was that ministers became, in process of time, the ministers of the Parliament and answerable to that body not only for their own acts but for those of the sovereign as well. The personal liability of ministers tended to limit the freedom of action of the Crown so considerably that it gradually became the constitutional practice for the king to act solely in accordance with their advice. This control over ministers was practically secured by the limitation of the revenue and the Mutiny Act to the period of one year only; thus the annual summons of Parliament became necessary for their renewal. The transference of power to Parliament, however, was not really complete till the time of George I. During the reigns of William and Anne Parliament fully realized the nature of the change which was slowly springing up, but that was all. It had no idea as yet how to exercise the authority which had fallen to it, no practical means of coercing the king except by a total stoppage of the whole machinery of government. It was at once powerful, irresponsible, and discontented; and it vented its discontent in factious opposition, virulent abuse, and occasional outbreaks of wild animal rage, which showed that a popular assembly could be as unreasonable, as violent, and as tyrannical as even the most despotic of kings. Parliament, in fact, felt that it had really acquired a right to a voice not only in the internal government but also in the foreign policy of the ountry, and it found, with undisguised rage, that William would iear of no interference on the latter point even from his own ainisters, but was determined to manage the whole business of reaties and alliances with the most complete autocracy. The Commons could only criticise his policy severely, without being ble to influence it very much, and without any prospect of having o make good their criticisms or execute any counter-policy of heir own. The result was that they criticised it more severely han they would otherwise have done; that they quarrelled with Villiam savagely on all points on which his administration was ulnerable; that they adopted the unjustifiable tactics of forcing heir most obnoxious votes through the hostility of the Upper House by the odious process of "tacking" them to Bills of supply, and thus compelling the Lords to choose between refusing the king the means of carrying on the government or passing the whole bill with the objectionable clause attached o it. This unhappy discord turned the Act of Settlement, which should have been the firmest support to William's government, into a vote of censure on his whole conduct, and led to furious attacks on his ministers, by which their lives were openly threatened by the strong measure of impeachment on the most insufficient grounds, simply because it was impossible to effect their removal in any other way when they had ceased to be in harmony with the majority in the Lower House.

An important result, however, sprang from this war of faction which should almost surround it with a halo of sanctity in the eyes of posterity. The obstacles thrown by this opposition in the way of William's policy embarrassed his Government so much in the prosecution of the continental war, that at last he was obliged to give up entirely his original view of ruling by means of the best men of all parties. Acting on the advice of the elder Sunderland, he gradually formed an united Cabinet, consisting of men drawn from the same party, who relied on the consistent support of a majority of their own partisans in the Commons in order to pass the measures needful to carry on the government. This policy was complete by 1697, when the last remnants of the Tories were excluded from the Cabinet and their places filled by Whigs. The Cabinet which resulted was known as the "Whig Junto"—a Spanish expression which practically meant "an executive union." In 1698, however, a reaction took place in the country, a Tory majority was returned to Parliament, and ministers once more became out of harmony with the Commons, without, however, deeming it necessary to resign their offices, as would be the custom now. In consequence open war broke out at once between the executive and the legislative, with the result that for the time there was almost a deadlock in the public business of the country. In 1700, however, William was obliged to replace his Whig Ministry by a semi-Tory Ministry, with the curious result that the king and Lords were opposed to the ministers and Commons on nearly every point of policy, and that the latter had recourse in consequence to every form of violence in order to force the king to give his assent to their views.

This period of bitter warfare between the king and Commons was marked by many important measures, which were all more or less designed to curtail the power of the Crown. In 1694 a Triennial Bill was passed, limiting the duration of Parliament to three years, and requiring that not more than three years should intervene between the termination of one Parliament and the meeting of its successor. The last clause has not much importance as long as the practice of voting the revenue year by year is retained; but the first was intended to prevent any repetition of the Long Parliament of Charles II., to render it impossible for a king to retain a Parliament that is agreeable to his wishes, regardless of any changes of feeling in the country. The same year, 1694, was also remarkable for the commencement of a policy which was really of vital importance to the independent existence of Parliament. This was an attempt to limit the king's corrupt influence among members, acquired by the creation and subdivision of places for the purpose of bribery and actual purchase of votes in Parliament. This systematic corruption had begun under the Cabal, had been carried to excess by Danby, and was revived in despair by William III. as apparently the only means of securing anything in the shape of consistent support in the ̄ ̄wer House. In 1694 therefore, on the formation of a new

ard for managing the stamp duties, a clause was inserted in
e bill disqualifying its members from sitting in Parliament.
1699 this disqualification was extended to the commissioners
d some other officers of excise.

In 1700 the death of the young Duke of Gloucester, the only
rviving child of the Princess Anne, rendered it necessary for
irliament to make some further provisions for the succession to
e throne, and these were embodied in the Act of Settlement,
oo-1 (12 and 13 W. III. c. 2). " There was no question," says
allam, "that the Princess Sophia was the fittest object of the
tion's preference." For though many persons stood between
r and any direct hereditary right, they were all Catholics, and
e was at least nominally a Protestant. All prior claims of
heritance were therefore set aside and annulled; and the
incess Sophia was made the source of a new royal line. It
is determined to accompany this settlement by additional
curities for the liberty of the subject, consisting for the most part
those clauses which had been originally proposed in the rough
aft of the Declaration of Rights and subsequently dropped
it in deference to the wishes of the Prince of Orange. Taken
erefore independently, these clauses may be regarded for the
ost part as a supplement to the Bill of Rights, with some
w additional innovations. Practically, however, they were an
ireasonable vote of censure on William's conduct during the
ign, passed in a spirit of bitter hostility by a Tory Parliament.
hese articles were seven in number :—

1. The sovereign must be a member of the Church of England.
2. If the sovereign is a foreigner, the country shall not be
   obliged to go to war for the defence of his foreign
   dominions.
3. All matters connected with the government and laws of the
   kingdom shall be transacted by the advice of the Privy
   Council, who shall be responsible.
4. Aliens born shall be incapable of holding any office, of
   sitting in Parliament, or of receiving grants of lands in
   England.
5. Holders of places of profit or pensions under the Crown,
   shall be incapable of sitting in the House of Commons.

6. Judges shall hold their places during good behaviour, and shall be removable only on petition of both Houses of Parliament.

7. A pardon under the great seal cannot be pleaded as a defence to a parliamentary impeachment.

Of these, the seventh represents a determined attempt to sweep away the last shadow of protection which the sovereign could still afford to an obnoxious minister. The third is a reactionary measure, an attempt in short to suppress the growth of Cabinet government, which was identified with the Whig Junto in the minds of the Tories, and which was proportionately hateful to them. The fifth article is short-sighted and preposterous; it carried to excess the policy of excluding placeholders from Parliament. As it stood, the king's ministers would have been entirely shut out from Parliament, and the legislative and executive bodies completely separated, without either having the power of influencing the other except by roundabout or violent measures. The Cabinet, however, had fixed too firm a hold on the Constitution to be thus rooted up; and it was obviously unjust that the Privy Council, without a shadow of power, should be loaded with the whole responsibility of the government. On the other hand, the short-sighted policy of the fifth clause was too obvious not to become immediately apparent when once the equilibrium of the State was restored. In 1705 therefore, these two articles were repealed. The spirit which had prompted the Place Bills of 1694, 1699 was still shown, however, in a provision which was enacted in 1707 as a further amendment to the Act of Settlement :—

"That any member of the Commons accepting an office of the Crown (except a higher commission in the army), shall vacate his seat, and a new writ shall be issued."

"And that no person holding an office created since Oct. 25, 1705, shall be capable of election or re-election."

Perhaps, however, the peculiarly irritable temper of Parliament was most glaringly exhibited in a burst of arbitrary violence excited by what they deemed a breach of their privileges in the " Kentish Petition."

During the quarrels between the Whigs and the Tories in the session of 1701, an opinion gradually rose in the country that the 'ories were pressing the king far too harshly and ungenerously, nd moreover that their peace-policy was no longer timely in the ice of the open aggressions of France. The Whigs who shared ie warlike views of the king, thereby got an opportunity of iaking head against their rivals in the country, though they were ntirely overmatched by the large Tory majority in Parliament. 'his change in feeling was first shown in Kent. At the Kentish)uarter Sessions, held at Maidstone, William Colepepper, the hairman, drew up a petition to the House of Commons, which 'as signed by the deputy lieutenants, about twenty justices of the eace, and a large number of freeholders. It started on the rinciple that no nation could be happy if disunited; it begged ie House to lay aside all variance, and especially all "mistrust f his sacred Majesty, whose great acts were engraven on the earts of the nation"; and it implored them "to turn their royal ddresses into Bills of Supply." It was sent up to London by the ands of William Colepepper, and presented by him in company rith four other justices. The House of Commons was amazed nd indignant at one county setting itself in opposition to the nited wisdom of the country, and still more, by the indirect way a which it was first brought before their notice by one of their wn members.

Seymour and Howe, both violent Tories, united in denouncing he Petitioners: "double war-taxes should be imposed on them, heir goods seized, an example made of them, how many soever hey might be." In their fury they rivalled the most extravagant tterances of the most despotic advocate of absolute power. The Commons moreover voted that the petition was "scandalous, nsolent, and seditious," and ordered the five gentlemen who had resented it into the custody of the Serjeant-at-Arms. Public pinion, however, was strongly excited in their favour, and a etition drawn up by Defoe was presented for their release, rith such an enormous number of signatures attached to it that it vas called the "Legion Memorial." It ran "in the name of the gentlemen freeholders, and many thousands of the good people of England," and emphatically claimed that the House should submit ts conduct to some control on the part of the people: for the people, from whom the House of Commons drew its authority, had a right to withdraw it again. No attempt, however, was made to free the prisoners by *Habeas Corpus*—so far the authority of the House was recognised—but the open manifestations of public opinion created such an impression that the prisoners were released at the end of the session.

The arbitrary temper of the Commons was still more conclusively shown, early in the next reign, by what was called "the Aylesbury case," in which they put forward a claim to a privilege which, if successfully asserted, would have involved a real derogation of the rights of the subject.   The question was merely the outcome of the ill-feeling produced by disputes between the two Houses over the Occasional Conformity Act.   The returning officer of Ayles-bury had been guilty of tampering with the returns of that borough in favour of his own friends, and, among other instances of sharp practice, had rejected the votes of several burgesses entirely at the last election.   Matthew Ashby, one of the rejected voters, brought an action against William White, the returning officer, and obtained a triumphant verdict.   A good deal of legal shuffling of courts and jurisdictions followed.   On an application for arrest of judgment, three out of four judges of the Queen's Bench decided that all questions concerning votes and elections belonged solely to the jurisdiction of the House of Commons. The case then went to the House of Lords, on a writ of error, and the Lords reversed the decision of the Queen's Bench.   The Commons at once interfered, and declared that the determining of all suits connected with elections was a special privilege of their own, and that electors were not at liberty to bring actions on election questions in the Common Law courts.   The Lords, how-ever, stoutly maintained that the right of voting was annexed to the freehold, and could not be taken away; it followed naturally that, like any other right, it could be supported in an ordinary court of law.

The position taken up by the Lords, seems incontrovertible to the impartial observer, but the Commons were inspired with an overweening sense of their own importance, which rendered them very unwilling to brook the slightest contradiction.   The quarrel, however, lapsed for a time, owing to the more important ques-tions involved in the changes in the Ministry, produced by the ismissal of the extreme Tories, and in the battles which began fresh over the Occasional Conformity Bill. Meanwhile, however, ve other burgesses of Aylesbury, encouraged by the verdict of 1e Lords, brought actions against the constables of the borough. 'he Commons took advantage of this to renew the contest, and ommitted the Aylesbury men to Newgate for contempt. The risoners applied for their writs of *Habeas Corpus*, but the judges eld that the Commons were sole judges of their own privileges, nd that the writ could not be issued. The Commons seized the pportunity to declare the counsel, solicitors, and agents of the laintiffs guilty of breach of privilege, and sent them all to prison. 'he prisoners, with indomitable obstinacy, applied for a writ of rror to bring the refusal of the *Habeas Corpus* before the House f Lords. The Commons, now thoroughly enraged, resolved that o writ of error lay, and petitioned the Queen not to grant it. 'he Lords, who acted all through with great calmness and 1oderation, pointed out that writs of error are writs of right, nd cannot be refused; and this view was confirmed by ten out f the twelve judges. At last the Queen determined to put an nd to this tragi-comic squabble, and prorogued Parliament, March 4, 1705. The Aylesbury men and the other prisoners were in onsequence set at liberty, and at once took advantage of the erdict and support of the Lords to proceed with the actions, in hich they were uniformly successful. The question was thus ractically adjudged against the Commons, and they have never lised the claim to decide the rights of the electors again.

One useful lesson, however, the Commons drew from the irbulent strife of William's reign—they learnt the mode of cercising the power which had fallen to them. It was easy to ie that a united Cabinet, relying on a strong majority in Parlia1ent, and thereby holding the control both of the army and the :venue, could practically enforce their views on any king, owever resolute, by a united threat of resignation, when xperience proved that the attempt to carry on the government 1 opposition to the majority in the Commons could only result 1 a hopeless deadlock which brought the country dangerously ear a revolution. Such a lesson could not remain long unfruitful.

SECTION 2.—*Anne* (1702–14).

The transition period, however, between the old system of personal government and the new era of the Cabinet, did not end with the death of William III.   Queen Anne, under the inspiration of the Duke and Duchess of Marlborough, formed at the outset an almost purely Tory Ministry; but it very soon included men of all parties.   Nor was this unnatural; Marlborough himself was a Tory, but the Tories were very lukewarm supporters of the war, at most they maintained that it ought to be carried on chiefly at sea, and, therefore, there was really more sympathy between Marlborough and the Whigs than his own party.   Gradually, in fact, he was forced by the stern logic of facts to recognise the utter impracticability of his system of government, and to eject section after section of the Tories from the Ministry, until at last, in 1708, the Whigs completely triumphed over their enemies, and the reins of power fell in a very short time into the hands of a united Whig "Junto."   So little, however, were the principles of party government understood as yet, that when the General Election of 1710 sent up a Tory majority to the House of Commons, the "Junto" would have remained in office to battle on with their enemies in the same hopeless deadlock which had wrought such evil effects at the end of William's reign.   They had lost the favour of the queen, however, and she gladly hailed the opportunity to dismiss them and instal in their places a Cabinet drawn from the different sections of the Tories.   Discord at once arose between the two Houses.   The Whig majority in the Lords pitted themselves against the Tory majority in the Commons, and a great constitutional battle was fought over the peace of Utrecht, which the Lords were determined to reject. Harley, the Tory Prime Minister, was equally resolved to ride down all opposition, and force the bill through the Lords at all hazards.   At the opening of 1712, the Whig majority ·was therefore swamped entirely by the creation of twelve new peers at one stroke from the ranks of the Tories; the peace of Utrecht was carried triumphantly through the Lords, and this thorough break-up of the old system proclaimed that the transference of political power to the House of Commons was complete.   Much et remained to be accomplished. The House of Commons ıust be emancipated from its dependence on the king and Lords, ıust obtain the uncontrolled right of appointing its own minister ; ut from the day that Harley executed this astounding *coup d'état,* became a recognised principle that a minister cannot carry on the overnment by the support of the Lords alone in the face of a ostile majority in the House of Commons, nor can the Upper Iouse permanently oppose itself to any scheme of policy brought ırward by a minister who is supported by a majority in the ower House. These principles did not, it need scarcely be dded, work with the unvarying accuracy that would have been esirable ; but with occasional aberrations of action they may be ·garded as regularly incorporated in the constitutional ma-hinery.

One natural and inevitable result of the triumph of Cabinet overnment, was the total disuse of the royal veto on legislation. : had been frequently used by William III. He had vetoed a 'riennial Bill, a Place Bill, and other bills intended to limit his ower. It was last used by Anne in 1707, when she refused her ssent to a Scotch Militia Bill ; and as it has never been used nce, it may be regarded as obsolete through long disuse.

SECTION 3.—*Early Years of George I* (1714–20).

" To George I. and his supporters, it naturally seemed that the 'ories wished to deprive him of the crown, and that the Whigs ad secured it to him.[1] The result was, that he relied entirely n the Whig party, and his Cabinet was drawn solely from their ınks. This threw all power into their hands, and they ruled the ountry, almost without a break, down to the accession of George II. He can scarcely be blamed for trusting the men to whom e owed the crown, but had a certain amount of room been left ır the Tories, they would not have been driven over to Jacobitism, ıd so many of the troubles of the reign might have been averted. 'he immediate result was, that the power of the ministers was ıcreased greatly by union, and that they relied more on par-

[1] The greater part of this section is quoted verbatim from an earlier work, 'Our Hanoverian Kings."

liamentary support and good government than on royal favour. Moreover, George's interests being bound up mainly in those of Hanover, he interfered rarely in the management of affairs, and so from his accession the true period of ministerial government may be said to begin. At the same time this must not be pressed too closely. The king still possessed great powers, and at times, when thoroughly roused, he could make use of them. The dismissal of Townshend for conduct personally displeasing to George I., the dismissal of Walpole by George II., and his reappointment, equally without constitutional reason, give striking instances of the fact that ministers were not yet solely responsible to Parliament, but were still responsible to the monarch himself. The existence of the Pretender was really a good thing for the growth of the Constitution. It compelled the king, naturally despotic in temper, to trust his ministers more than he might otherwise have done, and thereby strengthened the Cabinet system.

The result of this purely Whig triumph was *apparently a total change in the principles of both parties.* The Tories had formerly been the ardent supporters of monarchy and legitimacy, of passive obedience, the English Church, and the Divine right of kings. The Whigs had formed the opposition. They had brought in the Exclusion Bill; they had led the Revolution; they had always been the strenuous advocates of the Nonconformists. Now however, the Whigs suddenly became the strong partisans of the monarchy, while the Tories developed into a virulent opposition, and in most cases drifted into Jacobitism and treason. The explanation, however, was extremely simple. Neither party had really changed their principles in the slightest. It was the circumstances that were entirely altered. The Tories still maintained their old doctrines; but their reverential feeling was reserved for the Stuarts alone—the "Elector" they regarded as a usurper. Their attachment to the Church was likewise unchanged, but in their eyes the latitudinarian Church of George I. was not the Church of England. To the Tories, therefore, resistance was the only means of remaining true to their old faith. The Whigs, on the other hand, now assumed the position of the supporters of monarchy. But it was the constitutional monarchy of the Re-

)lution, of the Bill of Rights, and the Act of Settlement, not the
:rsonal rule of the Stuarts. The government was in their own
inds, and was carried on on purely Whig principles; the
)edience they advocated was constitutional, legal, orderly.
[oreover, the Church had now taken a different position. Di-
:sted of High Toryism and purged of Jacobitism, it became
)nverted to Whig principles and Low Church views. The
issenters moreover, though still proscribed by law, were practically
:ed. The Whigs therefore, in supporting the monarchy and
hurch under the early Hanoverians, were really staunchly main-
ining their old principles. A purely Whig Cabinet was formed
ider Lord Townshend—an amiable, but imperious and over-
:aring character, and, supported by a large majority in Par-
iment, the Whig party undertook the government of the country.
was during this Ministry that the sittings of Parliament were
olonged to seven years by the Septennial Act, 1716 (1 Geo. I.
38), which may be regarded as setting the seal to the work of
.e Revolution by emancipating the Commons from their de-
:ndence on the Crown and Lords. " In the then corrupt state
' the representative system, a General Election merely meant a
:sh exercise of the influence of the Crown and Lords to secure
embers favourable to their views. These members, elected in
.is way, naturally became to a great extent mere mouthpieces of
.eir patrons, and were held well in hand by the prospect of
.other election in three years, when their re-election could only
: secured as the reward for unquestioning obedience. The
iuntry members contrived to preserve a certain amount of
dependence, but the representatives of the small corrupt
)roughs, which existed in such numbers, were merely the no-
inees of the great landowners or the Crown. The result had
:en to give an undue importance to the Lords. Their seats
:re quite safe, and so they were guided in their political conduct
)lely by their own personal views. While, as a rule, each peer
id a number of vassals in the Commons whom he could rely on
act as the exponents of his opinions, it naturally became of
e highest importance to ministers to stand well with the Lords,
id so for the first twenty years after the Revolution the govern-
ent was carried on mainly from that body. The Prime Minister

L

usually was a peer himself, or became one shortly after his accession to office. Nothing, in fact, is more surprising to our modern ideas in the annals of that time than the readiness with which Harley, St. John, Stanhope, and other great ministers, were moved up to the Lords without any adequate motive, and without considering the gap which their departure would make in the Lower House. The Septennial Act went a long way to remove these anomalies. The Commons, having now a longer lease of life, began to act independently of their patrons, and assuming a more senatorial character, were guided by their own opinions in legislation and action, instead of acting merely as the instruments of the Lords. The result was that the Commons gradually wrested the government of the country from the hands of the latter, and though this fact was not definitely realized till the next century, yet from this time the Prime Minister is usually content with a seat in the Commons. Walpole, Pelham, and the younger Pitt, governed from the Lower House. So did the elder Pitt during his first great Ministry ; nor was it till his powers were failing, and he was really unable any longer to cope with the turbulence of a popular assembly, that he retired to the Upper House, and thus prepared the way for the speedy downfall of his Government.

"The immediate result, however, of the Septennial Act was undoubtedly to render possible the gigantic systems of bribery by which Walpole, Newcastle, and, later, George III., held in hand their docile majorities in the Commons. The removal of the slight check exercised on members by their patrons and constituencies, at a time when public opinion had little or no influence on the proceedings of Parliament, naturally rendered their support more valuable to ministers, and themselves more open to corruption. It became customary, therefore, for ministers to strengthen the attachment of doubtful allies and reward the devotion of sturdy partisans by considerations, sometimes in hard cash, sometimes in the equally acceptable form of office or pension.

"The results of the Septennial Act were, in the long run, decidedly beneficial to the Constitution. The publicity of debates and the growth of parliamentary reporting since then has enabled

e constituencies to keep a watchful eye on their representatives,
ile the balance of public opinion is pretty faithfully indicated
the Press. Corruption has therefore died a natural death, and
minister has to rely mainly on the value of his measures to
tain the support of Parliament. . . . Shortly after the
ssing of the Septennial Act, a bill was carried which disqualified
sitting in the House of Commons any person holding a
nsion from the Crown during pleasure or for a number of
ars. This indicates that the dependent state of the Commons
d its causes were beginning to be realized."

The year 1716 practically ends the period of transition which
lowed the Revolution. The modern system of parliamentary
vernment is now complete in form and principle. From this
ae the country is really ruled by the leader of the majority in
e House of Commons, and a Cabinet whose members are
pointed mainly by him, though neither royal influence nor cor-
otion are as yet excluded from the machinery of government.
ie details of ministerial practice, of the relations between the
ime Minister, the king, the Cabinet, and the Parliament, as they
ist at the present, are the result of over a century of imper-
ptible and gradual development, altogether unassisted by any
sh efforts of legislation.

An attempt was made in 1719 to restore to the House of
rds the power which had slipped away from its control since
e Revolution. This was the Peerage Bill of 1719, introduced
the specious ground of obviating "any dangerous attempts on
e part of the Prince of Wales, when he ascended the throne, to
amp the Whig majority in the Lords in his exasperation against
father's ministers: for the memory of the creation of twelve
ers to force the Peace of Utrecht through a hostile House was
fresh in the memory of man. The king was easily induced to
nsent, and little opposition was expected from the Lords. The
l provided that the English peers should not be increased
yond six, except in the case of princes of the blood; that for
ery extinction there might be a fresh peerage created; that the
teen elective peers of Scotland should be transformed into
enty-five hereditary peers, whose numbers should be filled up,
occasion required, from the remainder. The bill was a purely

party measure, and would have had very dangerous consequence to the Constitution.   It would have shut the House of Lord against any reinforcements from the ranks below them, an thereby made them an exclusive body.   Moreover, as they wer entirely irresponsible, and had no fear of a General Electio dangling before their eyes, they would have been extremel difficult to influence, even when they were opposed to the gener: voice of the people.   The present century has given repeate instances in which the Lords have found themselves in direc opposition to public opinion, and have only yielded after cor siderable pressure has been applied.   It is easy to imagine tha they would not have yielded at all, had it been impossible t apply such pressure, and that in consequence many necessar and salutary measures must have been thrown out.   It migh well seem fraught with impending evil that such a body, irre sponsible, permanent, drawn from a particular class only, an that class one which has by no means shown itself the most eage for political progress, should be entrusted with a general veto o1 legislation.   Fortunately, however, public indignation was arouse(against it.   Steele employed all his wonderful talent in exposin; the secret evils of the measure.   Walpole, still in opposition both spoke and wrote against it, and on this occasion his hostilit to Stanhope was undoubtedly of great service to the countr) The landowners were indignant that the House of Lords shoul! be thus effectually closed against them, and that there should b no future possibility of obtaining that honour, 'save through th winding-sheet of a decrepit lord, or the grave of an extinct nobl family.'   Therefore, though the measure passed easily in tl Lords, it was thrown out in the Commons, after an animat debate, and the Constitution was saved."

CHAPTER XI.

THE SCOTCH PARLIAMENT AND THE UNION.

THE earliest meetings of the Scotch Parliament may be dated with considerable certainty at the beginning of the four-enth century, though a feudal council undoubtedly existed for ome time before, and traces of the appearance of representatives : the boroughs are, in the opinion of some authors, distinctly iscernible before that era. "It resembled an English one," says [r. Hallam, " in the mode of convocation, in the ranks that com-osed it, in the enacting powers of the king, and the necessary onsent of the three estates ; but differed in several important spects." The right of suffrage in the counties belonged to the nall tenants-in-capite solely, who originally came in person to ie council, along with the greater barons ; but, in accordance ith a law of James I. in 1427, ceased to attend in person, and ected " two or more wise men, chosen at the head court," i represent them instead. The law of James, however, only tablished this representative system as an alternative to personal rvice ; it was still open to any, who possessed the right, to attend . person. Nor was it till 1587 that the representation of the)unties was declared by law. There was no distinction, how-'er, between the estates of the realm, nor was there any division to two Houses, though apparently the latter innovation had ?en contemplated also by James I. : and so the different estates ways sat and voted promiscuously together.

The grand difference, however, between the representative 'stems of England and Scotland consisted in the existence of committee, known as the *Lords of the Articles*, who appear to ave been introduced by David II. in the year 1367, though the iodern form of their powers must be dated more accurately from ie year 1369, when their original constitution and rights were thoroughly revised. It was their business to prepare all matters for discussion in Parliament, and it gradually became the general rule, with some few exceptions, that nothing was laid before Parliament without their previous recommendation. From the reign of James IV., the Lords of the Articles are regularly named in the records of every Parliament.

"It is said," remarks Mr. Hallam, "that a Scots Parliament about the middle of the fifteenth century consisted of nearly one hundred and ninety persons. We do not find, however, that more than half this number usually attended. A list of those present in 1472 gives but fourteen bishops and abbots, twenty-two earls and barons, thirty-four lairds or lesser tenants-in-capite, and eight deputies of boroughs. The royal boroughs entitled to be represented in Parliament were about thirty; but it was a common usage to choose the deputies of other towns as their proxies "to save expense, which appears to have always been the great object of the Scotch Parliament."

There are no chronicles of constitutional struggles in Parliament, no records of limitations imposed on the royal power, no traces of the purchase of privileges by payments in hard cash as in England. The whole tendency of the existence of Parliament appears to have been to augment the royal power. The king, moreover, possessed such large domains that he was practically independent of subsidies granted in Parliament. There was naturally, therefore, hardly any opposition to the measures proposed by the Lords of the Articles. Discontented barons stayed away from Parliament altogether, to avoid the chance of being arrested or assassinated; and the Constitution would have worked extremely smoothly but for the fact that what was lost in constitutional opposition was amply made up in armed rebellion, private war, and open defiance of the law.

Parliament having only the right of accepting or rejecting in its entirety any measure proposed by the Lords of the Articles, without the power of amendment, the latter were practically able to force any obnoxious proposal through Parliament by "tacking" it on to some bill of vital importance. It was by the employment of dishonourable tactics such as these that Charles I. succeeded in procuring the acceptance of his new

'rayer-Book by the Scotch Parliament, in spite of their repug-
ance to the innovation. The Stuart kings, moreover, acquired
uch complete control over the election of the Lords of the
rticles that they degenerated into mere instruments of mis-
overnment. The very name became hateful, and one of the
rst acts of the Convention Parliament, which met in 1689 to
econsider the Constitution, was to abolish them.

In the year 1702, by leave of the English and Scotch
'arliaments, commissioners met to make arrangements for the
nion of both assemblies. Neither party, however, were very
much in earnest, and they eventually separated—1703—without
aving effected any settlement. The Scotch Parliament in the
ame year passed a number of limitations on the authority of
he Crown, and finally introduced a Bill of Security authorizing
'arliament to name a successor from among the Protestant
lescendants in the royal line, but asserting that whoever that
uccessor might be, he was not to be the same as the successor
o the Crown of England, unless proper security was given for
he freedom of religion and trade. The royal assent was refused
o this bill, but the refusal excited so much discontent that the
ill was allowed to become law in 1704. In 1705 the Duke of
Argyle was appointed High Commissioner to carry out the Union,
which was now regarded by all as necessary. There were three
oarties in Parliament—the Government, the Opposition, and
he Squadrone Volante, who trimmed between the two first,
endeavouring to hold the balance, though, as a rule, they inclined
o the Government. After many long debates and mixed con-
:essions and menaces on the part of the English Government,
n April, 1706, the commissioners, thirty-one on each side, met
o arrange the terms of the Union.

The debates and skirmishes between the two parties were long
und tedious, but on the whole it was recognised that the Union
was a necessity. So at last a number of terms were agreed on
und embodied in a regular treaty :—perhaps the most important
being the stipulation that the two Parliaments should be united
under one head. The Scots were to have forty-five members
in the House of Commons, amounting to about a twelfth of the
whole number of members. The numerous peerage of Scotland

were to be represented in the House of Lords by sixteen of their number, who were to be elected at each General Election by the whole mass of the Scotch peers, and were to sit during the session of Parliament. It was further arranged that no new Scotch peerages were to be created in the future.

This treaty was strongly disliked by a large section of the Parliament, and a grand scheme of opposition was concocted, which, however, failed at the last, owing to the pusillanimity of the leader. The Act of Union was in consequence carried successfully through the Scotch Parliament January 16, 1706/7, and shortly afterwards received the ratification of the English Parliament (6 Anne c. 7). The first Parliament of the United Kingdom of England and Scotland met in October, 1707.

The result of the provision prohibiting the creation of any fresh Scotch peerages is that the old ones are gradually becoming extinct, or practically absorbed in the English peerage by grants of English patents. It may be as well to mention that in most cases a Scotch peer who has obtained an English patent prefers to retain his old style and title on account of its superior antiquity, and, in most cases, superior rank. There are, therefore, many Scotch peers sitting in the House of Lords who are only known by their Scotch titles, but who owe their seats to some utterly ignored and unknown title of an English peerage. Thus the Duke of Argyle sits and votes as Baron Sundridge, and the Duke of Buccleuch as Earl of Doncaster. Neither Scotch peers nor their eldest sons are allowed to sit in the House of Commons. A Scotch peer, therefore, who cannot gain the suffrages of his fellows, or the esteem of the English Prime Minister, is practically debarred entirely from political life.

CHAPTER XII.

PARLIAMENTARY EXCESSES.

DURING the first half of the eighteenth century it almost seemed as though a tyranny of Parliament had succeeded the tyranny of the king. On various points this body showed itself as arbitrary and unreasonable as the most high-flying of the Stuarts. Party feeling ran so high that the majority would fain have crushed their opponents entirely without giving them any hearing at all. The privilege of freedom of speech was practically limited by the condition of saying nothing distasteful to the Court or Ministry.

The weapons by which the Commons attacked all obnoxious to their power were very diverse. Sometimes they were contented with the infliction of a reprimand, of greater or less severity, by the mouth of the Speaker. More frequently this was followed by fine and imprisonment. It was by no means rare for these penalties to be supplemented by the harsher measure of expulsion. There is little doubt, moreover, that in many cases a majority made an unfair use of their power to revenge themselves on a political enemy, or even to diminish the ranks of the minority. For greater delinquents or more important victims the ancient weapon of impeachment was revived, and with it political criminals were vigorously attacked, whether they were members of Parliament or not. The House, moreover, extended its sphere of action by constructive renderings of the term privilege, and dealt out severe punishment to all who incurred its wrath. Reprimands, fines and imprisonment, prosecutions by the Attorney-General, were decreed at will against offenders whom it would have been wiser to leave to the ordinary process and penalties of the common law. Among other encroachments the two Houses assumed a complete censorship of the press, and the annals of Parliament teem with records of the summons of unfortunate authors and printers to the bar of either House for the crime of issuing some obnoxious fly-sheet, there to be condemned to humbly acknowledge their error and sue for pardon on their knees, with the alternative in the event of disobedience of whatever penalty the clemency or fury of the House might mete out to them. The period between 1700 and 1715 is especially replete with numerous cases of singular violence on the part of the Commons, which gave rise to a suspicion that this outrageous licence was partly due to indignant irritability at their helplessness and incapacity to grasp the power which had really fallen to them, and to assume their true position as rulers of the kingdom ; partly, no doubt, due as well to their feeling of irresponsibility, which rendered them at once extraordinarily captious and utterly reckless of consequences. The gradual development of the Cabinet system and its establishment on a firmer basis put an end to the old scenes of confusion and injustice which had disgraced the early part of the century, and they were gradually succeeded by the steady, respectable stagnation and utter absence of incident, almost of business as well, which reduces the parliamentary history of the later years of George II. to the dead level of the dullest of annals.

In May, 1702, a complaint was made to the Lords concerning a pamphlet, called the *History of the Last Parliament*, which stated that there had existed in the House of Commons "a numerous, corrupt and licentious party," which had treated the Princess Anne with "constant neglect, slight, and disrespect." The printers were ordered to attend Parliament; but one Dr. Drake, having meanwhile owned himself to be the author, he was called in and interrogated by the Lord Keeper. Failing to offer a satisfactory defence, he was ordered to withdraw. The House proceeded rather intemperately to a resolution that the pamphlet contained several expressions that were "groundless, false, and scandalous," and directed the Attorney-General to prosecute Dr. Drake for writing the offending paragraph.

Shortly afterwards the attention of the Lords was directed to another book, which was called *Animadversions upon the two last 30th of January Sermons.* Several paragraphs were read out, and excited their ire so much that they denounced the pamphlet in question as "a malicious, villainous libel, containing very many reflections on King Charles I. of blessed memory, and tending to the subversion of the monarchy"; and ordered it to be burnt by the common hangman.

The Lords next fell foul of a sermon preached by one Dr. W. Binckes, Proctor of the Bishop of Lichfield, in the preceding year before the Lower House of Convocation. In this heated discourse Dr. Binckes had outraged all ordinary sense of decency, by drawing a blasphemous parallel between the sufferings of Christ and the execution of Charles I.; hinting, moreover, in very transparent language, that there was but slight difference in heinousness of offence between the Jews who rejected the Saviour and all who rebelled against an anointed king. This was a little too strong even for the Lords ; the highest of High Tories in that assembly could scarcely endorse such blasphemous adulation. They voted that the book contained "several expressions that give just scandal and offence to all Christian people," and that the Bishop of Lichfield should be directed to inflict suitable punishment on his feather-brained subordinate.

In the session of 1703 the Commons proceeded to attack more powerful game in the person of the Earl of Ranelagh, who had been Paymaster of the Forces since the reign of James II., and during the whole of that period had omitted to send in any accounts of the public money which was passing through his hands. He was now suddenly called upon to exhibit his accounts of twenty-one millions of money, the total sum received by him in fourteen years. His statements were considered highly unsatisfactory ; and there were, in truth, a few items in them which were certainly calculated to excite remark even in a more impartial house. The question, however, was much more one of party politics than public purity ; and the majority in the Commons would have been quite satisfied with a much less plausible excuse for revenging themselves on a political opponent. Lord Ranelagh was expelled, and obliged to resign his place. The latter part of the penalty appears to have been considered a decidedly severe punishment by contemporaries; the former not even as a disgrace—so thoroughly was the true character of Parliament and parliamentary expulsions understood at the time.

The greatest infringement, however, of the rights of the subject attempted by Parliament during this era, undoubtedly occurred in the case of *Ashby* v. *White*, before alluded to, though fortunately the pretensions of the Commons were destined to suffer defeat.

In the session of 1705 a bill was brought down from the Lords for "the better security of her Majesty's government and person, and of the succession to the crown of England in the Protestant line." Mr. Charles Cæsar thereupon stood up and spoke, but his words excited the ire of the House to such an extent that they were taken down, and he was ordered to withdraw. The obnoxious portions of his speech had referred to "a noble lord, without whose advice the queen does nothing, who in the late reign was known to keep a constant correspondence with the Court of St. Germains," and this disrespectful allusion to the Jacobite intrigues of her Majesty's counsellors was resolved to be highly dishonourable to her Majesty's person and Government. Mr. Cæsar expiated his offence, like many other victims of parliamentary wrath, in the Tower.

In 1706 the passions of queen, Lords and Commons, appear to have been equally excited to fever heat by a pamphlet called a *Memorial of the Church of England*, more especially as the authors could not be found, and the printer had absconded. The queen sent indignant messages to Parliament; Parliament was indefatigable in replies breathing the utmost sympathy and even greater indignation. Matters came to a climax when David Edwards, the printer, who had been left apparently in the lurch by his employers, gave himself up on the strength of a promise extended by Harley that he should be granted a full pardon if he disclosed the true authors. He accused three members of the House, stating, however, that the actual contract had been made with him by a woman in a mask, accompanied by another who wore no disguise, and that he had delivered the printed sheets to four porters. The persons he pointed out were arrested, but even then it was found impossible to collect enough evidence to establish the charge against the accused members, and it was suffered to drop accordingly.

In another case the summary method of the Commons can

be more easily justified. The House was informed in November, 1707, that Mr John Asgill, one of their number, had written a profane book, in which he asserted many things contrary to the Christian religion ; among others that a man might be translated from this world into eternal life without previously passing through death, "although," as the Commons declared with an odd affectation of theological learning, "the human nature of Christ Himself could not be so translated till He had passed through death." A committee was appointed to inquire whether Mr. Asgill were really the author, and as they reported in the affirmative, the House resolved that the pamphlet contained "many profane and blasphemous expressions, highly reflecting on the Christian religion," and ordered it to be burnt by the common hangman; further, that Mr. Asgill himself be expelled the House. Asgill appears to have been more knave than fool in this transaction : his opinions springing not from conviction but merely a desire to delude his readers. His previous private life had been tainted, moreover, with many backslidings, and no doubt the Commons were actuated as much by the desire to get rid of a thorough black sheep as to punish the author of this particular pamphlet.

In 1709 the ancient weapon of impeachment was once more dragged from its resting-place, to be used against the person of Dr. Henry Sacheverell, ostensibly to procure his condign punishment for preaching and printing a sermon "with a wicked, malicious, and seditious intention to undermine and subvert her Majesty's Government and the Protestant succession as by law established." The charge was as sensible and moderate as the Doctor's sermon was seditious ; but the issue really in question was not stated in the formal accusation, though it peeps out in the speeches of the managers at the trial. The impeachment was as much intended to solve the important problem whether the duty of the subject could ever be compatible with resistance, as to punish the intemperate and foolish oration of the Doctor; and from this point of view it acquires an importance entirely apart from the actual circumstances from which it sprang. Never, in fact, to decide a more important issue was the cumbrous machinery of parliamentary impeachment put in motion, though never perhaps at a more paltry provocation.

On December 13 a complaint was made to the Commons of two sermons, preached and published by Dr. Henry Sacheverell, and especially of certain paragraphs of a highly objectionable nature. The subject was fiercely debated ; and Sir Peter King, among others, inveighed very bitterly against the presumption and audacity of the Doctor. It was finally resolved that he should be summoned to the bar of the House to explain himself if he could. The explanation proving highly unsatisfactory and somewhat insolent in tone, it was resolved to impeach him in the name of the Commons of England, and Mr. Dolben was ordered to carry the impeachment up to the bar of the House of Lords. A committee was promptly appointed to draw up articles against the offender, who was given into the custody of the Serjeant-at-Arms. By way, moreover, of expressing their opinions still more definitely, a vote of thanks was passed to Mr. Hoadley, Rector of St. Peter's Poor, London, for the extremely able way in which he had at different times vindicated the Revolution, and the queen was humbly entreated to bestow a bishopric on him. Hoadley, however, was a Low Churchman, and the queen's memory was very short for Low Churchmen ; so though she promised to comply with their request at a suitable opportunity, it never came. It is worthy of notice that when the impeachment was brought up to the Lords, Lord Haversham delivered himself of a speech to the effect that men had been rewarded in other times with bishoprics for saying what Sacheverell was now to be impeached for—a true but somewhat misleading criticism, for the times had changed. Sacheverell in due course petitioned that he might be admitted to bail, but there were no precedents for such a concession, and it was denied.

On January 12, 1710, the ever-useful Mr. Dolben carried up to the Lords the articles of impeachment which had been drawn up with much labour by the committee of the Commons. They began very tediously with a grandiloquent account of the " glorious Revolution of 1688," and the numerous advantages which had flowed from that glorious event : proceeding

fterwards to charge Dr. Sacheverell with attempting to stir
p sedition, to subvert her Majesty's throne, and finally to
ring into hatred and contempt the aforesaid "glorious Revo-
ation"—all this at great length, and in the most tedious
ossible style. Briefly the first article accused the defendant
f asserting "that the necessary means used to bring about the
aid happy Revolution were odious and injustifiable. That his
ate Majesty, in his declaration, disclaimed the least imputation
f resistance ; and that to impute resistance to the said Revo-
ation is to cast black and odious colours upon his late Majesty."
The second article declared that the defendant had asserted
hat "the toleration allowed by law is unreasonable ;" that
ny who defended it was "a false son of the Church," in
vhich category he scurrilously reckoned Archbishop Grindal,
if pious memory, for the latter's refusal to persecute the
Puritans in the reign of Elizabeth. The third article was of
a general nature, and charged the defendant with maintaining
hat the Church was in danger. The fourth was more sweeping :
t averred that the defendant had endeavoured to instil dis-
rust of her Majesty and her ministers, both in Church and State.

In reply, Dr. Sacheverell, with great arrogance, greater
ediousness, and some slight disregard for truth, denied, explained, or evaded each article in turn. He acknowledged his
assertion that William III. had disclaimed resistance, and
cited in proof William's own declaration to that effect. He
maintained that toleration had never been granted by law,
and therefore the second charge was unfounded and self-con-
radictory ; his own assertion about Archbishop Grindal was,
moreover, historically true ; and it could scarcely be a high
crime and misdemeanour to criticise the conduct of a prelate
who had been dead 120 years. With regard to the third and
fourth articles, he declared that his words had been misun-
derstood, for when he had pronounced the Church to be in
great peril, he had referred simply to the "outrageous
blasphemies against God and all religion, natural as well as
revealed, which were vented publicly with impunity with a
freedom and frequency that was unheard of before in any
Christian kingdom."

The Doctor's answer was sent to the Commons, and referred to the committee. Mr. Dolben, in a few days, reported that "it was in many things foreign to the charge, unbecoming a person impeached, and plainly designed to reflect upon the honour of the House." An attempt was made by the Doctor's friends to induce the House to leave him to the ordinary course of justice, but this was naturally a failure in the electric state of the parliamentary atmosphere. A reply was therefore sent up to the Lords, and the 9th of March appointed for the commencement of the trial. Every artifice, however, was employed by Sacheverell's friends to produce delay, that they might have time to rouse the passions of the High Church mob against the Commons. Accordingly they raised the question whether the House should attend in a body or in a committee of the whole House, and after a tedious debate carried it by a very narrow majority for a committee.

Next they moved that the trial might be conducted publicly in Westminster Hall, so that the whole House might be present; and the success of this motion necessarily involved a further postponement in order that Westminster Hall might be properly fitted up for the occasion. The trial did not, in fact, begin till February 27, when the managers of the Commons opened the case. Their names were Sir John Holland (Comptroller of the Household), Mr. Secretary Boyle, Mr. Smith (Chancellor of the Exchequer), Sir James Montague (Attorney-General), Mr. Robert Eyre (Solicitor-General), Mr. Robert Walpole (Treasurer of the Navy), Sir Joseph Jekyll, Mr. Lechmere, Mr. Dolben, Sir Thomas Parker (afterwards Lord Macclesfield), Sir Peter King (Recorder of the City of London), Sir John Holles, Lord William Paulet, Lord Coningsby, Mr. Spencer Compton (afterwards Earl of Wilmington), Mr William Thompson, General Stanhope (afterwards Earl Stanhope), General Mordaunt, Mr. Spencer Cowper, and Sir David Dalrymple.

It fell to Sir James Montague, the Attorney-General, with the assistance of Mr. Lechmere, to state the grounds of the impeachment. Sacheverell's counsel having acknowledged the sermon and dedication in question, they were read out at length. The

ıree following days were occupied by the case for the prosecu-
on, which was entered into by all the managers in turn. Sir
oseph Jekyll, in a speech of wonderful clearness, maintained
ıe existence of an original compact between the king and his
eople which had been broken by the acts of James. The ex-
·emely difficult question of William's own proclamation denying
ny intention of rebellion was got over with some slight disingen-
ousness by the assertion that the prince had merely intended to
isclaim all imputation of "resistance that tended to conquest,"
ıut that "the principle of the utter illegality of resistance upon
ny pretence the Commons must always resist with the utmost
letestation; for if the resistance at the Revolution was illegal, the
Revolution must have been settled in usurpation, and the Act of
iettlement can have no greater force and authority than an Act
)assed under an usurper." It fell next to Mr. Walpole to defend
he impeachment itself—a far harder task than to vindicate the
:onstitutional principles on which it was based; nor can Walpole
)e said to have put his explanation very happily when he de-
:lared that the object of the Commons was to prevent any
' seditious, discontented, hot-headed, ungifted, unedifying
)reacher, who had no hopes of distinguishing himself in the world
)ut by a matchless indiscretion," from venturing in the future to
ıdvance "doctrines destructive of the peace and quiet of her
Majesty's Government and the Protestant succession," or to
' prepare the minds of the people for an alteration by alienating
:heir minds from the Government and the new settlement."
General Stanhope, following Mr. Walpole, denounced in the
:learest language the dangerous tendency of this doctrine of in-
lefeasible, unalienable hereditary right. He asserted that it was
ıothing less than rank Jacobitism thinly disguised. "The true
)bject of these doctrines," he declared, "is a prince on the other
iide of the water. If they are in the right, my lords, what are
the consequences? The queen is not a queen: your lordships
ıre not a House of Lords, for you are not duly summoned by
legal writ: we are no House of Commons for the same reason:
ıll the taxes which have been raised for this twenty years have
been arbitrary and illegal extortions: all the blood of so many
brave men who have died (as they thought) in the service of their

M

country, has been spilt in defence of an usurpation, and they were only so many rebels and traitors." With the bitterest scorn he went on to allude to " the pious son of the Church, the honest citizen, the loyal subject," who was after all but " the inconsiderable tool of a party, no ways worth the trouble we have given your lordships," but who must for all his insignificance be visited with condign punishment " to deter others from the like insolence for the future." The reports of the trial say that this scathing contempt disturbed even the brazen front of Sacheverell, who had listened with a smile of amusement to the invectives of the preceding speakers. He grew deadly pale, and endeavoured to stop the stream of fire by protesting, with considerable confusion in his manner, that such a tone of vehement contempt was a reflection on his order.

To Sir Peter King fell the task of vindicating the Toleration Act, which he maintained was notoriously the "toleration" which the Doctor had reviled, though by the use of a disingenuous evasion he had had the effrontery to deny it in his reply to the charge. King was succeeded by Mr. Cowper, the two speeches forming a most eloquent appeal against the inhuman bigotry which had eulogised the intolerant cruelties of a bygone age and commended them for revival in the present. Mr. Dolben then spoke in defence of the third article ; and his eloquent harangue was productive of a curious scene, for he concluded with a breach of etiquette which can only be excused on the plea of inadvertence in the heat of the moment. "We hope," he exclaimed, "the record of this proceeding will remain a lasting monument to deter a successor that may inherit her Majesty's crown, but not her virtues, from attempting to invade the laws or her people's rights ; and, if not, that it will be a noble precedent to excite our posterity to wrestle and tug for liberty as we have done. Hard is the fate of that people who are betrayed at home to a perpetual condition of bondage by such false brethren as are at your lordships' bar." Great confusion at once arose, for the bar was thronged by a dense mass of the defendant's friends, including a number of reverend divines and learned lawyers, and the sweeping plural of Dolben's concluding invective seemed levelled at them all. Lord Haversham, a friend of

.cheverell, at once moved that the House do adjourn to con-
ler the matter. The Lords thereupon withdrew according to
stom to their own House, and on their return demanded an
planation of Mr. Dolben. The latter in some confusion ex-
ained that he had merely referred to the prisoner at the bar in
s inadvertent use of the plural.

The most eloquent oration was undoubtedly that of Sir Thomas
ırker, who opened the proof of the fourth article. He ex-
nined the sermon point by point, and proved that it was a
neral condemnation of the Government. He asserted that the
:ople of England had the highest possible respect and rever-
ıce for the clergy as long as they remained in their proper
ace, but that their proper place was not in the forefront of the
ıemy's ranks, nor was it in accordance with their temporal or
ıiritual duties to declaim against the Government, "crying to
ms and blowing a trumpet in Sion to engage his country in
ditions and tumults, . . . and this with Scripture in his
outh." Perhaps, however, the most brilliant piece of oratorical
:ill was the prompt dexterity with which the Speaker seized on
ıe of Sacheverell's illustrations from Scripture, and caused it to
:coil with crushing effect on the latter's own head. "There is a
:markable story in the Bible about a mistake of danger, which
ıe Doctor makes a handle for his purpose. Accordingly he
ıys, 'When Elisha, the great prophet of God, was surrounded
ith a host of enemies that sought for his life, his blind servant
ebeld not the peril his master was in until his eyes were opened
y a miracle, and he found himself in the midst of horses and
hariots of fire.' This story thus told is extremely happy for him,
ır hence the people are to understand him to be the inspired
rophet, and the Queen, Lords and Commons blind at least,
ıough not his servants. But the story in Holy Writ is directly
ontrary, and it was only the blind servant fancied they were in
anger when really they were not."

The speeches of the managers, which formed by far the most
ırilliant display of eloquence that the parliamentary annals as
et had furnished, were concluded on the third day, and then
ıacheverell's counsel began the defence. They were in every
ray worthy opponents of the great champions who had preceded

them. Sir Simon Harcourt and Mr. Phipps were two of the most distinguished lawyers of the day. Mr. Dodd, Mr. Dee, and Dr. Henchman, though inferior to their leaders in reputation, were experienced and skilful lieutenants. Sir Simon Harcourt took his stand on the paradox that resistance in itself was utterly unlawful, though it might become lawful under extraordinary circumstances ; but the Revolution itself was not a breach of the general rule, because at the Revolution there was no resistance. This singular statement he justified on the ground that the supreme power in the kingdom is the legislative power, and that the Revolution had been effected by the legislative power—a most unworthy quibble, which neither expressed Sacheverell's real meaning when he originally wrote the sermon, nor accorded with the historical facts. He appealed to a host of citations from the homilies, articles, and even sermons of existing and deceased divines, to prove that it was and always had been a tenet of the English Church that resistance to the supreme power was unlawful. "Is it criminal," he exclaimed with irresistible logic, after reading the homily against rebellion, "for a man to preach that doctrine which it is his duty to read?" He quoted the Militia Act, which declared "that neither both nor either of the Houses of Parliament can or lawfully may raise or levy any war, offensive or defensive, against his Majesty, his heirs or lawful successors"—there was no exception. Could it then be, he asked, a high crime or misdemeanour "to assert in general terms" that which was so specifically stated by Act of Parliament?

Mr. Phipps, an extreme High Tory, flew eagerly at the unsubstantial original compact which had been advanced by Sir Joseph Jekyll, and showed its emptiness. He asked when it was made; why it was not included in Magna Carta, when all the liberties of the subject then existing were claimed; whether it was before the great statute of treason of 25 Edward III. He declared that he had never heard of it before; it had never been pleaded to any indictment of treason; and until it had been declared to exist by an Act of the Legislature, all resistance except in the case of the Revolution was still treason within 25 Edward III. Mr. Dee, with daring sophistry, insisted that the Prince of Orange,

eing a sovereign Prince himself, " owed no allegiance to any
ne, so could not be said to resist in the sense resistance bears
ι the Doctor's sermon, which is the resistance by subjects to the
ιpreme power."

An amusing scene occurred during the reading of the quota-
ons which were brought forward to vouch for the orthodoxy of
ιe sermon. Among them was a passage from a sermon preached
y the Archbishop of York before the House of Lords in 1700.
So long as the text of St. Paul stands in our Bibles, the doctrines
f non-resistance and passive obedience must be of obligation to
ll Christians." Walpole, as it happened, was acquainted with the
ιrmon and the context. Much to the discomfiture of his oppo-
ents, he directed the clerk of Parliament to continue reading,
ith the following result:—" Care must be taken that this general
octrine be not misapplied: as the laws of the land are the
ιeasures of our active obedience, so are also the same laws the
ιeasures of our submission; and as we are not bound to obey
ut where the laws and Constitution require our obedience, so
either are we bound to submit but as the laws and Constitution
o require our submission." This proof of the disingenuousness
f the advocate for the defence was received with an outburst of
heers and laughter, and for the moment the sympathy of the
ssembly ran wholly with the managers of the Commons.

After his counsel had exhausted their ingenuity in the effort
ɔ prove that the words of the sermon bore really a meaning
ery dissimilar to that directly apparent, Sacheverell himself, by
ιave of the Lords, addressed his judges in his own defence.
Ie justified his intentions towards the queen and the Govern-
ιent, and maintained that he could be charged with no dis-
ιspect towards the Revolution and the Protestant succession.
Ie declared with considerable shrewdness that the best proof
f his innocence was the enormous time which it had taken to
rove his guilt. Then, adopting an altogether different tone, he
enounced all resistance under any pretence whatever, throwing
side the flimsy veil of pretence with which his counsel had
ought to conceal his real opinions, and standing forward openly
s the champion and martyr of his faith. He asserted that non-
esistance was a vital doctrine of his Church, and he appealed to

God and the holy angels to witness that he was inspired by no
wicked, seditious, or malicious intentions.

His defence was a triumph of art, and its effect on the assembly
was prodigious. All the efforts of the managers in reply were
utterly inadequate to destroy the impression which Sacheverell
had so successfully created. To the ladies, the clergymen, the
Tory peers, the High Church mob who were burning and pillag-
ing outside, he appeared like some pure and high-souled martyr
of the olden days, who suffered the cruellest persecutions for his
faith's sake ; and though his condemnation by the Whig majority
in the Lords was a foregone conclusion, such a party triumph
was likely to be more ruinous to the victors than the victim.

On March 16 the debate on the articles of impeachment began
in the Lords. The House was crowded ; even the queen herself
was present *incognita.* The discussion was opened by the Earl of
Wharton, who moved that the Commons had made good the first
article against Dr. Sacheverell. He was opposed by Lord Haversham, who, in a lengthy speech, re-stated all the arguments for
the defence. In the course of the debate, the Bishop of Oxford
defended the doctrine of the lawfulness of resistance ; the Bishop
of Bath and Wells supported passive obedience. The Duke of
Argyle expressed the very sensible opinion that the clergy should
not meddle in politics at all ; the Earl of Anglesey, on the contrary, maintained the opposite view, that political sermons were
useful, and at times even necessary. The Duke of Leeds (Danby)
declared that at the dawn of the Revolution itself, he, for one, had
never contemplated settling the crown on the Prince of Orange :
but that, owing to the fortunate and fortuitous abdication of the
king, there was no question of resistance in that settlement ; a
quibble which, though perhaps pardonable in a counsel retained
for the defence, was utterly unworthy of a great peer sitting in
judgment in the House of Lords. Burnet, Bishop of Salisbury,
justified the Revolution, on the broad historical ground of tyranny,
in a long and eloquent speech. The motion was eventually
carried by a majority of nineteen ; and, after a long debate of a
not very dissimilar character upon each, it was finally affirmed in
turn that the Commons had made good the remaining articles.
On March 20 the question was put to each lord severally, begin-

ing at the junior baron first; sixty-nine peers voted "guilty," and fty-two "not guilty." The defendant was therefore pronounced 'guilty"; and the Usher of the Black Rod having brought him ɔ the bar, caused him to kneel down, in which humiliating ɔosition, according to the old-established custom of Parliament, he received his sentence—"that he should be suspended or three years," a sentence that was a mere mockery. The House, moreover, ordered that the decrees of the University ɔf Oxford, passed in 1683, by which the Divine right of kings ınd the duty of passive obedience were asserted in a very high train, should be burnt by the common hangman, together with Sacheverell's sermon. And with this paltry result the celebrated rial ended.

The Tory majority which was returned in the General Election ɔf 1710 did not hesitate to equally misuse, for party interests, the veapons of Parliament which had been forged for very different ɔurposes. In the following year (1711) Mr. Ridge, a wealthy ɔrewer, was expelled the House for "notorious embezzlement" vith regard to a Government contract; and though he proved his ɔomplete innocence, and was allowed to retain the right of supplyıng beer to the navy, he was not restored to his seat. In 1712, moreover, Colonel Cardonell, the Secretary to the Duke of Marlborough, was expelled for receiving a petty gratuity from the army contractors, which had been invariably given unquestioned to the secretary of the commanding officer. In these two cases there seems little doubt that the political opinions of the offender were really the crime which excited the wrath of Parliament; and in dealing with Cardonell, they were most probably additionally stimulated by the hope that his expulsion would indirectly touch his principal, the then obnoxious Duke of Marlborough.

This expeditious mode of diminishing the ranks of their enemies appears to have been a very favourite one with the Government in this Parliament; and it was very effectively employed in January, 1711/12, to get rid of a far more formidable adversary than the two preceding victims. This was Robert Walpole himself, who was expelled for "notorious corruption in receiving the sum of five hundred guineas, and taking a note of five hundred more, on account of two contracts made by him when Secretary at War, pursuant to a power granted by the Lord Treasurer." Whether Walpole was guilty or not will always remain a mystery which is hardly worth inquiring into ; it is quite certain, however, that he was very obnoxious to the Tories. He was committed to the Tower and expelled the House. He was then re-elected immediately for King's Lynn ; but on petition of the rival candidate, Samuel Taylor, was declared by the House to be incapable of being elected to serve again in Parliament. Nor does there seem much reason for doubting, from the wording of the motion, that he was held to be incapacitated by reason of his expulsion.

The censorship of the press, assumed by previous Parliaments, was reasserted in 1712 by the passing of numerous resolutions denouncing its licentiousness in violent terms ; and more effectively in individual cases, by the old harsh measures of censure, expulsion, or imprisonment. In June, the preface to four sermons published by the Bishop of St. Asaph was ordered to be burnt, on the ground that it was " malicious and factious, highly reflecting upon the administration of public affairs, and tending to create discord and sedition among her Majesty's subjects." In March, 1714, the Lords similarly attacked a pamphlet written by Dr. Swift, and entitled *The Public Spirit of the Whigs,* which vilified the Union, the whole Scotch nation in general, and the Duke of Argyle in particular. The publisher and one Mr. John Barber, who was suspected of complicity, were ordered into custody ; their guilt, however, being disproved, they were released in three days. A reward of £300 was forthwith offered for the discovery of the author ; but Dr. Swift contrived to maintain his incognito more successfully than other like offenders, a circumstance which he attributed to the goodwill of the Ministry.

Few, perhaps, were more obnoxious to the Ministry than Mr. Richard Steele, and it was very quickly resolved to attack him by means of his political writings. Mr. Hungerford therefore, on March 11, moved that the House should give effect to a clause in the Queen's Speech relating to the suppression of seditious libels, and referred especially to several scandalous papers lately published under the name of Richard Steele. The next day Mr. Harley (Oxford's brother) specially moved the consideration of certain

pamphlets, all said to be written by Mr. Steele, and among others
of *The Crisis*, which reflected with bitter sarcasm on the conduct
of her Majesty's ministers, hinting in no enigmatical language
that they were hostile to the Hanoverian succession. Mr. Foley
and Sir William Wyndham continued the attack, and several
obnoxious passages from the pamphlet were read to the House.
It may be as well to state that there was nothing really scurrilous
or licentious in them, nor did they in any way exceed the bounds
of legitimate controversy. On the day appointed for examination
Steele appeared at the bar, standing between Stanhope and Walpole, the two great leaders of the Whigs. After his acknowledg-
ment of the authorship, the attack was opened by Mr. Foley, who
spoke with so little oratorical effect or argumentative power, that it
was quite clear that he regarded the trial as a mere form with a foregone conclusion. Steele defended himself with great ability, and
such unusual moderation, that the story got round very quickly
that his speech was composed for him by the cautious Walpole
or fear of any indiscretions. The defence was continued by
Walpole, Stanhope, Lord Finch, and Lord Hinchingbroke. Lord
Finch especially distinguished himself on this occasion ; and by a
strange chance his own nervousness contributed indirectly to his
success. Anxious to speak for Steele, he was at the same time
such a victim to self-consciousness, that after trying in vain to
address the House, he sat down in confusion, murmuring with the
utmost vexation, " It is strange I can't speak for this man, though
I could readily fight for him." His words were whispered from
mouth to mouth with electric rapidity, and the fickle assembly,
filled with sudden admiration and sympathy, cried out as one
man, " Hear him ! hear him !" Inspired with new courage, Lord
Finch sprang to his feet again, and addressed the House with
such force and fire, that he provoked a torrent of acclamations
from the very men who were determined beforehand to condemn
the friend for whom he pleaded so earnestly and generously. For
it is almost superfluous to add that, in spite of the eloquence of
the defence, party feeling carried the day ; and on the motion of
Mr. Foley the offender was expelled by 245 votes against 152.

If any further proof were needed of the despotic temperament
of this Parliament, it is to be found in a vote of February 12, 1712,

which condemned Viscount Townshend—for his share in negotiat-
ing a treaty with the United Provinces for securing the succession
to the Crown of Great Britain, and for settling a barrier for the
Dutch against France, which treaty was destructive of the trade
and interests of Great Britain—as a traitor to his country.   With
far greater justice was a well-merited punishment inflicted in the
last session, on one Mr. Quin, who had the audacity and credulity
to offer the Speaker a sum of money to procure the passing of a
certain Act of Parliament in which he was interested.   Mr. Quin,
who was an Irish gentleman, as the report mentions with unconscious irony, was promptly committed to prison ; but on alleging
inadvertence and ignorance, and humbly entreating pardon, he
was discharged with a severe reprimand.

The Whig Parliament of 1715 showed to the full as eager a
desire to employ the weapons of Parliament for vengeance on
their opponents as their Tory predecessors had done.   They
impeached the Duke of Ormond, the Earls of Oxford and
Strafford, and Viscount Bolingbroke for high treason, on grounds
that were at the most but a scanty foundation for a prosecution
for misdemeanour.   They further ordered Mr. Matthew Prior,
who had filled a post under the late Government, into custody
for examination.   Perhaps, however, their vindictive and tyrannical spirit was most glaringly shown in their attack on Sir
William Wyndham, who incurred their anger by referring to a
royal proclamation conceived in rather dictatorial terms, as " not
only unprecedented and unwarrantable, but even of dangerous
consequence to the being of Parliament."   He refused to justify
his charge, stoutly maintaining that every member had a right to
speak his thoughts.   The Ministry, however, thought otherwise
—certainly no Tory member had this right, would have been
their view.   It was moved that he had been "guilty of a great
indignity to his Majesty, and a breach of the privileges of this
House."   It was eventually decided that he should be reprimanded
by the Speaker, and reprimanded he accordingly was.   The
Speaker—it was Sir Spencer Compton—told him of the greatness
of his offence, and the lenity of the Commons in inflicting so
slight a punishment; but the impenitent Wyndham, while submitting to the commands of the House, expressed himself in the

highest degree insensible of the lenity of the House in inflicting a punishment at all where none was deserved.

The expulsions of Mr. Pryse for refusing to take the oath of allegiance, and of Mr. Forster for open and armed rebellion, were justifiable and natural ; as also were the impeachments of the Earl of Derwentwater, Lord Wintoun, and three other Jacobite lords, for their share in the rebellion of 1715, nor could there be much doubt as to the nature of the sentence, for they were all taken *in flagrante delicto.* A curious and pathetic scene occurred during the trial of Lord Wintoun, who either was half-witted or professed to be so in the hope of escaping the penalty of his crimes. He endeavoured to insist that his counsel should cross-examine the witnesses, alleging his own ignorance of law. He was informed that he might ask any questions he liked of the witnesses, but that his counsel might not examine for him—such was the unjust and barbarous law of the time. He persisted, however, in repeating his request again, every time the question was put to him whether he would cross-examine on the evidence. At last, in sullen despair, he exclaimed in reply to the Lord High Steward, who presided, "Since your lordship will not allow my counsel, I don't know nothing."

Ormond and Bolingbroke had fled at once on hearing of their danger : they were attainted of high treason. Oxford, however, stood his trial and was acquitted, owing to a quarrel between the Lords and Commons on a question of privilege, in consequence of which the latter declined to prosecute before the former. With the exception of the attempted impeachment of Walpole in 1742, this cumbrous weapon of Parliament was not dragged from its rusty sheath by party malice again during the whole course of the century. Lord Chancellor Macclesfield's impeachment, 1724/5, was grounded on a charge of corruption in the exercise of his powers of judicial patronage, and was as well deserved as beneficial to the State. The Jacobite lords impeached in 1745-6 were put on their trial for open and avowed high treason in levying war on the king or adhering to the king's enemies. The impeachment of Warren Hastings, 1785-8-95, rested on entirely different grounds to those of the earlier cases, and was mainly due to the influence and enthusiasm of Burke, and a certain feeling that

India was governed far worse than it need be. The impeachment of Lord Melville, 1805, was founded on frauds committed
in the public service, mainly owing to Melville's negligence, and
formed a salutary warning to public servants for the future.

The right of expulsion was used lavishly and violently during
the crisis of the South Sea Bubble (1720–1). Messrs. Vernon,
Sawbridge, Aislabie, Eyles, Sir Robert Chaplin, and Sir Theodore
Jansen were all expelled for their connection with the Company:
Aislabie for speculating, contrary to his oath of office, in the
funds of the Company, and for showing a suspicious-looking
deficit in his balance-sheet, which he was unable to account for
satisfactorily.   These expulsions, however, like those of Mr. Elde
(1725) for corrupt practices, Mr. Ward (1727) on his conviction
for forgery, and Sir Robert Sutton (1730) for his connection with
a swindling company, were not only justifiable but necessary,
and show a recurrence to a more moderate frame of mind on
the part of Parliament, and a return to the earlier principles on
which the right was founded as a means of clearing the House
of unworthy members.   Since that time the strong measure of
parliamentary discipline has been exclusively reserved for its
appropriate purpose, and the necessity for its use was fortunately
rare.

Before, however, finally retiring into the more decorous
demeanour which became them so much more than the barbaric
fury of the past, the House indulged once more in an outbreak
of wild, mad rage, which too aptly recalled the violent days of
Anne.   In 1751 Mr. Alexander Murray, brother of Lord Elibank,
was accused before the House of Commons of inciting to
violence at the Westminster election, was condemned to be committed to Newgate, and according to custom was ordered to
receive his sentence on his knees.   But to the general horror
and indignation, Mr. Murray refused to kneel.   The Speaker
commanded, Mr. Pelham protested, equally in vain—Mr. Murray
would not kneel down at the bar.   The House began to surge
and roar in its fury like a great sea, until at last, the tempest
rising to its height, they carried an angry resolution, " That Mr.
Murray, having in a most insolent and audacious manner at the
bar absolutely refused to be upon his knees, is guilty of a high

ınd most dangerous contempt of the authority and privilege of his House." He was then committed to Newgate, without pen, nk, or paper, and without permission to see his friends, and here he remained till the prorogation. Nor was it till near he end of the century (1772) that the odious necessity for kneel-ng at the bar of the House was repealed. Culprits brought)efore the Lords on the impeachment of the Commons were ;till, however, required to kneel.

CHAPTER XIII.

PARLIAMENT UNDER THE WHIG OLIGARCHY.

THE policy which had been begun by the Cabal, continued by Danby, and unwillingly revived by William III., which different Parliaments had attempted in vain to restrict or destroy by means of pension-bills, became during Sir Robert Walpole's long ministry of twenty years (1721–42), a regularly organized system for the maintenance of the Government, for the continuance of a consistent policy, and for a safeguard against the disputes and violence which had hampered the Cabinets and disgraced the Parliaments of William III. Unusual facilities were undoubtedly supplied for this by the already corrupt state of the representation, and the influence of the Septennial Act. From the very earliest days Parliament had never been really representative of any but the leading men in town and country, whose influence in most matters was entirely undisputed by their inferiors. The Tudors had set the example of creating small borough constituencies in which the influence of the Crown was paramount. It was also part of the royal electioneering tactics to appoint on occasion High Stewards to particular boroughs, whose business it was to secure the return of satisfactory candidates, and in most cases these officers were naturally chosen from the ranks of the neighbouring landowners. The Crown, in consequence, possessed the full control of a large parliamentary interest by way of direct nomination to a number of seats, besides considerable Powers of influencing elections in other constituencies by the votes of the revenue officers and other Government officials. In much the same way, though on a less ambitious scales there was a large amount of parliamentary interest in private hands. It was easy for a great landowner to create new votes, and to buy up old ones, either by direct payments in hard cash or by making it a practice to distribute

s custom, to grant privileges and favours, and to use a hundred
d one modes of benefiting his inferiors directly or indirectly,
lely with a view to insuring docility among them in electioneer-
g matters. In many cases, moreover, the original borough had
:cayed entirely, and in the words of Lord John Russell on the
eform Bill, nothing was left but a park, a mound, or a wall to
ark the site of the old constituency which originally really
eeted the two members, who now were simply nominated by the
rd of the manor. By the beginning of the eighteenth century,
, fact, most of the small boroughs were practically in the nomi-
ation of some one man, or at most were divided among
ie adherents of two, who invariably avoided contests by an
nicable arrangement to halve the representation. In the larger
oroughs, such as Liverpool, there were still some vestiges of a
opular election, as there was also in the most of the counties.
y this phrase, however, was simply meant that there was a
:ver-ending contest between the influences of rival families or
val coalitions of families, and that the side which bribed with
ie greatest freedom and recklessness would probably be able
) reinforce the votes of their own dependants by a sufficient
umber of comparatively independent votes to carry the day
gainst the enemy.

The nomination boroughs being practically the property of
ieir owners, were treated as property with a cynical disregard for
ught but the advantage of the proprietor. In many cases the
:ats were directly sold to the highest bidder, and this custom
ecame very prevalent as a wealthy middle class arose in the
ountry, which possessed plenty of money but no land. The rich
ierchants and Indian nabobs who desired to get into Parliament,
urchased land, votes, and seats, in order to acquire parliamentary
iterest. In many cases they bought the whole interest in a
iorough from its needy proprietor; oftener they contented them-
elves with purchasing the right of nominating to the seat at the
iext vacancy—it being always easy to create a vacancy in a
ery short time by arrangement with the sitting member. Rich
nen, moreover, possessed advantages in contesting big county or
iorough constituencies, which in many cases would outweigh the
greatest talents, if the latter were unsupported by more solid

considerations. It is not, therefore, strange that a change gradually came over the face of Parliament, and that political power ceased to be the monopoly of the landed interest. It was with the view of excluding from Parliament the rich landless merchants, who were generally Whigs, that the Tory Government of Harley brought in a Property Qualification Law, 1712, which enacted that the candidates for the boroughs should possess freehold or copyhold land to the annual value of £300, a similar qualification of double the value being required for candidates for the counties. A law like this, however, was too obviously opposed to the general pecuniary interest and too easily evaded, to be of much practical value. Its utter inefficiency and speedy defeasance may be best estimated by the fact that it never even occurred to the Whigs in the hour of their triumph to move for its repeal.

The value of nomination boroughs was considerably increased by the Septennial Act, owing to the longer lease of life conferred on the member; for the vendor of the seat might now fairly charge at least double as much as under the old system of triennial Parliaments. The seat itself was worth more to the buyer, and he was not likely to grumble at the increased price. " Popular elections," moreover, naturally became more expensive; bribery had to be conducted on a more extensive scale than ever. Altogether there was a general rise in prices, owing to the increased value of the commodity. From this sprang two very important consequences: first that the members, when once elected for their term of seven years, felt themselves comparatively independent of their constituents, vendors, or patrons; secondly, that in most cases they regarded the money spent in procuring their admission to Parliament as so much capital sunk which should bear a rich harvest in the shape of lucrative places, comfortable pensions, or round agreeable bags of hard cash. They borrowed a lesson from the electors, and they expected to be treated as they had treated the latter—only, as the commodity which they had to sell was so much more valuable, the tariff of prices was naturally arranged on a far higher scale.

Therefore, when Walpole sought for his majority, he found it ready to his hand. Voting-power might be had in great abun-

nce, provided he could give the *quid pro quo*. In order to
rnish the necessary rewards to the faithful, he misused his
ntrol of the enormous Crown patronage; places and pensions
are multiplied and subdivided to an extraordinary extent, to
ovide for the numerous hungry claimants; peerages, ribbons,
d stars were bestowed in equal profusion on those who pre-
rred them; in many cases there appears to be no doubt that
ms of money were directly handed over to individuals on the
casion of some particular division of great importance. The
ormous secret service fund was employed, in a great measure,
r the purchase of votes. Half the members at least were in
gular receipt of public money in some form or other. It is
ositively asserted in Wraxall's memoirs that the supporters of
e Government usually expected handsome gratuities at the end
each session, and were not disappointed. Lord Hervey
cidentally mentions that he heard from both Sir Robert Wal-
le and the queen that a particular ministerial triumph only
st £900—£500 to one man and £400 to another; nor does
express any surprise at the disclosure, except perhaps at
e marvellous cheapness of the bargain. There is a popular
gend that Walpole's code of morality and his opinion of man-
ind were so extremely low, that he was wont to declare derisively
at "all men have their price," and that in reply to the question
hat Sir John Barnard's price might be, he answered, "Popu-
rity." The phrase that he really used was, "All *these* men have
eir price," and was spoken with contemptuous reference to
veral members of the Opposition, who, though conspicuous for
eir uncompromising invective against the corruption by which
e government was carried on, might, it was well known, have
sily been converted into supporters of that very government by
e offer of what they so ardently panted for—office. Still, though
e motto attributed to him be delusive, there appears to be no
asonable doubt that Walpole did practise corruption on a very
rge scale as an engine of government, but it is impossible to
iew his conduct in this respect with any great disapprobation.
n the first place, it was absolutely necessary to insure the easy
orking of the parliamentary machine at a time when old lines
f politics were half effaced, the old parties were breaking up,

N

and the new parties, with new principles and organizations, had
not yet arisen in their place to form the foundation of a systematic party government.   Secondly, this mode of rewarding
the devotion of sturdy partisans, and strengthening the more
doubtful allegiance of waverers, was not regarded as unusual or
discreditable, and did not involve so much moral degradation as
a similar course of conduct would at the present day.   Men,
manners, and morality were different.   The members did not
see any harm in receiving a gratuity in return for a vote.   They
would have voted, in most cases, just the same had they been
left solely to their own impulse.   There are few instances of the
direct purchase of votes from the Opposition, for Walpole knew
better than to place a premium on resistance.   Thirdly, the
system, such as it was, was not his own invention; he received
it from the hands of his predecessors, an instrument still bright
with recent use.   He was not guilty of the fabrication of it, but
in his hands it was swiftly ground so sharp and keen that it would
be a dangerous engine in the hands of a dangerous man.

Perhaps the most singular form of interference with the
representative system is to be found in the manipulation of
election petitions for party purposes.   This jurisdiction had been
originally claimed by the House of Commons to insure their
elections against royal interference.   In the eighteenth century,
however, it became a mere weapon of party.   Members voted
on election petitions strictly with an eye to the politics of the
candidates.   Men were unseated, and the seats given to their
rivals; minorities were declared larger in numbers than majorities; elections were annulled, and fresh writs issued; all because
the man who had been returned at the head of the poll happened
to be odious to the Government.   The right of expulsion no
doubt played a very prominent part in party tactics during the
reign of Anne; but under her successors the more gentle and
plausible mode of elimination by means of an election petition
was usually preferred.   In many cases petitions were presented
against returns solely in order that the choice of the constituency
might be overruled by Parliament.   It is this fact that explains
why Walpole resigned on the side-issue, as it seems, of the
Chippenham Election Petition.   If there was any question, he

doubt argued, on which his party ought to have held by him,
rtainly it was with regard to a question affecting the increase
decrease of their own numbers. If, therefore, he was unable
carry such an important party measure as an election petition,
was clear that the hour of his resignation was nigh at hand.

By the help of a majority constituted in this peculiar way, the
vernment was carried on during the whole period between the
ars 1721–1760; the means were the same all through, though
e ministers might be different. The Government, in fact, was
ally in the hands of a *clique* of wealthy aristocratic families
aded by the two Pelhams—the Duke of Newcastle and his
other Henry Pelham. This governing class is known in the
cords as "the Great Whig Houses"; their power rested on
eir vast parliamentary connection, built up entirely by an un-
rupulous use of local, political, and family influence. As a
le, they committed the actual management of the government
some leading statesman, usually a commoner, who ruled the
untry by means of their docile majority in the House of
ommons. In most cases the great personality of the minister
tirely eclipsed the silent, insignificant potentates to whom he
ved his power; and it is the measures, the triumphs, the govern-
ent of the strong men of action with which historians are wont
fill their pages, without reflecting that no Ministry, however
rong in talent and oratory, could have stood for a day without
e support of the Duke of Newcastle. Newcastle really governed
e country, in a sense, during the whole of this period. It was
e defection of Newcastle which broke the strong majority of
alpole; the hostility of Newcastle which caused the overthrow
Carteret; the support of Newcastle which preferred Henry
elham to the Premiership. Even Pitt himself, the chosen
ght of the people and the bitterest opponent of Newcastle's
fluence, found himself totally unable to form a stable govern-
ent without the assistance of the man he had reviled and
espised, and was at last compelled, in spite of his previous
otestations, to submit to the unutterable humiliation of taking
fice under him again in 1757. The period, therefore, between
720–1760 is that of the supremacy of the Whig Oligarchy,
hich continued without a break or check down to the death of

George II. The two most remarkable results which flowed from this continuity of governing influence were the almost unbroken continuity of foreign policy and the very slight mutations which occurred in the *personnel* of the less prominent members of the Administration.

At the same time there are very distinct characteristics to mark the different Ministries of this period from one another. Walpole's policy may be described as based on exclusion, and his motto was, "discipline before all things." To his dependants he was absolutely tyrannical. The slightest insubordination was punished by instant dismissal. He appears to have been inspired with a haunting fear of a rival, and to have determined to suppress all possibility of sedition by the most stringent precautions. John, Lord Carteret, one of the most remarkable men of the century, very early excited his jealousy by his talents for foreign policy; he was compelled to surrender his office of Secretary of State, and retire to the seclusion of Dublin Castle, where he remained till 1730, when he threw up his post and joined the ranks of the Opposition. William Pulteney, a skilled and powerful debater, a statesman of consummate talents and power, who had stood by Walpole in office and opposition for years, was rewarded on the accession of the latter to the Premiership by the offer of the insignificant post of Cofferer of the Household—an offer which was an insult in itself, but which he strangely enough accepted. He soon wearied of political nullity, broke out into open opposition, voted against the Government, and was promptly dismissed. In 1730, Walpole quarrelled with his brother-in-law, Lord Townshend, and compelled him to resign his post, thereby certainly depriving himself of the ablest man left in his Cabinet. In 1733, in pursuit of the same idea, he revenged himself on all those place-holders who had voted against the Government on the Excise Bill; Lords Chesterfield, Clinton, Burlington, Marchmont, Montrose, and Stair, were dismissed. Most iniquitous of all, Lord Cobham and the Duke of Bolton were compelled to surrender their commissions in the army, and this stretch of arbitrary power was very shortly followed by a similar measure dealt out to William Pitt on the like ground of his opposition in Parliament. It is easy, therefore, to perceive that as he relied neither on the

rilliance of his supporters nor the solidity of his measures, cor-
uption was to Walpole a necessity, and that his Government,
rithout deriving much lustre from the presence of Newcastle,
wed its existence to the latter's support.   One of the most
mportant results of this system was to break up the old lines
f party politics entirely.   The original Opposition consisted of
ories and Jacobites.   It was reinforced gradually by the ad-
ition of the Whigs dismissed or rejected by Walpole.   The
ond of union between them was the ex-minister Bolingbroke,
rho, restored in property but not in peerage, and finding his
iffers of service rejected contemptuously by Walpole, was eager
or revenge.   It became Bolingbroke's business to build out of
hese dissimilar elements an united opposition to Walpole.   He
naintained that the old meaning of parties was now obsolete,
hat it was not now a question of Whigs and Tories, but solely
rhether Walpole should be allowed any longer to exclude every
capable man from the Government: and he was undoubtedly
ight.   There *was* no difference between the Government Whigs
ind the Opposition Whigs, except the possession of office ; there
ras no connection between the Opposition Whigs and the Tories,
ixcept the desire for office.   And so the latter united easily in
opposition to all the Government measures.   In the ranks of the
Government itself there was no great principle, good or bad,
which marked them off from their opponents.   Party politics, in
act, had become a war between the Walpoleans and the anti-
Walpoleans, and the personal nature of the struggle only rendered
it more bitter and vindictive.   The total inversion of principle
which resulted was shown most decisively by the great debate on
the repeal of the Septennial Act, moved by Mr. Bromley in 1734.
The repeal was supported by the united ranks of the Opposition,
among others by many men who had voted for the Act itself
when it was originally introduced in 1716.   A grand passage of
arms occurred on this occasion between Sir William Wyndham,
one of the principal Tory chiefs, and the Prime Minister himself.
The former began by a fierce declamation against the evils of
corruption, and thence diverged into a well sustained attack on
Walpole, whom he accused of maintaining himself in office by its
means.   He drew a picture of an abandoned man of no family

or real influence, but who, armed with money extracted from
the people, might maintain himself and his creatures in office for
seven whole years by means of corruption, even though under
his rule the interest of the nation was neglected, her honour and
credit lost, her trade insulted, her merchants plundered, and her
sailors murdered. Walpole, in reply, ignored the invective of
Wyndham, and openly denounced the unseen figure of Bolingbroke, whose influence had prompted the attack. He drew a
picture in turn of an "anti-minister," a mock-patriot actuated only
by self-interest, who, being rejected by the side he had offered
himself to, was stimulated to the bitterest hostility by envy and
revenge. He depicted Bolingbroke—for no one could doubt
who was meant—as the dishonoured leader of desperate, disappointed men, striving to gain credit with the enemies of his
country by divulging any State secrets which he could pick up,
and endeavouring to spread alarm over the country by raising
false cries, solely in order that he himself might be restored to
office : though, save for the grace of the Government (in removing
the attainder) he would be an exile flying from the terrors of the
law. Supposing then that it were possible that such a monster
could really exist, he concluded with scathing sarcasm, "can
there be imagined a greater disgrace to human nature than such
a wretch as this ? "

The attack of the Opposition failed entirely, and the Septennial
Act remained uninjured ; but the result of these repeated dis-
appointments was that they became desperate and furious. They
were ready to embrace any tactics, to support any measure which
afforded a hope of expelling their enemy from office, and actuated
by this motive they urged on the Spanish war with the utmost
vigour, almost with ferocity. Had his party clung to him, Walpole might have defied them to the last ; but " the Thanes were
flying from him," Newcastle and the Whig houses withdrew
their support, and though he adopted the policy of his enemies
and declared war, yet his majority dwindled into a minority, and
he was forced at last unwillingly to resign. Nothing can show
more conclusively how little the true principles of Cabinet
government were understood as yet, than his determined attempt
to retain office, even after the total reversal of his policy, and the

esperate efforts of his enemies to attack him on his resignation
y an impeachment. All the influence of the Court was exercised
) protect him, however, and the impeachment dropped at last
)r want of evidence. Never more would that antiquated weapon
e raised against a minister of the Crown by the impulse of
olitical animosity.

The new Ministry included a large number of Walpole's
)llowers ; it was founded on the support of the Pelhams. It
ras almost inevitable, therefore, that though Carteret's influence
ras at first supreme, he should be unable to stand long against
he intrigues of Newcastle. His dismissal enabled the Pelhams
) inaugurate the policy which caused the Ministry to be known
s the Broad Bottom. They included in it all the principal
:aders of the Opposition, and in consequence practically stifled
ll hostility by the soothing influence of office. They reckoned,
n fact, that by bribing the leaders they would silence their
)llowers as well. This policy was extremely distasteful to
;eorge II., who saw himself forced thereby to receive men
rhom he hated personally, and it induced him to intrigue against
iis ministers. The latter, with some astuteness, forced his hand
)y resigning in a body during the crisis of the Jacobite invasion ;
.nd finding himself unable to form a new Ministry, he was
)bliged to submit to their terms. The result was that the Broad
3ottom in time included all the great men of the age, Whigs,
["]ories, even so-called Jacobites. By 1751 all opposition in Parlia-
nent ceased entirely, and the debates attained a condition of utter
:tagnation. This singular coalition, however, only made it more
)bvious that the true meaning of party names and cries had
:ntirely disappeared, and that the country was passing through
i transition period, when there were really no parties at all, in
he proper sense of the word, though personal and sectional
:nmities abounded.

This became more decidedly apparent after the death of Henry
Pelham, in 1754. He had been able to hold the discordant
:lements in suspension ; but the accession of Newcastle to
)ower set them at once in active motion again. There was still
no real constitutional opposition in the proper sense of the
word ; but fierce disputes continually arose in Parliament be-

tween different members of the Government; in many cases his subordinates openly reviled and ridiculed their nominal leader without his venturing to dismiss them. This singular period lasted down to 1756, when Newcastle found himself at last obliged to dismiss Pitt and the principal mutineers. His own utter incapacity, which had been conspicuous from the first, now became so glaringly apparent in the crisis of war, that he was obliged to resign. It soon became evident, however, that though he could not rule himself, he could prevent any one else from doing so successfully At last, therefore, as it was impossible for any Government to exist without him, a coalition between the discordant elements was arranged. The influence of Newcastle and the talents of Pitt were united in one Cabinet, and under them were gradually included all the principal men in the kingdom, till at last all opposition ceased in Parliament, and the whole nation joined in one grand effort to carry on the Seven Years' war.

This period is rendered glorious by the eloquence of William Pitt, subsequently the great Earl of Chatham. Unfortunately, however, owing to the stringent rules against parliamentary reporting, there are but very few fragments of his speeches existing, and they have been extracted rather from magazines and collections of speeches than regular reports. His first speech was delivered on the occasion of the Prince of Wales' marriage. A contemporary historian describes it as superior even to the models of ancient eloquence. In the opinion of Tindal, it was more ornamented than the speeches of Demosthenes, and less diffuse than those of Cicero. It certainly contained such a lofty eulogium of that worthless princeling as to almost seem like a satire in the eyes of posterity. In 1739 he delivered in committee a speech on the question of the "right of search," which has justly become celebrated. He declared that England's trade was her last entrenchment; she must defend it to the last. There was a plan on foot to sacrifice it to the exigencies of ministers, and such a plan would be odious throughout the kingdom. He declared that the exercise of the right of search on the part of Spain was "an usurpation, an inhuman tyranny"; the claim of Spain to seize and confiscate ships which approached

er colonies was "an injury, an indignity, an intolerable griev-
nce"; even if the claims were good, "the excesses admitted
o have been done in consequence of this pretended right were
tterly unjustifiable." He asserted that the treaty for compen-
ation was fraudulent, illusory, and wholly to the benefit of Spain,
nd the honour of England was sacrificed solely that ministers
night remain in office. " The complaints of your despairing mer-
hants and the voice of England have condemned it. Be the guilt
f it upon the head of the adviser. God forbid that this committee
hould share the guilt by approving it." On the 5th of February,
740, he opposed a bill which would have conferred extraordinary
owers on the press-gangs and justices for the seizing of seamen.
Ie denounced it as cruel and arbitrary, and declared that it was
npossible that it could be executed. Horace Walpole attacked
im in reply, and taunted him on the score of his youth and
heatrical gestures. Pitt's answer was a model of caustic satire.
'The atrocious crime of being a young man," he replied, "which
he hon. gentleman has with such spirit and decency charged
pon me, I shall neither attempt to palliate nor deny, but content
nyself with wishing that I may be one of those whose follies
nay cease with their youth, and not of that number who are
gnorant in spite of experience. Whether youth can be imputed
o any man as a reproach, I will not assume the province of
letermining; but surely age may become justly contemptible,
f the opportunities which it brings have passed away without
nprovement, and vice appears to prevail when the passions
ave subsided. The wretch who after having seen the conse-
juences of a thousand errors, still continues to blunder, and
rhose age has only added obstinacy to stupidity, is surely the
ibject of either abhorrence or contempt, and deserves not that
lis gray head should secure him from insults." He then dealt
rith the charge of theatrical behaviour in the same tone of
cathing satire. Mr. Winnington, however, called him to order
rith such bitterness of language that Pitt retorted on him. " If
his be to preserve order, there is no danger of indecency from the
nost licentious tongue; for what calumny can be more atrocious,
or what reproach more severe, than that of speaking without any
egard to truth? Order may sometimes be broken by passion or

inadvertence, but will hardly be re-established by a monitor like this, who cannot govern his own passion while he is restraining the impetuosity of others."

On December 10, 1742, in a speech against the Hanoverian subsidies, he made use of the celebrated expression : "It is now too apparent that this powerful, this great, this mighty nation is considered only as the province to a despicable electorate." Numerous utterances of his exist, containing fierce criticisms of the Hanoverian policy of Carteret, and especially the sums paid to Hanoverian troops, and the indignities suffered by the English soldiers at the hands of the allies.   His opposition, however, ceased on the dismissal of Carteret, and in 1746, when the objections and hatred of George II. had been finally crushed, he was admitted into the Cabinet as Paymaster of the Forces. Naturally, the period which followed was one of considerable parliamentary inactivity, nor was it till 1754 that he again became really a prominent figure on the parliamentary stage.   To the period, however, which followed the death of Pelham belong many of his best known speeches.   It was at this time that he obtained such a command of the House that he was able to take liberties with it such as no other statesman could or has ever dared to do.   It is recorded that on one occasion he rose after Mr. Delaval had convulsed the House by a witty speech in his own defence on a charge of bribery, and addressed them in a tone of the severest censure.   He was astonished, he declared, when he heard what had been the occasion of their mirth.   Was the dignity of the House of Commons on so sure foundations that they might venture themselves to shake it? and so on.   It was observed that by his two first periods he brought the House to a silence and attention that, in the words of Mr. Fox, you might have heard a pin drop.   On the 26th of February, 1755, he attacked Murray, the Attorney-General, with regard to a bill for subjecting the tenure of office of Scotch sheriffs to the king's pleasure, and delivered one of his best worded and most spirited declamations in favour of liberty.   He declared he had more dread of arbitrary power dressing itself in the long robe than even of military power.   He added that he would not recur for precedents to the diabolic divans of the second Charles and

ames—he did not date his principles of the liberty of this
ountry from the Revolution : they are eternal rights; and when
God said, *Let justice be justice,* He made it independent.

By common consent, however, it is agreed that the greatest of
is speeches during this period was the magnificent burst of
ratory in which he attacked the degrading coalition of Fox and
Newcastle (November 13, 1755). It was delivered during one
f the longest debates then on record, and was at once the cause
f his own dismissal from office, and in the end the fall of the
Newcastle Ministry. "But," he cried, referring to the King's
peech, "there are some parts of this address which do not seem
o come from the same quarter with the rest. I cannot unravel
his mystery—yes (suddenly raising his hand to his forehead),
, too, am inspired. Now it strikes me ! I remember at Lyons
o have been carried to see the conflux of the Rhone and the
Saone ; the one a gentle, feeble, languid stream, and though
anguid, of no depth ; the other a boisterous and impetuous
orrent. But they must meet at last, and long may they continue
mited, to the comfort of each other, and to the glory, honour,
nd security of the nation." The whole speech, on the authority
of Lord Orford, lasted above an hour and a half, and was kept
ip with inimitable spirit, though it did not begin till past one in
he morning, after an attention and fatigue of ten hours. And
et for theatrical effect even this fine effort must yield to the
peech with which he opened the session of 1758 on November 17.
n the course of it he did not attempt to disguise the expense
nd difficulties under which the country laboured—heaps of
millions, he said, must be raised ; we could not make the same
var as the French, or as our ancestors did, for the same money.
He described in the most glowing terms the advantages which
had sprung from the war, the victories, the glories which had
followed our arms in both hemispheres. Then suddenly, assuming
n attitude of stern but dignified defiance, he shouted till the
ild rafters of the House of Commons rang again and again,
' Is there an *Austrian* among you ? Let him stand forward and
eveal himself. I invite him now to speak out instead of dis-
persing anonymous pamphlets among the people." Such a *coup
le théatre* would now only excite contempt and laughter, but

then the effect was magical. There was a dead pause, a silence during which a man might have heard the beating of his own heart ;—but no one dared rise and attack him ; Mr. Dodington, against whom the challenge was really levelled, was too utterly cowed by the impressive dignity of the speaker and the silence of the House to attempt a reply.

The principal orators of this period, besides Pitt, were Henry Fox and Murray. Granville (Carteret) still continued to be a well-known figure in Parliament, but his influence was entirely gone. Chesterfield, who had given great promise both of oratorical and diplomatic power, was afflicted by an attack of incurable deafness, which practically withdrew him from active political life. Bath (Pulteney) had too entirely lost all power and popularity to be of any importance. George Grenville's time had not yet come. The great figures of the past—Walpole (Orford), Shippen, Cotton, Barnard, Wyndham, all in turn were quitting the troubled stage on which the greater portion of their lives was spent, leaving the field clear for younger men ; of these, as yet, the most prominent figures were Pitt, Fox, and Murray ; the annals of the time bear copious evidence of the part they played in the wild guerilla warfare of Newcastle's Ministry. Murray, however, was determined to get on in his profession : he sacrificed politics to the bar. Fox was bent on accumulating money : he sacrificed honour to avarice. Pitt alone preserved at once the unity of his career and the purity of his character. By the side of Fox his figure assumes a majesty and a dignity almost like that of Olympian Jove himself, which inspired awe and terror even in the reckless soul of his rival, and which appears portentous, and almost inconceivable, even at this distance of time.

CHAPTER XIV.

INNER LIFE OF PARLIAMENT IN THE EIGHTEENTH CENTURY.

WHAT was Parliament itself like? is a question which must often have occurred to our readers. Well, it was not very unlike the modern Parliament; the resemblances were far greater than the contrasts. And yet the latter were numerous enough, and being, as it were, concerned more with the inner life, the private as opposed to the public business, were quite sufficiently marked to have rendered the by-laws of Parliament almost a *terra incognita* to many a modern M.P.

The Speaker—to deal with the highest first—may be regarded as completely independent after the Revolution. He is from that date the servant of the House solely, appointed by their choice alone. The last remnant of royal influence—the right of *veto* on his election—which had enabled Charles II. to peremptorily decline to receive the haughty Sir Edward Seymour as the chosen Speaker of the Commons, was suffered to fall into oblivion, along with the royal *veto* on legislation. The Speaker improves, too, in dignity and privileges. He becomes really and truly the First Commoner in England. He is appointed a regular official salary of suitable dimensions, is given an official residence during his term of office, and is allowed certain other comfortable perquisites in the shape of hogsheads of wine, and other solid comforts. At the beginning of the century, it was still the custom to make the election of a Speaker the first business of the session, and, in some cases, the first trial of party power. Sir Spencer Compton's Speakership was remarkable for its prolongation throughout the whole reign of George I. Speaker Onslow (1727–1761) may be regarded as the man who did most to establish the Chair on its modern footing, to create for it that character for impartiality which is so essential to the position, to endow it with the dignity which it has since so uniformly preserved. The Speaker's business was then, as now, mainly to preserve order. This he was empowered to do by naming any individual who was creating disorder : a formality which was the prelude to the more severe punishment of fine or imprisonment. He also acted as the instrument of the House in administering reprimands, ordering the imprisonment or pronouncing the expulsion of recalcitrant members, of which discipline we have given proofs that the House was by no means niggard early in the eighteenth century.

The arrangement of the House of Commons was considerably different from the modern one. There was no regular division into Government and Opposition benches ; there was merely a bench reserved for the members of the Privy Council, and on this were usually seated, side by side, the leaders of both Government and Opposition. It was, in fact, quite a common thing for a man, after indulging in the bitterest sarcasms on the conduct of some individual statesman, to take his seat again by the side of the object of his invective, and inquire how he had done, which inquiry the latter would answer with the utmost good nature, ere rising to return with double force the hail of words which had rattled so savagely about his ears. There is a story that Walpole, sitting down as usual near to Pulteney, after an earnest and pathetic appeal to the House, was informed by his enemy, in a whisper, that he had made a misquotation. Walpole betted him a guinea that he had not. The matter was referred at once, and decided against the minister, who tossed a guinea to Pulteney. The latter caught it triumphantly, and holding it up to the House, cried, in a perfectly audible tone, " This is the first public money I have received for years, and it shall be the last ! "—a sarcastic allusion to the pecuniary gratifications bestowed on Walpole's supporters.

With regard to the members themselves : by law they were all landowners, duly qualified by the religious tests. In actual practice, the property qualification laws were continually evaded : perhaps the tests may not have proved a greater stumbling-block to elastic consciences. It is worthy of notice, that in 1708 the eldest sons of Scotch peers were specially incapacitated from sitting in the Commons ; though there was no such restriction

placed on those of English peers, or of Irish peers after the Irish
Act of Union. Apparently, however, the privilege which was
debarred to the eldest sons aforesaid, was not valued extraordinarily highly by every sitting member. There are numerous resolutions against the continued absence of members; there are
even tragi-comic attempts to "whip" in the absentees by sending
round officers in search of them. In 1710, it was formally resolved
that those who stayed away were neglecting their duty. But all
these efforts to insure a better attendance were ineffectual; those
who came more regularly than the mass, seem to have seized
any excuse for an adjournment or a count-out. The claims of
the East India Companies had to give way to a tiger-baiting.
Private theatricals, fêtes-champêtres, races, any form of amusement would lure away the House, and cause the postponement
of public business. It is said that the practice of adjourning
from Friday night to Monday originated in Robert Walpole's
determination not to miss his Saturday's hunting at Houghton.
During the latter part of George II.'s reign, when parliamentary .
business consisted chiefly in budget-voting, varied by an occasional
pæan of triumph from Pitt at the news of some victory, there was
almost invariably a count-out on Wednesday, in addition to the
regular Saturday *dies non.*

The debates, however, grew longer, and the sessions lasted
farther into the year as the eighteenth century slowly drew out
to its close. The sessions in the earlier days had lasted for a
week or fortnight, at most; but they had extended their duration
from October or November, over a Christmas recess, to the middle
of April even before the Revolution. They were prolonged later
and later, deeper into the spring; by the reign of George III.,
they often trenched on a portion of the summer; and their length
was in no small measure owing to the waste of time over Satur-
days, and other adjournments. The debates, too, which had
begun under the Tudors at seven or eight in the morning, and
were ended before the afternoon, had gradually slipped down the
clock, until the regular hour of opening business at the beginning
of the eighteenth century was one or two in the afternoon, sometimes even as late as four. The latter became the usual hour
under George III. The committees, however, on whom the

main burden of the work fell, had always sat in the afternoons, and their hours suffered no alteration. The usual hour of closing the debate was two o'clock in the night; sometimes, of course, it might be prolonged to much later. In 1722, a debate on the suspension of the Habeas Corpus Act lasted till seven. In 1727, the House wrangled over the Address from two to six. The debate on the Excise Bill, which was conducted amid a hoarse, rolling murmur of angry voices outside, lasted for twelve hours. The division on the Address in 1783 was moved at half-past seven; Fox's India Bill was put to the vote at half-past four. Clearly, however, the idea of a forty-eight or more hours' sitting had not yet presented itself to the minds of our legislators; and after the Reform Bill of 1832, it became the established custom to adjourn, as a rule, at the midnight hour.

It was natural, perhaps, that as the debates grew longer, the speeches should similarly increase in volume. The good old rule of Parliament was, that "if any one speak too long and speak within the matter, he may not be cut off; but if he be long and out of the matter, then may the Speaker gently admonish him of the shortness of the time or the business of the House, and pray him to make as short as he may." As early as 1738, however, Horace Walpole spoke for two hours and a half on the Spanish question. Lord Chatham is recorded to have spoken on one occasion for more than two hours; and this was regarded as quite a notable event. Under George III., long speeches became the rule rather than the exception. Pitt, Burke, Fox, Sheridan, Windham, and other lights of Parliament, used frequently to speak for hours. The speeches on Warren Hastings' trial would have been intolerable but for their extraordinary power. During the exciting debates which attended the close of the American war, consisting chiefly of a series of violent attacks on the Prime Minister, Lord North, it was by no means unusual for two or three speakers to occupy a whole evening in denunciations worthy of our own times. From the Speakership of Onslow, however, the rule was strictly enforced, that no one should speak more than once, except in committee.

The standard of age was much lower before than after the Reform Bill of 1832. It was found necessary even to pass a

atute (7 Will. III.), rendering null and void the election of any
:rson who should not be of full age. Still, there were always a
rge number of young, rising men in Parliament, introduced, as
rule, by some patron who had been attracted by their ability or
ratorical power. It was, in fact, urged as one of the strongest
·guments in favour of the nomination system, that it secured
constant infusion of good, fresh blood into the parliamentary
rstem by admitting able young men, who had no experience to
hich they could appeal as a recommendation to a large, popular
onstituency. It must also be mentioned that many eminent men
referred standing for a close constituency, in order that they
ight enter Parliament with their hands free, unfettered by
ledges such as the larger constituencies were accustomed in
iany cases to demand from their candidates. It may be added
iat the two Pitts, and many other distinguished statesmen, made
ieir first appearance on the parliamentary stage by the help of
pocket-borough.

We have referred elsewhere to the corruption of Parliament
nd of the representative system. It must not, however, be in-
:rred from this that patriotism and purity were wholly dead in
ie land. The counties remained tolerably pure; most of the
irge· constituencies were very sensitive to popular opinion; and,
i spite of the powerful levers of influence and corruption by
·hich individuals and families controlled the elections, Parlia-
ient to a very great extent reflected the feeling of the country.
'he idea of popular representation of course was a farce. But
npopular ministers were frequently rejected for large constituen-
ies; unpopular men at times would have been excluded from
'arliament altogether but for the close boroughs; and it was
enerally found perfectly impossible to keep the most docile
iajority together in hours of great popular excitement. More-
ver, before the reign of George III., ministers themselves were
iirly susceptible to popular influences. Sunderland could not
arry the Peerage Bill (1719). Walpole withdrew the Excise Bill
1733). The voice of the nation forced Parliament to declare
·ar on Spain (1740–1). Not all the corruption or royal favour
·hich Newcastle commanded, enabled him to defy the general
·ish that Pitt should manage the war (1756–7). The greatest

blot on the policy of George III. is, that the popular element did not enter into it at all. And yet, if we examine the principal events of his reign, it will be found that in most of his most arbitrary acts he was supported by the majority of the nation; that his success against the Whig Oligarchy was due mainly to popular support, given, it is true, under the influence of a delusion; that his complete triumph in the end was solely due to his union with the popular statesman William Pitt the younger; and that whenever he set himself directly against the majority, he found himself overmatched in the end. The corruption of Parliament, however, was more fully realized and bitterly resented by the opposition under Walpole, because they thoroughly under-- stood that they were excluded from their rightful share in it solely- by the inveterate jealousy of one man. They were obliged to make good their invective to some extent when they came into office by passing a Place Bill (1742); it was, however, an extremely inadequate bill, which really produced but little result. Corruption, no doubt, they considered was too valuable a weapon to be surrendered now that they had attained the seat of power. Probably it was some similar train of thought which had prompted the elder Pitt to avail himself of the influence of Newcastle for the government of the nation, which he felt himself inspired to save. Nor was it till the edged tool had fallen into the hands of the king, and was used by him to restore the old powers of prerogative, that the danger was really appreciated; then there arose a cry for economical and parliamentary reform, as the surest method of averting it.

Among the privileges of Parliament, the most important was undoubtedly the right of regulating and deciding every question connected with their own Houses. The Lords, under this head, included all bills with regard to themselves, their privileges and peerages, and any disputes which might arise about the latter. The Commons claimed the right of deciding all election petitions. The latter jurisdiction, however, became, as we have seen, a mere abuse. An attempt was made to remedy it in 1770, by Mr. Grenville's Election Petition Act, by which the trial of election petitions was transferred to a committee of thirteen, selected from forty-nine members chosen by ballot. In a very short time, how-

er, the majority realized that by packing the committee with
ir own friends, a very real control over the elections might be
intained, and the abuse was but very slightly diminished in
nsequence. The valuable right of freedom from arrest, which
s in its origin necessary to the very existence and independence
 Parliament, degenerated in the eighteenth century into an
trument of oppression. It was extended, not merely to the
rsons of members and their servants, but also to their whole
usehold, property, and appurtenances. The shield of privilege
s cast in some cases over the rabbits, fish, trees, even the foot-
n, of members. Members themselves claimed immunity from
actions of law and claims of creditors. In many cases worth-
s spendthrifts were inducted suddenly into a seat in order to
ble them to defy the just demands of their creditors. To put
 end to these abuses, an Act was passed (1770) by which the
vilege was reduced to its ancient dimensions, affording protec-
n to the persons of members only, and leaving the course of
tice with regard to their property and servants entirely free
 Geo. III. c. 50).

rhe privilege, however, that was most jealously claimed and
rded was that of complete secrecy of debate. It was even
npetent for any member to suddenly call attention to the fact
t there were strangers present, and procure their instant expul-
n. In ancient times this rule, however, does not seem to have
n strictly enforced, for in 1675 Lord Shaftesbury complained
f the droves of ladies" that attended Parliament, and added
t it was quite the custom for men to hire or borrow of their
nds " handsome sisters or daughters to deliver their petitions."
e rule was more stringently enforced in the eighteenth century;
ruders who ventured into the Gallery were liable to be expelled
 taken into custody. Even as late as the year 1740, the
sence of a stranger in the Gallery was considered a crime. In
77, however, Mr. Luttrell moved the reconsideration and
endment of the rule. He was supported by Mr. Fox, and
posed by Lord Norton and Mr. Rigby. The motion was
gatived, but the rule appears to have been relaxed in execution.

1779, however, during an interesting debate, an immense
wd of ladies attended. As many were unable to obtain seats,

the Speaker directed that the House should be cleared of all the male strangers. This was followed by such an irruption of ladies that all the seats below the bar and both galleries were filled. A member, irritated by the expulsion of some male friend, insisted on the removal of all the strangers, and a ridiculous scene ensued. The ladies refused to go at all, expostulated and resisted violently, so that it took the officers nearly two hours to turn them out, during which time there was such a rustling of dresses and clatter of voices, and altogether such an extraordinary turmoil and confusion, that ladies were for the future rigorously excluded until after the Reform Bill. They were still allowed to appear in the House of Lords, but the place allotted to them was behind the curtains on each side of the throne. After their exclusion from the Commons, they resorted to disguise in order to obtain admission. The Duchess of Gordon went to the Strangers' Gallery disguised as a man, and the beautiful Mrs. Sheridan imitated this example in order that she might listen to her husband's oratory. The strict rule that any member might call the attention of the Speaker to the presence of strangers, and procure their expulsion, was not modified till quite late in the next century (1875).

The exclusion of strangers was no doubt originally connected with the prohibition of reports, which was enforced under heavy penalties. The earliest records of Parliament consist of notes jotted down surreptitiously for subsequent entry in diaries, which were not intended to be printed—at least till after the writer's death. Regular reports in outline were thus preserved of many important debates under Elizabeth and the first Stuarts by Sir Symonds d'Ewes. The Long Parliament in 1641 permitted the publication of its proceedings in the "Diurnal Occurrences of Parliament," but prohibited the printing of speeches without leave of the House. This practice continued till the Restoration, and the prohibition extended beyond it. In 1680, with the view of preventing inaccurate accounts of the business actually done, the Commons directed that a bare statement of their votes and proceedings, without any of the speeches, should be printed. Regular reports, however, were sent to his constituents by Andrew Marvell, member for Hull (1660–1667), and similar notes were taken by Anchitell Grey, member for Derby, between 1667 and

74, which were published long after their deaths. Somers has ansmitted in the same form valuable accounts of the debates of e Convention, 1689. Under the Hanoverians the rule was ry stringently enforced; Parliament became more jealous and spicious; printers were frequently punished for disobeying it. spite, however, of these severities, reports were published con-ually, but in a very different form from the modern elaborate ansard. Notes jotted down surreptitiously of the main gist and sult of a debate, with barren outlines of speeches, and an occa-nal metaphor inserted, like a flower culled here and there, ere afterwards taken to the nearest tavern, where the whole bate, speeches and all, would be constructed partly by the help the dry bones in hand, partly by memory, partly by imagina-n. In many cases, speakers may have said the exact contrary the words placed in the mouths of their representatives, who ured under the thin disguise of ancient Romans, or easily cognised initials, or some well-known nickname, in the pages of *he Gentleman's Magazine, The London Magazine,* and Boyer's *litical State of Great Britain.*

In many cases the wit and eloquence of one side may have en due to the talents and political sympathy of the writer, quite much as the dense stupidity of their opponents was due to his atred. Sir Robert Walpole, in a debate which arose on the bject in 1738, put the case very forcibly : "I have read some bates of this House," he observed, "in which I have been ade to speak the very reverse of what I meant. I have read thers in which all the learning, the wit, the argument, were rown into one side; and on the other nothing but what was w, mean and ridiculous ; and yet when it comes to the question e division has gone against the side which upon the face of this ebate had reason and justice to support it."

Dr. Johnson, who compiled a large number of the speeches in *he Gentleman's Magazine,* is actually reported to have gloried in e fact that he never let the Whig dogs have the best of the rgument. The inaccuracy of these stolen reports was advanced ery frequently as a reason for allowing regular reporting, in order hat political partisans should no longer be able to hoodwink the eople by false or partial reports. The matter, however, was brought to a crisis in 1771, when the foolish irritability of Colonel George Onslow plunged the Government into a contest with the printers. He drew attention to the publishing of parliamentary reports, which was now done openly. For this he was vilified in various papers by the title of "Little cocking George," and other opprobrious epithets. A number of printers were in consequence summoned before the House, and reprimanded on their knees. One Miller, however, refused to attend, and gave the messenger, who tried to arrest him, into custody for assault. The Lord Mayor, Crosby, and Aldermen Oliver and Wilkes, before whom the case was brought, committed the messenger for an infringement of the privileges of the City. The king was furious; insisted on the punishment of Crosby and Oliver;—he had had enough of Wilkes. The two were committed to Newgate, but the question of reporting was wisely dropped, and has never been interfered with since, though it was not officially recognised, or any regular provision of places made for reporters, till the new Houses of Parliament were built, in 1834.

The licence taken by reporters after their victory might well excuse their previous exclusion. Under the influence of party feeling they would ruthlessly cut down the most beautiful oratory of Burke, Fox, or Sheridan into a few bald lines; pure malice sometimes induced them to place ridiculous ineptitudes in the mouths of distinguished men, solely with the view of making them ridiculous. Mr. Wilberforce on one occasion read out and bitterly complained of an extract from a newspaper, in which he was reported to have recommended the cultivation of potatoes in the following terms: "Potatoes make men healthy, vigorous, active; but what is still more in their favour, they make men tall; more especially was he led to say so as being rather under the common size, and he must lament that his guardians had not fostered him under that genial vegetable." The passage was naturally received with peals of laughter, though the evil was only too apparent. These outbreaks, however, of indecent ridicule gradually became more rare as the freshness of the triumph wore off a little, and then the value and importance of parliamentary reporting became incalculably great and exercised an enormous influence, not only in modifying the licence of Parliament

self, but in widening the sphere of political life and awakening
the nation from the long dream in which they had lain, gazing at
the world like children who see, and yet only half appreciate, the
things which appear to their view.

"The entire people," says the late Lord Farnborough (Sir
Erskine May), "are now present as it were and assist in the
deliberations of Parliament.   An orator addresses not only the
assembly of which he is a member, but through them the civilized
world; his influence and his responsibilities are alike extended.
Publicity has become one of the most important instruments of
parliamentary government.   The people are taken into counsel
by Parliament, and concur in condemning or approving the laws
which are there proposed."

An altogether meaner, though much cherished, branch of privilege was that of franking, which had its origin in a settlement of
the revenues of the Post-Office during the Long Parliament of
Charles II.   Sir Walter Erle introduced a proviso that the letters
of members of Parliament should be free during .the session.
Several members spoke against it, and the whole House seemed
ashamed of it.   The Speaker, Sir Harbottle Grimston, even
declared that he was ashamed to put the question.   Interest,
however, appears to have outweighed shame, for the question was
not only put, but carried.   Nor was the privilege long confined
to the period of the sessions merely; it was very shortly extended
to the whole duration of a Parliament.   By 1715 the abuse had
become great.   It was declared that his Majesty's revenue was
lessened, that scandalous and seditious libels were transmitted by
their medium, and that these evils were due to a reckless use of
the privilege, which extended even to the franking of enormous
numbers of letters, without examining them in the slightest, and
sending franks themselves by post to be used by persons not
members for any length of time.   It was, therefore, directed that
for the future the franks must be in the member's own hand-
writing.   Even then the most remarkable abuses were perpetrated.
Hampers of game, baskets of fish, parcels of all sorts—even in
some cases able-bodied men and girls—were carried at his
Majesty's expense by the magic of a member's signature.
Wraxall says that, "till 1784, neither date nor place was neces-

sary. Not only were covers transmitted by hundreds, packed in boxes," to be used at some future time, but " far greater perver-sions of the original principle took place." He then quotes a case where a member "decorated with the Order of the Bath"— which he appears to consider an aggravation of the offence—sent thirty-three letters to London full of garden seeds, and though the Postmaster-General had them carried to the Speaker, yet the matter was hushed up because the offender was one of the Government majority. In 1760, the privilege was limited to franking parcels not exceeding two ounces in weight. Later, during the American war, Lord North proposed to relieve the strain on the revenue by suppressing the exemption altogether, but his statement was received with such a general howl of dis-approbation, that the idea was dropped at once for fear of alienating votes. Mr. Pitt succeeded, however, in placing some limits on the abuse. He proposed that all franks should be dated with the time and place. This measure, which practically limited the right to the personal use of members,—for which it was originally intended,—was carried unanimously. From this time the privilege was watched with considerable jealousy ; and though innumerable frauds must have been perpetrated—especially on the eve of an election—yet they were no longer done openly and unblushingly in the light of day. The privilege was not finally given up till the establishment of the penny post, in 1840.

The old rule that Parliament, being the creation of the Crown, was *ipso facto* dissolved by a demise of the Crown, was con-siderably reduced in effect by a statute of Anne (6 Anne c. 7), which provided that it should continue for six months after such event. A further statute of George III. (37 Geo. III. c. 127) in view of a very possible contingency, added that if there should be no Parliament in existence at a demise of the Crown, the last one should reassemble for six months. The connection, however, between a demise of the Crown and a Dissolution of Parliament was not finally severed till late in the next century (Reform Act, 1867).

CHAPTER XV.

PERSONAL GOVERNMENT OF GEORGE III.

SECTION I.—*Struggle with the House of Commons.*

THE policy of George III. may be described as a last attempt to restore the waning authority of the Crown to its original ustre. He fancied that it laboured under a temporary eclipse; ie did not see that personal government had become an anachronism. With this object well in view, he designed to break ıp the strong phalanx of the great Whig houses, which had so ong curbed the royal power to utter ineptitude. Pitt's Ministry must fall; Pitt himself be driven from office; a new Government ıe formed, in which every member should be, to a certain extent, lependent on the Crown. George intended to avail himself of he rivalry already existing between his ministers, in order to lestroy the Cabinet; and by holding out hopes of supremacy to hose who should be submissive, to produce a general subervience to his will. Working thus on the general thirst for ıffice, which was the common attribute of most of the prominent ıtatesmen of the time, he proposed to patch together a Ministry ıut of the most heterogeneous materials, which could never unite nto a coherent whole, which should be held together by his will ınd by the individual greed of its members, and which must ıventually fall hopelessly to pieces under the influence of internal action. In this way he would ruin the credit of the Whig leaders ıy debasing their motives, and destroy their influence by pitting hem one against the other in a personal scramble for the seat of ıower. Then, when the favourable moment came, he would seize he opportunity to commit the government to some mediocre ıtatesman, who would be thoroughly obedient to his authority, ınd who would rely not so much on the solidity of his measures, ır any parliamentary influence of his own, as on the steady ıupport and parliamentary interest of the king. To give effect to

his plans, George intended to resume the *Crown patronage* which
had for so long formed the main prop and stay of the Whig power,
to employ it in a precisely similar manner, and to create thereby
for himself a party in Parliament which should be thoroughly
devoted to his service, and should owe obedience not to the
minister, or to the Cabinet, but to the king alone. The command
of such a troop of " King's Friends " as they were later called,
would give him a very considerable control over the House and
his ministers. He could at least insure that no measure which
he disliked should be carried through Parliament, unless all
parties united against him. There was, moreover, the further
advantage that ministers, conscious of the uncertainty of their
majority, would be apt to shirk or suppress any measures to which
the king was known to be hostile.

To find the raw material for the creation of this party, he
intended to avail himself of the regeneration of the Tories, who,
now that Jacobitism was practically extinct, and the throne
occupied by an English king whose views were worthy of the
Stuarts themselves, were quite ready to transfer their allegiance to
George, and even invest him with all the attributes of Divine
authority which they had hitherto reserved exclusively for the
exiled line. This new-born loyalty of the Tories supplied George
with a convenient nucleus for the foundation of his party. He
found that he could rely on the consistent support of a small but
united body from the first; that his natural opponents were
incapacitated from any vigorous action by their own dissensions ;
and that he might expect continual accessions to his own list of
supporters in the shape of deserters from the enemies' ranks,
He had, moreover, at the outset, the sympathy of the people, who
felt that, the significance of the old watchwords being practically
obsolete, there was no reason why men of ability should any
longer be excluded from office simply because they were Tories.

It was easy to attack the Whigs in their existing state, for the
apparently united and patriotic Ministry, which had borne the
burdens and reaped the glory of the Seven Years' War, was a house
divided against itself, split, rent, and tottering to its foundations
under the secret influence of the factious disputes and personal
quarrels which had broken out during the first Ministry of

Newcastle, and, lingering on in a smouldering state, thinly surfaced over by the temporary pressure of national feeling, were ready to burst forth again into a conflagration the moment that pressure was removed. No sooner was the question of peace mooted, than the Cabinet fell at once to pieces. This was the king's opportunity. Had he made use of his early popularity to form on their ruins a Ministry including the ablest men of all parties, public opinion would have applauded, and the country would have trusted and supported him. But his narrow intellect and restricted education had inspired him with a violent prejudice against the whole Whig party, and induced him to rely entirely on a man who had neither administrative talents, oratorical powers, nor personal popularity to recommend him as a constitutional adviser. Bute's fall—there is no space for details—was as rapid and complete as his rise had been sudden and unusual, leaving his master to engage single-handed in an obstinate contest with the various sections of the disintegrated and discomfited Whig party, extending down to 1770, amid the strangest alternations of victory and defeat to both sides. The king, however, gained steadily. The very victories of his opponents were triumphs like those of Pyrrhus, which were as bad as defeat, for the king almost invariably contrived to have a hand in the formation of every new Ministry, and his influence was marked by the introduction of some element of disorder and weakness. All through the balance of success lay wholly with George, and in the end his triumph was decisive and complete. The Whig party was broken and scattered. The four sections into which it was divided were at daggers drawn with each other. It was impossible for them to unite as a coherent whole on any question of principle. It was easier for the followers of Bedford and Grenville to join themselves with the Tories, than to act with their old comrades of the Whig Oligarchy. The King's Friends, moreover, were now a large and well disciplined party, whose influence in Parliament gave George a very real control of its action. Beginning merely with the personal friends of the king and Lord Bute, it had naturally attracted the sympathies of the Tories, it had been quickly recruited by a number of self-seeking statesmen of the type of the elder Fox, and its numbers were continually enlarged by accessions from the ranks of the Whigs when the advantages of adhering to the king began to be more distinctly understood. Relying therefore on the implicit obedience of his followers, and the utter disorganization of the Opposition, which became clearly apparent on the downfall of the Grafton Ministry in 1770, George seized the opportunity to grasp the reins of power into his own hands, and to thrust into the first place his own lieutenant, Lord North, a man after his own heart, in whose subservience he had the utmost confidence. The year 1770 dates the commencement of a new period, during which George was really endeavouring to carry into practice the principles of personal government, which were so deeply implanted in his character, and which he fondly imagined would be at once beneficial and acceptable to the English people.

One of the most important results of the changes effected in the decade 1760-70, was the rise of modern Radicalism, almost as if by natural antagonism to that revival of high Tory principles which prompted the stringent measures of repression directed against Wilkes. The Radicals advocated sweeping parliamentary reforms of an entirely original character. They proposed that members of Parliament should put off their senatorial character, to become the delegates of their constituents. They advocated annual Parliaments, the payment of members, universal suffrage, vote by ballot, and other measures, the result of which would have been partly to destroy the reviving power of the Tory party, and partly to transfer the entire control of the executive to the people in the widest sense of the term. At first, however, they were but a small party, and the violence of their principal orators, among whom were Wilkes, Glynn, Oliver, Sawbridge, Townsend, and John Horne Tooke, discredited them in the eyes of the governing classes. The principal result of the movement in its early stages was to instil new life into the decrepit Whig party, to compel them to abandon their old purely selfish, oligarchical, place-hunting characteristics, and take up an entirely new and advanced position as the advocates of Parliamentary Reform. This development, however, was not yet apparent in Parliament.

Lord North began with an enormously strong Government. He could rely of course upon the Tories; he could also rely on two sections of the Whigs, respectively known as the Bedford and

Grenville Whigs, from the names of the leaders. It may be readily imagined that these two sections contained many of the most unprincipled statesmen of the time. The only opposition was that of the two remaining sections, headed by Chatham and Rockingham; but, unfortunately for the cause of progress, there existed between them almost as much personal hostility as between each and the Government. Of the two, the party of Chatham was undoubtedly the most disinterested, and the most enlightened; the Rockingham Whigs were really the old party of Newcastle, the successors of the great Whig Oligarchy, with their principles only slightly developed, and adapted to suit the requirements of the new era. This Ministry, founded on corruption, held together by the basest feelings of personal interest, untrammelled by any effective opposition in Parliament, was naturally fitted to be the instrument of the prerogative which had created it.

Its strength seemed irresistible, and it was governed solely by the king. "Not only did the king direct his ministers in all important matters of domestic and foreign policy, but he suggested the management of debates in Parliament, what motions should be made or opposed, and how measures should be carried. He reserved for himself all the patronage. He arranged the cast of the Administration; the places of ministers, law officers, members of the household. He nominated and promoted the English and Scotch judges; managed all the preferments in the Church; disposed of the military governments, regiments, and commissions." All this patronage was used solely to create a party in both Houses, and the control of this party enabled the king to do exactly what he pleased in Parliament. The result was that, in the words of Burke, the power of the Crown, almost as obsolete as prerogative itself, revived and flourished with extraordinary vitality under the new title of *influence.* In the earlier days, in their ignorance, the Opposition had attacked the supposed secret influence of Bute as the cause of all the evils; they now realized to the full that it was the influence of the king himself. To George is directly due all the disasters of the time. He it was who refused to yield an inch to the Americans; who insisted on the prosecution of the war; who persuaded Lord North not to

"desert" him when the latter's own convictions were against
continuing the struggle. He it was who persistently opposed
Economical and Parliamentary Reform, and marshalled his forces
steadily night after night to oppose the motions of Chatham,
Burke and Dunning. He insisted on continuing the proceedings
against the printers, even when Lord North considered it advisable
to drop them. The Whig Governments, corrupt as they were, had
at least avoided open conflict with the people. But now the
Ministry was brought disastrously into collision again and again
with public opinion by the narrow-minded obstinacy of the king.
During the American war it is true that public opinion was with
the king against the rebels; but this agreement was short-lived,
was soon broken by the unsuccessful issue of the war, and was
due, not to affection for George, but hatred for America.

Perhaps one of the most important elements from which the
new-born power of the Crown derived its exuberant vitality was
the vast wealth which flowed into the country from India, and
was used by the Indian civil servants and officers to purchase
parliamentary influence. These men were accustomed to the
despotic principles of government which were necessary in
India. They naturally therefore leant towards the royal power,
and swelled the party of the King's Friends. Lord Clive and
Warren Hastings, two of the most distinguished of the Company's
officials, supported the king steadily both in and out of Parliament.

The well-head, however, from which this royal influence
flowed was to be found in the corrupt state of the representative
system, and the unprincipled policy by which the whole Crown
patronage was uniformly dispensed for purely party purposes.
Matters had grown worse since the days of Newcastle. In 1770,
192 members of the House of Commons held places under
Government. In 1782 no less than 11,500 revenue officers were
employed. All these public officials were bound to vote as
bidden on pain of instant dismissal. An attempt was made, as
we have noticed above,[1] to restore purity in 1770 to the decision
of contested elections, but with very little result. The corruption

---

[1] *v.* p. 194.

xisting among the constituencies and in Parliament was too xtensive to be dealt with except by sweeping measures. To uch an extent was the practice of directly or indirectly buying p votes in Parliament carried, that in 1776, in spite of the rugality of the king and queen, there was a deficit of £600,000 n the royal accounts. Servants, tradesmen, and such unim- ortant people had been kept without their money for years in rder that the glorious work of maintaining the influence of the Crown by bribing members of Parliament might proceed un- hecked.

To maintain this system of government the king professed him- elf ready to adopt the most extreme measures. On one critical ccasion he threatened to use the sword rather than surrender. Several times he announced his intention of returning to Hanover f certain measures were carried. He warned Lord North that if ecessary he would refuse his assent to an obnoxious bill, though he royal veto had not been used since the beginning of the entury.

There is no reason for supposing that Lord North himself was lirectly responsible for this policy, or even approved of the de- ails in all cases. He was merely the mouthpiece of the king; nd he carried out the king's orders even in opposition to his own iews. He appears to have regarded George in the light of a ommander-in-chief, whom he was bound to obey implicitly as ong as he remained in office; while to quit his post without ermission would amount to desertion. On this principle he ontinued to prosecute the American war, although he held in is heart that its continuance must end in ruin to the king and ountry.

One of the principal results of this period was a considerable hange in the policy of the Whig party. Formerly they were the nain supporters of corruption; they now became staunch advo- ates of Economical and Parliamentary Reform as the only neans of securing some limitations of the royal power. The ransformation, however, was effected very slowly. The principal eaders of the old Whigs, Chatham, Burke, Rockingham, and even Junius himself, did not contemplate any lowering of the ranchise. The utmost that the most enlightened among them aimed at in the early days was a complete excision of rotten boroughs.   Charles Fox himself had not yet taken up the cause of Parliamentary Reform; Burke was even opposed to it, on the ground that the franchise was a right with which Parliament had no power to interfere.   The Radicals of course advocated their sweeping programme to the full, both in and out of Parliament; but it was not till the entrance of the younger William Pitt into Parliament that the question was seriously taken up by any prominent Whig.   Burke and the others concentrated their attention on Economical Reform; and, despairing of any success in Parliament, they organized a system of extra-parliamentary agitation, in 1779–80, as a weapon wherewith to oppose the impenetrable royal majority.   This important movement may be regarded as the starting-point of the modern system of parliamentary petitioning.   Twenty-three counties and a number of large towns sent up simultaneously petitions for economical reform, and this manifestation of popular opinion undoubtedly strengthened the hands of the Opposition considerably.   But so entirely had George and his minister reversed all the known rules of ministerial government, that though the Opposition, on the motion of Mr. Dunning, succeeded in carrying against them (April, 1780) the celebrated resolution "that the influence of the Crown has increased, is increasing, and ought to be diminished," it is highly probable that North would not have resigned had he seen his way to continuing the American war with the faintest prospect of success.

   The resignation of North in 1782, consequent on his determined conviction that it was impossible to continue the American war or the government any longer, marks the temporary failure of the king's policy; and had his enemies proceeded at once to carry out vigorous reforms, personal government might have been destroyed for ever.   The House, however, was really too corrupt; the oligarchical leaders of the Rockingham Whigs—the lineal successors of Newcastle and Henry Pelham in policy if not in power—did not sincerely desire reform.   Burke, and others of the more earnest of the rank and file of the party, had not sufficient influence to effect as much as they desired.   The Shelburne Whigs, who represented the remnants of the old party of Chatham,

ere divided and weakened by the refusal of young William Pitt
) enter the Government in company with his nominal leader.
'he result was that though the Whig Ministry of 1782 did carry
irough a bill for economical reform, it was extremely inadequate
i its effect.   They then devoted themselves to the more con-
enial task of quarrelling among themselves for the principal
laces, as in the old days, and thus afforded the king again the
pening for interference which he desired.

He succeeded in making his opinion felt in the formation of the
.ockingham Ministry of 1782, and it was short-lived in con-
:quence.   Moreover, though the unscrupulous union of the old
nemies, Fox and North, in the coalition of 1783, for the moment
:emed the death-blow of his hopes and his policy, they really
layed entirely into his hands.   Their conduct in this matter
ave a tremendous shock to public feeling, completely ruined the
haracter of each for political honesty and consistency, and
nabled the king to execute, for their destruction, a *coup d'état*
'hich is perhaps the most extraordinary instance of the undue
iterference of the Crown in the ordinary working of the Consti-
ition that the reign of George III. affords.   A ministerial bill,
nown as Fox's India Bill, was passed by an overwhelming
iajority in the Commons and sent up thence to the Lords.   The
ill itself was highly obnoxious to the king ; it was also extremely
npopular in the country, not only on its own merits, but also by
reflection of the unpopularity of its authors.   George was de-
:rmined that it should not pass, and to this end he gave an
utograph letter to Earl Temple, authorizing him to inform the
eers individually that whoever voted for the bill was not a friend
f the king, and, moreover, to use stronger language if necessary.
'he result of these tactics was that the bill was thrown out.   A de-
:a: in the Lords, however, was not reckoned of much importance,
s a rule, when the ministerial majority in the Commons was so
verwhelming as that commanded by Fox and North ; but the king
'as determined to accept the decision of the Lords as final, and,
iy an extraordinary exercise of his prerogative, immediately dis-
iissed his reluctant ministers, calling in the younger Pitt to wage
. desperate struggle against the huge majority of the Opposition.
in that struggle he and his scanty band of followers must have

P

been beaten but for the steady support of the King's Friends. His ultimate triumph therefore implied really the final victory of the king in the long contest between the Crown and the Whig party; for though Pitt's earlier administration was conducted on a liberal basis, and he even ventured to propose a bill—a most inadequate bill, it is true—for Parliamentary Reform, 1785, still it was impossible for him not to fully realize that he was, in fact, the king's minister, resting primarily on the royal support—or, if any doubt existed in his mind on the subject, the desertion of a large number of his own majority on this very question must have furnished the most convincing proof of it. It was only natural therefore, that he should gradually abandon as impracticable all details of policy which the king objected to, and should become more and more identified with the royal policy and the royal principles of government. And if it be attributed to him as a reproach that he voluntarily gave up at the king's pleasure measures which he undoubtedly deemed would be beneficial to the country, it must be remembered that he did not consent to dismiss them from his programme until experience proved that on these points he would be opposed by the Whigs as well as the king ; and he knew that a return of the Whigs to office would be followed by the very smallest changes in policy, but would involve the unusual phenomenon of a Government depending on a small disunited minority in Parliament, and in consequence subject to the dictation of the strong and fairly coherent majority in opposition.

Circumstances, moreover, were shortly to drive the great mass of the nation into Toryism of the strictest kind, and to unite them under the royal banner as the sole hope of escape from a plunge into the wildest anarchy.

SECTION 2.—*Triumph of the King.*

" The stirring events which occurred in France in the years[1] 1789-92 were viewed at first with the greatest sympathy by those Englishmen who had devoted their lives to the improvement of

---

[1] The greater portion of the earlier part of this section is quoted almost *verbatim* from an earlier work, " Our Hanoverian Kings."

eir own country. The excesses, however, which followed the
rlier constitutional reforms, alarmed the Conservative instincts
' many who considered that the maintenance of order was the
ghest object of government, and who disapproved of any
)litical changes whatever, unless they were accomplished in a
adual and orderly manner. The two extremes of opinion on
is subject were equally dangerous, though diametrically opposed
one another. These were the Tory party proper, headed by
e king, and the Radicals, whose leader was Lord Stanhope :
e former distrusting all change, and reprobating alike the
'ench Revolutionists and the moderate efforts of the reforming
irty in England ; the latter hailing with enthusiasm the wildest
)nstitutional vagaries of the Jacobins, and panting eagerly to
litate the example thus conspicuously set them. There was,
)wever, no clear line of demarcation between the various
ctions at first. Many who admired the talent for destruction
hich the French had developed, would have regarded it in a
:ry different light had it manifested itself in England. Few had
)y real desire to substitute the tyranny of the Jacobin Club for
ie comparatively mild government of George III. On the other
ind, many of those who proved the strongest and bitterest
)ponents of the French Revolution, had themselves in quieter
mes led the van of reform in England, had advocated the
·oadest principles of toleration and free trade." For a long time
itt wavered beween the two middle parties. His policy towards
ie Revolution was one of strict neutrality. He still remained
)nestly in favour of progress ; and, though he considered that
iy attempt at Parliamentary Reform, in the electric state of the
)litical atmosphere, must be productive of anarchy, yet he advo-
ited strongly the concession of relief to the Catholics, and sup-
)rted a measure brought forward on the subject by Mitford in
792. Nor was it till France had announced decidedly to the
orld her utter disregard for international obligations, and had
roclaimed a Crusade against all existing Governments, that Pitt
:luctantly threw in his lot with the party of repression.
One of the most important results in England of the events of
789 was a total change in the political opinions of Burke, and a
uarrel between him and Fox. Burke's intense veneration for

everything that was old extended even to the mouldering antiquity of the French Constitution. He could see in the Revolution nothing but a great and terrible crime, unrelieved by any redeeming feature whatever. He entirely recanted his old political creed. He gave up all attempts at progress as leading inevitably to the anarchy he condemned.

On the mind of Fox a very different impression was produced by the events of 1789, as might be anticipated from his character. He failed to see anything but unmixed good in the progress of the Revolution. At the same time, he never went beyond intense sympathy with the French, and abhorrence of their would-be conquerors. Inspired by their example he aimed now at a complete reform of the representative system in England, the removal of the grievances of the Dissenters and Roman Catholics; but he had no desire to adopt the sweeping programme of the extreme Radicals.

The Radical party were really extremely scanty in numbers as yet, but they acquired an undue prominence owing to their demonstrative affection for the French Revolution, which was manifested most conspicuously on every possible occasion.

They were never numerous, however, during the eighteenth century, and they were at first almost unrepresented in Parliament.

" The immediate result of the French Revolution therefore in England was to divide the country once more into two distinct parties of Whigs and Tories, whose comparative importance was faithfully reflected in Parliament. The new Tory party consisted of those who, alarmed at the extravagance of the French, rallied round the king as the only barrier against similar excesses, and determined to resist all attempts at reform of any kind in this country, for fear that it should prove, as in France, but the prelude to a bloody Reign of Terror. This party at first included only the remnants of the King's Friends, the country gentlemen, the propertied classes, and the Tories generally. It was powerfully reinforced by the accession of Burke and many other Whigs, who, while strongly approving of progress in itself, sacrificed it readily to the cause of order. Lastly, Pitt himself, the Duke of Portland, and the personal followers of both, were driven to swell the ranks of the Tories, when the outbreak of war swept away the thin con-

:itutional illusions with which they had endeavoured to invest
1e savage figures of the French leaders.   They fancied they had
) choose between repression and anarchy; and the choice was
asily made."

On the other side, however, there grew up a new Whig party
f very diverse elements.   There was the extreme wing of the
.adicals, whose motto was violence, and who unfortunately
rought discredit on the whole Whig party.

" Next to them came the section headed by Fox, small in
umbers and declining in influence, who admired in theory the
'hole progress of the Revolution, who denounced the war against
: as wicked and wanton ; but who had no desire to assassinate
King George, or to establish a republic in England, or to mas-
acre the principal men of the Government.   Higher still in the
cale came the third section, headed by men like Mr. Grey (after-
/ards Lord Howick and Earl Grey), who, setting aside entirely
he question of the excellence or unmixed evil of the French
Revolution, maintained that the panic which had resulted from it
/as wholly unreasonable ; that there was no fear of its influence
:xtending to England in any dangerous shape ; and that therefore
here was no reason for refusing to pursue the path of Constitu-
ional Reform in a moderate and peaceful manner.   The great
juestion of Parliamentary Reform, in fact, was the bond of union
)etween the three sections of the Whigs ; and it was the common
ympathy of the moderate Whigs on this topic with the Radicals
vhich enabled the writers of the *Anti-Jacobin*, a magazine of
trongly anti-revolution principles, to falsely represent them as all
:qually eager to show their admiration for the reign of Blood and
Terror existing in France, by setting up an English republic on
he murdered corpses of the king and loyalists.

" Unfortunately, too, the opinions of the *Anti-Jacobin* became
he opinions of the great majority of Englishmen.   The cause of
Reform was viewed with abhorrence and fear by most as an
.nsidious advance towards Revolution.   Pitt and the more mode-
:ate men even considered that the extreme danger of the question
must render it a sealed book, at least until a stable Government
should be established in France.   Grey and his party, while
maintaining the necessity for Reform and the iniquity of post-

poning it, recognised, after two overwhelming defeats in 1793 and
1797, the utter uselessness of pursuing the question in the then
hostile state of the nation.   The cause of Reform therefore fell
wholly into the hands of the Radicals after 1797, with the disastrous consequence of strengthening the almost universal belief in
the dangerous nature of the movement.

"The formation of these two parties may be dated in the year
1792, when Pitt first began to abandon the attitude of neutrality
towards the Revolution which he had hitherto assumed."

The principal result of the strong Tory reaction, which set in
steadily after 1793, was a material increase of the power of the
king.   By his own unaided action he had expelled one Ministry
and retained another in defiance of the House of Commons.
Public opinion had declared its approbation of his conduct, and
given his minister an overwhelming majority at the General
Election.   That minister had tacitly consented that his policy
should be to some extent limited by the prejudices of the king.

Circumstances had aroused in the country the feeling that the
best safeguard of the Constitution lay in the royal power; half
the Whigs or more had deserted to the king's banner, and the
desertion was led by the very man who had hitherto been the
warmest opponent of personal government, and the most strenuous advocate of Constitutional Reform.   The result was that from
this date to the end of the century there was no real opposition
of any practical value, and in 1798 Fox and his friends withdrew
at last in despair from Parliament altogether, leaving the task of
offering the little in the way of opposition and criticism that was
still possible, to Mr. Tierney and a scanty remnant of the Whigs.
During this period there was naturally complete harmony between
the king and his minister: their policy was the same; their parties
were practically identical.   The old organization of the King's
Friends assumed a state of suspended animation, though it still
remained in latent existence.   The real power of the king was
more clearly shown at the beginning of the next century, by the
ease with which he was able to dismiss Pitt on the Catholic
question at the very height of the latter's power and popularity
(1801); to dictate the exclusion of Fox from Pitt's second Ministry (1804-6); and even to exact from Pitt himself a promise that

ie would never arouse the Catholic question again, though he had
vowed that he considered it of the most pressing importance.
n the absence of any other possibility, George was forced reluc-
antly to accept the Talents Ministry on the death of Pitt (1806),
nd even to consent to the inclusion of his pet aversion, Mr. Fox,·
)ut he obliged them as the price of their victory to find places for
Lord Sidmouth and many others of the King's Friends, and he
dismissed them at once when they ventured to revive the Catholic
question (1807). Their successors, the Ministries of Portland
and Perceval, were essentially his own creation ; they possessed
neither ability, oratory, nor voting power ; the royal influence
was the one mainspring of their existence.

Perhaps, however, no single event more clearly testified the
strength of the royal influence than the perfect readiness with
which, on the outbreak of the king's malady in 1810, the Opposition, headed by Lord Grey and Lord Grenville, agreed to accept
the task of governing the country in the face of a hostile majority
in both Houses, relying solely on the support of the Prince
Regent. The personal opposition of the Crown was the principal
cause of the delay of the settlement of the Catholic Relief Question till 1829, and the postponement of many other useful and
necessary reforms. The death of George IV. (1830) was regarded
as decidedly favourable to the progress of Parliamentary Reform,
because the Duke of Clarence (William IV.) was not so deeply
pledged against the movement, nor had he ever received pledges
on the subject from any of the leading statesmen who had bound
themselves to his father and brother, or considered themselves
bound by the promises of others. It is, moreover, a remarkable
fact that the opposition of the Lords to the Reform Bill of 1831-2
was eventually overcome by an effort of royal influence very
similar to that which had overthrown the coalition of 1783—the
personal order of the king to the Lords with regard to the
exercise of their votes on the question.

CHAPTER XVI.

THE IRISH PARLIAMENT AND THE UNION.

A N Irish Parliament was, at the outset, merely a wider form of the Ordinary Feudal Council of the Lord Deputy, the latter consisting of those barons who lived in the vicinity of the vice-regal whereabouts, the former including in addition others from more distant provinces, who were summoned only on important occasions. In 1295, however, the Lord Deputy Wogan issued directions to the sheriffs of every county and liberty to return two knights to Parliament. The date of the admission of the burgesses cannot be fixed with anything like accuracy; but it is improbable that it was earlier than the reign of Edward III. They appear for certain in 1341, and they are mentioned as an essential part of Parliament in an ordinance of 1359.

In 1495, the famous statute of Drogheda, known as Poyning's Law, produced an essential change not only in the parliamentary constitution of Ireland, but also in its jurisprudence. It enacted that no Parliament should, for the future, be held in Ireland, until the king's lieutenant has certified to the king, under the great seal, "the causes and considerations, and all such acts as it seems to them ought to be passed thereon," and until the assent of the king and Council, and permission to hold a Parliament, be obtained. It further enacted that all statutes made lately in England should be deemed good and effectual in Ireland. The result of the first clause was to secure the initiative of all Acts of Parliament to the English Council. The second was construed to mean that Acts of the English Parliament passed after the eighteenth year of Henry VII., had no operation in Ireland unless specially adopted by the Irish Parliament.

The Irish representative system was manipulated with even greater facility than the English, for not only were boroughs created or suppressed at will, but writs were issued or denied to

irticular counties for no better reason. The first trace of oppo-
tion to the Crown appears in a Parliament summoned by Sir
ienry Sidney in 1569, in which a strong country party ranged
self against the Government, denounced the illegalities com-
itted. with regard to the elections and returns, and proceeded
rther to discuss general business, including taxation. By the
ign of James I. the number of counties had reached thirty-two ;
id during the same reign the boroughs were augmented by forty
:w creations. The number of the Commons was at this time
}2 ; it gradually increased until it amounted to 300, which in
i92 became the final limit. Two hundred and sixteen of these
:presented nomination boroughs. The numbers of peers in 1613
is 122, of which 66 were present at the Parliament of that year.
hey had the privilege not only of voting by proxy, but also of
·otesting in the same vicarious fashion, and there are instances
: the infliction of fines on those who omitted to send their
·oxies to Parliament. Their numbers became enormously en-
rged under the Hanoverians, Irish peerages being lavished right
id left as a cheap and easy mode of corruption, or reward for
oubtful political service. They were also used in many cases as
step towards an English peerage for military services which
ere regarded as worth more than a baronetcy, but not quite up
) an English barony. The Catholics appear to have been at all
mes hopelessly excluded from the Irish Parliament by prevailing
istom, though not directly by law till after the Revolution, in
iite of one or two attempts, at different intervals, to procure the
:gislative adoption of the oaths of supremacy as a qualification
ir membership. The Act of the 2nd of Anne, 1704, required
oters to take the oaths of allegiance and abjuration, but the
lective franchise was not taken away from Roman Catholics in
reland till the 1st of George I., 1715.

For a long time it was doubtful whether the English Parliament
ad power to bind Ireland by laws, without the subsequent assent
f the Irish Parliament. The former always maintained the
ight, the latter denied it. Before the Revolution, however, it
·as only in very rare instances that the English Parliament
xtended the operation of its statutes to Ireland. After that date,
iowever, several laws of great importance passed in England were

made binding on Ireland as well. There was no opposition to this practice till 1719, when the Irish Lords resolved that no appeal lay from the Irish Court of Exchequer to the king in the Parliament of Great Britain. In consequence, a bill was brought in (6 Geo. I.) for the better securing the dependence of Ireland upon the Crown of Great Britain. It declared that the king and the Parliament of England could make laws which should be binding on Ireland, without any necessity for the consent of the Irish Parliament.

The parliamentary history of Ireland begins in the year 1753, when, for the first time, the Ministry were opposed by the House of Commons on a question of finance; the former claiming to dispose of a surplus, the Commons maintaining their right to appropriate it to whatever purpose they pleased. The Ministry triumphed, but from this date begins a " period of splendid eloquence, and of ardent though not always uncompromising patriotism, which lasted down to the Union." The rise of a national party naturally led to the rise of national feeling, and a desire for independence from the yoke which had so long galled the necks of the Irish. The magnificent oratory of Grattan was the strongest impulse to this Home Rule movement. He became the leader of the popular party, the soul of the opposition to England. The American war, and the reverses of England, gave the Irish at last the opportunity they so eagerly panted for, and the demand for legislative independence was unwillingly conceded in 1782. Poyning's Law, and 6 Geo. I., were repealed, and Ireland started on a chequered period of Home Rule, which was as illustrious for the splendid eloquence of the many brilliant orators who adorned it, as despicable for the deep-rooted corruption and low party spirit of the governing class. The parliamentary system naturally became more and more corrupt ; all attempts at reform were rejected by the aristocratic *clique* who monopolised the places and profits of the Administration ; the English Government could only carry any measures in Parliament by direct bribery; there was always the danger that the latter might, on its own initiative, decree something utterly incompatible with the continued connection with England. The necessity for restoring legislative union gradually forced itself on the understanding of ıost responsible statesmen, and the blunders and cruelties of the ɽish Rebellion only precipitated the event.

Legislative union, however, could only be effected with the ɔnsent of the Irish Parliament, and as both the Catholic and ɽotestant sections of the Opposition steadily declined the idea, ıere was nothing left but to buy up a majority. Borough-mongers ıust be compensated; influential men given peerages and ɽensions; many prominent people bribed directly with hard cash. ɽearly a million and a half of money was spent in this laudable ıause; and when a new Parliament met in 1800, the Government ɽas confident of success. The first night, however, was the scene ſ a tremendous contest and a striking *coup de théatre*. An ɽmendment was moved to the Address, pledging the House to ɽphold legislative independence. Orator after orator, in true Iibernian fashion, hurled forth denunciations, promises, warnings, ɽke torrents of molten lava on the heads of the cowards, the ɽaitors, the renegades who would betray their country to the ıvader. The Ministry defended themselves with equal spirit. ɩnd so the long watches of the night dragged slowly out, till ɽfteen hours had been spent in wordy warfare, and through the ɩll windows the gray dawn peeped curiously in on the angry ɽcene. Then at seven o'clock in the morning Grattan, weak, ill, ɽlmost dying, the shadow of his former self, was suddenly led into ɽhe House, dressed in the old patriotic garb of the volunteer army ɩf 1782, which had won Home Rule for Ireland. He had been ɽastily elected after midnight for Wicklow, that he might come ɽke a ghost from the grave of patriotism to speak against the Jnion. His speech was worthy of him—a splendid piece of ɽloquence—but its results were zero. The amendment was ɽhrown out, and on the 18th of February the resolutions for the Jnion were carried by a majority of forty-six. They were con-ɽrmed by act of the English Parliament, which received the royal ɽssent August 2, 1800. By the bill it was provided that four ɽishops [1] sitting in annual rotation, and twenty-eight representative ɽeers chosen for life by the whole peerage of Ireland, should ɽepresent that country in the English House of Lords. The

---

[1] The Irish Church Act, 1869, removed the Irish bishops from the Lords.

Commons of Ireland were to be present at Westminster in the
persons of one hundred members elected on the old franchise.
Provisions were also added to insure the reduction of the numbers
of the overgrown Irish peerage. It was arranged that only one
fresh Irish patent could be granted for every three that fell extinct.
This rule was to hold good till the number was reduced to one
hundred, which was to be maintained by fresh creations. It was
also specially provided that Irish non-representative peers could
sit in the House of Commons for English boroughs.

The first Parliament of the United Kingdom met January, 1801,
without a General Election.   The members of the Parliament then
sitting for England were declared, by royal proclamation, to be
members of the first Parliament of the United Kingdom of Great
Britain and Ireland, which was to meet on January 22, 1801.

CHAPTER XVII.

MEN AND DEBATES. (1760–1800.)

THE period of George III. ranks extremely high in the oratorical annals of this country. Seldom indeed has Parliament been adorned with such a galaxy of brilliant stars as those
which coruscated in the political firmament at the close of the
eighteenth century. It seems to the student almost like entering on a new and unknown country to cross the barrier which
interposes its unsubstantial shape between the reign of the third
George and that of his grandfather. There is no break in the
political history, hardly any change of policy at first, and yet it is
evident that the old era has given place to a new, that the age
of Pitt and Pelham, Granville and Bath, Newcastle and the elder
Fox, must be reckoned in the annals of the past. Pitt, it is true,
remains, but how changed from the Pitt we used to know—his
identity shrouded in the title of Chatham, his eloquence shrilling
at times to mere bombast amid the dull decorum of the House
of Lords, his brilliant genius ruined by disease, his own majestic
bearing fallen to a wreck of insolence and pride,—

" Quantum mutatus ab illo."

His whole political life during the years 1761–1770 was a grand
mistake, and it was only when he again renewed the struggle in
behalf of liberty, during the early stages of the American contest,
that he appeared to become once more inspired with all the fervour of his youth. In 1774, he came down to the House to lead
the Opposition on this question, and in the course of the debate
he delivered one of his best known speeches. He dwelt with
anxiety upon the importance of the contest into which the
country had been plunged, and with indignation upon the measures which had provoked it. He declared that the Government's imperious doctrines of submission would be insufficient

to enslave their fellow-subjects in America. "This resistance," he cried, "to your arbitrary system of taxation might well have been foreseen; it was obvious from the nature of things and of mankind; and above all from the whiggish spirit flourishing in that country. The spirit which now resists your taxation in America is the same which formerly opposed loans, benevolences and ship-money in England; the same spirit which called all England on its legs, and by the Bill of Rights vindicated the English Constitution; the same spirit which established the great fundamental, essential maxim of your liberties—that no subject of England should be taxed without his own consent. This glorious spirit of Whiggism animates three millions in America, who prefer poverty with liberty to gilded chains and sordid affluence." It was given to Chatham to die in harness, protesting to the very last his adhesion to those principles which had formed the pole-star of his brilliant though erratic career. On the 7th April, 1778, the Duke of Richmond brought forward an address in which, after recapitulating the disasters which our arms had sustained in America, he moved that it was impossible to carry on the present system of reducing that country by military force. Lord Chatham listened with the deepest attention to the Duke's extremely able speech. He had come to the House wrapped up in flannel and supported by two friends; ill, racked with gout, emaciated, the shadow of his former self, he was there in his place to oppose with his last breath the idea of separation. When he rose to reply he was received with the deepest silence; the reverence and attention of the House was most affecting. At first he spoke in a very low and feeble voice, but as he continued his tones rose to the old pitch, and thrilled his hearers as he had never thrilled them before in that House. He looked like a dying man, and yet his very weakness was impressive in its supreme dignity. He reviewed the whole history of the American question and the fatal measures which had evoked it. He protested earnestly against the idea of separation. Never would he consent to deprive the offspring of the House of Brunswick of their fairest inheritance. When he had finished, the Duke, in reply, restated his opinion and the grounds which induced him to dissent reluctantly from the noble lord. Chatham listened

'ith composure and attention, and when the Duke sat down
gain, made an eager attempt to rise, as if inspired with some
lea ; but his strength failed him, and he fell backwards. In-
tantly all was confusion. His friends pressed near to support
im ; his son sprang forward from behind the bar; the Lords,
iends and enemies alike, all crowded round. Party enmities
'ere forgotten for the moment ; every feeling was lost in the
ingle thought that the greatest soul in England was passing
lowly away, that never again would the hearts of Englishmen
eat high at the stirring eloquence of Chatham. He was re-
noved from the House in a state of insensibility, and died in
our days.

Very different indeed was the career of Lord Bute—the
ninister of the king as Pitt was of the people. Inducted into
he office of Secretary of State, and thence into the Premiership,
vithout any natural abilities for the position, he was inevitably a
onspicuous failure as a statesman. Nor was he an orator of
ny ability ; his words came slowly amid long pauses, which
ave rise to Charles Townshend's gibe of " minute-guns," and he
iever acquired the slightest control of Parliament. It is not
ingular that he resigned the administration after a year's ex-
lerience of its thorny path, and retired to the private life which
ie was so eminently calculated to adorn.

His successor, George Grenville, a haughty dictatorial man of
noderate ability, has been described as " a Speaker spoilt." He
vas essentially qualified to fill the Chair, both owing to his con-
ummate knowledge of the forms of the House and the exquisite
leasure they afforded him. He would have made an excellent
Speaker, but he preferred to become an inferior leader of the
House under Bute, and later a blundering Prime Minister. He
vas an extremely tedious orator, and his best known speech is
he one which he might have preferred not to be remembered
by. It was during the debate on the Cider Tax in 1763 :—
Grenville replied to Pitt's attacks with the assertion that if the
ionourable gentleman objected to this particular tax, he was
bound to tell them where else he would have taxes laid. " Let
iim tell me where," repeated the Prime Minister in a peevish
whine several times, " I say, sir, let him tell me where." " Gentle

shepherd, tell me where," hummed Pitt in a tone that was a most felicitous imitation of Grenville's own, quoting a popular song. "If," cried Grenville in a transport of rage, amid shrieks of laughter from the House, "gentlemen are to be treated with this contempt——" At this moment Pitt, who was leaving the House in token of the utmost disdain, turned round and made a sarcastic bow to the infuriated speaker. The nickname of the "Gentle Shepherd" clung to Grenville in consequence for several years.

Foremost among the opponents of Grenville and Bute comes the name of John Wilkes, who, having aroused the indignation of the Grenville Ministry by his pungent criticisms on the King's Speech, was accused of a seditious libel and expelled the House (1764). This circumstance, comparatively unimportant in itself in a history of Parliament, led to ulterior consequence of great moment. Later, in 1768, Wilkes stood for Middlesex, was elected by an overwhelming majority, and claimed to take his seat. He was expelled again ; was unanimously re-elected, again expelled, and once more returned to Parliament at the head of the poll. This time the Commons were determined to end the matter; and so, having solemnly expelled him again, they declared him incapable of ever sitting in the House. Moreover, though he had been returned by an overwhelming majority, they adjudged the seat to his opponent Colonel Luttrell, who had contrived to obtain some two or three hundred votes. This at once provoked a great outcry, for it was felt that ministers had done a grossly illegal and arbitrary act. The right of expulsion was undoubted, but expulsion did not create a disability, far less did it give the seat to Luttrell. The Ministry quoted the case of Walpole, but it appears doubtful whether Walpole's incapacity was grounded on his conviction of corruption or on the expulsion alone.

Wilkes was re-elected in 1774, and was allowed to take his seat by Lord North. After repeated motions on the subject, he finally succeeded in getting all the records of the proceedings against him expunged from the journals of the House.

Charles Townshend, who served in various capacities under Bute, Grenville, and Chatham, was a man of striking though very erratic genius. There appear to be considerable grounds for

spicion that during his later years he even suffered under
ental aberration. It was his ready wit which invented the
rm "minute-guns" for Bute's measured sentences. He it was
ho brought forward the ill-omened tea-tax for America in 1767,
which measure it is said that he was goaded by the taunts of
renville. His abilities are best summed up in the powerful
ilogy of Burke, to whom he seemed "a splendid orb rising
. the eastern heaven, lord of the ascendant." Of his oratory,
iat great master of the art declared that "he stated his matter
:ilfully and powerfully; he particularly excelled in a most lumi-
ous explanation and display of his subject; his style of argument
as neither trite and vulgar nor subtle and abstruse; he hit the
[ouse just between wind and water, and not being troubled
ith too anxious a zeal for any matter in question, he was never
iore tedious or more earnest than the preconceived opinions and
resent temper of his hearers required to whom he was always
i unison. He conformed exactly to the temper of the House,
nd he seemed to guide because he was always sure to follow it."
.nother writer has described him as a beautiful vessel driven
idderless before the wind and dashed to pieces at last on the
ocky bulwarks of the American coast.

Space will not permit of more than a passing allusion to
ie rough veteran Colonel Barré, and the courtly soldier-
tatesman General Conway. Many others must be dismissed
rith equal brevity. Short and inadequate notices must suffice
or even leading men like the Marquis of Rockingham, who
ucceeded Newcastle as the chieftain of the Whig houses,
iut whose talents were infinitely more calculated to enable
iim to shine in the hunting-field than in the House of Com-
nons. For though he actually twice filled the post of
'rime Minister,[1] his oratorical powers were so slender and his
:apacity for retort so utterly wanting, that even his enemies at
imes felt a certain amount of compassion and refrained from
orturing "the poor dumb animal." The Duke of Grafton,
inother of George III.'s Prime Ministers,[2] would have been
:emembered solely for the profligacy of his private life had not

---

[1] 1765-6. 1782.   [2] 1766-70.

his contests with Wilkes, the anonymous writer Junius, and the American Colonies, gained him an unenviable coign of vantage in political history. Lord North, his successor,[1] has already been touched on to some extent. In appearance he was an awkward, bulky man, with swollen cheeks and staring eyes, which earned him the nickname of "the Blind Trumpeter": and oddly enough there was also a very noticeable resemblance between him and his royal master which completed the shadow-like relation which he bore to the latter. North was an extremely able and business-like statesman, was possessed of great common-sense, a singularly sweet temper, and an extraordinary capacity for sleep under the most trying circumstances, which enabled him to score more victories over his opponents than he ever gained by mere eloquence,—clever, witty, and sparkling as his speeches always were. He was extremely short-sighted, and his weakness of vision on one occasion provoked a ridiculous scene. Happening to rise suddenly at the same time that Mr. Welbore Ellis was stooping forward, the point of his sword caught in Mr. Ellis's wig and twitched it off. The Prime Minister, however, all unconscious of this unusual ornament, walked solemnly down the House amid peals of laughter, and would probably have not discovered the cause of the general mirth for some time but for the intervention of a friend. Had Lord North been guided in his political action more by fixed principles, his reputation would have been clearer to his contemporaries and to posterity. But he covered himself with unpopularity by his early subservience to the king, and he ruined himself entirely by his coalition with Fox in 1783.

The Duke of Bedford, though concerned in the making of many Ministries and always of importance in Parliament, has more claim to be remembered as the leader of the party known as the Bedford Whigs or the "Bloomsbury gang," than any special talents as a statesman or orator. Lord Hillsborough, the first Secretary of State for the Colonies, whose secretaryship was rendered disastrously memorable by the early

---

[1] 1770-82.

ages of the contests with America; Lord Sandwich, the
ofligate companion and subsequently the equally profligate
:cuser of Wilkes, whose conduct during the Wilkes debate in
e House of Lords, in 1763, earned him in the country the
:le of "Jemmy Twitcher" (a nickname derived from the
Beggar's Opera" and equivalent to Judas Iscariot), and secured
m a place in Lord North's Ministry by the gratitude of the
ng; Lord George Germaine, whose shoulders bore the main
irden of the American war and the largest share of the
)use; Mr. Rigby, the principal friend and follower of the Duke
Bedford;—these and a host of the King's Friends must make
iy for others of greater weight.

Dunning, the great Opposition lawyer, the brilliant champion
Economical Reform, the able opponent of Lord North and
ie North system, the proposer of the celebrated resolution
ith regard to the undue influence of the king. Wedderburn
fterwards Lord Loughborough), who began life as a Whig,
it forsook his party and principles for the king's favour on
e accession of Lord North to power; whose celebrated
iilippic on Mr. Franklin's honesty is supposed to have thrown
ie latter over to the ranks of the irreconcilables. By a curious
)mbination of characteristics it was Wedderburn, Lord North's
ttorney-General, who, alone among all the Privy Council, took
)on him the responsibility of advising the king to use the
oops to suppress the Gordon Riots: and it was Lord Lough-
)rough who excited the resentment of the king against Pitt's
)ntemplated proposals for Catholic relief, in the hope of
icceeding the latter in the Premiership in the event of his resig-
ition. It may be added that he was deservedly disappointed,
id that his conduct on this occasion practically ruined any
·ospect of high office in the future. Lord Mansfield, the
:illiant orator and judge, fulfilling to the utmost the high
:omise of the youth of Murray, yet for the moment soiling his
·mine by a partial and unconstitutional vindication of the action
f the Commons in disqualifying Wilkes and giving the seat to
uttrell. Lord Camden (Chief Justice Pratt), who earned the
·atitude of his country by his bold refusal to connive at the
legal acts of the Ministry, and his uncompromising denunciation

of the practice of issuing general warrants—though the path to favour and distinction lay in submission to the royal will. The rough, haughty, and obstinate Lord Thurlow, who was known as the " King's Chancellor," and who in that capacity was inducted into Ministry after Ministry for the purpose of looking after the king's interest. In person he was imposing, almost Olympian, with rough-hewn limbs and heavy beetling brows. His oratory has been compared to rolling thunder : the language was often as forcible as the volume of sound was stupendous. "When I forget my king," he perorated on one occasion with tears rolling down his cheeks, "may my God *forget* me ; " but the wags of the Opposition suggested that the Chancellor must have amended the original version in the delivery.

One of the most curious figures of Parliament must surely have been Mr. Gerard Hamilton—Single-speech Hamilton— the man who made only one really good speech in his life, and that far surpassing all the oratorical efforts of his contemporaries. The popular theory, that he acquired his nickname from the fact that he condemned himself to silence in Parliament ever after for fear of injuring his reputation, is an exaggeration.

Many other figures well known in Parliament must pass rapidly before us. Lord Shelburne, more distinguished as the successor of Chatham and the early leader of the second Pitt, than for his own administration. Earl Temple, afterwards Marquis of Buckingham, who carried the king's orders to the Lords, to vote against Fox's India Bill. Mr. Jenkinson, afterwards Earl of Liverpool (father of the Premier of 1812-27), who acted as the mouthpiece of the king to the *King's Friends* during Lord North's Ministry ; Townsend, Glynn, and Sawbridge, the leaders of the Radicals.

Lower down the historic roll we find the name of Windham, "a man of great and original genius, with a mind cultivated with the richest stores of intellectual wealth," and a trained faculty of debate which must have rendered him the admiration of the House but for the dazzling lustre of the many brilliant stars which shone beside him in the parliamentary firmament. Of Dundas, afterwards Lord Melville, who began his olitical life under Lord North, and later attached himself with emarkable sagacity to the rising fortunes of the younger Pitt. t was his fortune to be the first President of the Board of :ontrol for India, and the last minister ever impeached by 'arliament. Of Tierney, who led the forlorn remnant of the Vhigs during the weary time when Fox and his friends seceded :om Parliament in hopeless despair (1798).

Even the brilliant Richard Brinsley Sheridan must receive ut a passing notice. We hurry on instinctively past the lesser iminaries to the three glorious constellations—Burke, Fox, Pitt.

Edmund Burke made his maiden speech in Parliament in 1766, rith striking success : from that day he became a power in ie nation, though never fully appreciated by his audience or is contemporaries generally. He took a prominent part 1 the constitutional struggles that followed, and his burning ttacks on the North Ministry, their American policy, and the ecret influence of the king, undoubtedly must be reckoned mong the most powerful of the forces which finally expelled hem from office in 1782. Then his light appeared suddenly ɔ wane. He was not appreciated by the Rockingham Min- itry ; he incurred the taint of the coalition without reaping he expected profit of the plot; he exposed himself to the harge of factiousness in his opposition to the younger Pitt ; nd it was not till the question of the impeachment of Warren Iastings attracted universal interest and attention, that he ecame once more an important figure in Parliament.

Charles James Fox, the younger son of the elder Fox, began fe as a Tory, but was soon dismissed from office by Lord Iorth for a glaring act of insubordination. He promptly went 1to opposition, and soon became a convert to Burke's views rith regard to Economical Reform. His powers of debate, rhich were of the highest order, were pushed to their utmost ɔ effect the ruin of Lord North, and in 1782 for a very short ime the sympathy of the people went entirely with the young rator ; but he was soon out of harmony with them again, nd this discord lasted for the rest of his life. There was so ttle consistency, such an apparent absence of any guiding rinciple in the whole tenour of his political conduct, that he exposed himself to the gravest charge of factiousness and political immorality. Even when undertaking what he considered to be the great public duty of the impeachment of Warren Hastings, the suspicion of party malice hung around all the action of the managers, and neutralized to some extent the salutary effects of this impressive pageant of parliamentary fudicature.

The impeachment of Hastings is of sufficient importance to justify a somewhat lengthy digression. It took its first origin from a resolution moved by Mr. Dundas in 1782, which in somewhat violent terms denounced the conduct of the Governor-General during his career of office. In February, 1785, when the question of the Nabob of Arcot's debts was raised in Parliament, Burke seized the opportunity to attack the Company's mode of government in India; and during the whole of the session of 1785, Burke, in conjunction with Philip Francis, the deadliest personal enemy that Hastings possessed, was busily engaged in collecting evidence of every kind and description that they imagined could be dragged in as a ground for his impeachment. There was still, however, such a general conviction in the country that be Hastings' faults what they might, he and he only had preserved India to us in a crisis of incalculable magnitude and his errors ought really to be accredited to the rapacity of the Company rather than his own depravity, as to render it highly probable that the question might have been allowed to drop in sheer desperation of ever obtaining a conviction. The incautious confidence of Major Scott, however,—Hastings' blundering agent, —led him to challenge an inquiry, and Burke at once replied by demanding the production of papers. At first, the Ministry were disposed to discourage all proceedings against the late Governor-General. Dundas, now President of the Board of Control, naturally felt, however, that he could not disavow his resolution of 1782, and as the question was taken up vigorously by the Opposition, the Ministry decided not to hinder the impeachment. Burke proceeded, therefore, to draw up twenty-two Articles of charge against Hastings. The latter desired to be heard in his own defence at the bar of the House.

The request was granted after some dispute, and for two days e defended himself mainly by recitations from a lengthy and xtremely prosy document. The House immediately afterwards roceeded to take evidence in support of the various charges, and ufficient ground having been thus established for going further, 1e prosecutors began to explain the various Articles in detail. "he first related to the Rohilla war, that is, the letting out of he English army of Calcutta for a large sum to the Nabob of)ude, to be employed in the conquest and massacre of a free and ndependent people, the Rohillas. The charge was true, and the leed iniquitous ; but it had practically been condoned, as Dundas 1ointed out, by Hastings' subsequent reappointment as Governor-3eneral. Therefore, though Burke, North, Fox, Francis, all in urn dilated on the villainy of such conduct, and the silence of Pitt vas a tacit condemnation of perhaps greater weight, yet the sense if the House was against the revival of the accusation, and a arge majority declared that Warren Hastings, Esq., should not 1e impeached on that Article. This failure disconcerted the 1rosecutors so thoroughly that the impeachment would have been it once abandoned in despair had they not felt they had no :hoice but to go through with it in order to justify its inception.

The second charge was based on the facts that Hastings had lemanded of Cheyte Sing, Rajah of Benares,—a tributary of the Company—an extraordinary war contribution of £50,000 ; that in the refusal of the latter to pay, and offers of a bribe for remission if the claim, the late Governor-General had raised his demand :o half a million ; and on further refusals to pay, had seized the :ity of Benares, and deposed the Rajah. On this point Mr. Pitt, :o the astonishment of many, expressed himself in favour of the impeachment. He considered Hastings perfectly justified in demanding the war contribution and in inflicting a further fine for contumacy and attempts at bribery, but the fine imposed was monstrous and exorbitant. He passed a high eulogy on Hastings, and denounced the party malice which had distorted into a design of ruining Cheyte Sing a very simple intention to exact to the uttermost farthing all that could be claimed for the Company. But he avowed that in his opinion the charge of violence and exorbitancy was so far made out that he must vote for this Article of the impeachment. The result of his example was a complete

triumph for the prosecution. The Benares charge was agreed
to in a week; the Begum charge was carried early in the next
session; twenty Articles of impeachment were drawn up and
passed, and Burke was ordered to take them up to the House of
Lords. Black Rod in due course effected the arrest of Hastings,
but the prisoner was subsequently released on heavy bail. A
motion was also made for the impeachment of Sir Elijah Impey,
late Chief Justice of India, who was charged with complicity in
many of the criminal transactions of which Hastings was accused.
Impey, however, met the charges with such courage, promptitude,
and skill, that he escaped. He had been obviously engaged in
many questionable matters, but there were strong extenuating
circumstances, and he produced testimonials in his favour from
men of the most unblemished character. The Commons, therefore, voted that there was not sufficient ground for putting him
on his trial.

The proceedings opened February 18, 1788. Westminster
Hall had been fitted up with red cloth and other decorations for
the occasion. The queen and three princesses were present.
The ambassadors' box was full of the representatives of all
nations. The peeresses' gallery shone with a dazzling mass of
rainbow hues and glancing jewels; the brightest eyes in the kingdom gazed now with pity and commiseration at the illustrious
prisoner, anon dilating with horror at the monstrous cruelties of
which he was accused. The peers were present in their robes,
headed by the hereditary Earl Marshal of England, Charles
Howard, Duke of Norfolk;—among them might be seen the
numerous princes of the blood royal. The Lord Chancellor sat
on a throne as president of the court; opposite to him, on one
side was the space assigned to the prisoner and his counsel; on
the other the managers' box, in which were congregated some of
the greatest orators of the day, among others Burke, Windham,
Sheridan, Fox. The preliminaries occupied two days, and then
Burke was called upon to open the first charge.

His speech extended over nearly four days. He began with
a rapid and brilliant survey of the history of the British settle-
--ment in India. Then he devoted himself to the Herculean
· of proving, by an accumulation of quotations from various

)riental books of law, that the gentle and kindly natives of Hin-
ostan were wholly unaccustomed to cruel and arbitrary treatment
ll they became oppressed by the heavy yoke of the bloodthirsty
'nglish—a statement which, had the audience possessed the
lightest acquaintance with India and Indian history, must have
een received with shouts of mocking laughter which not even
ie dignity of the court and the importance of the occasion would
ave been sufficient to repress. On the third day he entered into
)ose and general charges of bribery and peculation. The fourth
ras occupied by the horrible details of atrocities alleged to be
erpetrated by one Deby Sing, a native lieutenant appointed by
Iastings, for all of which horrors Burke insisted that Hastings
iust be regarded as personally responsible. This part of his
ration was couched in the most tremendous and awful language,
nd it produced an extraordinary effect on its audience. " The
rhole statement," says his biographer, " is appalling and heart-
ickening in the extreme ; a convulsive sensation of horror, affright,
nd smothered execration pervaded all the male part of his
iearers, and audible sobbings and screams, attended with tears
.nd faintings, the female. His own feelings were scarcely less
)verpowering; he dropped his head upon his hands, and for some
ninutes was unable to proceed; he recovered sufficiently to go
)n a little further, but being obliged to cease from speaking twice
t intervals, his Royal Highness the Prince of Wales, to relieve
iim, at length moved the adjournment of the House."

His peroration at the end of this four days' labour was ex-
essively fine. He drew a striking picture of this heinous criminal,
his monster of iniquity, this Warren Hastings, standing at the
iar of the most renowned tribunal in the world, and in the actual
)resence of an assembly illustrious not only for the high birth
.nd ancient lineage of many of its members, but for the legal
alents and the ecclesiastical dignities of the rest. Nor was a prose-
:utor wanting to this great trial : all the Commons of England
tood forth to prosecute, " resenting as their own the indignities
hat have been offered to the people of India. . . . There-
ore it is," concluded Burke, in his last impassioned appeal, " that,
)rdered by the House of Commons of Great Britain, I impeach
Varren Hastings of high crimes and misdemeanours. I impeach

him in the name of the Commons of Great Britain, whose parliamentary trust he has abused, whose national character he has dishonoured. I impeach him in the name of the people of India, whose laws, rights, and liberties he has subverted, whose properties he has destroyed, whose country he has laid waste and desolate. I impeach him in the name of human nature itself, which he has cruelly outraged, injured, and oppressed in both sexes. And I impeach him in the name and by virtue of those eternal laws of justice, which ought equally to pervade every age, condition, rank, and situation in the world."

When Burke had concluded, the managers proposed that the charges should be heard and disposed of separately; but after a debate this course was rejected, as obviously unjust and oppressive to the accused. Lord Thurlow denounced, with justifiable severity, the extraordinary extravagance of the language of Burke's opening speech, and declared that he ought to be held to the strictest proof of his allegations. If the charges were true, the severest punishment could not be too harsh for such a criminal; but they must be proved in a regular way before any punishment or even annoyance ought to be offered to the prisoner. To this decision of the Lords must be mainly attributed the enormous length and tediousness of the trial. The whole series of charges had to be stated one after the other before any evidence could be taken. The opening speeches, moreover, were delivered in turn by the greatest orators of the day, and were of extraordinary power and brilliancy. Men flocked to hear them as to a rhetorical display, without regarding much their true importance to the accused or to the country; nor was it possible to attach any very inordinate weight to them at a time when no scrap of evidence had been advanced in their support. Then when the time came at last for taking the evidence, the opening speeches were a thing of the past; the impression produced by them had faded faintly away, and the evidence adduced seemed poor and mean and wholly insufficient as a foundation for an impeachment. The invectives of Burke were listened to with disgust, and great as undoubtedly were the crimes of Hastings, it was felt that the magnitude of his services should fully outweigh them. In 1792, Burke himself renounced sixteen of his charges, and in consequence all interest in the trial disappeared, though it was not till 1795 that Hastings was finally acquitted. The trial is chiefly remarkable, besides the efforts of oratory that it elicited, for the fact that in 1791, a dissolution having occurred since the last session of Parliament, the question was raised again whether an impeachment did not terminate on a dissolution. After a full discussion, it was voted in both Houses, by large majorities, that by the law and custom of Parliament, an impeachment continues from one session and from one Parliament to another until it is ended by judgment given.

Next in oratorical power to Burke's opening speech must be reckoned Sheridan's vigorous appeal on the Begum charge, which accused Hastings of torturing and robbing the princesses of Oude, or at least of conniving at the evil deeds of others and condoning them for a share in the spoil.

Returning to our original subject, the verdict of history gives to Burke the palm for oratory; to Fox, the superiority in debating power. There is abundant evidence that Fox could on occasion rise to heights of rhetoric almost emulating the pitch of his great rival; but no speech of Fox's ever surpassed the tremendous invective, the graphic descriptions, the impassioned appeals of Burke's opening speech against Warren Hastings.

The third of this brilliant trio, William Pitt, the second son of the great Earl of Chatham, produced at once a striking impression in Parliament by his maiden effort, which dealt with the question of Economical Reform. Old members said that no such speech had been heard there since the days of Chatham, except perhaps from Fox. From this time he occupied a distinguished place in the ranks of the Opposition that hunted North from office.

He was Chancellor of the Exchequer and Prime Minister before he had attained the age of twenty-four. His Premiership, moreover, lasted for nearly a quarter of a century. His career, like that of Burke, is divided into two parts. During the first he played the part of a liberal and enlightened statesman; the second saw him drifting gradually to the harshest measures of reaction and repression. The point of divergence is, roughly, the year 1792, the eve of the French revolutionary war. The same year saw the outbreak of the quarrel which severed the long friendship of Burke and Fox.

The question of the Revolution was first discussed in Parliament on the 6th of February, 1790. Mr. Fox, speaking in opposition to the army estimates, declared that he " had never thought it expedient to make the internal circumstances of other nations the subject of much conversation in that House, but if ever there could be a period at which he should be less jealous of an increase of the army from any danger to be apprehended to the Constitution, the present was that precise period. The example of a neighbouring nation had proved that former imputations on armies were unfounded calumnies, and it was now universally known throughout Europe that a man by becoming a soldier did not cease to be a citizen."

On the 9th of February, Mr. Burke spoke in a far different strain. He declared that " France was at this time in a political light to be considered as expunged out of the system of Europe. Whether she could ever appear in it again as a leading power was not easy to determine ; but at present he considered France as not politically existing, and most assuredly it would take much time to restore her to her former active existence. . . . In a political view France was low indeed. . . . He regretted that his right hon. friend (Mr. Fox) had dropped even a word expressive of exultation on that circumstance, or that he seemed of opinion that the objection to standing armies was at all lessened by it. He attributed this opinion of Mr. Fox entirely to his known zeal for the best of all causes—liberty." He protested, however, that grieved as he was to differ from his friend, in whose opinion he had hitherto had such confidence, on this occasion he was obliged to dissent. He then drew a broad distinction between the Revolution of 1688 and the French Revolution— expatiating on the wisdom of the legislators of the former period, the folly and wickedness of the agitators of France.

Mr. Fox rose next to declare that "it gave him a concern which it was almost impossible to describe on perceiving himself driven to the hard necessity of making at least a short answer to the latter part of a speech to which he had listened with the greatest attention, and which, some observations and arguments excepted, he admired as one of the wisest and most brilliant flights of oratory ever delivered in that House. There were parts of it, however, which he wished had either been omitted or deferred to some more fit occasion." He declared his affection and esteem for Burke, and passed a very warm eulogy on the latter's character. He declared himself a friend to liberty, but he would never lend himself to any scheme for introducing any dangerous innovation in our excellent Constitution. He was not, however, an enemy to every kind of innovation. "That Constitution which all revered, owed its perfection to innovation; for however admirable the theory, experience was the true test of its order and beauty." . . . "The scenes of bloodshed and cruelty which had been acted in France no man could have heard of without lamenting; but still, when the severe tyranny under which the people had so long groaned was considered, the excesses which they committed in their endeavour to shake off the yoke of despotism might, he thought, be spoken of with some degree of compassion; and he was persuaded that, unsettled as their present estate appeared, it was preferable to their former condition, and that ultimately it would be for the advantage of this country that France had regained her freedom."

Burke thereupon expressed his pleasure at Fox's explanation; but Sheridan, who appears to have wished to create a complete rupture between them, rose and defended the cruelties of the French Revolutionists on the ground that the accursed rule of the Bourbons had stripped the people of all feelings of justice and humanity, concluding by denouncing Burke as the advocate of despotism. Burke retorted angrily that henceforth he and his honourable friend were separated in politics. He had been cruelly misrepresented. "All who knew him could not avoid acknowledging that he was the professed enemy of despotism in every shape, whether it appeared as the splendid tyranny of Louis XIV., or the outrageous democracy of the present Government of France, which levelled old distinctions in society."

Fourteen months, however, elapsed before an open rupture occurred between the two statesmen. On the evening of April 21, 1791, at the close of a speech with regard to the Russian armament, Fox took the opportunity to pass a high eulogy on the

French Revolution. " With regard to the change of system which had taken place in that country, he knew different opinions were entertained by different men, but he for one admired the new Constitution of France considered altogether as the most stupendous and glorious edifice of liberty which had been erected on the foundation of human integrity in any time or country." Burke would probably have replied to this by an outburst, but he was prevented.

On May 6, 1791, however, a curious scene occurred when the Quebec Bill was re-committed. This being a period which members usually select for airing grievances, Burke without any preliminary plunged into a denunciation of *The Rights of Man*, a book lately imported from France. Fox accused him of wandering from the point, and the House called him to order. Burke replied bitterly in the words of Lear, that he saw all parties, " Blanche, Tray, and Sweetheart, all barking at him now." Pitt endeavoured to obtain a hearing for him, but Fox insisted that the French Constitution had nothing to do with the Quebec Bill, and added a sarcastic taunt that " minute discussions of great events without information did no honour to the pen that wrote or the tongue that spoke the words." Burke, furious and resolved, rose, accused Fox of disorder and a personal attack on himself, and declared their friendship at an end. He then adverted once more to the crimes which had accompanied the progress of the Revolution, and avowed that with his last breath he would exclaim, " Fly from the French Revolution." Thus in disorder and insult ended the friendship between the two Whig leaders.

In January, 1792, Mr. Pitt declared his intention of reducing the military and naval establishment in view of the favourable prospects of peace—by the irony of events only a year afterwards a war was destined to break out which would desolate the whole of Europe for nearly a quarter of a century. The peroration of this celebrated speech is the most perfect specimen of the stately and majestic flow of Mr. Pitt's eloquence. After alluding to the accumulation of capital and the growth of commerce he continued :—

" Such are the circumstances which appear to me to have

:ontributed most immediately to our prosperity. But these again
ire connected with others yet more important. They are ob-
/iously and necessarily connected with the duration of peace, the
:ontinuance of which on a secure and permanent footing must
:ver be the first object of the foreign policy of this country.
They are connected still more with its internal tranquillity and
vith the natural effects of a free but well-regulated government.
What is it which has produced in the last hundred years so rapid
in advance beyond what can be traced in any other period of
)ur history ? . What but that during that time, under the mild and
ust government of the illustrious princes of the family now on the
hrone, a general calm has prevailed through the country beyond
vhat was ever before experienced; and that we have also enjoyed
n greater purity and perfection the benefit of those original
)rinciples of our Constitution which were ascertained and
:stablished by the memorable events that closed the century pre-
:eding? This is the great and governing cause the operation of
vhich has given scope to all the other circumstances which I
iave enumerated. It is this union of liberty with law which, by
aising a barrier equally firm against the encroachments of power
ind the violence of popular commotion, affords to property its
ust security, produces the exertion of genius and labour, the
:xtent and solidity of credit, the circulation and increase of
:apital; which forms and upholds the national character, and sets in
notion all the springs which actuate the great mass of the com-
nunity through all its various descriptions. The laborious industry
)f those useful and extensive classes (who will I trust be in a
)eculiar degree this day the object of the consideration of the
House), the peasantry and yeomanry of the country, the skill and
ngenuity of the artificer, the experiments and improvements of
he wealthy proprietor of land, the bold speculations and successful
.dventures of the opulent merchant and enterprising manufacturer,
—these are all to be traced to the same source, and all derive
rom hence both their encouragement and their reward. On this
)oint, therefore, let us principally fix our attention, let us pre-
erve this first and most essential object, and every other is in
ur power. Let us remember that the love of the Constitution,
hough it acts as a sort of natural instinct in the hearts of Eng-

lishmen, is strengthened by reason and reflection, and every day confirmed by experience ; that it is a Constitution that we do not merely admire from traditional reverence, which we do not flatter from prejudice or habit, but which we cherish and value because we know that it practically secures the tranquillity and welfare both of individuals and the public, and provides, beyond any other frame of government which has ever existed, for the real and useful ends which form at once the only true foundation and only rational object of all political societies. . . .

" The season of our severe trial is at an end. . . . This is a state not of hope only but of attainment. . . . On this situation and this prospect, fortunate beyond our most sanguine expectations, let me congratulate you and the House and my country, and before I conclude, let me express my earnest wish, my anxious and fervent prayer, that now in this period of our success, for the sake of the present age and of posterity, there may be no intermission in that vigilant attention by Parliament to every object connected with the revenue, the resources and the credit of the State which has carried us through all our difficulties and led to this rapid and wonderful improvement ; that still keeping pace with the exertions of the legislature, the genius and spirit, the loyalty and public virtue, of a great and free people may long deserve and (under favour of Providence) may insure the continuance of this unexampled prosperity; and that Great Britain may thus remain for ages in possession of these distinguished advantages under the protection and safeguard of that Constitution to which, as we have been truly told from the throne, they are principally to be ascribed, and which is indeed the great source and the best security of all that can be dear and valuable to a nation."

CHAPTER XVIII.

THE OLD TORY MINISTRY.

THE resignation of Pitt on the Catholic question may be conveniently accepted as the commencement of a new a of the internal life, and above all, the prominent figures in arliament. The line must not, however, be drawn too hard id fast. The two periods to a great extent overlap one another. urke, indeed, has departed from the scene, but Pitt and Fox irvive till 1806. Windham, Sheridan, Tierney, Dundas have ot yet ended their career. Canning, Grenville, Grey, Wellesley, ddington, Scott, Wilberforce, and many others of the new men ad made their mark in Parliament before the historic milestone f 1801 had been actually passed. From this date, however, ie old order changes surely, giving place to the new.

The resignation of Pitt, moreover, was followed by a rearrange-
ient of parties in consequence of a total disruption of the old 'ory party, which had supported him so faithfully through the risis of the revolutionary war. One section, headed by Lord irenville, gradually formed relations with Fox, which drew them i time entirely away from the side of Pitt, and definitely com-
iitted them to advanced views on Catholic Relief. Another, eaded by Addington, took up the position of Tories and yet ot Pittites—recalling the old intermediate attitude of the King's 'riends during the first decade of George's reign, and assuming ery much the same relation to the king. It was obviously ievitable that in the end the two sections of Pitt and Adding-
on should unite once more to carry on the government on the ld lines, and the followers of Fox and Grenville should imilarly coalesce into a coherent Opposition.

At first, however, disunion was rife. Grenville would not join 'itt without Fox; Addington was jealous and resentful of Pitt's uperiority. Pitt's second Ministry was, therefore, necessarily a ailure, weakened as it was by the defection of Grenville, the hostility of Fox, and the treachery of Addington. The death of Pitt rendered a temporary union of All the Talents of every party necessary in order to carry on the government at all; but where the sole bond of coherence is necessity, the appearance of amity which results is necessarily hollow, and the Ministry really existed but at the sufferance of the king, and inevitably fell when they excited his hostility.

The ensuing years were a period of doubt and expectation. The Tories were seeking for a man and a Government which should be worthy of the name. The Opposition, now united under the leadership of Lords Grey and Grenville, were momentarily expecting the hour when the Tories should be finally weighed in the balance and found wanting, or when the malady of the king should commit the government into the hands of the Prince of Wales, to be delegated of course by him to his old comrades, the Whigs. The actual seizure of the king (1810) was, however, attended by very different results from those anticipated. The Prince of Wales had no special liking for Lord Grey or Lord Grenville personally, nor had they ever assumed towards him the intimate relations of his old rollicking companions, Fox and Sheridan. He now took it into his head to be offended with the amount of support they were ready to afford him in the Regency question. The result was a quarrel, which threw him over to the Tories. The Tories, moreover, by making Catholic Relief an open question, were able to get rid of a great bone of contention in their own ranks, for it was widely felt that whatever respect might have been previously due to the king's religious scruples, whatever reluctance might have existed against a course of action so calculated to re-arouse his mental disease, all such considerations were now entirely robbed of their weight by his madness, and the very general disbelief in the principles or scruples, religious or otherwise, of the Prince Regent. Under these conditions the Tory Ministry of Lord Liverpool was formed (1812), which was destined to such a long span of existence. Its chiefs were drawn from the party of Addington, but it relied in addition on the remnants of the party of Pitt,—the young men,—headed by Canning. The more liberal

rinciples for which Canning was afterwards celebrated were as
et in the future of his career, and it was inevitable that the
;overnment should be conducted on the strictest Tory lines of
epression and reaction. It was this same Government, with its
iews modified in no small measure by the ever-increasing import-
nce of the more liberal or Canningite section of the party, and
:s *personnel* similarly altered by the irresistible hand of death or
he course of natural development, which lasted under the
uccessive premierships of Lord Liverpool, Mr. Canning, Lord
;oderich, and the Duke of Wellington, right down to 1830.
*he Administrations of Canning and Goderich were but an inter-
ide, however, lasting barely over a year (1827). Goderich has
ven the distinction of being the only Prime Minister who never
net Parliament, owing to his resignation before it had assembled.
*he true successor of Lord Liverpool was the Duke of Welling-
on.

The great questions of the time, apart from the conduct of the
rar, are Catholic Relief and Parliamentary Reform—the latter
rill be dealt with separately in the next chapter. The former
ras undoubtedly the most prominent subject in Parliament during
his period, and it progressed but slowly,—beginning with total
uppression by the royal will, rising gradually to the position of
n open question in Lord Liverpool's Ministry, obtaining at last a
najority in the Commons, forcing the unwilling hands of the Lords
nd the Government by repeated triumphs in the Lower House
)acked up by a vigorous extra-parliamentary agitation, until
inally, on the proposal of the Duke of Wellington's Govern-
nent, the Catholics were admitted to Parliament by the Emanci-
)ation Act, 1829.

Among the leading men in Parliament during this period, the
iame of Addington cannot fail to strike the imagination very
:arly, if chronological order be alone considered. Mr. Addington,
ifterwards Lord Sidmouth, was an excellent Speaker ; he became
ater, however, a very inferior Prime Minister, and he filled the
)ffice of Home Secretary in a manner of which it is difficult to
;peak in measured terms of dispraise. He was a remarkable
nstance of successful mediocrity and the power of interest. His
:arly rise was due to the patronage of Pitt ; his later success to

the friendship of the king.   He was naturally marked out as
the butt of the wags of Parliament.   His father's profession
furnished the nickname of the " Doctor," his own career that of
the " Speaker."   Probably the fact that is most generally known
about him is the gibe in which Canning summed up his comparative merits—

> " As London is to Paddington,
>   So is Pitt to Addington."

The Duke of Portland occupied in two Cabinets the position
which a figure-head holds on board a vessel—not expected to do
anything, but supplying a name to the whole.   Mr. Percival, the
third in order of the Tory Prime Ministers, was a brilliant speaker
and an able and patriotic statesman, who had, however, too little
influence to be of much real importance.   Perhaps the most
noticeable event in his Ministry was his assassination by a lunatic
named Bellingham while leaving the House of Commons, May,
1812.   Lord Liverpool's chief claims to notice are purely official.
He became Foreign Secretary to Addington in 1801, under the
courtesy title of Lord Hawkesbury, by which he was known till his
father's death in 1808.   In 1804, he accepted the Home Office
from Pitt, to which, after the interlude of the Talents Ministry,
he returned in 1807.   Two years later, as Secretary for War and
the Colonies, he undertook the management of the Peninsular
Campaigns.   In 1812, he became Prime Minister, and began a
career of office which is memorable in the annals of Parliament
for its unusual duration, over fourteen years, though it is but just
to add that Lord Liverpool was really as little responsible for the
great historical events with which it is associated, as for the
mistaken policy with which it attempted to govern the country.
Like his father, he was not eminent in debate, and he wisely
refrained from exhibiting the fact.   His talents were far inferior to
his virtues ; and though he may be entitled to respect, it would
be difficult to leave him with any feeling of admiration.

Among the nominal subordinates in the Tory Ministry there is
only space to briefly mention a few.   Scott (Lord Eldon), like
Dundas, attached himself very early to the fortunes of the younger
Pitt, and later acquired such a hold on the affections of the king,
that in the latter's own words he gave him the Great Seal in 1807

from his heart." He filled the high office of Lord Chancellor
n two successive occasions—the last period extending over
venty years, during the whole of which he proved himself the
reconcilable and most dangerous opponent of every project of
:form mooted in Parliament. Earl Bathurst was Foreign Secre-
iry between the years 1809-1812, after which he went to the War
nd Colonial Office, and remained there till 1827; but in neither
ipacity did he show enough administrative talent to rescue him
·om the Slough of Despond, in which all the "old stumped-up
'ories" lie. Mr. Vansittart, during his career at the Exchequer,[1]
arned the unenviable distinction of being the worst financier that
ver brought forward a budget. His successor, Mr. Robinson
ifterwards Lord Goderich and Earl of Ripon), whose extra-
rdinary cheerfulness in the face of the most unfavourable revenue
tatements gained him the nickname of "Prosperity," was hope-
:ssly feeble at the Exchequer. Nor was the brief period of
Goody Goderich's" Ministry remarkable for anything except
ie fact of its existence and the rapidity of its termination. Mr.
²esey Fitzgerald (afterwards Lord Fitzgerald and Vesey) will
robably be remembered for his rejection at the Clare Election
1 1828, and the impetus which this event gave to the Catholic
lelief movement, long after the merits which caused his elevation
o the Board of Trade, and consequent necessity for re-election,
.ave been forgotten.

The Whig Opposition was neither a strong nor a compact body.
ts natural leaders, after the death of Fox, were Lords Grey and
;renville, who both suffered under the disadvantage of being in
he House of Lords. William Wyndham Lord Grenville (son
.f George Grenville) began his parliamentary career as a. sup-
.orter of Pitt in the struggle with the Coalition, 1783, and was
ewarded with the Foreign Office in Pitt's Ministry. The Catholic
[uestion shook his ancient loyalty, and drew him over to the side
.f Fox. The part that he played in Parliament from this time
vas not very important; and it has been aptly remarked that his
·efusal to join Pitt in 1804 practically placed his new party on the
.helf for over a quarter of a century, with the exception of the

---

[1] 1812-23.

brief year of his Ministry of All the Talents. Lord Grey, after his transference to the House of Lords, took very little active part in politics for some time; and, indeed, in the face of the overwhelming Tory majority which was the result of Pitt's lavish creations, any vigorous action was for some time impossible. Except Lord Grey, the Opposition had no leader fit to inaugurate a policy or lead a party. Mr. Tierney and Mr. Ponsonby were the nominal chiefs in the House of Commons; but Mr. Tierney's views were too moderate for many of the Liberal sections; and Mr. Ponsonby, on one occasion, avowed at a meeting of the whole party that he neither knew what proposal the Government intended to make, nor what course it would be advisable to pursue.

Disunited, however, as the Opposition might be, it contained in its ranks many distinguished men—Sir Samuel Romilly, celebrated for his philippics on the slave-trade and the criminal laws; Mr. Joseph Hume, the leader of the parliamentary Radicals, who, with indefatigable industry, perseverance, and ability, devoted himself to attacking the reckless financial policy of Lord Liverpool's Government; Mr. Horner, whose name is also associated with the question of economical and currency reform; Mr. Wilberforce, the zealous champion of freedom, the leader of the crusade against the slave-trade; Sir Francis Burdett, who sustained the whole weight of the Parliamentary Reform movement, during the period of its greatest discredit and absence of hope; Lord Henry Petty, afterwards the celebrated Marquis of Lansdowne; Mr. Whitbread, the able coadjutor of Wilberforce in the campaign for the release of the slaves; Earl Fitzwilliam, a true representative of the old Whig grandees, who, having begun life amid the traditions of the Whig aristocracy, lived to be reckoned in the ranks of the reformers. Mr. Brougham was beginning to make a great name in Parliament, though his time had not yet fully come. Mr. Holborne, Mr. Denman, and many others, must be disposed of with the barest allusion.

The most interesting figure and most prominent statesman on the Tory side before 1822 is Lord Castlereagh. His career embodies the parliamentary and political history of the time.

Robert Steward, Lord Castlereagh, afterwards Marquis of Londonderry, held various offices in the different Tory Cabinets.

As Foreign Secretary, under Lord Liverpool, he rose to the position of real leader of the whole party, and his name is identified with the repressive policy which formed the mainspring of government till his death in 1822. He was an obscure orator, and what was still more remarkable in an Irishman, a dull one. He appeared neither to know the way to his meaning, nor to possess the power of conveying it to others; he rarely attempted to illustrate or adorn his argument by classical quotation or historical example; his metaphors were, as a rule, extremely confused. He took three-quarters of an hour in telling the House of Commons that he did not intend to make any motion on the Treaties of Vienna, but that any private member was at liberty to do so; though another man would have occupied some five minutes at most. On another occasion, in the midst of a long and unintelligible oration on some unknown topic, he stopped suddenly and exclaimed, "So much, Mr. Speaker, for the law of nations." He once declared to the House that he had "now proved that the Tower of London is a common law principle," and he committed himself in perfect good faith to the following remarkable historical estimate of the condition of Spain:—"That the pendulum had swung so far on the side of Jacobinism, that it afterwards swung quite as far on the side of anti-Jacobinism, which had prevented its settling in a middle point." In the excitement of a moment he entreated the country gentlemen not to turn their backs on themselves; and it is even asserted that he accomplished the incomprehensible feat of concluding one of his speeches with the monosyllable "its."

With regard to the two great questions of the day he held divided views. He was a firm opponent of Parliamentary Reform, and, indeed, of all measures which had the faintest democratic origin or tendency; but he was favourable to the claims of the Catholics. He took a prominent share in introducing the Six Acts, 1819, saying with his usual boldness, "I rise for the purpose of proposing to the House measures of severe coercion." He obstructed, and successfully obstructed, all the efforts of Sir Samuel Romilly for the reform of the criminal law and the suppression of the slave-trade; and he listened unmoved to the accusation of buying colonies at the Treaty of Vienna with "the blood of Africa." As long as he lived he formed an insuperable barrier across the path of progress; his death marks an epoch in the history of Lord Liverpool's Cabinet, of Parliament, and the world. Yet one of his warmest opponents, Grattan, the old Irish patriot, on his death-bed said to his friends, " Don't be hard on Castlereagh—he loves our country."

His suicide, in 1822, transferred the reins of power to his great rival, Canning, and began a period which was remarkable not only for a considerable change in home and foreign policy, but also for the brilliance of the oratory in the House of Commons. George Canning was a shining wit and an orator of the most dazzling type. The speech in which he explained that a few days had sufficed for the decision, preparation, and despatch of the armament to Portugal to resist the designs of Spain, is, perhaps, the one which produced the greatest effect on his contemporaries; but his declaration that, by acknowledging the independence of the South American Republics, he had "called in the New World to redress the balance of the Old," has become almost an idiom in the English language. He had begun life in Parliament as the friend of Pitt, and clung to the latter's fortunes till his death. He took office in the Portland Ministry, but his quarrel with Castlereagh ended in his resignation, and practically condemned him to parliamentary insignificance till 1822.

On the resignation of Lord Liverpool, he was pointed out as the natural successor, and yet no man could have been more unfitted for that position. He was personally unpopular with the great mass of the Tory party; his views were regarded by most of his then colleagues with intense suspicion of their progressive character; his own party was too small to be of much value; his ideas were scarcely advanced enough to enable him to unite with the Opposition. As soon as his acceptance of office was known, six of his colleagues resigned. This wrung from him a bitter declaration to the House that his "position was not that of gratified ambition," and that he would never consent to be a mere "helot," executing the orders of some man who was his real inferior. The result was that his Cabinet was necessarily recruited by a number of moderate Liberals, and that Canning himself, during the short space of his Ministry, became the butt of Parlia-

nent, baited by both Tories and Liberals with a savage ferocity
which recalls the memory of the fierce debates on the American
war, and which exercised a terrible—nay, fatal—effect on Canning's excitable nature. Like Burke, he saw " Blanche, Tray, and
Sweetheart, all barking at him," and it needed Lord North's sweet
temper and somniferous character to bear the fearful strain.
Easily exasperated by the most insignificant gad-fly, howled at by
the Tories as a renegade, distrusted by many of his own party,
thwarted continually by the king, it is no wonder that his temper
and his health gave way, and he sank into his grave—literally
killed by Parliament.

This period was also graced by two orators of remarkable power.
Mr. Brougham, afterwards Lord Brougham, and Chancellor in the
Reform Ministry, well earned his great reputation. "With prodigious force of argument," says a contemporary, "he struck
down any common adversary, pouring fiery sarcasm and unsparing,
overwhelming refutation upon his head, and leaving him an object
of ridicule or of pity, crushed beneath the weight of accumulated
epithets, and a burning mass of invective."

Of the three principal stars of Parliament, Mr. Plunket has the
pre-eminence for the most perfect oratory, the most thorough
command of his fancy, the greatest skill in elucidating and adorn-
ing his argument. As a rule, he spoke chiefly on the Catholic
question; but Earl Russell declares that his defence of his own
conduct, in answer to Mr. Brownlow, was a great triumph of
oratorical art; and his answer to Brougham, on the proposal to
make a provision for the Roman Catholic clergy, is deservedly
celebrated.

The substitution of Mr. Peel for Lord Sidmouth at the Home
Office, in 1822, was almost as important an advance on the Tory
side as the succession of Canning to Castlereagh. The adoption
of the Reform question by Lord John Russell relieved it in a
great measure from the odium which had clung round it while in
the hands of Burdett. The growing importance of Copley was to
provide the Tories with a successor to Lord Eldon (1827) in the
person of Lord Lyndhurst. Long years of service as Secretary
at War were preparing Lord Palmerston for higher things when
the Reform period should be overpast. All four belong really to

the later days. No part of their parliamentary career before 1830 can compare with the great deeds which followed.

Last, but by no means least, almost like the-chief figure in a pageant, comes the soldier-statesman Wellington, who brought to the government of the country, and the management of Parliament, the principles of strict military discipline. Discipline must be obeyed; waverers, as he esteemed the remnants of Canning's party, must resign or be expelled from the Cabinet; the king's orders must be paramount; above all, the trust conferred on himself must be defended to the very last, not to be renounced but by the king's own command. This singular theory induced him to drive Ireland to the very verge of insurrection on the Catholic question before he would yield a jot. Even then he did not think it necessary to resign. Just as he had accepted a defeat on the Test and Corporation Acts (1828), and consented to their repeal, so now he forced his unwilling Cabinet to bring in the Catholic Emancipation Act (1829). The part that Wellington played in Parliament up to 1832 was altogether disastrous to the country and his own reputation; but it was amply atoned for by the great parliamentary services of the after-years.

CHAPTER XIX.

PARLIAMENTARY REFORM.

SECTION 1.—*Early History* (1745–1830).

THE question of Parliamentary Reform, which had been first aroused by Cromwell, was suffered to drop again at the Restoration, not to be revived till the year 1745, when Sir Francis Dashwood, a Tory,—afterwards Bute's Chancellor of the Exchequer,—moved an amendment to the Address, advocating the reform of Parliament. It was also strongly advanced by the elder Pitt in opposition, though it must be confessed that he did absolutely nothing in that direction when he was actually in office. The question was brought forward again in different forms by the various sections of the Opposition under George III. as the true means of effectually curbing the corrupt power of the king. Wilkes, however, was the first to give actual expression to these views. In 1776, he introduced a bill proposing that additional members should be allotted to London, Middlesex, Yorkshire, and other large counties; that a number of rotten boroughs should be disfranchised and added to the county constituencies; that Manchester, Leeds, Birmingham, and other large towns should be enfranchised. This bill was, however, rejected, as were also a motion for reform moved by the Duke of Richmond in 1780, and two motions moved by Pitt in favour of considering the representation, in 1782, 1783. The Reform question, in fact, was as yet really in the hands of the extreme party led by Wilkes, Horne Tooke, and the Society of Friends of the People. The king was steadily opposed to it. Burke and the mass of the Whigs disliked the idea excessively; Fox only coquetted with it as yet, as seeming to open a way to break the power of the king and facilitate his own return to office. The only prominent public man who was sincerely anxious for the

reform of the representation was the younger Pitt, who had inherited his father's views.   In 1785, therefore, he brought forward
a bill which would have disfranchised thirty-six rotten boroughs,
and admitted copyholders to the franchise, giving the seats
gained to the large towns and counties.   It also proposed to
compensate the owners of the disfranchised boroughs—in fact, to
buy them out.   This bill was liked neither by the king nor the
Whigs ; and was, in consequence, thrown out.   The outbreak
of the French Revolution shelved the question almost entirely
till 1809, when it revived once more under the auspices of
Sir Francis Burdett and the extreme Radical party.   Burdett's
advocacy did the question more harm than good, nor was it till
Lord John Russell, in 1820, took it up and identified himself
with it, that it can be said to have come within the range of
practical politics.   In 1821, he succeeded in carrying a bill disfranchising Grampound, a very notorious Cornish borough, and
from that date motions for reform of different kinds were moved
almost every year, but without any success.   The repeal of the
Tests, however, in 1828–9, gave a tremendous stimulus to the
Reform movement, and in 1830 it was generally felt that its advocates were within measurable distance of success.   In 1830 the
Bourbons were expelled from France without the popular rising
being stained by any of the horrors which were supposed to be
inseparable from a revolution.   The quiet and orderly manner
in which the events of these " Days of July " were accomplished
proved quite a revelation to the English people.   They saw that
even a revolution was not necessarily accompanied by violence,
and that an orderly reform might be effected without bloodshed.
This awakening produced such a revulsion of public opinion that
it was now merely a question of time, and no doubt the settlement of the question was considerably facilitated by the death of
George IV. in June, which rendered a General Election imminent.
The Duke of Wellington, however, the Premier, directly chal-
lenged the question by eulogising the state of the representation
at the opening of Parliament.   Mr. Brougham thereupon gave
notice of his intention to move for reform.   Before the day
arrived, Wellington, defeated on the Civil List, had resigned, and
Lord Grey succeeded him with a Ministry pledged to reform.   A

ill was drawn up by the united efforts of Lord Grey, Lord John
ussell, and Lord Durham, and the difficult task of piloting it
hrough the House of Commons was entrusted to Russell.

SECTION 2.—*The Reform Debates* (1831-2).

On the first of March, 1831, the day appointed for bringing in
1e Reform Bill, the state of the House and of its approaches
stified to the intense interest with which the event was regarded
y the public. The avenues leading to the House were all
1ronged with eager pushing crowds for hours before the meeting
f Parliament, and through the long delay caused by the business
n which the House was first engaged the crowd waited anxiously
ll nearly five o'clock in the afternoon. Then the doors were
1rown open, and a tremendous struggle took place, which was
onducted with so much noise and confusion that the Speaker
1reatened to order the galleries to be cleared if the tumult were
ot instantly suppressed. Order was restored by this threat, and
1en the mob of visitors settled themselves gradually and quietly
1to every nook and corner of the space allotted to them, until
1ey were packed as close as the House could bear. There was
ut a thin assemblage of members as yet, but every unoccupied
2at in the body of the building bore a label with a name on it,
nd it was only too evident that there would be a very full House
lter on. By six o'clock, in fact, when Lord John Russell entered,
1ere was scarcely a single unoccupied place. He was received
'ith a loud burst of cheering, which subsided as if by magic when
e rose, and in a low voice and an almost deprecatory manner
lid the scheme of reform before the House. He began by a
light historical sketch of the origin and anomalies of the repre-
entative system, and he drew a curious picture of the corrupt
tate of the franchise with marvellous skill. "A stranger," he
xclaimed, "who was told that this country is unparalleled in
realth and industry, and more civilized and more enlightened than
ny country was before it,—that it is a country that prides itself
n its freedom, and that once in seven years it elects representa-
ives from its population to act as the guardians and preservers
f that freedom,—would be anxious and curious to see how that
epresentation is formed, and how the people choose their repre-

sentatives to whose faith and guardianship they entrust their free
and liberal institutions. Such a person would be very much
astonished if he were taken to a ruined mound and told that
that mound sent two representatives to Parliament; if he were
taken to a stone wall and told that three niches in it sent two
representatives to Parliament; if he were taken to a park, where
no houses were to be seen, and told that that park sent two
representatives to Parliament. But if he were told all this and
were astonished at hearing it, he would be still more astonished
if he were to see large and opulent towns, full of enterprize and
industry and intelligence, containing vast magazines of every
species of manufacture, and were then told that these towns sent
no representatives to Parliament. Such a person would be still
more astonished if he were taken to Liverpool, where there is a
large constituency, and told, ' Here you will have a fine specimen
of a popular election.' He would see bribery employed to the
greatest extent and in the most unblushing manner; he would
see every voter receiving a number of guineas in a box as the
price of his corruption; and after such a spectacle he would be
no doubt much astonished that a nation, whose representatives
are thus chosen, could perform the functions of legislation at all,
or enjoy respect in any degree. I say, then, that if the question
before the House is one of reason, the present state of representation is against reason." With this eloquent appeal to the understanding of his audience, he proceeded to explain the ministerial
scheme. He proposed to disfranchise entirely sixty-two boroughs
containing less than 2,000 inhabitants; and to reduce to one
member forty-seven others containing less than 4,000 inhabitants;
to extend the franchise in the boroughs to all householders
paying rates for houses of the yearly value of £10 and upwards,
subject to certain conditions; and the franchise in the counties
to all copyholders to the value of £10 a year, and leaseholders
for twenty-one years, whose annual rent was not less than £50.
These were the principal clauses of the bill. The 168 seats
gained by disfranchisement were to be distributed among newly
created boroughs and county districts, though not all the vacant
seats were to be filled up,—in accordance with the opinion of
ministers that the number of members in the House was incon-

niently large. Seven large towns—including Manchester,
:eds, and Birmingham—were to receive two members apiece ;
neteen others were to receive one; four districts—Tower
amlets, Holborn, Finsbury, Lambeth—were to be created out
the unrepresented parts of the metropolis, with two members
.ch ; lastly, twenty-six counties were each to receive two ad-
.tional members. Rules were also mentioned for registration
id shortening the hours of polling ; and proposals were added
r reform in Scotland and Ireland. At the end, in obedience
the loudly-expressed wish of the House, Lord John Russell
ad out amidst shouts of contemptuous laughter the list of the
>roughs which the bill would wholly or partially disfranchise.

The motion was opposed by Sir R. H. Inglis, member for the
'niversity of Oxford. He appealed to the history of the repre-
:ntation to prove that it had never been conferred on strict
rinciples of population or taxation, and that therefore the bill
as not restorative, it was Revolution. He then advanced the
:rongest argument that could be urged for the old system.
The great benefit of the constitution of the House of Commons
s it now exists (though if the noble lord's plan be adopted that
enefit will cease) is, that it represents all interests and admits all
ilents. If the proposed change takes place it will be almost
ntirely confined to one interest, and no talent will be admitted
ut the single one of mob oratory. Many of those who sat for
close and rotten boroughs,' as they have been designated for the
rst time by a member of the Government, have constituted the
hief ornament of the House and the support of the country ; but
?ould, if this plan had been adopted in their days, never have
reen received into the House. I ask the noble lord by what
aeans the great Lord Chatham came into Parliament. By the
ye, the first borough for which that great man sat was Old Sarum
tself. Mr. Pitt sat for Appleby. Mr. Fox came in for a close
>orough ; and when rejected for a populous place he again took
efuge in a close borough. Mr. Burke first sat for Wendover ;
ind when by that means he became known, he was transposed
n his glory to Bristol, as Mr. Canning, who also sat for Wendover,
vas transposed to Liverpool. When their talents became known,
:hey were the honoured representatives of large towns ; but would

such places ever have thought of selecting Mr. Canning, Mr. Burke, or Lord Chatham, if they had not previously had an opportunity of showing their talents in the House? It is only by this means that young men who are unconnected by birth or residence with large towns can ever hope to enter this House unless they are cursed—I will call it cursed—with that talent of mob oratory which is used for influencing the lowest and most debasing passions of the people."

Mr. Hume, the enlightened leader of the moderate Radicals, expressed his satisfaction with the bill, as far exceeding his expectations from the present Ministry, at the same time adding that he regarded it as but a temporary measure. Mr. Hunt, however, the spokesman of the extreme party, inveighed against it as utterly inadequate, and declared that nothing would satisfy him but universal suffrage. "Honourable members," he continued, "had predicted revolution, murder, and massacre from any wider measure. Could any massacre be worse than that perpetrated by the drunken yeomanry at Manchester in 1819 on the unarmed and unresisting people?" Here the cries and interruptions which had followed his whole speech became so overpowering that the speaker for the moment was unable to proceed. Nothing daunted, however, he raised his voice to its loudest pitch, and in stentorian tones shouted high above the din his denunciation of the conduct of the late Lord Liverpool's Government. Finally, he expressed his determination to support the bill.

He was followed by Sir Charles Wetherell, the ablest champion of the Tory party. He denounced the bill as "corporation robbery." He declared that there was little difference between the proceedings of the Government and the Radical reform executed by "Cromwell & Co." when they cut off the head of Charles I. "I have now performed," he said in conclusion, "and I trust within reasonable limits, the duty which I owe to myself, to the British public, and the House of Commons, in making the observations on this bill which I have felt myself compelled to make, and I have now but a few more words to utter. There existed in Cromwell's time a purge of the House of Commons (laughter). That purge was called Colonel Pride's Purge (laugh-

r and cheering). The gentlemen on the opposite side of the
ouse are close imitators of the Cromwellian system; not only
his system of parliamentary reform, but also of his sanitary and
ırgative system; for they are prepared tó expel by one strong
ıse no fewer than 168 members from the House. I do not
ıow what name should be attached to this specific; for I did
ıt conceive it possible that the country would see a repetition of
ch a process. Within the last three days, however, the country
ıs been promised a purge, to which, as no name has been
tached, I will attach the name of ' Russell's Purge' (roars of
ughter and great cheering for some time). I say that the
ïnciple of the bill is republican at the basis; I say that it is
ːstructive of all property, of all right, of all privilege; and that
e same arbitrary violence which expelled a majority of mem-
ːrs from that House at the time of the Commonwealth is now,
ter the lapse of a century from the Revolution, during which
ıe populace has enjoyed greater happiness than has been en-
ıyed by any populace under heaven, proceeding to expose the
[ouse of Commons again to the nauseous experiment of ,a repe-
tion of Pride's Purge." This peroration was followed by an
ıtburst of cheering which effectually prevented the continuance
f the debate for several minutes.

Lord Palmerston next spoke in favour of the bill. He declared
ıat if concessions had been made at the right time, if advantage
ad been taken of the opportunities offered by the conviction of
ɔrrupt boroughs to bring the great unrepresented towns gradually
ıto connection with the House, the sweeping measures proposed
y the bill might have been averted. All concessions, however,
ad been refused, and the inevitable result had followed. He
efended himself from the charge of inconsistency in now advo-
ıting reform when formerly, under the leadership of Canning, he
ad opposed it. He declared that changes of the utmost moment
ad taken place since the death of Canning, which justified any
onourable man in changing his opinions; and for his part he
rmly believed that had Canning lived he also would have become
convert to the necessity for reform.

Sir Robert Peel, on the other hand, complained of the means
dopted for forcing the bill down the throats of Parliament, the

S

menaces of dissolution, the violence of the mob. He declared
his intention to oppose the bill, and to seek re-election with the
utmost confidence at the hands of his constituency. He protested that the bill tended to separate all the ties which connected
the higher and lower classes, maintaining that the great recommendation of the existing system was that it enabled every class
in the community, in some way or other, to have a voice in the
election of the members of the House. He proposed that no
voter should be disfranchised at all—that were a crying injustice
to which he would never consent, and he considered the disfranchising of all who did not possess the £10 qualification
in boroughs one of the most objectionable clauses of the bill.
He argued in favour of the rotten boroughs that the results were
good, that the House was full of men of ability, and that nothing
would tend to lower it more in public estimation than that it
should be below the average ability of educated gentlemen. He
ran over a long list of the distinguished men of the preceding and
present centuries, who had all been returned originally by boroughs
which would be disfranchised by the bill. "Nor is the mere
facility of admission the only benefit. The introduction, by
affording them an opportunity—the essential condition of successful talent—for displaying their legislative ability on a larger
scale, recommended them to a more extended franchise at a more
mature age; and again, when they, by caprice, or want of money,
or otherwise, were deprived of their larger seats, those close
boroughs, which the noble lord's bill would destroy altogether,
received them and secured their invaluable labours to their
country. Such was the case when Mr. Sheridan was defeated at
Stafford: he found shelter at Ilchester. Mr. Windham, having
failed at Norwich, took refuge at Higham Ferrers; and Lord
Castlereagh, in like manner, having lost his election for the
county of Down, was returned for Orford. Mr. Tierney also,
when he lost Southwark, was returned for Knaresborough; and
Lord Grey for Tavistock, when defeated in Northumberland.
All this proves that the tendency, and not the mere accident of
the close-borough system, is to facilitate the entrance of men of
ability who otherwise could not obtain a seat in the House." He
declared, moreover, that the example of the United States was

delusive, owing to the brief span of the existence of that State ; in that country, moreover, there were circumstances existing so different to those in England as to render it dangerous to apply any conclusions drawn from thence. He pointed to the miserable failure of democracy in South America; and he wound up with an eloquent denunciation of the " firebrands of agitation," which the Government had hurled far and wide through the length and breadth of the country.

He was met by an opponent in all ways worthy of him—Mr. Stanley, subsequently to be known as the great Earl of Derby. Mr. Stanley began by warning the Opposition that any danger which might ensue would be due to their having denied reform so long, and then obstructed it to the last when brought forward. He declared that it was useless to talk of a gradual reform— that had been attempted at every opportunity, but had been invariably opposed and rejected by the Tory party. Some advantages, it was true, had alleviated the evils of the nomination system ; but they were not great enough to outweigh the fact that the nominees were not in any way representative of the people. It was absurd to talk of the party of reform as the party of re- volution, of socialism, of universal destruction. The names of the men who supported the bill in Parliament were a sufficient guarantee against this.; they all had a stake in the country them- selves. Lord John Russell was hardly likely to propose a redistribution of property ; Earl Grey would be the first to resist any encroachment on the rights of the aristocracy. " By the bill," he maintained, " the influence of the aristocracy will be upheld—I mean the influence which they ought to possess ; not the influence of bribery or corruption, not the influence of direct or indirect nomination."

The debate had lasted for five nights when Mr. O'Connell rose to address the House, but it was not till early on Thursday morn- ing, March 10, that Lord John Russell was called on to reply. Seventy-one members had spoken altogether, and of them thirty- four spoke in favour of the measure and thirty-one against it. Lord John Russell replied very briefly, and then the Speaker put the motion for leave to bring in the bill, which was granted with- out a division in consequence of an agreement between the leaders on both sides of the House. The bill was read a first time on the 14th of March. The second reading was moved on the 21st, and carried after a warm debate by a majority of one only—the numbers being 302 to 301. The situation now resolved itself into the alternative of allowing the bill to be hacked and hewed in committee at the pleasure of the Opposition or to dissolve Parliament. The ministers offered concessions—some boroughs should be taken out of the disfranchisement list; additional members should be given to populous counties; existing franchises should be continued not only to existing holders but to their sons as well. The Opposition, however, were determined on no surrender, and the trial of strength eventually came on a resolution moved by General Gascoyne in committee to the effect that the number of representatives for England and Wales should not be changed. This motion was carried against ministers after a lengthy debate by a majority of eight, and the Government determined at once on a dissolution. The Opposition decided for their part to move an address to the Crown beseeching that Parliament might not be dissolved.

A curious scene occurred in consequence in the Lords, while the king was actually on his way to dissolve Parliament, and the Park guns could be distinctly heard announcing his approach. The object of the Opposition was to carry their address before his arrival, of the Government to delay it as long as possible. The House surged and foamed in all the uproar and confusion hitherto peculiar to the Commons. Lord Londonderry, furious at the tactics of the Ministry, broke out into a wild denunciation of ministerial conduct, and thereby played into the hands of his opponents, who only wished to gain time, prolong the tumult, and avert the moving of the address. At last, Lord Wharncliffe was allowed to move his long delayed resolution, and he was in the act of reading it when the king was announced. A storm of angry voices arose as the Lord Chancellor hurried out to meet his Majesty, but the game was up, and an hour later Parliament was dismissed to fight the battle of reform among the constituencies. Sir Robert Peel was similarly in the act of speaking amid an uproar of interruption when the Serjeant-at-Arms knocked at the door of the House to summon the Commons to the House of Lords.

A large reforming majority was returned to Parliament, and when it was opened by the king in person on June 21, the anti-Reformers found themselves in a hopeless minority. On the 24th the Reform Bill was again introduced by Lord John Russell, and his speech was delivered with a boldness and confidence very different to the hesitating, deprecatory tone in which he had addressed the last Parliament—it was obvious that he felt he was in the presence of an assembly of a very different temper. He expressed a hope that the bill would not be received with the taunts, jeers, and interruptions which had impeded its progress in the last Parliament, for the Government, the king, and the people were alike bent on pursuing the course which they considered necessary for the welfare of the nation. In the midst of a loud tumult he acknowledged that the late elections were governed not by reason but by passion, and asserted that that passion was the noblest of all feelings—patriotism. He then announced some modifications of the old bill, which he intended to introduce. Afterwards the bill was read a first time. The trial of strength, however, between the two parties was fought over the second reading, which was moved on July 4, and carried after a warm three nights' debate on Thursday morning, July 7, by a majority of 136—a striking proof of the change of feeling in the country. A further attempt was made to save their cause on the part of the Opposition by a concerted system of obstructive tactics worthy of the political warfare of modern times. Accordingly when it was moved that the Speaker do now leave the chair in order to go into committee, Lord Maitland, the member for Appleby, urged that the return of population for his borough was erroneous, and that his constituents should be heard in person or by counsel at the bar of the House. Russell admitted the statement of the return, but thought that the present time was not suitable to discuss the question. The motion was negatived, and it was immediately moved that the Speaker do now leave the chair. A debate was promptly raised on this question, and the adjournment of the House moved and defended with as much interest and fire as if the Reform Bill itself were the subject under discussion. The motion for adjournment was negatived by an overwhelming majority, but the motion that the Speaker do now leave the chair was again placed before the House, and no less than eight successive motions for adjournment were moved, each involving a lengthy debate, and each followed by a motion that the Speaker do leave the chair, before the House was allowed to resolve itself into committee *pro formâ*, only to be adjourned at once at half-past seven in the morning.

In committee the same tactics were pursued. Clause after clause was debated with an eagerness hitherto unknown in parliamentary annals. Every rotten borough furnished a fresh subject for a fresh battle, which was fought out with the same gallantry and determination which inspired the Greeks and Trojans in the desperate *mêlée* over the body of Patroclus. The grand object of the Opposition was delay, and to effect it they rang over and over again with unflinching energy the same eternal changes of defence which had been dinned into the ears of the House day after day since the introduction of the bill. It was proposed in turn that every individual borough of Schedule A (the total disfranchisement clause) should be exempted entirely from the operation of that clause on its own peculiar merits, should return two members, should return one member, should be united with one of its fellows to form a new constituency, and every other permutation of the possibilities of the case. It was similarly proposed that every borough in Schedule B (the partial disfranchisement clause) should be in some way exempted from the operation of that clause. There was a regular division of work in the labour of obstruction, which was arranged by a committee presided over by Peel. The leading anti-Reformers spoke night after night in opposition to different parts of the clauses. Peel spoke forty-eight times, Croker fifty-seven times, Wetherell fifty-eight times, and other prominent members of the Opposition vied with them in obstructive eloquence. Hour after hour in all the heat of July, when the thermometer at times ranged from 75° to 80°, the weary debates dragged on with endless iteration. The one solitary achievement of the anti-Reformers, however, was the carrying of the Chandos clause (August 18), which gave a vote to all occupiers of land at a yearly rent of £50. But they returned to the charge with untiring energy, and so well did they labour in the cause that it was not till the 22nd of September at the bill was eventually passed by a majority of 106, the members being 345 to 239.

The same evening Lord John Russell carried it up to the Lords, and Earl Grey moved the first reading. The real struggle, however, began on the second reading, which was moved by Earl Grey on the 3rd October. Strangely enough the scene reads in the old records. When he advanced to the table to address the House, such a flood of conflicting thoughts rushed through his brain that for a short time his agitation rendered him speechless. And when amid the encouraging and sympathetic cheers of the House he essayed once more to speak his thoughts, the recollections of the past and the responsibilities of the future, which had momentarily overcome him, perceptibly influenced the whole of his address.

" In the course of a long political life," he commenced in low, earnest tones, which gradually increased in volume till they rang through the House like the blast of a trumpet, "which has extended to half a century, I have had the honour of proposing to this and the other House of Parliament, amid circumstances of much difficulty and danger, in seasons of great political convulsion and violence, many questions affecting the government of the political interests of this country as well as the government of its domestic concerns. If at such times, speaking as I did in the presence of some of the greatest men that have ever graced his country, I experienced awe and trepidation, it was, as your lordships will readily believe, nothing to the emotions which affect me now when I am about to propose to the consideration of your lordships a question involving the dearest interests of the nation—a question for the consequences of which I am more responsible than any man—a question which has been designated as subversive of the Constitution, as revolutionary, as destructive of chartered rights and privileges, and as tending to produce general confusion throughout the empire, but which I solemnly and deliberately feel to contain changes that are necessary ; to be a measure of peace and conciliation, and one on the acceptance or rejection of which I believe depends, on the one hand, tranquillity, prosperity, and concord ; on the other, the continuance of a state of political discontentment, from which those feelings

must arise which are naturally generated by such a condition of
the public mind. Those members of the House who have observed the political conduct of so humble an individual as myselt
are aware that I have always been the advocate of reform." He
then touched briefly on his connection with the Reform movement, and portrayed in vivid language the evils which had resulted from the iron check placed on the aspirations of the people
by the utter refusal of Parliament to grant even the most moderate measure of reform. "Is it possible," he continued, "that the
boroughs called nomination boroughs can longer be permitted to
exist when the people see the scenes which disgrace every election : when they witness the most gross and scandalous corruption practised without disguise : when the sale of seats in the
House of Commons is a matter of equal notoriety with the open
return of nominees of noble and wealthy persons to that House :
when the people see these things passing before their eyes as
often as a General Election takes place : and when, turning from
such sights, they read the lessons of their youth, and consult the
writings of the expounders of the laws and Constitution, where
they find such practices to be at once illegal and inconsistent
with the people's rights, and where they may discover that the
privileges which they see a few individuals converting into a
means of personal profit, are privileges which have been conferred
for the benefit of the nation? It is with these views that the
Government has considered that the boroughs called nomination
ought to be abolished. In looking at these boroughs we found
that some of them are incapable of correction, for it is impossible
to extend their constituency. Some of them consisted only of
the sites of ancient boroughs, which, however, might in former
time have been very fit places to return members to Parliament ;
in others the constituency was insignificantly small, and from
their local situation incapable of receiving any increase, so that
upon the whole this gangrene of our representative system bade
defiance to all remedies but that of excision." He then dwelt at
some length on the provisions of the measure itself, combated the
objections which had been urged against it, and warned the
House of the dangers to which they would expose the country and
themselves in particular if they rejected it. He appealed to the

archbishops and bishops in the House not to let it be said that
t was by their votes that the measure was rejected, and he hinted
n no obscure language at the dangers which they would expose
themselves to by the exercise of their votes against the bill.
Finally, he declared that if the bill were thrown out, the matter
would not end there, but that greater concessions would be demanded.

Lord Wharncliffe, in a moderate speech, in which he acknow-
edged the necessity of some reform, led the Opposition against
his particular bill. Lord Melbourne declared that he would
upport the bill because he felt that there was considerable
langer in refusing the demands of the people at that time. The
Juke of Wellington spoke strongly against the measure; and
gave it as his opinion that under the system it established the
king would not be able to carry on the government of the country
on the principle on which it had been conducted hitherto. Lord
Brougham made a most eloquent appeal to the House not to
eject the bill, and then Lord Lyndhurst rose to reply to his
great opponent.

He began by complimenting Lord Brougham on his eloquent
oration, and then he attacked the bill. He denounced it as
revolutionary; he heaped up argument on argument against
it; he declared that it would be utterly subversive of the
existing order. "The bill takes 157 members from the aristo-
ratic part of the House of Commons. It gives back 65 in the
shape of county members; but it gives also 50 members to the
populous towns to be elected by such a constituency as I have
escribed. What would the representatives of such places be?
We may judge by the persons who are at present the favourite
candidates. The difference is not a difference of 50 members,
ut a difference of 100; for 50 are taken from the aristocratic
art and given to the democratic part of the House. But then
there are 35 more to be taken away; so that, in fact, the aristo-
ratic part of the House will lose 135 members. The same
consequences will result in Scotland, where the democratic part
of the members will utterly overwhelm the aristocratic part.
Then look at Ireland. Three-fourths of the representation of
Ireland will be in the power of the Catholics. I must say that

I think that the whole will form what the noble duke near me
has described—namely, a fierce and democratic assembly." There
was considerable danger, he asserted, that Earl Grey and his
associates would be unable to control the storm they had raised,
and that they would be swept away by its violence ; that a
republic would be established ; that the Protestant Church in
Ireland would be destroyed, and church property in both king-
doms confiscated.   Finally, he concluded with an eloquent and
brilliant appeal to the Lords not to betray the trust confided to
them, but to preserve it unimpaired for posterity.

Late on the morning of October 8, after a hard night's sitting,
Lord Grey rose to reply, and especially to the attacks of Lord
Lyndhurst.   He declared, in conclusion, that his sole object was
to serve his country, and that when the king and Parliament had
ceased to repose confidence in him, he would gladly sink once
more into retirement.   On the division, it was found that the
numbers were, for the second reading, 158 ; against it, 199.   The
Lords had thrown out the Reform Bill by a majority of 41.

The result caused an outbreak of excitement and disorder
almost unprecedented, except in time of civil war.   Riots broke
out in all parts of the country.   The peers were hustled and
assaulted in the parks and on their way to the House.   Tory
members had to fly for their lives over housetops to escape the
attack of infuriated mobs.   Angry debates arose in the House of
Lords, in which fierce recriminations were exchanged between
the parties—the bishops even plunging into the fray with all
the activity and zeal of laymen.   The Commons wrangled furiously,—the Ministry openly menacing their opponents, the latter
denouncing the threats of the Ministry as a breach of the Constitution.

At last, on Monday, December 12, Lord John Russell brought
forward the third Reform Bill.   There were very few changes.
There was a little shuffling of the boroughs from Schedule A to
Schedule B, a slight rearrangement of the members, and a few
other changes ;—all of which had been borrowed from the proposals of the Opposition in committee, as Sir Robert Peel pointed
out, with some dexterity, in the debate on the second reading.
Two nights' debate were sufficient on this occasion for the second

ιding, which was carried Sunday morning, December 18, by
najority of 162—a marked gain on the majorities of the pre-
ding bill.

The question was now, what would the Lords do? The non-
inisterialists were divided into two bodies: the Tories, the
compromising foes of reform, headed by Wellington; and the
averers, headed by Wharncliffe, who, though objecting to the
eeping nature of the bill itself, recognised the necessity of
ιnting some measure of reform. The key to the situation lay
ιlly in the hands of the king. If he would give his promise to
ιate enough peers to swamp the Tory majority, it was only too
ιvious that the Waverers would give way; if not, they would
ιite with the Tories to throw out the bill on the second reading,
to alter it to their liking in committee. This latter was what
tually happened. The king, who favoured the Waverers, refused
create peers. The bill was passed on the second reading; but
committee, Lord Lyndhurst moved that the consideration of
e disfranchising clauses should be postponed until the enfranch-
ng clauses had first been considered. Earl Grey declared that
e true meaning of this motion was to take the control of the
ll out of the hands of ministers. In spite of this, the motion
ιs carried, and Earl Grey at once moved the adjournment of
e House. All appeals to the king, however, were useless, and
ι Grey resigned. Peel, however, refused, and Wellington found
mself wholly unable, to form a Ministry. The state of the
ιuntry became every day more alarming; organized unions
ιrang up in every town, breathing defiance and determination
ι adopt any measures to carry the bill. The king was mobbed
ιd cursed in London. No Government could be found that
ould exist for a day unless it was headed by Lord Grey. And
ι in the end the king gave way, and definitely promised, in
riting, "to create such a number of peers as would insure the
assing of the Reform Bill, first calling peers' eldest sons."

In order to avert this contingency, the king ordered a circular
ιtter to be sent to Wellington and the principal Opposition
ιaders, to the effect that all difficulties might be obviated by
declaration from a sufficient number of peers that they would
bstain from opposition. In consequence, Wellington and a

number of others withdrew entirely, leaving a small, determined minority to bicker and bandy insults with the Ministry over what was now a foregone conclusion.   The Lords, in fact, entirely put off any little shreds of dignity they had retained hitherto, and described one another's conduct as "unparliamentary, disorderly, abandoned, and atrocious," with the utmost candour and freedom. Eventually, however, after a wearisome repetition of these scenes, the third reading of the bill was carried by 106 to 22 (June 4).

On the 5th of June, the Lords' Amendments were sent to the Lower House, and assented to with some slight discussion. It was on this occasion that Lord John Russell made his celebrated "finality" declaration.   He said : "I think, so far as ministers are concerned, this is a final measure.   I declared on the second reading of the bill, that if only a part of the measure were carried, it would lead to new agitation; that is now avoided by the state in which the bill has come from the other House." The royal assent was given by commission, and the bill became law. It was followed shortly by Reform Bills for Scotland and Ireland.

The English Act disfranchised 56 nomination boroughs, which returned 111 members; semi-disfranchised 30 more; took away 2 members from the united boroughs of Weymouth and Melcombe Regis;—thus gaining 143 seats. It gave 65 additional members to the counties; 2 members each to Manchester, Leeds, Birmingham, and 19 other large towns (among which were included the 4 metropolitan districts); 1 member each to 21 towns, all of which had previously returned no members at all. The county franchise was given to copyholders and leaseholders as arranged in the first bill, and to the £50 tenants at will of the Chandos clause. The borough franchise was given to all holders of houses to the annual value of £10.

By the Scotch Reform Bill, the number of members was increased from 45 to 53, of whom 30 were to sit for the counties, and 23 for the cities and boroughs. The county franchise was extended to all holders of property to the annual value of £10, and to some classes of leaseholders. The franchise in the burghs was conferred, as in England, on all £10 householders.

The Irish Reform Bill increased the number of members from 100 to 105. The existing county franchise was higher even than

ǝ English, for in 1829, when the Catholic Emancipation Act
ıs passed, it was raised from 40s. to £10, in order to take the
:ctions from the control of the priests, who were omnipotent
ıong the 40s. freeholders. Now the same changes were intro-
ıced in counties and boroughs as in England. The occupation
ınchise in the counties, however, it was considered desirable to
: at a higher level than the English; it was, therefore, conferred
ıly on occupiers to the value of £20.

CHAPTER XX.

THE AGE OF PEEL.

THE General Election of 1832 was regarded with very different feelings by the two parties. The Conservatives were anxious and fearful, wondering whether the sun of their political power had set for ever. The Reformers awaited with considerable anxiety the result of the changes which they had effected. No man could foretell the event, and it surprised them all. The disturbances at the elections were not by any means greater than usual, though no doubt this was in no small measure due to the law which closed the poll in two days, instead of keeping it open for a fortnight. The new assembly did not differ so very materally from the old ones, and though the Tories were now in a small minority, most of the old faces were there. Peel was re-elected for Tamworth, Goulburn for the University of Cambridge, Herries for Harwich; Hardinge found a seat at Launceston, Charles Wynn was returned again for Montgomeryshire; Mr. Baring and Sir R. Vyvyan, both among the most uncompromising opponents of the bill, were chosen respectively by Essex and Bristol. These triumphs, however, were balanced by important losses. Sir Charles Wetherell, Sir E. Sugden, and Mr. Murray were rejected by the constituencies, and Mr. Croker withdrew altogether from public life, vowing that he would never sit in a reformed Parliament. The Radicals were disappointed in their hopes of large gains; the real triumphs lay with the Whigs.

The new constituencies had on the whole acted with considerable sense and discrimination. The representatives of the new boroughs were above all creditable to their electors. Manchester chose Poulett Thomson, the Vice-President of the Board of Trade; Leeds, Macaulay, who had made his mark as an orator during the Reform struggle; Birmingham, Attwood, the founder f the Birmingham Political Union, which had played such an mportant part in the Reform agitation. London selected Grote, he historian of Greece; Westminster chose its old member, Sir 'rancis Burdett, and Sir J. Cam Hobhouse, the Secretary at War : Iarylebone returned Sir William Horne, the Attorney-General ; outhwark gave a seat to Brougham, the Chancellor's brother.)n the other hand, there were five O'Connells chosen by five Irish onstituencies, and Pontefract rejected a highly respectable Irish eer in favour of Gully, a retired prize-fighter. Noticeable among 1e new men was Joseph Pease, the Quaker, whose election 'as rendered memorable by his claim at the opening of Parlia- 1ent to be allowed to substitute a solemn affirmation for the arliamentary oaths, in accordance with the provisions of the 'oleration Act, and his claim was allowed ; but in order to remove ll doubt for the future, a relieving statute was passed in the same ear. Of the Whig leaders, Lord Althorp was re-elected for Iorthamptonshire, Sir James Graham for Cumberland, Charles irant for Inverness-shire, Lord John Russell for Devonshire, Lord 'almerston for Hampshire ; Mr. Stanley, in company with Mr. /ilson Patten was returned for the northern division of Lancashire.)n the whole, the result of the election was to make the iovernment one of the strongest that had ever existed in .ngland, to disappoint all extreme views, and to render it ecessary for the Tories to abandon for ever their old unreasoning ostility to all reform, and take up an entirely new position.

A change, in fact, was inevitably coming over the character of arties, which was directly due to the bill. Lord Eldon and Sir C. /etherell may be taken as the type of the old bigoted Tories ; but .ord Eldon's influence was now on the wane, and Wetherell was xcluded from Parliament. The man who had succeeded them in 1e leadership of the Tory party, was Sir Robert Peel, and Peel)ok the very earliest opportunity of explaining that his position 'as altered. He declared that he accepted the reform of the :presentative system as an accomplished fact, and that, far from eing opposed to all reform, as had been falsely stated concerning im, " he was for reforming every institution that really required :form, but he was for doing it gradually, dispassionately, and eliberately, in order that the reform might be lasting." It may be imagined that this speech was likely to be very unwelcome to a large body of his followers.

Just as a division had arisen in the ranks of the Tories in consequence of the Reform Bill, so the Reformers were splitting up into two bodies. There were the old Whigs, timidly clinging to traditions of the pre-Reform period ; and a more advanced body of Radicals, Reformers, and Repealers, who regarded the Reform simply as a repair of the old, almost useless, parliamentary machinery, and were anxious to employ it in its restored state with the most untiring energy. The extremists among them were ready to begin at once the reform of everything, and it must be added that most of their propositions of reform, violent and impossible as they were considered at the time, have been accepted by the maturer wisdom of later generations. Such men were not likely to be content with the apathetic Whiggism of the Ministry, the limitations imposed on further action by the rash promises of "Finality Jack" (¹) or the truly ministerial principle that everything must be sacrificed to the grand duty of keeping the existing Government in power. So irritated did they become at last, that the boldest of them crossed the floor of the House and took up their position on the front Opposition benches. In consequence, Peel, the leader of the recognised Opposition, found himself pushed from his usual place and forced to go up nearer to the Speaker. Mr. Disraeli, then beginning to be known as a clever young man, even imagined that it would be possible to unite the two divergent sections of the Opposition for the purpose of destroying the Whig Government—a project which was really as feasible as an attempt to mix oil and water, and met with unqualified failure when carried into practical application at the Wycombe elections of 1831–2. The Radicals themselves, however, were by no means an united band. They were mostly men possessed with a fixed idea, which they brought forward again and again, and endeavoured but with little success to thrust down the throat of an unwilling House. There was very little *esprit de corps* among them, and a total lack of organization. On many topics they would find themselves in the same lobby as the Whigs. On

(¹)   A nick-name given to Lord John Russell, *v.* p. 268.

her occasions, sheer disgust at the inadequate shilly-shally policy oposed by the Government would drive them into the same bby with their natural enemies, the Tories.

The natural consequence of these changes was a further change party names. The advanced section of the Tory party dis-aimed entirely the name of Tories, and the undesirable sociation with which it was connected. They preferred to :scribe themselves as the party of *conservation* rather than action in Church and State, and the new name of Conservatives as in process of time invented. Natural development had simi-rly rendered it necessary to provide some new designation to clude all sections of the Whigs, for the Radicals and Reformers ttirely rejected the name of Whig, and covered it with as much pprobrium as that of Tory. The singularly suitable name of the iberal Party was borrowed from continental politics, and was sed indifferently to include the timid and old-fashioned views of le true Whigs, and the advanced views of the most extreme oliticians, as well as the great mass of the party of Reformers.

The hostility between the Radicals and the Whigs was dis-layed at the opening of the Parliament of 1833, when the Iouse of Commons met to elect a Speaker. Mr. Manners utton had filled this important post since 1817, and in spite f his decidedly Tory views the Ministry determined to avail lemselves of his experience again, for they imagined that an lexperienced Speaker might find it extremely difficult to ac-uire the necessary control over a Parliament elected under such ifferent conditions. The Radicals were annoyed at this deter-lination of the Ministry, for they considered that a Tory Speaker 'as by no means suited to the changed condition of Parliament. Ir. Hume, who may be regarded as the leader of the Radicals, herefore, without waiting for the ministerial nomination, proposed Ir. Littleton in spite of the latter's objections. The Ministry, owever, persisted in their original plan, and in the contest which nsued the ministerial candidate triumphed by a large majority— he Radicals only numbering 31 votes. Thus war was declared etween the Ministry and the Radicals, but at the same time it 7as made conclusively evident that there could be no settled ourse of united action between the Tories and the Radicals.

T

Among the leading men of this Parliament may be mentioned Lord Althorp, the eldest son of Earl Spencer, who presented the singular spectacle of a Chancellor of the Exchequer who was possessed of little oratorical and smaller financial power, whose budgets appeared to be brought forward solely that they might be amended.   His efficiency as a leader was not due to his capacity but his honesty.   He was trusted by the country and the House of Commons as no minister ever had been before, or in all human probability will ever be again. He said himself that nature had intended him for a grazier, but that men insisted on his being a statesman.   There was so much truth in the latter part of the remark, so really popular and influential was he in the House of Commons, that when he resigned in 1834 all possible pressure wás brought to bear on him to induce him to reconsider his determination ; and on his elevation to the House of Lords by the death of his father, William IV. gladly assumed that the Ministry could not carry on without him as an excuse for dismissing them abruptly. The Prime Minister, Earl Grey, was now almost at the close of his public career ; he had accomplished the great end and aim of his life, and the results so alarmed him that he was glad to escape their unwelcome presence.   He found himself in the trying position of a man of a bygone age who has outlived the manners of his youth, and is terrified by much that seems so easy and familiar to the later generations.   His timely withdrawal in 1834 enabled him to avoid the unpopularity which must infallibly have fallen to his lot, had he remained to become identified with the vacillating apathy which gradually took the place of policy in the once triumphant and energetic Reform Ministry.   Lord Palmerston's time had not yet come, though he was already winning golden opinions at the Foreign Office.   Wilberforce died in 1833, just as the great work of his life—the emancipation of the slaves—was at its completion.

The most prominent man on the Whig side in the House of Commons after the withdrawal of Lord Althorp, was Lord John Russell, the pilot of the Reform Bill in the Lower House. He was even suggested for the leadership, and though the claims of Lord Melbourne were most unaccountably preferred to iis, he became the real leader of the House of Commons. His name is associated with most of the reforming measures of the time, and in spite of his frequently reiterated " Finality " assertion, is inseparably connected with the progress of a further Reform of Parliament until his death, though not one of his proposals but proved inadequate and abortive. "Johnny" was, during the whole of his parliamentary career, an un-failing subject for ridicule. He was caricatured by *Punch* repeatedly, during the period of the alliance between Lord Melbourne's Government and O'Connell, as "the beggarwoman's baby," with the features of the Liberator peering through the hood of the Irish mamma : later on he figures in the cartoons as Britannia's "boy in buttons," who was "hardly strong enough for the work " : later still, as the "do-nothing minister," whom all men are vainly invoking to work. Stanley wrote to Sir James Graham that "Johnny had upset the coach," when Russell, in 1834, insisted on explaining at a most inopportune time that the proposition of nationalizing church revenues was not excluded from the Irish policy of the Government. Mr. Disraeli sneered at him as "Lord John Straw," the leader of the modern Peasants' Rebellion. His oratory was of the cold and acrid type, which is convincing enough when it is fairly listened to, but which produces a feeling of repugnance and unwillingness to be convinced in the mind of the listener. He could state the most difficult case with great clearness and consummate logical power, but there was no trace of passion in his speeches, nothing that appealed to the emotions of his hearers, and nothing but frigid and unsympathetic argument.

At the defeasance, for it can scarcely be called withdrawal, of Lord Melbourne, "Johnny's" turn at last came, but he signally failed to make use of it. Many of his friends had thought from the first that his confidence was far greater than his ability, and their opinion seemed to be justified by the event. Nothing could have shown less judgment than his unwise revival of the cry of "No Popery" in the middle of the nineteenth century. The vigorous and aspiring personality of Lord Palmerston gradually overshadowed the less resounding reputation of Lord John Russell, until the latter suddenly found that Palmerston was the real head of the Liberal party, and he himself must be content with a subordinate position. On the death of Palmerston Earl Russell became once more Prime Minister, though it was fully recognised that the ablest man in the Cabinet was Mr. W. E. Gladstone. Not even in his own department, the Foreign Office, was Russell satisfactorily successful during his last term of power, and the general feeling when he retired, after a premiership of a year, was not so much regret, as wonder that so much enthusiasm could ever in the earlier days have attached itself to the name of Lord John Russell.

For a short time it seemed as though Mr. Stanley (afterwards Lord Stanley and Earl of Derby) would be a possible rival to Lord John Russell in the leadership of the Liberal party. The Irish Church question, however, caused his secession from the Ministry; and though he held aloof from Sir Robert Peel in 1835, he joined his Ministry in 1841 as Secretary for War and the Colonies. During the struggle over the Repeal of the Corn Laws he took the side of Protection so decidedly that on the great split in the Conservative ranks he became the leader of the Protectionist party in the House of Lords, and on the death of Lord George Bentinck, two years later, the recognised chief of the whole party. By the irony of fate, therefore, he was marked to be the principal opponent of Lord John Russell, later of Lord Palmerston,—doomed to constant opposition, with only the hopeless prospect before him of forming occasionally a stop-gap Ministry during the dissensions of the Liberal party, and the certain knowledge of defeat and dismissal again as soon as they were once more composed. He was, perhaps, a brilliant parliamentary swordsman rather than a great statesman; he had too little knowledge, too little thoroughness in his grasp of a subject, for the latter. But as the leader of a forlorn hope, such as the remnant of the Tory party was after 1846, he was admirable. His energy was fitful and uncertain, he was wanting in patience and perseverance, but his courage was indomitable, his honesty was indisputable, and his oratory was brilliant and irresistible in its effect on even an unsympathetic audience. Its effect was amply testified to by a generous opponent: "I have heard the Right Hon.

Secretary often taunted with his aristocratical bearing and demeanour. I rather think that I should hear fewer complaints on that head if the right hon. gentleman were a less powerful opponent in debate." His very blunders, which drew for him from Disraeli the nickname of "the Rupert of Debate," and which even his brilliance was unable to hide or atone for, mattered little where his party was unable to comprehend them. To Mr. Disraeli is no doubt due the organization of the later Conservative party, and the re-creation of a Conservative feeling in the nation just as much as the "education" of his followers may be; but undoubtedly, without the able assistance of a man of recognised birth as well as ability like Lord Stanley, the Jewish "adventurer" would have found it hard, if not well-nigh impossible, to maintain his position at the beginning.

Among the less conspicuous figures of the Reforming party in 1833, we may notice the artistic and somewhat doctrinaire Lord Morpeth, better known to a later age as the Earl of Carlisle; John Lambton Lord Durham, Grey's son-in-law, the Radical member of the Cabinet, oddly enough to be known in later days as the Dictator of Canada, and to die of a broken heart at the cruel accusations of his enemies; Mr. Littleton, the Irish Secretary, whose indiscreet negotiations with O'Connell, and subsequent exposure by the duped and indignant Liberator, gave the first shock to Earl Grey's Ministry; Sir James Graham, one of the seceders with Mr. Stanley in 1834, who also joined Peel in 1841, and on the practical extinction of the latter, seemed for a short time as if about to become the leader of the new party of the Peelites; Lord Ashley, better known to us as the Earl of Shaftesbury, the humane and philanthropic champion of the factory children, and the miserable unsexed women who toiled away their lives amid the darkness and filth of the coal mines; Sir William Molesworth, the polished leader of the philosophical Radicals; Mr. Grote, the historian of Greece, who was identified in Parliament with the question of the ballot; Mr. Tennyson, who was similarly connected with the repeal of the Septennial Act; "Honest Tom" Duncombe, the Radical member for Finsbury; Mr. Hume, now as ever devoted to the question of economy, and a fervent advocate of a further reform of Parliament; Mr. Ward, the energetic leader of the crusade for the diminution of the overgrown Establishment of the Irish Church; Mr. Roebuck, whose name is associated with the abolition of the duel; the brilliant Macaulay, who had already made a lasting impression on the House by his powerful speeches during the Reform debates, and who was to win yet higher honours in the future; the Marquis of Lansdowne the Whig Duke of Wellington, whose presence in a Whig Cabinet was as indispensable as that of *"the* Duke" in a Tory one; the Earl of Ripon, hiding under a respectable old age the follies of " Prosperity Robinson" and " Goody Goderich"; and last, but by no means least, the eccentric William Lamb Viscount Melbourne, and Lord Brougham.

Lord Brougham was by no means the conspicuous figure in the Government that he had been. His influence was on the wane, and his extravagant conduct disgusted his allies. It was never exactly explained why, on the reconstitution of the Ministry under Lord Melbourne, there was no place found for Brougham, but it may be easily conjectured that his colleagues thought it intolerable to serve with him. He took up, therefore, the position of " candid friend" to his ungrateful party. His eloquence had lost nothing of its biting sarcasm and tremendous invective, and though he remained still for some time the principal opponent of Lord Lyndhurst's reactionary views in the Lords, he never omitted to point out to the Whigs any errors or follies which he could detect in their proposals, and to tell them frankly and cuttingly when he thought them in the wrong. He drifted slowly, however, over to the Tories, and especially showed a disposition to court the Duke of Wellington, thereby exciting the malicious attacks of his former friends. He became the constant butt of the Liberal press in consequence, which had a strong tendency to overrate his really rapidly declining influence.

The leading figure in the House of Commons was undoubtedly Sir Robert Peel, the chief of the new Conservative party. Peel's career presents a number of extraordinary paradoxes. He was in his earlier years the bitterest opponent of Catholic Emanci-

ation ; he became converted to the necessity for it, and was a
member of the Government which brought in the bill. He was
similarly opposed to Parliamentary Reform, on the ground that
s results must be disastrous to the country; he became con-
inced, however, that Reform was inevitable, and he therefore
refused to help in forming a Tory Ministry in 1832, during
the final crisis, and thereby destroyed the last chance of
'oryism. Later still, he became converted from Protection,
nd came into office expressly to repeal the Corn Laws, of which
e had spent his life in maintaining the expediency and necessity.
t does not appear that he possessed a highly impressionable and
somewhat shallow nature, as might perhaps be expected ; it was
ather that he was gifted with an unusual talent for perceiving
nd recognising afar off the approach of the inevitable. He was
ever really converted to Emancipation and Reform, but he saw
heir time had fully come. It is impossible to estimate how far
he latter consideration influenced his conversion to Free Trade.
n 1833 he was, as he declared, ready to accept the established
settlement, and his object was to " build up a great middle class
parrier, combining popular progress with constitutional prin-
iples," as ·the one hope of protecting the country from the
uinous advance of Radicalism. He wished to effect the complete regeneration of the Tory party, to clear them from all
suspicion of retrogressive policy, to " educate " the country up
o Conservatism, and to build up a new and great Conservative
party. He made it his business to cry to his followers uninter-
mittently, " Register, register, register," and the result of his
efforts was shown in the Conservative reaction of 1841. So much
of his career is necessarily dealt with apart during this and other
chapters, that this short notice must suffice for the man who
was certainly the leading figure in the country between 1832
and 1846. As an orator he was clear, lucid, and convincing,
and essentially a great debater, and a thorough master of the
House of Commons and its ways ; but nothing more. He
narrowly missed attaining the rank of a great orator, but he had
no passion and little imagination, and no man ever really appealed
to the passions and hearts of an audience by addressing their
reason only. The man whose oratory perhaps his own most

resembled was Richard Cobden ; fate placed them, as a rule, on
opposing platforms, but their methods and modes were almost
identical, and in the hour of a nation's frenzy, whether sprung
from panic or enthusiasm, both would be brushed aside, the
common-sense arguments of the logician and debater would be
drowned in the stirring eloquence of the true orator that rings
through the soul like the blast of a trumpet.   His principal
supporters were, in the Lords, the Duke of Wellington, and Lord
Lyndhurst ; the Earl of Aberdeen, who was to become the head
of the weakest and most unsuccessful Coalition Ministry of
modern time, composed of men of all parties, from the extreme
Tory to the extreme Radical, which drifted along in a rudderless
condition until it struck at last helplessly on the rocky bulwarks
of the Crimean shore ; in the Commons, Mr. Henry Goulburn,
one of the most successful Chancellors of the Exchequer ever
known ; Sir Henry Hardinge, Messrs. Herries, Sidney Herbert,
Alexander Baring (afterwards Lord Ashburton), and Mr. W. E.
Gladstone, now entering Parliament for the first time as the
elected of Newark, and oddly enough as a Tory.

The real leader of the Conservatives in the Lords was the
Duke of Wellington, who endeavoured to take up the position
assumed by Peel in the Commons, and to induce the Lords to
recognise the change effected in their position by the Reform
Bill, and to accommodate themselves gracefully to it.   He was
always liable, however, to find his influence disputed, and a
mutiny organized by the active and somewhat mischievous energy
of Lord Lyndhurst, who took up the position of the leader of
the ultra-Tories, and on many occasions carried the whole mass
of the Lords along with him, in defiance of the wiser counsels
of Wellington and Peel.   " Peel ! what's Peel to me ?   Damn
Peel," was his concise reply to a remonstrance that his action
was in opposition to the wishes of his leader, and these words
gave rise to an impression that he might have some lurking idea
of superseding Peel altogether.   Lord Lyndhurst was one of the
most effective and most equal parliamentary debaters ever
known, but he had neither the passion nor the genius of an
orator.   In the delivery of clear, correct argument, he was unrivalled, and in the compass of his voice and grace of his manner

e had all that a speaker could desire. But he never rose above
he level of a practised debater, and in capacity he was inferior to
iis great opponent, Lord Brougham.

Standing in the gap between the two parties, we discern the
olossal form of O'Connell, the Irish leader, venerated by many
is the "Liberator of Ireland," laughed at by more as a "fire-
rand extinguished on the floor of the House"; but deemed by
he common consent of posterity the greatest Irishman of the
entury, and the greatest orator of his time. He had extorted
mancipation from the Government by a peaceful but determined
gitation; he hoped to obtain the Repeal of the Union by the
ame means. His method was simple enough. He had full
ontrol over the Irish constituencies, and he used this power for
iis own ends. He created what was known as "O'Connell's
ail," the first germ of the modern Home Rulers—a party of
iis own, consisting of his sons, nephews, and sworn adherents,
vho, putting aside all connection with English party politics,
tood between the Reformers and the Conservatives, ready to
iccept concessions from either, ready to throw the entire weight
)f their votes on that side which would give them most. O'Con-
iell knew, of course, that he had nothing to gain from the
Conservatives, that his hopes must rest on the Reformers, but
ie was determined to do nothing blindly, and he kept aloof at
irst from the both parties, so as to hold the balance between
hem, and make his profit out of their political necessities. The
lismissal of the Whigs in 1834 brought about a *rapprochement*
)etween them and O'Connell, which may be described as the
irst type of the "Treaties of Kilmainham," and the "Unholy
Alliances" with the Parnellites, of which later years have had
:xperience. It was denounced with quite as much vigour,
lenied with equal circumnavigation of the truth, and at least as
insuccessful in its ultimate result. To O'Connell's credit it
nust be recorded that he went to his end strictly by peaceful
ind constitutional means; he set his face decidedly against
)utrage and violence, and he used his influence to the utmost on
he side of order. Whether he really believed in the possibility
)f obtaining the Repeal of the Union, or merely maintained the
igitation because it was his *métier*, and because agitation "paid";

whether, in short, he was the unprincipled swindler that the average Englishman of the day imagined him to be, who waxed fat and kicked under the stimulating influence of the tribute wrung from the pockets of his miserable dupes, or merely—to quote a later view—a high-souled and magnificent hero, with just that slight twist in his moral nature which is so attractive to "the sensuous and passionate Celtic nature," and which has been so admirably caricatured in Mr. Christie Murray's portrait of the Irish "patriot," Hector O'Rourke;—these, and questions such as these, must ever remain a subject of controversy.

Of O'Connell's oratorical powers, an impartial and learned authority has remarked that he was "a perfect master of every form of argument—potent in ridicule, sarcasm, and invective, rich in imagination and humour, bold and impassioned, or gentle, persuasive, and pathetic—he combined all the powers of a consummate orator." Unfortunately, however, for his reputation, his extraordinary powers were frequently disgraced by the worst abuse, by a violence and scurrility which transcended all that this century has yet produced, a vulgar coarseness of epithet and attribute that was more suitable to the purlieus of Drury Lane than the Chamber of the Legislature, and a truculent defiance of tone and manner which, however calculated to impress the "passionate Celtic nature," must ever be regarded by all educated men as a revolt from the ordinary code of decency almost approaching brutality.

It was this Parliament which passed the Act for the emancipation of the slaves in the West Indies, shortened the hours of labour of the factory children, attempted to extend the blessings of education by a national grant, removed the curse of the old poor-law from the agricultural system, reformed the Municipal Corporations, and endeavoured to deal with the then (as now) extremely dangerous and difficult Irish question. A proposal to reduce the Irish Church Establishment in the interests of the Irish nation produced the first rent in the Ministry. Lord Grey, Sir James Graham, Mr. Stanley, the Duke of Richmond, and Lord Ripon, disapproving of the principle of diverting Church revenues to lay purposes, sent in their resignations, and the subsequent failure of an attempt to deal with Irish tithes afforded Lord Grey a welcome pretext for withdrawing from political life (1834).

t was on this question that Mr. Stanley, in his new character of
ritic of the Government measures, made his once celebrated
thimble-rigging speech." " He had never witnessed," he said,
 anything like the principle on which the Government were pro-
eeding, except among a class of persons who were not generally
ːceived in society, and the instruments of whose calling were a
eal table and four or five thimbles. The skill of these persons
·as shown by dexterous shifting of the pea—placing it first under
ne thimble and then under another, and calling on the bystanders
ɔ bet where the pea was.   The Government," he continued,
·ere doing the same with the rights of property in Ireland, and
when the thimbles were taken up, it would be found that the
roperty had ~~altogether~~ disappeared, and the dupes would be
ughed at."

Lord Grey was succeeded by Lord Melbourne—no one could
ɪake out exactly why.   He had never been a conspicuous
olitician, and he was by no means gifted with oratorical power.
Ie was, as a rule, troubled with great hesitation and embarrass-
ɪent when speaking, he was totally devoid of eloquence, and he
nly became even fluent when he was really excited.   His speeches
·ere usually direct and sensible enough, but the merits of the
ɪatter of them were not great enough to balance the defects of
.elivery.   It was, moreover, a singular foible of his to hide his
ɛal good sense and businesslike capacity in an affectation of
ɔppishness and trifling that was very embarrassing to the plain
nd serious men with whom he was necessarily brought con-
ɪnually in contact.   Deputations from different interests, who
.iscovered Lord Melbourne dandling a cushion or playing with
 feather, and had no knowledge of his real character, no doubt
eported to their principals the view which found favour with
ɪany prominent Whigs, that Lord John Russell would have made
. better leader.

William IV.'s confidence in him was so slight that on the with-
lrawal of Lord Althorp from the Commons, he dismissed the
Vinistry and summoned Peel to office.   The Conservatives, how-
·ver, were still in a minority, and after a very brief interval, the
Reformers naturally returned to power again.   From this time
heir history was very extraordinary.   Their names are connected

with a number of valuable and remedial measures, and yet they gradually became more and more unpopular, until the great Conservative reaction of 1841 overthrew them.   This was partly, no doubt, due to an unwise junction with O'Connell and his "tail," partly to the extraordinary apathy of the Whigs, who were really satisfied with the reforms already effected, and desired to rest and be thankful, an aspiration which excited the utmost indignation in the breasts of the Radicals, and at least was scarcely calculated to sustain the enthusiasm which had gathered round them during the Reform crisis; but it was mainly due to the natural change of opinion which invariably succeeds a period of vigorous action and which had been so studiously fostered by Sir Robert Peel. Peel could now boast that he had created the Conservative party, and the General Election of 1841 was followed by his return to power.   This event might have been accomplished even earlier but for Peel's disinclination to take office without the right of disposing afresh the offices in the Queen's bedchamber to the exclusion of the Whig ladies, and the refusal of the Queen to submit to this request.   The Whigs in fact, laughed the wits of the day, during the last three years of the Melbourne Ministry were merely hanging on by the petticoats of their ladies.   " Was there ever," said Lord Lyndhurst, " in the history of this country a body of men who would have condescended so low as to attempt to carry on the Government under the circumstances?   In this House they are utterly powerless ; they can effect nothing.   Yet thus disgraced and trampled on, they still condescend to hold the reins of Government.   Proud men, eminent statesmen, distinguished and high-minded rulers ! "

The Parliament which had given the *coup de grace* to the Whigs did not meet in the old historic House of the English Legislature, for on the 16th of October, 1834, the latter had been burnt to the ground.   This was due to the stupidity of some workmen who were employed to get rid of large masses of the old Exchequer tallies, and could think of no better method than burning them in the stoves of the House of Lords.   The stoves and pipes being subject to such an unusual amount of combustion, became so intensely hot that at last the dry wood with which they were surrounded charred, smouldered, and finally broke out into leaping ɪngues of flame, which sprang forth with startling effect near the ɪtrance. In half an hour, in spite of all the efforts of the fire-ɪen, the whole building roared up to heaven with the blast and ɪme of an open furnace. Westminster Hall was with difficulty ɪved, but the two Houses, the greater portion of their libraries, ɔme tapestry which dated back to the Armada, many works f art which it was difficult to replace, many records which it as impossible to replace, were all swallowed up in the greedy ɔnflagration. The accident was universally regretted, for the old hamber was invested with memories that rendered it almost ɪcred in the eyes of all. Yet there were undoubted advantages ɔringing from the catastrophe, which commended themselves ɪore especially to the sitting members. The old Houses of 'arliament were ill-adapted to the needs of the Reformed Legisla-ɪre. The deficiency of room in the House of Commons had ecome painfully apparent on crowded nights. In our own days ɪe difficulty has revived afresh. Members who have realized ʻhat it is to be seatless, though entitled to a seat, to be crushed ɪto the side galleries, flattened out below the bar, or driven to aze with envious eyes from the vantage of the Peers' Gallery on he more fortunate ones within the precincts of the House itself, ɪay enter into the feelings which had prompted even the ɔonomical Mr. Hume, in the sessions of 1833 and 1834, to urge ɪe construction of a new House of Commons. The argument, ʻhich had fallen unheeded on the ears of the House, acquired ɪresistible force in consequence of the fire. The Commons were ɪow homeless: new buildings had become a necessity. Temporary ɔcommodation was fitted up among the ruins until the new ɪuildings could be completed, and for some time the two Houses at, like Marius, among the ruins of the mighty past.

The Ministry of Sir Robert Peel may be briefly summarised ɪs the progress of the conversion of England and of Peel him-elf to the principle of Free Trade; and on the slow and exces-ively gradual development of their education, the outbreak of he Irish famine produced the sudden and decisive effect of the Harlequin's wand in a transformation scene. The absolute ɪecessity of providing food for the starving peasants brought ɔoth Russell and Peel, convinced and repentant, to sit at the feet of the man who had started the Free-Trade agitation—Mr. Richard Cobden.

Cobden was one of England's greatest orators. His style was persuasive and sweet, his voice clear and well toned, his delivery essentially free and conversational, and marked by an obvious sincerity that was convincing by its very simplicity. His speeches were characterized by great common sense and a total absence of passion. Unreasoning enthusiasm was a power which he did not comprehend; he could neither appeal to it, nor control it, and he was always rather disposed to underrate its effect. The calm judicial clearness of his mind, which enabled him to steer his way straight to his object, prevented him from appreciating the devious modes by which the majority of men attain the same result, and in consequence he never could place his finger exactly on the pulse of the nation, and he was never really in harmony with them. During the Crimean war he was even intensely unpopular. He was greatest undoubtedly in the Anti-Corn-law Crusade, and yet there is little doubt that, with the exception perhaps of Peel, few men in Parliament recognised his true share in the Repeal. Most men would have said it was the work of the Prime Minister, perhaps even have characterized it as a deliberate act of successful treachery. Few saw, beneath the turmoil of party strife and party vicissitudes, the irresistible influence of Richard Cobden. During the whole of his career Cobden was never exactly a member of either of the great historical parties. He was an independent Radical, at first a free-trader merely, ready to accept Repeal wherever he could get it; later, in conjunction with Mr. Bright, he became the founder of the peace-at-any-price party, or the Manchester School, which excited so much of the national odium during the Crimean and Chinese wars, and were regarded as little better than avowed traitors to their country. He held aloof entirely from Lord Palmerston, and reprobated Lord Palmerston's methods of policy. His hostility to Palmerston kept him out of the latter's Cabinet, and threw him at times into a singular alliance with Mr. Disraeli. The Manchester party in fact were an utterly unreliable factor in politics, always developing into the unexpected, until they were drawn into more regular courses by the admission of Mr. Bright to Mr. Gladstone's Cabinet in 1868.

When Parliament met in 1846, Peel, speaking third on the Address, explained that his views on the Corn Laws had undergone a considerable change, and that the force of events had brought him to the conviction that the protective system which he had so long supported must be abolished. The Tories were raging with indignation against the man whom they regarded as a traitor, and yet were hardly possessed of sufficient oratorical power to effectively denounce. Just at the right moment Mr. Disraeli stepped into the breach and stood forth as the apostle and champion of the Protectionists. By this act he raised himself at once to the position of a great parliamentary tactician, and a power of no small importance in the House of Commons. Hitherto, from his entrance in 1837, he had been more or less of a failure—listened to under protest, and scarcely regarded—continually saying brilliant and bitter things of persons who excited his wrath, and yet with all his brilliance and bitterness never exactly producing the effect on the House, or the victim, which he aimed at. He had attacked Peel already on the subject of his apostasy from Protection. He had denounced him as " the political Petruchio, who has tamed the political shrew of Liberalism with her own tactics." He had accused him of "catching the Whigs when bathing, and walking away with their clothes." He had rated the Conservative Government of Peel as "an organized hypocrisy," and sneered at the Prime Minister himself as " a sublime mediocrity." But there is no doubt that these brilliant sallies attracted far more attention later on than at the moment of delivery.

Now, however, his opportunity had come. At the right moment he made himself the spokesman of a voiceless multitude. He expressed the rage and indignation boiling in their breasts with all the biting sarcasm and furious invective of his fluent tongue. By so doing, he stepped at once into the foremost rank of the politicians of the day, and became the recognised mouthpiece of the Tory party. As he listened to the loud shouts of the Protectionists, which italicised every point of his attack, he must have felt triumphantly that he had rolled back the charge of failure, that he had fulfilled at last the prophecy which he had flung at the House when he sat down discomfited by the per-

sistent interruptions of the followers of O'Connell on the first
occasion of his attempting to address Parliament, and that he
would never sit down unheeded in Parliament again.   As a
specimen of oratory, his speech is hardly worth recording, but
as a striking instance of a crushing attack levelled at exactly the
right moment, in the right way, and with telling effect, it must
be regarded as inimitable.

"I should have abstained from intruding myself on the House
at this moment had it not been for the peculiar tone of the right
hon. gentleman ; I think that tone ought not to pass unnoticed.
At the same time, I do not want to conceal my opinions on the
general subject.   I am not one of the converts.   I am perhaps
a member of a fallen party.   To the opinions which I have
expressed in favour of Protection in this House I still adhere,
They sent me to this House, and if I had relinquished them I
should have relinquished my seat also.   I must say that the tone
of the right hon. gentleman is hardly fair towards the House while
he stops discussion upon a subject which he himself has entered
on with a fervency unusual to him.   Sir, I admire a minister
who says that he holds power to give effect to his own convictions.   I have no doubt that the right hon. gentleman has
arrived at a conscientious conclusion on this great subject.   The
right hon. gentleman says it is not so much by force of argument
as by cogency of observation that he has arrived at this conclusion.   But surely the observation which he has made might
have been made when he filled a post scarcely less considerable
than that which he fills at present.   What, sir, are we to think
of the eminent statesman who, having served under four
sovereigns, who, having been called to steer the ship on so
many occasions, and under such perilous circumstances, has
only during the last three or four years found it necessary
entirely to change his convictions on that important topic which
must have presented itself for more than a quarter of a century
to his consideration?   Sir, I must say that such a minister may
be conscientious, but he is unfortunate.   I must say also that
he ought to be the last man in the world to turn round and
upbraid his party in a tone of menace."   He then compared
Peel to a Turkish Admiral who took the command of the

urkish fleet, only to steer straight away to the enemy's port. Now, sir, the Lord High Admiral on that occasion was very uch misrepresented. He, too, was called a traitor; and he, o, vindicated himself. 'True it is,' said he, 'I did place yself at the head of this valiant Armada; true it is that my vereign embraced me; true it is that all the muftis offered p prayers for my success. But I have an objection to war; see no use in prolonging the struggle, and the only reason I id for accepting the command was that I might terminate the ntest by betraying my master.'" So had Peel done. He might lk about posterity, but the party of Protection had raised him power, and now he had betrayed them. He had assumed very lofty attitude; but after all a great statesman was a man ho represents a great idea, not "a man who takes his obser- itions, and when he finds the wind in a certain quarter, trims is sails to suit it. Such a man may be a powerful minister, but e is no more a great statesman than a man who gets up behind carriage is a great whip." And so he went on at great length, nid the loud and ringing cheers of the Protectionists.

This speech ruined Peel, and divided the Tory party. But r Disraeli's interference, the Protectionists might have still hung illenly on to the Prime Minister, true to their old habits of bedience. Now, however, there was a definite split in the Tory imp. Graham, Gladstone, Cardwell, Sidney Herbert, and many ther men of note went along with Peel, but the bulk of the Tory juires refused to follow his lead any longer, and sought for iemselves new chieftains in Lord George Bentinck and Mr.)israeli. Lord George Bentinck was no orator, and at times his >eeches degenerated into mere nonsense. He had attracted very ttle attention in Parliament, and, indeed, had as yet no oppor- inity of showing that he possessed any aptitude for politics. lis high birth naturally marked him out for the leadership if he iowed any capacity for fulfilling the task; and his patience, ood humour, persistent energy and sincere honesty, enabled him amply satisfy the trust reposed in him. Mr. Disraeli, however, ho acted as his faithful lieutenant, was really by far the ablest ian of the party, and the most skilful debater. On Lord George's remature death, in 1848, Disraeli became the recognised leader

U

of the Opposition, the untiring opponent of Lord John Russell, Lord Palmerston, and later, Mr. Gladstone.

The secession was quickly organized, and the seceders prepared for revenge. The Corn Bill of course passed, but the Coercion Bill for Ireland which followed was thrown out. Some eighty of the Protectionists, headed by Bentinck and Disraeli, walked into the same lobby with the Whigs, the Free-traders and the Irish, and Peel's Ministry fell to the ground—slain by Protection. Lord John Russell naturally succeeded, with a Cabinet principally composed of Lord Palmerston and Mr. Macaulay. There could be very little opposition at first, for the Protectionists and the Peelites were at daggers drawn, and neither cared for the responsibility of turning out a Government which neither could venture as yet to succeed.

CHAPTER XXI.

LORD PALMERSTON.

ORD JOHN RUSSELL'S Ministry was but the dying
embers of the fire which had destroyed the old system
personal government; it lingered on merely until some one felt
ong enough to blow it out. The dismissal of Lord Palmerston[1]
insubordination in the management of the Foreign Office, pre-
)itated the crisis before any one was ready. Lord Palmerston,
10 had seemed so utterly extinguished by his dismissal that
israeli spoke of him as a man of the past, revived with unex-
cted alacrity in the spring of 1852, carried an adverse vote
ainst his late leader, and puffed the last faint flicker of the
inistry completely out. But there was no one really able to
ke Russell's place as yet. Lord Derby and his skilful lieutenant,
israeli, attempted the experiment of governing with a minority
thout much success. Next Lord Aberdeen formed a coalition
Whigs, Peelites, and Radicals, which lasted till the crisis of
e Crimean war, and then fell to pieces quite naturally amid the
sasters of the terrible winter of 1854–5. Its contribution to
e annals of Parliament consisted mainly in Mr. Gladstone's
)nderful Budget-speeches, which showed that it was possible to
vest what was usually regarded as rather a dry and tough sub-
ct with so much of the sparkle of genius, as to transform it from
mere dull financial statement into a brilliant and fascinating
scourse, which brought him at once into the foremost rank of
ırliamentary orators. Much of his extraordinary success in
tracting and charming the ears of the House was due to the
:quisite tone of his voice, the perfect ease of his delivery, and
e energetic action with which he *italicised* his words. Much,
) doubt, was forgiven him on this account which would have

---

[1] *v.* pp. 310–11.

been severely criticised in a speaker less favoured by nature: for even as early as the first Budget-speech of April, 1853, many of the blemishes had become visible which time was to develop at last into positive defects—the long-involved sentences which at times almost bewildered the brain of the listener, the copious flow of words, by which the orator seemed himself to be carried entirely away, the extraordinary redundancy of language without which he appeared to be unable to express the simplest thought. But in spite of all he was recognised, then and ever after, as one of the greatest parliamentary speakers of his day, second perhaps only to Mr. Bright. During the Reform debates it almost seemed at one time as if Mr. Lowe were about to make good his supremacy over Mr. Gladstone; but whereas Mr. Lowe waned almost immediately after he had attained his zenith, and sank rapidly into obscurity, Mr. Gladstone remained steadily at the same high level, recognised by all not only as a brilliant speaker, but a consummate master of the art of debate; an opponent whose retorts were withering in their intensity, whose invective was crushing in its tremendous vehemence.

The downfall of Lord Aberdeen's Government brought Lord Palmerston to the head of affairs, for it seemed to be agreed by unanimous consent that he alone could carry England through the crisis of the war; he alone could satisfy the national desire for vigorous action. At first there were few changes in the Cabinet; the Premier and the Minister of War, Lord Panmure, were the only new figures. Very shortly, however, the Peelites retired in a body, and Palmerston became the head of a purely Whig Government.

Lord Palmerston was essentially an Englishman, and this must account for the extraordinary fascination which he exercised for so many years over the mass of his contemporaries. In all his foreign escapades, when he was lecturing or bullying foreign Governments, coercing and trampling on the "insolent barbarian" in different parts of the world, interfering generally in everybody's business, it was thoroughly understood by his countrymen that all this was for the sake of "British interests"; and there was a general feeling that England was a greater nation, that Englishmen were far more feared and respected by the foreigner,

d that the nation got on much better in the world at large when
rd Palmerston had the control of the Foreign Office than when
r international relations fell to less vigorous hands. All this
s very pleasing to the average Englishman of the day, who was
ll closely enveloped in a thick crust of insular Philistinism, and
lo regarded foreign nations as the natural enemies of England,
er on the look-out to do her an ill turn. There was something,
o, in Palmerston's method of oratory which exercised an ex-
lordinary influence over his generation. It was brilliant and
lling, but it was also extremely practical and opportune. He
peared to have the knack of always striking the right chord at
lce, and putting himself in complete harmony with the feelings
ld prejudices of his audience. The most remarkable instance
his success in this respect is to be found in what is known as
e Don Pacifico debate. Don Pacifico was a naturalised British
lbject resident at Athens. He had suffered considerable ill-
lage at the hands of an Athenian mob in 1847 without any
rovocation, and his claims of redress had been enforced by
almerston against the Greek Government with a very high hand.
[any members thought that the Foreign Minister had acted in
le matter with undue violence. They said as much in Parlia-
lent, and Palmerston found himself practically on his defence.
lis reply was a masterly appeal to the passions and prejudices of
ls hearers. · He declined to discuss the accusations of knavery
rought against Pacifico himself, the charges of dishonest dealing
l the estimation of the damages he had sustained, the exposure
f the mean and miserable character of his life, so utterly at
lriance with his extravagant assertions; still less whether the
ccasion was worthy of the extreme measures which had been
sed, whether the question of compensation might not with greater
ourtesy have been left to the good faith of the Greek Govern-
lent, or whether the tone adopted towards the latter was one
hich it was feasible or desirable to sustain towards foreign
lovernments in general. No; he took his stand on clearer grounds
lan these. They might be true, but that was not the question.
he question was one solely of British interests. Other men
light raise shouts of laughter from an unthinking House, by
lsts " at the poverty of one man, or the miserable habitation of

another; at the nationality of one man, or the religion of another;"
but he would have no share in it. He would never acknowledge
that "because a man was poor, he might be bastinadoed and
tortured with impunity; or that a man who was born in Scotland,
might be robbed without redress; or that because a man was
of the Jewish persuasion, he was a fair mark for any outrage."
In a peroration of thrilling power, he declared that the House
must decide between such men and the interests of their country;
must decide "whether, as the Roman in the days of old held
himself free from any indignity when he could say 'Civis Romanus
Sum,' so also a British subject, in whatever land he may be, shall
feel confident that the watchful eye and the strong arm of England
will protect him against injustice and wrong." This remarkable
effort is said to have lasted for five hours, during the whole of
which period Palmerston continued to speak with the utmost
fluency, with all the passion of a man moved to the very soul by
generous indignation, and without the help of a single note. The
success of his appeal was striking and irresistible. The Ministry
came out triumphant, and from that day Palmerston was recognised in the country as the "patriotic Minister," the unswerving
champion of England.

The death of Peel made Palmerston beyond doubt the foremost
man in English politics, though several years were to elapse before
this fact was recognised by his contemporaries. His aspiring
spirit ill brooked the orders of another, and that other his true
inferior, and it was his constant delight to make "strokes off his
own bat," his ill-disguised insubordination to Lord John Russell's
opinions, which caused his dismissal from the Cabinet. Sunk
irremediably as he seemed, he came to the surface again almost
directly, and on the break-up of the Aberdeen Cabinet the full
direction of affairs passed to his hands. From this date a period
of active foreign policy ensues, during which the question of
Reform was suffered to languish and almost die of sheer neglect.
The opinion of the country supported his "patriotic policy" to
the full. It seems singular, by the light of modern Imperialism,
to come across in old volumes of *Punch* the figure of Mr. Disraeli
oddly attired now as "the bear-leader," anon as the "China
merchant," later the "unhorsed jockey scrambling out of the

itch," while Lord Palmerston wins the Grand National Steeple-hase on " Patriotism." But still it is undeniably true that Mr.)israeli was regarded as an " outlandish person," the sworn com-anion of Jews, Quakers, Mr. Bright, Mr. Cobden, Russia, China, .ustria, and other strange allies—any one, in fact, who got in ,ord Palmerston's way and thwarted his "patriotic policy." The ne thing the English people and Parliament could not forgive ieir pet was his friendship for Louis Napoleon. It was so un-nglish; it was truckling to the natural enemy of England; ιversing the traditions of Waterloo, and so on. At last, to the stonishment of all, none more surprised no doubt than them-ιlves, in February, 1858, Parliament carried an adverse vote ιn the subject. Of course Palmerston resigned, and there was ιothing for it but to commit the Government for a time to the ιands of Lord Derby and Mr. Disraeli, the "friends of Cobden, ιussia, China & Co." A Government relying on a minority ιeldom lasts long. This lasted only until the Liberal party had ιecomposed their differences, and then in June, 1859, a coalition, ιncluding all sections, and headed by Lord Palmerston, assumed ιhe reins of power; the third act of the Palmerstonian era began ιnd carried the drama on on precisely the same lines as in the ιreceding portions. The death of Palmerston, in November, 1865, ιnded the period of vigorous policy, and transferred the real ιeadership of the Liberal party to a more advanced section—the ιarty of Reform—headed by Earl Russell and Mr. Gladstone.

CHAPTER XXII.

GLADSTONE AND DISRAELI.

M R. GLADSTONE, it must be observed, had developed considerably since the days when he was first returned for Newark as a Tory. He had become converted to Free Trade along with Peel, and had formed one of the leading men of the anomalous party of Peelites. His Liberalism had gradually acquired a deeper tinge, a more precise development. He never was exactly in harmony with Lord Palmerston; he suggested at times that Palmerston's policy was another name for bullying and blustering; even in 1862, when he was actually a member of Palmerston's Ministry, he had hinted as a reproach to the nation that they had forced the Government to enter on a great deal of unnecessary expenditure for defensive measures, and the hint had drawn a rather severe reply from Palmerston. His rejection, however, by Oxford University at the election of 1365 gave a sharper impulse to his gradual progress. "Unmuzzled at last." as he declared himself to be, he sprang forward with a bound on the path of Reform, and from that date though he has frequently stumbled, even fallen, he has never swerved aside from the track. The death of Lord Palmerston made him the leader of the House of Commons and the acting lieutenant of the Liberal party. He had now at last an opportunity of giving full vent to his views, and expression to the reaction in favour of Reform which was coming over the nation.

Even as early as the first session of 1866, Mr. Gladstone in the discharge of his functions as leader of the House, gave tokens of that extraordinarily sensitive and conscientious anxiety which became gradually such a marked characteristic of that statesman, and has within the latest experience even formed a decided hindrance to the progress of public business. He listened attentively to every speaker, answered fully every question put

> him, spoke on every subject, and exhibited such untiring
earnestness and perseverance, that many of his friends feared
that he must soon overtask his powers, and disable himself for
the performance of his duties.

It was understood very early that the Ministry would endeavour to deal with the long outstanding question of Reform,
and a great and comprehensive bill was expected. Instead of
this an utterly inadequate and unscientific measure was introduced, which confined itself to reducing the county franchise to
fourteen pounds, and the borough franchise to seven pounds,
with some additional fanciful extensions based on no principle
whatever. That was all ! For over thirty years the Liberal party
had inveighed against the inadequacy of the Reform Bill of 1832,
the unjust inequality of the franchise in county and borough,
the iniquitous disfranchisement of "millions of capable citizens,"
and the imminent danger of delaying any longer the pressing
question of a fresh reform. It had been not obscurely hinted
that Palmerston was to blame, that Palmerston cared only for
constitutional reforms abroad—thought them good enough for
the "miserable foreigner," but a decided mistake at home.
Lord Palmerston's carriage had long blocked the way ; but now
had at last been moved on by the irresistible commands of the
great watchman Death, and the road was clear for the passage
of Reform. What was the result? A petty, paltering, miserable
measure too mean to arouse the slightest enthusiasm, too impotent
to excite alarm in the most reactionary. The franchise was to
be distributed with a cautious hand. There was to be no rash
admission of too many fresh voters all at once. A few hundreds
were to be enfranchised here and there ; the rest were to be left
to the "dim and distant future." "Unenfranchised millions," in
fact, were on their own statements thundering at the doors of
Parliament impatient to enter in, and the Government, after
superhuman efforts, were going to open a little wicket gate so as
to admit the rush of men cautiously one at a time.

The measure, in fact, was too evidently a compromise. The
Russell and Gladstone section of the Cabinet wanted reform :
the remnants of Palmerston's followers still thought it unnecessary. The result was this wretched, tinkering measure, which

satisfied nobody, and disappointed the expectation of all earnest
Reformers. How Mr. Gladstone could have persuaded himself
that the scheme was anything but a sham and a farce, it seems
difficult to conceive ; but he did—nay more, he took an active
part in an agitation in its favour, and announced with the utmost
enthusiasm to the electors of Liverpool, that he and his colleagues
were determined to stand or fall by their Franchise Bill : they
had crossed the Rubicon and burnt their ships : there was no
thought or possibility of retreat.

The principal opposition came not from the Conservatives, as
might have been expected, but from Mr. Horsman and Mr.
Robert Lowe,[1] both members of the Liberal party, who from the
very first declared they would have none of it. Mr. Disraeli and
his friends were naturally only too glad to leave the unpopular
task to these able banditti, and the astute Conservative leader
must have smiled sardonically to himself when he saw Messrs.
Lowe and Horsman remorselessly tearing the entrails out of the
Government measure, and Mr. Bright rising in his wrath to hurl
Ætnas of oratory on the heads of the rebellious Titans. Mr. Bright
denounced them furiously as "Adullamites" ; all who were in
distress, all who were discontented, had gathered themselves together in the political cave of Adullam for the attack on the
Government. But Mr. Lowe, all unabashed by denunciation of
sarcasm, carried the war straight into the enemy's camp in a swift
succession of speeches of extraordinary brilliance and power. The
remarkable part of it was that Mr. Lowe really laboured under
the greatest possible disadvantages which could attack an orator.
His voice was so harsh and unpleasant that it reminded his
hearers irresistibly of the grating of a door-key in the lock ; his
appearance was peculiar and unprepossessing ; his eye-sight was
so weak that he was obliged to hold his notes up almost to his
nose in order to read them at all ; his action was so singularly
awkward as to render him the living realization of the wooden
Mr. Grewgious. Yet in spite of all these defects Mr. Lowe
made for himself a name which can only be compared with that
of Single-speech Hamilton in the last century. For the moment

---

[1] Afterwards Lord Sherbrooke.

ıe threw Mr. Disraeli into the shade, and to the astonishment
)f all stood forth boldly in the lists against the practised powers
)f Gladstone much as the stranger knight iń Ivanhoe astounded
:he onlookers by daring to the fight and triumphing over the
lreaded Templar, Brian de Bois-Guilbert. Gladstone and Bright
were at their best during the Reform debates of 1866, and yet
)y the unanimous consent of all it was agreed that Mr. Lowe
ıeld his own again and again against them amid hurricanes of
ıpplause from the House of Commons. Nay, more—Mr. Lowe
·uined the bill, and ejected the Government from office. The
)arty of two, which in its origin reminded Mr. Bright of "the
Scotch terrier which was so covered with hair that you could not·
:ell which was the head and which was the tail of it," was
gradually reinforced by deserters from the ranks of the Government, until at last the Adullamites were strong enough to turn
:he scale of a division. Then one wild night, after a hot and
·urious debate, the combined armies of the Adullamites and
Conservatives carried triumphantly an amendment brought
·orward by one of the Adullamite chiefs, Loŕd Dunkellin, to the
:ffect that a rating be substituted for a rental qualification; and
:he Government was at an end. Ivanhoe had triumphed in the
:ontest : the Templar rolled defeated in the dust.

The failure of the bill brought Lord Russell's official career·
:o its close. He formally handed over the leadership of the
)arty to Mr. Gladstone, and from this time took but little part
.n politics. Lord Derby, his opponent, was soon to follow his
:xample, and then the long-standing duel between Gladstone and
Disraeli would be pushed up to the very front of the parliamentary stage, right in the full glare of the footlights. Meanwhile, however, Lord Derby had taken office. Disraeli and
Gladstone were changing weapons and crossing the stage. Mr.
Lowe had steadily declined to join the ranks of the new Government. The other Adullamites were preparing to return to their
original obscurity. The exasperated Liberals, however, were
rousing a widespread agitation throughout the country in favour
of Reform : monster meetings were held in Hyde Park: the
Park railings were pulled down and trampled on by an excited mob, and the police regulations proved as unable to bear

the unusual strain as police regulations usually do on such occasions.

The result was that Mr. Disraeli became convinced that a Reform Bill of some kind or other was inevitable, and Mr. Disraeli's opinion naturally carried the day.   The Government, however, did not go straight to the point at once.   They began by proposing a number of resolutions on the subject, which were very soon laughed out of existence.   Then they brought a bill founded on them, which, however, was very shortly afterwards withdrawn after a very discouraging reception.   Finally, the Ministry, lightened by the loss of three of its members—the Earl of Carnarvon, Viscount Cranborne,[1] and General Peel— announced their intention of bringing in a comprehensive measure.

The measure in question proposed household suffrage in the boroughs subject to the payment of rates, and occupation franchise for the counties subject to the same limitation, and a variety of fanciful clauses, which would have admitted members of the liberal professions, graduates of the universities, and a number of other classes to the franchise.   The most novel feature was a clause which permitted a man to acquire two votes if he possessed a double qualification by rating and by profession. The great objection to the bill was that it excluded " the compound householder."   The compound householder is now as extinct an animal as the potwalloper found in earlier parlia- mentary strata, but he was the hero of the Reform debates of 1867, and as such deserves more than a passing reference.   He was, in fact, an occupier of a small house who did not pay his rates *directly* and in person, but paid them through his landlord. Now the occupiers of these very small houses were naturally by far the most numerous class of occupiers in the boroughs, and the omission of them implied a large exclusion from the franchise. The Liberal party, therefore, rose in defence of the compound householder, and the struggle became fierce and hot.   It must be remembered, however, that neither Mr. Gladstone nor Mr. Bright wished to lower the franchise beyond a certain point, and a meeting was held in consequence, in which it was agreed that

---

[1] The present Marquis of Salisbury.

:he programme brought forward in committee should begin by an alteration of the rating laws, so that the compound householder above a certain level should pay his own rates and be given a vote, and that all occupers below the level should be excluded from the rates and the franchise alike.

On what may.be described roughly as "the great drawing-the-line question," however, the Liberal party once more split up. The advanced section were determined that *all* occupiers should be admitted, and they would have no "drawing the line." Some fifty or sixty of them held a meeting in the tea-room of the House of Commons and decided on this course of action : in consequence they acquired the name of the "Tea-Room Party." The communication of their views to Mr. Gladstone made him excessively indignant. He denounced them in violent language, and his passion was emulated by Mr. Bright. If the Tea-Room Party had been a second set of Adullamites, sworn to resist all reform, they could scarcely have been attacked with greater fury. Their sole crime, however, consisted in opposition to Mr. Gladstone, for it is now universally recognised that their proposed policy was far the most enlightened and liberal of the two, and that the Gladstonian scheme must have ended in considerable confusion and injustice.

Mr. Gladstone had to give in, and his surrender was followed by that of Mr. Disraeli. The Tea-Room Party, in fact, were masters of the day, and were able to bring sufficient pressure to bear on the Government to induce them to admit the principle of household suffrage pure and simple, and to abolish all distinctions of rating. The *coup de grâce* was given to the compound householder, and a number of persons admitted to the franchise who would otherwise have been excluded. The rest of the debate may be characterized as a cutting and carving into symmetrical proportions of the measure which the Government had brought rough-hewn into the House. The bill in its final form, the details of which are reserved for the next chapter, differed very considerably from the form in which it had originally appeared. Not only was the household suffrage clause considerably extended, the dual vote abolished, and most of the fancy franchises swept away, but there were numerous additions which completely altered the character of the bill, and transformed it from a balanced attempt to enlarge the franchise without shifting the balance of power to a sweeping measure of reform.

In the course of the debate, Mr. Disraeli had to listen to attacks and denunciations very similar to those which he had hurled at the head of Peel in the Corn Law debate. Lord Cranborne described his action as "a policy of legerdemain," and "a great betrayal which has no parallel in our parliamentary annals, which strikes at the root of all mutual confidence, which is the very soul of our party Government, and on which only the strength and freedom of our representative institutions can be secured." There was this difference, however, in principle between the position of Mr. Disraeli in 1867, and in Sir Robert Peel in 1846, that Sir Robert carried the repeal of the Corn Laws by the help of the Opposition, in defiance of the well-known opinions of the mass of the men he professed to lead, and to rely on; Mr. Disraeli had on the contrary educated the great mass of his party—all except a few seceders—into the firm conviction that he could read the signs of the times better than most men, and that the moment had come when Reform of some kind was inevitable. Mr. Disraeli moreover was in a minority in Parliament; he had turned out Mr. Gladstone solely by the help of the Adullamites; he knew he could not carry the smallest measure of Reform without the help of the Liberals; the principle of compromise must in fact have been present to his mind from the first, or it were worse than useless to have brought in the bill at all.

The immediate result of the bill was a great Liberal triumph at the General Election, which returned Mr. Gladstone to power at the head of a Ministry drawn from all sections of the Liberal party. A period of active and aggressive Reform set in, of which the nation soon wearied, and the result was, that when Mr. Gladstone suddenly dissolved Parliament in 1874, a large Conservative majority was returned to power. A period of active foreign policy followed, which as naturally produced the inevitable reaction, leading up, in 1880, to a new period of vigorous legislation, and the Third Reform Bill of 1884–5.

CHAPTER XXIII.

PARLIAMENTARY DEVELOPMENT.

SECTION I.—*Cabinet Government.*

THE passing of the First Reform Bill may be regarded as the second Act of the English Revolution. The expulsion of the Stuarts had transferred the government of the country from the king to the aristocracy, who ruled for nearly a century by means of a well organized system of corruption. George III., by a crafty use of their own weapon, succeeded in wresting from them a large share of the authority which the Crown had lost. The Reform Bill put an end almost at once and for ever to personal government by influence, broke the power of the aristocracy, depressed the House of Lords very low in the political balance, exalted the House of Commons to unquestioned supremacy, and vested the real government of the country solely in the Cabinet.

Not that these important results were immediately apparent. All that the Reform Act appeared to do, was to destroy a vast deal of corruption, and admit the middle classes to political power. But the new constituencies, though extremely vulnerable to bribery in every form, were comparatively but slightly susceptible to personal influence. Rich men might buy seats at enormous expense, great landowners might command an overwhelming interest in some particular constituency, ministers might make an unfair use of the very considerable patronage in the public departments, and the army and navy, still left to them, to attach a large personal following to their cause. But anything like the deliberate and systematic formation of a party by wholesale purchase or intimidation of the electors was utterly impossible for the future. The character of this House of Commons naturally underwent a considerable change in consequence. There were more business men sent to it, fewer idlers. The standard of age became much higher than in the eighteenth century; the attendance far more regular; the House began to represent more widely the true interests and political sentiments of the nation; its policy was more liberal; it proved more susceptible to public opinion. The code of parliamentary honour naturally became more and more severe in the fierce light which the extraordinary development of parliamentary reporting tended very rapidly to throw on proceedings in Parliament. The widespread corruption which had existed among members during the preceding century dwindled, drooped, and died. The whole framework of corrupt influence fell to pieces almost of itself, and gave way to the modern system of government by the leading men of certain organized parties, which are held together mainly by community of principle and policy, partly no doubt by pure *esprit de corps* or loyalty to some particular leader, and partly also, in many individual cases, by the feeling that bad as things may be at present it is quite possible for them to be worse.

The exclusion of royal influence from active government involved the practical transference of the power of appointing ministers from the Crown to the House of Commons. William IV., it is true, did not at first comprehend this, and endeavoured in 1834 to assert his personal wishes with regard to the choice of his Ministry in a most exaggerated way by suddenly dismissing Lord Melbourne's Government, without the faintest shadow of constitutional pretext, and calling Sir Robert Peel to power, though it was well known that the latter could only rely on a small minority in Parliament. The General Election, however, showed that the country refused to ratify this high-handed act, and after a gallant but ineffectual struggle against a hostile majority, Peel was obliged to resign. With William IV. the long chapter of personal government came finally to its close, but so little was the fact appreciated at the time that when Victoria ascended the throne, and it fell to the courtly and lively Lord Melbourne as existing Prime Minister to make the first impression on the mind of the youthful sovereign, the Duke of Wellington openly declared that there was no hope for the Tories in the future. "I have no small talk," he said, "and Peel has no manners." It was difficult for him to imagine, with the

emory of preceding reigns before him, that the Tories could
ider these disadvantages ever hope to make themselves
ifficiently acceptable to the young queen to be permitted to
turn again to office. His fears, however, were utterly groundless,
r from that date, under the wise and constitutional rule of her
·esent Gracious Majesty, the right of selecting ministers has
?en exercised solely by the House of Commons. A faint
irvival of the old system is to be traced in the great Bedchamber
uestion of 1839, which made such a noise in its time—namely,
ie refusal of the queen to dismiss her Whig ladies of the Bed-
iamber to satisfy her new Conservative minister, Sir Robert
eel, and Peel's consequent resignation. The queen's action,
owever, was really due as much to the advice of the late Whig
[inistry as to her own personal views; and Peel was in a
iinority in the House of Commons, or he could easily have en-
irced his wishes ; nor does it seem that Peel was in the right in
:tempting to exact an unconditional surrender from the Crown
-above all, in the case of a youthful and inexperienced girl—in
matter where her feelings were mainly concerned, especially as
er good sense was sure to convert her to the justice of his views
hen the excitement of the moment had worn off. However,
ie difficulty did not arise again.

In constitutional theory and in the formalities of appointment
iere has been no change apparent in the formation of a new
overnment. The monarch, now as ever, on receiving the
:signation of one set of ministers, sends for some influential
:atesman, commits to him the duty of forming a new Govern-
ient, considers and approves of the names he may submit as
is proposed colleagues, and confers on those who meet with
pproval the insignia of office : the whole process of appoint-
ient terminating by the ceremony known as "kissing hands."
in intelligent person, however, standing behind the scenes of all
iis picturesque medieval pageantry would soon become aware
hat the monarch invariably sends for the statesman—whether
eer or commoner—who is recognised by common consent to
ie the real leader of that party in the House of Commons
fhich by its numbers and successful parliamentary tactics has
ucceeded in obliging the last Government to resign, and does

x

this usually on the advice and recommendation of the defeated
and retiring Premier: moreover, that the statesman in question is
practically guided in the work of filling up the principal offices
in the new Government by the necessity of conciliating the
support of the leading men of his own side in Lords and Commons, and securing the adhesion of their personal following;
therefore though his choice with regard to the minor posts is almost
unfettered, the appointments to the seats in the Cabinet are
dictated by the same power which has secured his own supremacy. Further, that the recommendations of the Prime Minister
of names for office are never rejected by the monarch, and that
the moment when the individual member accepts the offer of the
Prime Minister of a seat in the Cabinet is the actual date when
the appointment is practically complete. It is important to
remember, however, that by strict law the individual member in
question does not become a minister of the Crown, has no claim
to the title, and no right to exercise the duties of his destined
department, until the office has been formally conferred on him
by the monarch and he himself has kissed hands on accepting it.

By gradual development it has become the established rule
that a Ministry thus formed remains in office so long only as it
commands the confidence of the House of Commons. Want of
confidence may be expressed by a defeat on some important
question. It may be shown more pointedly by a distinct vote
of censure. It may be fulminated with paralysing effect in a
refusal to pass the annual bills for the levying of the revenue
and preserving the discipline of the army—the Appropriation Bill
and the Mutiny Act. The exact moment when a minister de-
cides that he has lost the confidence of the House necessarily
depends in a great measure on the character of the individual
minister, but when he is at last satisfied that such is the case,
there are by constitutional custom two courses open to him:
—he can resign, or he can dissolve Parliament and appeal to
the country. If, however, the General Election results in the
return of a hostile majority, it will inevitably become his duty
to resign. During the early portion of the century it was the
custom for ministers to struggle on strenuously to the very last,
and to obstinately delay their resignation until positively obliged

o send it in by a decisive defeat in the House of Commons. Lord Melbourne's Ministry in 1841 remained in office after the opening of Parliament, though the General Election had given the Conservative Opposition a majority of over eighty, nor did they resign till compelled to do so by a distinct adverse vote of the Commons. Mr. Disraeli, however, when the General Election of 1868 returned a hostile Liberal majority to Parliament, introduced the convenient and admirable practice of resigning before the meeting of Parliament—a custom excellently adapted to save time and to diminish the bitterness of party enmity. This example was followed by Mr. Gladstone after the General Election of 1874, and by Lord Beaconsfield again after the General Election of 1880. In 1885, however, Lord Salisbury, relying on the fact that the Liberal party, though in a decided majority over any other party in the House of Commons, did not outnumber the united strength of the Conservatives and Parnellites, decided to remain in office until defeated on some important question. The course of precedent has been therefore broken, and the practice in the future is necessarily uncertain. It is perhaps, however, as well to notice that the monarch's prerogative of dismissing ministers at discretion remains wholly unimpaired by law, and might conceivably be exercised in the event of any glaring defiance of the will of the House of Commons, with very beneficial results. The prerogative of dissolution similarly, and of creating peers to force the hand of the House of Lords, though nominally only exercised at the request of the minister, might be refused conceivably to a minister who was obviously out of harmony with the nation.

Into the intricate details of ministerial custom and practice it is impossible to enter at any length, owing to the impenetrable secresy which enshrouds the proceedings of the Cabinet. Cabinet Councils and their results are continually noticed in the papers. Interviews between ministers and the queen are similarly inserted among the items of news. But the details of the meetings and interviews are never reported and can only be conjectured. It is easy to imagine that the amount of influence which the advice and recommendations of the monarch were wont to exercise on the policy and government of the country must have tended to gradually diminish during the present century, as a natural consequence of the loss of any possible means of enforcing the royal views in the event of disagreement with ministers; and that in modern times the political influence of the monarch must depend in a very great measure on the character of individual Prime Ministers. It is easy to comprehend, however, that the advice and experience of an impartial, well-intentioned, and business-like constitutional sovereign must be of incalculable value and considerable weight to even the most self-confident of statesmen. It is impossible to do more than conjecture that the amount of influence which individual ministers may exercise on the policy of the whole Cabinet must depend in a great measure on their own character and that of the Prime Minister. In matters, no doubt, which affect a particular department, the head of that department may be expected to have an authoritative voice. In matters of national interest Mr. Gladstone has shown us, with regard to the Irish Government Bill and Irish Land Purchase Bill of 1886, that it is possible for the overwhelming personality of the Prime Minister to exclude the whole Cabinet, almost to the last, from even any knowledge of the proposals about to be brought forward in the name of them all.

Public men of all parties are agreed that when a Prime Minister has been returned to power by a particular party, with the view of carrying out by their help a particular line of policy, it would be a most unjustifiable breach of good faith, which no motive, however excellent, would atone for, if he decided to initiate a contrary policy and yet abstained from resigning. Nor could it possibly be regarded as any palliation of such conduct that he could rely on the support of a majority in Parliament for the measures which he contemplated by the help of his political opponents. The power committed to the leader of a party by the votes of that party is a trust which must be exercised in accordance with their views, or at least the views of the majority of them; to abuse it, therefore, by carrying out however successfully a policy which is diametrically opposed to the views of ? majority of them, can only be regarded as a glaring and ?stifiable breach of trust.

It is on these grounds that, putting aside all considerations of motive, of national benefit, and the intrinsic merit of the course of policy actually carried out, most public men have agreed that the conduct of Sir Robert Peel in repealing the Corn Laws (1846) by the help of the Liberal Opposition and in defiance of the main body of his Conservative allies who had raised him to power, cannot be dismissed without censure. The honesty and political morality of Peel himself were beyond dispute, but the example was an exceedingly dangerous one, which, in the interests of public morality and party faith, were best forgotten. Peel himself recognised that the act debarred him from power for the future, and the silent acquiescence of his contemporaries in his complete withdrawal testified to their concurrence in his opinion. It is difficult to imagine that the public opinion of the present day would permit its repetition.

It may be laid down with undoubted authority as a settled rule of Cabinet government, that if a minister decidedly disapproves of a course of policy proposed by the Premier, it is his duty to resign and decline the responsibility which he disapproves of. Sir James Graham, Lord Ripon, and Mr. Stanley left Lord Melbourne's Ministry in 1834, rather than consent to any measures affecting the endowments of the Irish Church. Lords Derby and Carnarvon resigned their seats in Lord Beaconfield's Ministry in 1878, because they objected to the proposed warlike measures on behalf of Turkey during the Turko-Russian war. Messrs. Chamberlain and Trevelyan retired from Mr. Gladstone's Government in the spring of 1886, in consequence of their disapproval of their leader's proposed legislation for Ireland. It also appears to be recognised that if a minister approves of a measure as an advance in a particular direction, though in his heart he considers it an inadequate advance—a position which may be perhaps expressed by the homely maxim that "half a loaf is better than no bread"—he is not bound to resign, nor is he bound to conceal his hope for a further advance in the future. The recognition of this principle has enabled the Radical leaders at different periods to enter Liberal Ministries with the view of helping on the cause of Reform at a slow pace since it was impossible to urge it on any faster.

There is indisputable evidence, documentary and otherwise, that the policy of each department and its special minister is regulated by the opinions of the whole Cabinet, and more especially by the Prime Minister. As regards details, no doubt a great deal is left to the discretion of the individual in the interests of expediency, to avoid continual delays and vacillation, but it would be regarded as a very extraordinary breach of good faith for a minister in some important crisis, or in any matter of moment, however transitory, to act independently of his chief and his colleagues, still more if he acted in defiance of their expressed views. If, in fact, he finds that any other course of policy seems to him more adapted to the present need than that which has commended itself to the Cabinet, it is his duty to resign—the least that can be expected of him if he elects to remain in office is to refrain from giving expression to his own views in any way. It was in accordance with this principle that Lord John Russell dismissed Lord Palmerston in 1851. Lord Palmerston had an impetuous way of acting in his own department, the Foreign Office, as if he were the supreme dictator of foreign affairs, and it were Lord John Russell's business simply to look after home matters. He had, in consequence, very naturally excited the anger of the queen and her Prime Minister. The queen even wrote a very sharp reprimand to him, which has become historical :—

" The Queen requires, first, that Lord Palmerston should distinctly state what he proposes in a given case, in order that the Queen may know as distinctly to what she is giving her royal sanction.

" Secondly, that having once given her sanction to a measure, that it be not arbitrarily altered or modified by the minister. Such an act she must consider as failing in sincerity to the Crown, and justly to be visited by the exercise of her constitutional right of dismissing that minister. She expects to be kept informed of what passes between him and the foreign ministers, before important decisions are taken based upon that intercourse ; to receive the foreign despatches in good time ; and to have the drafts for her approval sent to her in sufficient time to make herself acquainted with their contents before they must be sent off."

This, subject to slight modifications to suit individual instances, the recognised theory of the duties of individual ministers.

Palmerston promised amendment, and the way in which he ept his word may be expressed in the Premier's own language: The first important transaction in which Lord Palmerston took part since the end of the last session of Parliament was his :ception of a deputation of delegates from certain metropolitan arishes respecting the treatment of the Hungarian refugees by ie Turkish Government. On this occasion I thought that my oble friend exhibited some want of due caution, but I gave him ie credit of supposing that this was through an oversight. The ext occasion to which I think it necessary to refer, relates to the vents which took place on the 2nd of December in France.[1] 'he instructions conveyed to our ambassador by the queen's iovernment were to abstain from all interference in the internal ffairs of that country. Being informed of an alleged conversation between Lord Palmerston and the French ambassador epugnant to those instructions, I wrote to that noble lord ; but iy inquiries for some days met with a disdainful silence, Lord 'almerston having in the meanwhile, without the knowledge of is colleagues, written a despatch containing instructions to Lord. Iormanby,[2] in which, however, he evaded the question whether e had approved the act of the President. I consider the noble ird's course of proceeding in this matter to be a putting himself i the place of the Crown and passing by the Crown. Under hese circumstances I had no alternative but to declare that /hilst I was Prime Minister, Lord Palmerston could not hold the eals of office." And on these grounds, concluded Russell, 'almerston has been dismissed.

The results of the second Reform Bill on the government of he country and the constitution of the House of Commons were further continuation of the work effected in 1832. The balance f power was once more violently disturbed, and the weight of uthority was transferred to the small shopkeeper class, who were

---

[1] The *coup d'état*, by which Louis Napoleon destroyed the Republic and stablished the third Empire.
[2] British ambassador at Paris.

thus for the first time endowed with the franchise, and who constituted by far the larger mass of the new voters. The result was seen in the changes which took place in the House of Commons, where there was a great liberalization. There were more business men, more men of inferior social standing, more professional politicians; there were fewer of the younger scions of noble houses, fewer representatives of the aristocratic families. Altogether the new assembly was a much more democratic assembly than its predecessor, and a more democratic tone was naturally imparted to the Government.

SECTION 2.—*The House of Lords.*

The change in the position of the House of Lords, which was one of the principal results of the passing of the Reform Bill, was not immediately apparent, owing to the failure of the extreme Tory lords to recognise the fact. Before 1832, it had been the principal function of the Peers to control, amend, and modify measures sent up from the Commons, rather than to originate legislation or direct the policy of the country; after that date their principal function remained identically the same, and they exercised it for some years under the stubborn and somewhat spiteful leadership of Lord Lyndhurst, with precisely the same autocratic spirit that had actuated their decisions in the good old days of aristocratic government before the Reform Bill. In 1835 and 1836, they obliged the Commons to give up the principle of appropriating surplus ecclesiastical revenues to lay purposes in dealing with the Irish Church question. They inserted amendments at will in the English Municipal Reform Bill, in spite of the remonstrances of Wellington, and a serious quarrel would have ensued with the Commons but for the wise and statesmanlike conduct of the Conservative leaders which effected a compromise.

They resisted for years the removal of the Jewish disabilities In 1860, they even ventured to reject a bill for the Repeal of the Paper Duty, and successfully defied all the representations of the Commons that by this act they were infringing on the financial privilege of the Lower House.

The bitter experience of 1832, however, had convinced the

nore wary and intelligent among the Conservative peers,
hat it was no longer possible or tolerable for the Tory majority
n the Lords to relentlessly pit themselves against a Reforming
najority in the House of Commons, and to reject or assent to a
)ill solely because they happened to like or dislike it. The
:lement of discretion and enlightened forbearance must for the
'uture leaven their conduct in dealing with obnoxious measures.
:t was unlikely that an independent House of Commons,
,wayed by a large Reforming majority, would consent to allow
.ll their most cherished schemes to be hacked and hewed, and
n many cases turned completely inside out, for ever, with the ex-
,mple of 1832 before them. It might occur to them that the Tory
najority might be easily transformed into a Reforming majority,
)r at least that the two parties might be brought nearer equality
vith very satisfactory results. It became the constant care of the
)uke of Wellington, during the latter years of his career, to
mpress again and again on the extreme Tory peers that they
nust not act like spiteful children, still less must they imagine
hat their assembly was any longer co-ordinate in power with
he House of Commons. They must recognise that their true
)osition was to improve crude legislation, and to insure that
,weeping measures should not become law until they had been
horoughly discussed, and their tendency fully explained. It was
;till the business of the Lords to revise and modify legislation,
)ut they must understand that revision was not the same as a
·eduction to the lowest possible terms, nor was a modification
ikely to be satisfactory which was equivalent to total destruction.
[he Peers resisted his wise advice for a long time, but it steadily
;ained in effect, until at last it is possible to lay down a series of
·ules—the result solely of practice—by which the unlimited legal
·ight residing in the Peers of rejection and amendment is now
·egulated.

It appears to be recognised that in dealing with *unimportant*
)ills the Peers can do as they like—can exercise their revising
)owers so as to materially improve a crude measure and render
t far more effective of its original purpose, or, if the fit seizes
:hem, can mutilate it almost beyond recognition, and thus compel
ts abandonment ; or, if the people seem indifferent to its merits,

can kill it at once by simple rejection.   With regard to *important* bills, the unwritten code appears to prescribe that when the Commons and the country are resolved that a measure shall pass, the Lords confine themselves to tentative amendments which do not affect the main principle of the bill, and which they insist on with more or less firmness in proportion to the pressure exerted by the Commons.   If the pressure from below is unusually powerful and determined, and there appears to be no hope of compromise, the Lords as a rule find it advisable to give way.   The process therefore by which the most of the reforming legislation has been passed in the present century, consists of several stages :—first, the stage of being regarded by the Lords as an unimportant bill, and being hustled out of existence with scant courtesy ; secondly, the stage of uncertainty, when the majorities in the Commons were scanned with great eagerness, and the Peers confined themselves to amendments which they were not always sure of enforcing ; thirdly, the stage of importance, when the bill comes up supported by overwhelming majorities in the Commons and the country, and is accepted with a bad grace whole, like a pill.   It is well to note that the standard of importance and unimportance, of greater or less pressure, is based solely on the size and eagerness of the majority in the Commons and the enthusiasm visible among the people.

The political weight of the House of Lords has been undoubtedly considerably injured by the utter indifference displayed by the great mass of its members, the very scanty attendance, and the practice of voting by proxy.   The latter custom was very wisely suspended in 1868, and the attendance has in consequence become far more regular.   Regarded merely as a businesslike assembly, the House of Lords ranks far above the House of Commons.   The debates may be devoid of interest, the atmosphere dull and decorous, and the sittings short and uneventful, but this must be mainly attributed to the fact that the Lords do not waste any time in idle discussions and recrimination, that obstruction is a thing unknown, undreamt of, and their debates are intended for argument, not for display.   The result is that the Lords as a rule get through their work in less than half the time that the Commons take, and frequently dispose

f a bill in a single night which the Commons have wrangled
ver for weeks. Occasionally additional interest is imparted to
ıe debates, with the result of extending them, by the presence
f the Premier. The result, however, is but slight, for even
ıinisterial statements are found to be capable of considerable
ompression where there is no premium on words.

An attempt was made in 1856 to introduce the practice of
reating Life Peers—an innovation which must in the end have
een inimical to the hereditary principle, though it seems that
.ord Palmerston's Government was not actuated by any insidious
ıotive. There was nothing actually repugnant to existing usage
ı the idea of a life peerage itself. The archbishops, bishops,
nd the Irish representative peers all held their seats strictly for
fe only. Our own times have seen the fullest recognition of the
ıct in the creation of "the Law Lords." Still the principle was
ndoubtedly only recognised in official peerages; and when Sir
ames Parke was created Lord Wensleydale *for life* only, the
atent was distinctly irregular. The Lords therefore inquired
ıto the subject, and reported that there was no precedent [1] for
ıe grant of a patent of an *ordinary* peerage for life later than the
:ign of Richard II.; that the right was therefore as obsolete as the
ıyal veto, and could not be revived by prerogative. The Ministry
:adily yielded the point, and Parke was given a new patent of a
ereditary peerage.

The allusion to "the Law Lords" in the last paragraph renders
necessary to explain an important change which has lately been
fected with regard to the judicial powers of the House of Lords.
ustom had for a long time limited the exercise of the appellate
ırisdiction to those members of the House of Peers who had
ıme practical and official knowledge of law. The Judicature
.ct in its original form (1873) contemplated the entire extinction
f the appellate jurisdiction of the Lords. It did not, however,
ıme into operation immediately, and by 1875 a great Conserva-
ve reaction had passed over the country. The original statute

---

[1] There are numerous instances of ladies being raised to the peerage for
fe by their royal admirers, but as these grants did not involve the right of
tting and voting, they were not regarded as precedents.

was amended, so as to preserve to the Lords their rights of final appeal. In 1876, however, the Appellate Jurisdiction Act was passed, which placed matters on a far more satisfactory footing. It was provided that the right should practically be exercised solely by those members of the House who had at some period or other held high judicial office, and who were to be called the Lords of Appeal. In order moreover to insure further efficiency in this august tribunal, the queen was empowered to create other Lords of Appeal from among the judges, who were to rank as barons, with full rights as peers, except that their peerages were not hereditary, and they were liable to be removed on petition of both Houses.

Section 3.—*The House of Commons.*

It is almost to be expected that the lapse of nearly a century should not have left the internal details of the House of Commons exactly where they were before the passing of the Reform Bill of 1832.

The character of the members themselves has perhaps been the subject of the greatest change; numerous classes have been rendered eligible for Parliament who were not so before, others have been expressly disqualified by statute. The old Property Qualification Law, which had been evaded with impunity for over a century, was relaxed in 1838 so as to admit personal incomes of the same value as a qualification for membership; in 1858, however, the utter futility of attempting to enforce these laws being at last recognised, they were repealed. The successive lowerings of the franchise have in each case been followed by the admission of a larger number of business-men to the House, and the consequent diminution of the proportion of idlers. The last General Election has even been productive of a body of so-called "labour" candidates—a term which does not imply that the members in question are "working-men" at the present moment in the usually received acceptance of the word, whatever may have been their origin, but simply that they are sent to Parliament expressly to represent the interests of the working men more particularly than any others.

The Reform Bill of 1832, which Lord John Russell regarded

s a final measure, seemed to the Radical members very incomlete, and in consequence in the very next year motions were rought forward for the introduction of the Ballot, to secure the omplete freedom of elections, and for the re-establishment of riennial Parliaments, in order to insure to the constituencies a reater control over their members. Neither effort, however, was ttended with much success; but in spite of this, under the uccessive auspices of Messrs. Grote, Ward, and Berkeley the notion for the ballot became almost an annual one. The actual uestion of a further reform of the franchise was first really revived y Mr. Hume, in 1848, in a Radical measure which advocated ousehold suffrage, triennial Parliaments, equal electoral districts, nd the ballot. It was rejected; as equally was a measure ntroduced by Mr. Locke King, in 1851, for the assimilation of the orough and county franchise. Mr. Locke King, however, noays daunted by his defeat, continued to bring forward his notion again and again with varying ill-success. In 1852, Lord ohn Russell once more took up the subject of Reform, and ntroduced a bill the chief features of which were a slight lowering f the franchise and a partial redistribution of seats. This proosal, however, and another made in 1854, were failures; as also as a bill brought forward by Lord Derby's Government in 1859. Another abortive measure of Russell's, in 1860, practically shelved he question for the time, and it was not taken up again till 1866, hen Mr. Gladstone made an energetic but highly unsuccessful ttempt to deal with it. In consequence Mr. Disraeli, his uccessor, found it necessary to make Reform a Government neasure; and after his proposed bill had been subjected to a evere criticism and amendment at the hands of the Liberal)pposition, it finally assumed a form which may be briefly sumnarised as follows :—

In the boroughs household suffrage was established, and the ranchise was extended as well to persons occupying lodgings at a ent of £10 per annum and upwards. The existing county [ualifications were reduced by one-half, and a £12 occupation ranchise created. The principal effects of the disfranchisement lauses were the total disfranchisement of about eleven boroughs, artial disfranchisement of 35 others. Nine new boroughs and

two new metropolitan districts were created. Leeds, Liverpool,
Birmingham, Manchester, were to return three members instead of
two ; and several of the larger counties were to be re-divided with
additional members.   One of the most characteristic provisions of
this measure was the so-called Minority Clause, which declared
that in three-cornered constituencies [1] the electors should only
give two votes.   The object of this device was to insure the
representation of the minority in large constituencies ; but it was
immediately realized by the wire-pullers that where the majority
was sufficiently large it would be easy to neutralise the effect of
the minority clause by perfection of organization and a careful
arrangement of all available votes.   In Birmingham, for instance,
at every General Election between 1867 and 1880 the Radical
chiefs have invariably so carefully planned out the electoral
campaign that they have always succeeded in carrying their three
candidates in despite the desperate efforts of the Conservatives.
There were also bills introduced in the following year for
Scotland and Ireland providing considerable alterations of the
franchise, though not on so extensive a scale as in England.
Scotland was moreover given seven additional members.

The Reform Act of 1867, however, left the question of distribution of members in a very unsatisfactory condition, it made
no effort to remove the differences existing between the county
and borough franchise, and it made no provision for the introduction of the ballot.   Tke latter omission was soon remedied by a
temporary Act in 1872, which has since been made permanent.
In the same year moreover, Mr. G. O. Trevelyan introduced a bill
for the assimilation of the county and borough franchise which
became an annual measure, and in due time was adopted by the
whole Liberal party.   The Gladstone Ministry of 1880 were practically pledged to a further reform, and their pledges bore fruit in
1884-5 in two bills for the reform of the franchise and a redistribution of seats.   The former established a uniform household
and lodger franchise in county and borough, with further extensions with the object of insuring the enfranchisement of numerous
classes who were not actually owners or tenants of houses.

---

[1] Those returning three members,

The latter rearranged the country into districts containing on
.n average from 50,000 to 60,000 inhabitants apiece, and re-
listributed the existing number of members among them, with a
urther provision that there should be one member only to each
:lectoral district, except in the case of those old boroughs which
vere allowed to retain their original two members on the grounds
if sufficient population. Among the principal results of this
neasure were the increase of the members of metropolitan
nembers to 59, of the members for Birmingham and Glasgow to
even each, and those for Liverpool to nine. The redistribution
1 Scotland and Ireland necessarily could not be carried out on
xactly the same lines as in England; it was arranged, however,
o as to insure due proportion between population and repre-
entation. The number of members allotted to Scotland was
noreover raised to 70.

At different times during the century—to look at the other side
if the case—disqualifying laws have met with the approval of
'arliament. The custom which excluded clergymen from Parlia-
nent was embodied in a statute 1801. Minors, aliens, traitors,
elons, persons convicted of bribery, bankrupts, revising barristers,
iolice magistrates, returning officers, county-court judges, and
udges of the High Court of Appeal have in turn been declared
nsuitable persons to sit in the House of Commons. On the
ither hand, the legislation directed against holders of offices under
he Crown was so far relaxed in the interests of the public service
iy the second Reform Bill that a member actually holding one
iffice does not vacate his seat on his transference to another.
[he religious disqualifications were removed little by little after a
ong struggle. The admission of Dissenters and Roman Catholics
n 1828–9 was quickly followed by a law which allowed a Quaker
o substitute an affirmation for the parliamentary oath, and cleared
he way for the entrance of Moravians and Separatists. The
trong prejudices existing against the Jews rendered their relief in
his respect a far more difficult matter, and it required a long and
rduous struggle, diversified by one or two scenes in the House of
'ommons, before the obstinate resistance of the House of Lords
ras finally overcome (1858). Ten years later the law was finally
mended so as to provide one oath which could be taken by any

person who believed in any form of Supreme Being—it being open to the privileged sects to substitute a solemn affirmation for the oath in question. As it happened, there was no provision made in any of these statutes for an atheist, and the result we have seen in the Bradlaugh case. Mr. Charles Bradlaugh, the junior member for Northampton, in 1880 declared at the opening of Parliament that the oath would not be binding on his conscience, and claimed to be allowed to affirm instead. It was pointed out to him, in the summary way peculiar to the House of Commons, that there was no statute which would allow him to do so. The result, in fact, of the legislation of the century is that an atheist is almost the only person in the kingdom who is still excluded by conscientious motives from Parliament. It may be perhaps instructive to add that at the opening of the Parliament of 1886 Mr. Bradlaugh, once more elected for Northampton and tired of sitting out in the cold below the bar waiting for the remedial legislation which never came, swallowed his scruples and the oath and took his seat in the ordinary manner.

We have referred in an earlier chapter to the extraordinary mode by which election disputes were settled in the eighteenth century, and the ineffectual attempt to remedy the abuse in 1770.[1] Matters did not improve in the nineteenth century. The conduct of the election committees in 1838 drew from Mr. O'Connell a fierce denunciation that they were guilty of " foul perjury." A Mr. Poulter, who had been unseated on petition in the same year, declared that " the seat had been as completely filched from him as ever a purse was from a person on the common highway." This plain speaking was visited with public censure by the House, but the general truth that lay at the bottom of it was only too apparent. A further effort was made by Sir Robert Peel in 1839 to insure judicial impartiality in the decision of contested elections,[2] but the question was not really removed from the influence of party politics till 1868, when the trial of election petitions was transferred from the House

---

[1] *v.* p. 194.

[2] A general committee of elections was to elect a committee of six (later five), who were to decide all election disputes.

Commons to the judges. The Commons, of course, still tained the right of deciding all questions connected with their vn privileges, and also of determining whether an elected ndidate fulfilled the requirements of the laws in respect of igibility, capacity to take the oath or the affirmation, and any other points, but the actual decision as to the *validity of return* is now reserved for a strictly impartial and non-political bunal—an arrangement which seems only in accordance with mmon-sense and justice.

Prominent among the abuses of the old representative system as that of bribery. It survived the changes effected by the eform Bill, and developed largely in consequence of the great crease of the franchise and the almost parallel accumulations wealth. The old boroughs spared by the Act were the orst offenders : their unblushing corruption in many cases was eservedly punished by total or partial disfranchisement. But e new ones vied with the old, and improved on the lessons venality handed down from bygone generations. It became ecessary very soon to provide some general stringent remedies r the wholesale corruption which pervaded the electoral stem. Lord John Russell, in 1841-2, attempted to deal with e question. A further effort of a more searching kind was ade ten years later. In 1854, another statute was added to e roll, but its efficacy may be estimated by the fact that in 360 the writs for Gloucester and Wakefield were suspended consequence of the extreme corruption of those places. he payment of voters' travelling expenses was expressly cut ff in 1858, and the second Reform Bill added providing coneyances for voters to the long list of possible items of bribery. he Conservative Government, in 1880, on the eve of a General lection, thought fit to repeal the latter provision, but the onard march of legislation was very soon resumed again in the aape of the Corrupt Practices Act of 1883. This remarkble measure greatly increased the list of illegal payments and ctions with regard to elections, including, among others, the ld bone of contention, providing carriages ; established very tringent limitations on the election bills of candidates ; and xpressly defined the exact number of paid agents permissible.

Y

The strongest possible inducement is provided to deter all parties from illegal proceedings by the fact that corrupt practices of any kind, whether effected by the candidate himself, or by his agent with his consent, or even by his unwise followers without his knowledge or consent, are sufficient to vacate the seat. The unseating Messrs. West and Jesse Collings on the Ipswich election petition (1886), in consequence of the ill-advised energy of some of their supporters, is a sufficient and salutary warning that the election judges will not err on the side of lenity in interpreting the clauses of the Act.

Shortly after the Reform Bill, the House of Commons began to publish full reports of their own proceedings, which were supplemented later by the publication of the daily division lists and the questions put by members to witnesses before select committees. They further ordered, in the general interest, that their publications should be sold as cheaply as possible. This excellent example was imitated somewhat later by the House of Lords. One of the most important results of this complete opening up of all the dark places of parliamentary life, was the diminution of the senatorial and utterly irresponsible character of members; the rendering them far more amenable to the wishes and the censure of their constituents; and, above all, the purification of the moral atmosphere of Parliament, and the final sweeping away of the last remnants of the Augean corruption of the eighteenth century. It is, however, a curious instance of the tenacity with which ancient customs are preserved, that the privilege itself has never been relinquished, and that reporting is still a breach of privilege. Parliamentary censure, however, is reserved for wilful misrepresentation, an offence which is now almost unknown.

The extreme freedom of parliamentary utterances and the candid expressions of opinion on all and every subject, which is the prevailing characteristic of parliamentary papers, was likely to be extremely unwelcome to persons who might find themselves the object of animadversion in them; and in consequence the right of the Commons to publish statements affecting character was very shortly disputed in the celebrated ase of *Stockdale* v. *Hansard.* It appeared that in 1836 Messrs. Hansard, the parliamentary printers, published by order of the House a report of the Inspector of Prisons, in which a book published by Mr. J. Stockdale, and found among the prisoners at Newgate, was described as "obscene and indecent"—a very fair instance of the "call a spade a spade" style of parliamentary reports in general. Stockdale brought an action for libel against Messrs. Hansard, but as the book was proved to be actually obscene and indecent, the verdict went against him. Lord Chief Justice Denman, however, who tried the case, took the opportunity of mentioning that in his opinion the resolutions of either House of Parliament were not laws, and could not authorize that which was unlawful in itself; therefore the order of the House of Commons would not justify the publication of a libel on any man in a parliamentary paper. This ruling was naturally very offensive to the House of Commons, and when Stockdale brought another action and *won* it on the direct issue that the order of the House was no justification to the printer, they began to get very hot, and with the view, no doubt, of maintaining their dignity, directed the Hansards not to take any notice of any more actions.

The result was that the third of the series, brought in the recess of 1839, went by default; the damages were assessed at £600, and the sheriffs successfully levied them. The House of Commons now rose to the occasion. They imprisoned Stockdale and the sheriffs; and as the indefatigable Stockdale kept on bringing actions even during his imprisonment, they went on imprisoning a number of other innocent people connected with the actions or levying of the damages, until at last they had some thirty or forty prisoners on hand without the remotest idea what to do with them. The position of the House of Commons became very embarrassing, for their action was extremely unpopular, and the unlucky sheriffs naturally aroused a great deal of sympathy. Yet there is little doubt that the House behaved with great temper and moderation under very trying circumstances, and that they were really asserting a privilege which was indispensable to the due performance of their duty. The key-note to the whole situation was aptly

struck by Sir Robert Peel when he asked the House: " Do you
believe that slavery would have been abolished unless we
had published to the world the evidence of the abuses and
horrors of slavery?"   At the same time it was quite clear that
unless the House could protect its agents, the right of publication would be a dead letter, and that the old mode of enforcing
privilege by imprisoning innocent people was at once dangerous,
ridiculous, and ineffectual.   Lord John Russell therefore, acting
in obedience to the general opinion of the House, brought in
a bill conferring this useful privilege on both Houses, and the
bill rapidly became law.

Sir Erskine May is of opinion that had the Hansards carried
their case into a higher Court on a writ of error, the higher
Court might have decided in favour of privilege, for this actually
happened in the case of *Howard* v. *Gosset*, which arose out of
Stockdale v. *Hansard*.   Howard was Stockdale's attorney and
one of the arrested persons.   On his release he brought an
action against Sir W. Gosset, the Serjeant-at-Arms, for the arrest.
The lower Courts decided in favour of Howard.   The higher
Court, on a writ of error, decided in favour of privilege.   Undoubtedly, however, the termination of the question once and
for ever by the legislative power was by far the most satisfactory
solution.

It is almost natural that there should have been very few
illustrations of the older privileges.   The right of freedom of
speech has not been disputed by any outside power, and the
right of freedom from arrest has been conspicuous chiefly in
consequence of the recognition of certain very salutary limitations on it.   It was held not to cover contempt of court, and
Messrs. Whalley and Onslow, members of Parliament, who
were both committed for contempt of court during the progress
of the Tichborne case, were unable to protect themselves
under the shelter of privilege.   In 1883 moreover, in consequence of sundry speeches which appeared to amount to
incitements to violence and breach of the law generally, Mr.
Healy and some of his Irish colleagues were bound over to
keep the peace, and committed to prison in default.   The
question was raised in the House whether this were not a breach

privilege. The Marquis of Hartington, who was then leading
e House in the absence of Mr. Gladstone, declared that
·ivilege did not cover the refusal to give securities against
·each of the peace, and in proof of his statement he quoted
.e resolution of the Lords to that effect in the case of the
arl of Arundel,[1] 1626.

The privilege of controlling the conduct of its own members
ıd the progress of its own debates, which the House of Com-
ons has always claimed with the utmost jealousy, received an
ıusual amount of illustration during the century, especially with-
ı the last ten years. It is necessary, however, first to refer to
ıe two earlier cases. In 1847, Baron Lionel de Rothschild was
ected for the city of London. As a Jew, he was unable con-
:ientiously to take the parliamentary oath, and, in consequence,
ᴇ sat for two sessions below the bar of the House, waiting for
gislative relief, which never came. In 1850, he determined to
resent himself and take the oath, with certain omissions. He
ad no sooner done so, than he was directed to withdraw; and,
:ter a long discussion of the law and the situation, the House
ecided that he could not take his seat or vote until he had taken
ıe oath in the exact form prescribed by the statute. This decision
ıe House repeated in the case of Mr. Salomons, who, on his
lection for Greenwich, proceeded to take the oath in the same
regular way. Mr. Salomons, however, insisted on taking his
ᴇat as well, and a skirmish ensued between him and the Serjeant-
ᴛ-Arms before he could be removed. He carried the case at
nce into the law courts; but they decided unanimously in favour
f the Commons. The question which was at issue on both these
ccasions was, whether the House has the right to prevent a duly
lected member from taking his seat; and in each case they
ıccessfully asserted their claim to do so. Thrice moreover in
ıe century they have asserted their right to decide whether
ertain elected members were eligible for election; and they
eclared that Messrs. Mitchel and Davitt were rendered ineligible
ᴏr election by their previous conviction of treason-felony. This
ight of jurisdiction over their own members was retained even

---

[1] *v.* p. 69.

when the jurisdiction over election petitions was surrendered; but it would be impossible now-a-days to exercise it in a manner contrary to the spirit of the law, or subversive of the liberty of the subject.

During the last ten years, the obstructive tactics of the Irish members, who grouped themselves round the leadership of Mr. Parnell, have rendered it necessary to introduce several amendments of the old rules of privilege, and to entrust the House and the Speaker with far more stringent powers of coercing and defeating attempts at wilful obstruction than were found sufficient before.   Mr. Biggar, member for Cavan, in 1875 invented the ingenious idea of wilfully delaying legislation by the abuse of the privilege which still survived to each member, of calling for the expulsion of any strangers who might happen to be in the House, when, of course, a long pause would ensue in the debate in order that his request might be carried out.   These tactics Mr. Biggar repeated with striking effect on various occasions,—it happened that one of the persons hustled out unceremoniously at one time, in obedience to the mischievous will of the Irish pork butcher, was the Prince of Wales himself,—until at last the nuisance became so great that it had to be specially dealt with.   In order to put a stop to Mr. Biggar's unbridled hostility to strangers, the general body of members were obliged to surrender their ancient privilege.   It was resolved that for the future, when a member desired the expulsion of strangers, the question should be at once referred to the decision of the whole House.   The Speaker, however, still retained the right of ordering the House to be cleared at discretion.

In 1877, however, matters became worse and worse.   A small knot of men among the Home Rulers banded themselves together to systematically obstruct all legislation, in the hope of irritating the British Parliament into granting Home Rule to Ireland. Disclaimed by their nominal leader, Mr. Butt, they ranged themselves under the active chieftainship of Mr. Parnell, member for Cork, and Mr. Biggar, and abused all the rules of the House, for purposes of systematic obstruction, with tireless and intolerable ingenuity and perseverance.   "Day after day the House was harassed with their notices of amendments, motions of adjournment, and rganized delay, carried out with the all but avowed intention of ·ringing the proceedings of the British Parliament into disrepute nd slight regard." It was a favourite amusement moreover with /Ir. Biggar to relieve himself of the trouble of exercising his inven- ion in order to prolong his speech, by the simple expedient of read- ıg long and endless quotations from Blue-books, which, though hey were never strictly off the point, were aggravating, tedious, and ʀholly unnecessary. Every now and then moreover the Govern- nent would be goaded to fury, and personal altercations of the nost undignified kind broke out between them and the Obstruc- ives. Mr. O'Donnell would coolly complain of the waste of ɔrivate members' time by the Government. Mr. Parnell would .ttack the Government for their delays and general mismanage- nent of public business. Last of all, Mr. Chaplin would furiously lenounce these speeches as proofs of their "stubborn insensibility o the sentiments by which gentlemen in that House had almost nvariably been actuated," and would solemnly warn the Obstruc- ives that they would not be permitted to "bully" the House of Commons.

At last, Sir Stafford Northcote, Chancellor of the Exchequer, moved that a Resolution be passed to the effect that when a member has been *twice* declared out of order, a motion be made :hat he be not heard any longer, and put to the vote at once. In the debate which ensued, the Resolution was naturally not favoured by the Irish, though it was supported by the principal men on both sides of the House. Major O'Gorman, who was recognised as a standing joke, even rose and warned the House, in his richest style, to beware lest another Cromwell should come and bid them once more "take away that bauble"; but, in spite of this eloquent appeal, the Resolution became law.

It produced very little effect, however. Matters became worse and worse during the debates on the South African Bill. When the bill was brought forward in committee, seven members— Messrs. Parnell, Biggar, O'Donnell, Power, Gray, Kirk, and Captain Nolan—determined that it should not pass. Sir Stafford North- cote was equally resolved not to give way till the bill had gone through committee, and he was unhesitatingly supported by the leaders of the Opposition. The seven, however, held on with a

perseverance worthy of a better cause. Thirteen motions for
adjournment were made successively; and while the majority
varied from 150 to 77, the minority never rose above five. Repu-
diated by Mr. Butt and the true Irish party, denounced repeatedly
by the leading men on both sides, pitted against an overwhelming
majority, which maintained the struggle easily all through the
night, by means of well-organized systems of relief, the seven
Obstructives held on for twenty-seven hours, until at last they
gave way to threats of decided action on the part of the Government. Sir Stafford Northcote, it may be interesting to note,
remained at his post facing his foes all through the long sitting.

The question of obstruction was rather shelved by foreign policy
till 1879, when, during the debates on the abolition of the "cat,"
Mr. Parnell, Mr. Biggar, and their friends reappeared in the old
rôles, and moved an almost endless series of minute amendments
with the greatest zeal and apparent gusto. Mr. Biggar especially distinguished himself by hinting that the Chairman of Committees (Mr. Raikes) was incapable of conducting the business of
the House. He was promptly called to order; and, after a fierce
wrangle, he ultimately rose and, with the thumb of one hand in
the armhole of his waistcoat—a graceful action painfully familiar
to the House by now—delivered himself of the following remarkable sentiment: "Of course, Mr. Raikes, I withdraw any expression
I may have used; but I really don't remember what I am supposed
to have said."

In the session of 1880, the debates on the Address and the
Distress Bill were so unusually protracted by deliberate obstruction, that more stringent measures became necessary to enable
the House to deal with the offenders. Resolutions were passed
enabling the Speaker to *name* members whom he considered
guilty of wilful obstruction, when the question was to be at once
put, "That the member be suspended during the sitting." When
moreover any member had been suspended three times in a
session, the House was empowered to suspend him for a week or
more at discretion. This bold front shown towards obstruction
had a considerable effect on the business of the rest of the session,
but its beneficial influence was found in the long run to be purely
temporary.

The same session supplied an interlude from the eternal ques-
ion of obstruction in the shape of a breach of privilege of the
ood old-fashioned sort. Mr. Plimsoll, member for Derby, had
btained leave to introduce a bill intended to lessen the chances
f disaster to merchant ships at sea. Sir Charles Russell (West-
1inster), and Mr. Onslow (Guildford), had given notice of oppo-
ition to the second reading, that is, had " blocked " the bill, with
1e result that it could not be taken after half-past twelve. The
nly chance, therefore, was on the private members' day, Wednes-
ay, and as Wednesday evenings are disposed of by the ballot,
nd are moreover always liable to be seized on by the Govern-
1ent for their own ends, Mr. Plimsoll comprehended that his
ill was postponed to the Greek Kalends. Highly indignant, he
lacarded Westminster and Guildford, denouncing the inhumanity
f the two hostile members, and calling on their constituents to
how their resentment. The two denounced called on Mr.
'limsoll to apologise, and as he refused to do so, avowed their
1tention of formally complaining of the breach of privilege. To
void a scene, Mr. Plimsoll yielded and made an ample apology.
lut Sir Stafford Northcote was determined on a scene : the
rivileges of the House had been infringed and they must be
indicated. It was quite bad enough that the Irish members
eemed totally devoid of any respect for the House ; it would not
o to allow Mr. Plimsoll to fall into the same evil ways. So
ir Stafford denounced Mr. Plimsoll to the House, and moved
1at a Resolution censuring his conduct should be entered on the
1lls of the House—which was duly done after an animated
ebate raised by certain obstinate members who refused to ap-
reciate either the humour or pathos of the situation, and persisted
1 looking at the matter from a purely common-sense point of
iew, namely that as Mr. Plimsoll had apologised there ought to be
n end of the matter. An Irish member, one Mr. Sullivan, took
1e opportunity to rise at the end of the discussion, and with an
xcellent assumption of earnest indignation insisted that the
:ader of the House should support him in bringing before the
ar one Major Jocelyn, who had venture to stigmatise a section
f the members of the House as "a despicable lot of Irish rebels."
'his appeal was treated as a parody on the proceedings against

Mr. Plimsoll, but many members considered that on the strict
point of principle there was no real difference between the two
cases.

In the same year, after the General Election and the overthrow
of Lord Beaconsfield's .Government, the House found itself con-
fronted by a more appalling nuisance even than Mr. Biggar.
This was Mr. Charles Bradlaugh, the newly elected member of
Northampton. The great Bradlaugh question extended really
over several years, but for the sake of clearness it may as well
be disposed of at once. It originally arose, as has been already
mentioned, out of Mr. Bradlaugh's atheistic disinclination to take
the parliamentary oath, and the resolution of the House that the
statute did not permit an atheist to affirm. The obliging Mr.
Bradlaugh thereupon offered to take the oath itself as the House
was so particular on the subject—it would not be binding on his
conscience, of course, any more than an affirmation, but that was
no matter if the House wished it. The House debated and
quarrelled over the subject again and again. The Bradlaugh
question became a great party question, and at one time, when
the anti-Bradlaughites happened to be at their posts, the elected
of Northampton was solemnly denied the right of taking the oath.
At another, when the Bradlaughites were most *en evidence*, it
was decided that he might make an affirmation if he liked and
take the consequences as well—which he promptly did with a
lavish disregard for the latter that was almost sublime. For a
short time, therefore, the elected was actually member for Northampton, and he sat and voted with a liberality that would have
been alarming to a less heroic person. In the end he was evicted
from his seat by an action at law, and became liable to a bill of
£500 for each vote that he had given. Thereupon a new writ
was issued, and he was once more elected for Northampton,
April 9, 1881.

He now tried to take his seat by force, and a period of considerable excitement followed. It became almost a standing
order of the day for Mr. Bradlaugh to rush across the body of
the House and insist "firmly but respectfully" on being allowed to
take the oath. It was equally well understood that Captain Gosset
(the Serjeant-at-Arms) and sundry ancient retainers would at

once advance to the rescue and escort Mr. Bradlaugh "gently but firmly" away, and that meanwhile Mr. Gladstone, Sir Stafford Northcote, Mr. Labouchere, Lord Randolph Churchill, would fling personalities at one another, and rage round the body of Bradlaugh like the Greeks and Trojans over the corpse of Paroclus. So far there was little harm done.

Later, however, an awful rumour spread that Mr. Bradlaugh, like a second Lord George Gordon, was coming down to the House accompanied by a mob. Matters were getting serious. It was felt that the might of Serjeant Gosset would not be enough for the protection of the House; reinforcements were therefore called in in the shape of Inspector Denning and a number of policemen. When therefore Mr. Bradlaugh actually advanced to the siege of the House, he found it as impregnable as the lines of Torres Vedras. He was allowed to come alone into the lobby, but he was not allowed to advance further. On his attempting to force his way into the House there was a general "scrimmage," in which the Serjeant, the deputy-Serjeant, and a number of messengers and policemen all contended against the indomitable Bradlaugh, with the result that he was at last deposited outside in Palace Yard considerably shaken, and with his raiment very much the worse for the somewhat rough handling it had gone through. Once more the matter was concluded by a formal resolution of the House against Mr. Bradlaugh.

The case went again to the Courts in the shape of actions against Serjeant Gosset and deputy-Serjeant Erskine. The latter terminated in 1882, the former not till 1884. They were both grounded on allegations of assault, and in the end the verdict in each case was decidedly in favour of privilege. "The House of Commons," said Lord Chief Justice Coleridge at great length and in the due legal jargon, "has full control over everything within its own walls, and the law-courts cannot even inquire into any action of the House within the House. If therefore its actions were illegal in the ordinary sense of the word, there would be no possible remedy." This ruling, when finally given in *Bradlaugh* v. *Gosset*, practically ended the question, and formed the most conclusive legal decision on the subject of privilege which had yet been placed on record.

In 1882, the Bradlaugh episode reappeared in a fresh form. Mr. Bradlaugh, after vainly asserting his right to take the oath, determined on a bold stroke. On Feb. 21, he hurried up the floor of the House to the table, and to the utter stupefaction of the members on both sides took a New Testament from his pocket and proceeded to calmly swear himself in. He then produced a paper certifying that he had sworn himself duly in, signed this document, and turned to the House with an air of expectation. The House now broke out into insane rage. They howled and shouted in a manner that would have satisfied the oldest precedents. Lord Randolph Churchill denounced Mr. Bradlaugh and Mr. Gladstone with equal vehemence, and demanded vengeance. Mr. Bradlaugh himself took part in the wrangle, and from a seat below the gangway laid down the law to the Speaker with a coolness and a freedom that brought the House to the verge of madness. In the end, by formal motion of Sir Stafford Northcote, he was solemnly expelled for contempt.

The question cropped up again and again at different times, for Mr. Bradlaugh was never weary of the excitement of a fresh election at Northampton and triumphant return, a sudden descent on the House, a repetition of the process of swearing himself in, a fresh wrangle and a fresh expulsion, followed by a storm of indignation and recrimination in the papers. At last, however, in 1884, an action was instituted by the Attorney-General to settle the dispute once and for all, and after a solemn and careful trial, Lord Chief Justice Coleridge and his fellows decided that an avowed atheist could not take the oath in Parliament, and there was no statute empowering him to make an affirmation.

It may be as well to note that the loophole discovered to admit Mr. Bradlaugh to the present Parliament consists in the fact that he offered to take the oath without avowing his atheism, and that there is therefore no evidence to the mind of the new Speaker, Mr. Peel, that he is *still* an atheist.

The session of 1881 brought up the question of obstruction with greater vigour than ever. Mr. Parnell's followers had been considerably increased in numbers by the General Election, they had also increased in determination and daring. The threat of coercive legislation for Ireland was sufficient to incite them to

train to the utmost those powers which had been held to some
extent under control in the preceding years. Their indignation
was first shown by protracted debates over the Address, but it
reached a climax when the Protection of Property Bill was introduced. The first session lasted for twenty-two hours, during
the greater part of which the Irish members spoke almost un-
interruptedly—the speeches for the most part consisting of
wearisome iterations interspersed with occasional breaches of
order. On Monday, Jan. 31, however, matters went further.
Mr. Gladstone determined to take the vote on the introduction
of the bill at that sitting; and Mr. Parnell and his merry men
were equally determined to prevent it. The result was, that the
House sat all that night, right through the next day, and far into
the Wednesday, until forty-one hours and a half had elapsed
from the beginning of the struggle, and the longest sitting in the
history of the House of Commons had been placed on record.
In view of some such tactics, arrangements had been made between the Government and the Opposition for preserving a full
House by regular relays, and the Irish members similarly relieved
one another in the tedious work of speaking against time. The
unfortunate Speaker, Mr. Brand, was relieved at five on Tuesday
morning, by Dr. Lyon Playfair, Chairman of Committees, who sat
through the debate during the greater part of the day, until he
was in turn released from his post by the return of the Speaker.
The proceedings were not quite so dreary as usual, for there were
a number of Irish members who had not yet spoken on the
subject, and the comparative novelty of hearing their views was
quite refreshing after the wearisome iterations which formed the
staple of the course. Most of the Irish members moreover
contrived to be called to order at intervals, and thereby contributed a little excitement, and in this congenial task Mr. Dillon
and Mr. Finigan laboured with the greatest zeal, or, as the
Annual Register has it, "were the most prominent offenders,"
though later on their performances were emulated by those of
Mr. O'Connor Power, Mr. T. D. Sullivan, and Mr. T. P. O'Connor.
At eleven o'clock on Tuesday evening, Sir Richard Cross on
behalf of the Conservative Opposition rose and appealed to the
Speaker to use his power of "naming" obstructives, but Mr.

Brand declined to do so. Later on, Sir Stafford Northcote and
Mr. Childers both rose in turn and informed Dr. Lyon Playfair,
who had once more relieved the Speaker, that if he chose to use
his powers to stop any further obstruction he would be supported
by both sides of the House, but Dr. Playfair also declined their
handsome offer. The return of the Speaker, however, about nine
on Wednesday, was the signal for a *coup d'état* of the most impressive kind. The House was nearly full. Mr. Gladstone and
Sir Stafford Northcote were both in their places. Mr. Biggar was
in the act of addressing the House, and had already spoken for
over an hour. The Speaker at once declared that the time of the
House had now been wasted by systematic obstruction for forty-
one hours, and that the old rules having failed to insure orderly
debate, a new and exceptional course became necessary. He therefore declined to permit any more speaking, and having disposed of
the amendment actually before the House put the question at once.
The Irish members endeavoured to interpose, but they were put
down by unanimous shouts of " Order." When the question had
been put and carried, they sprang to their feet with shouts of
" Privilege," and then rushed tumultuously from the House.

The result of this "disgraceful exhibition" was that both sides
of the House became impressed with the view that the rules of
debate required amending, though naturally there were considerable differences of opinion as to the most suitable form of
amendment. This impression was considerably strengthened by
the events of Feb. 3, when Mr. Gladstone was called on to bring
forward the Government resolutions. Mr. Dillon rose before
him, and refused to sit down in spite of the order of the Speaker.
Immediately "there [1] were loud cries of 'Name him!' while
the Irish members cried 'Point of Order,' and at last the
Speaker in the terms of the standing order said, 'I name you,
Mr. Dillon, as wilfully disregarding the authority of the Chair.'"
Mr. Dillon was promptly suspended, but Mr. Dillon, amid frenzied
cheering of his friends, declined to leave the House, with the
ridiculous result that Serjeant Gosset and some of the messengers
had to be called in to effect his removal by force. As it was

---

[1] Ann. Reg., 1881, p. 54.

ıow quite evident that everybody was in earnest on this occasion, Mr. Dillon avoided the employment of force by walking out of he House, amid loud shouts of " Shame " from the Irish benches. A short wrangle ensued on the subject, and then " Mr. Gladstone[1] ıttempted to resume his speech, but was interrupted immediıtely by The O'Donoghue moving the adjournment of the House. Vo notice was taken of his motion, and Mr. Parnell, in an excited one, called out, ' I move that Mr. Gladstone be no longer heard.' There were loud cheers from the Irish members at this, and :ounter-cries of 'Name him,'" as Mr. Parnell repeated the notion; and The O'Donoghue called out that this was exactly he same motion which Mr. Gladstone himself had made in Mr. O'Donnell's case. The Speaker warned the hon. member hat if he persisted he should have no option but to enforce the :tanding order. Mr. Gladstone was allowed to proceed for a ew sentences, but Mr. Parnell having consulted with his friends, ose and again called out, " I insist on my right to move that Mr. Gladstone be no longer heard." The Speaker then "named" Mr. Parnell in the prescribed form, Mr. Gladstone moved that he e suspended, and the motion was carried. Like Mr. Dillon, Mr. Parnell declined to withdraw until removed by "superior orce," and the same farce of coercion was solemnly gone hrough. As Mr. Parnell retired from the House, his friends ' stood up and waved their hats, cheering vociferously."

Mr. Finigan was very shortly got rid of in a similar manner, ınd as the great body of the Irish members refused to vote on ıis suspension, twenty-eight of them were suspended *en masse* for lisregarding the authority of the Chair, and removed one by one ıy "superior force." Two more followed shortly, and then three, ınd so on, until by 8.30 thirty-six in all had been suspended. The result of all this was that resolutions were carried giving he Speaker special powers to restrict discussion when " urgency " ıas been voted in debate. This rule moreover was intended to ıpply not merely to the wilful and obvious obstruction of the Irish members, but also to more subtle forms of over-criticism of which the House had had occasional experience.

---

[1] Ann. Reg., 1881, p. 59.

The efficacy of the "urgency" rule may be measured by the fact that, in 1882, an autumn session was specially held to create new regulations of debate. A number of resolutions were passed, enabling the Speaker or Chairman of Committees to terminate the debate when the "evident sense of the House" was against its continuance, to suppress various abuses of the forms of the House which were very prevalent, and to keep the debate strictly to the subject in hand. Grand committees were to be appointed to relieve the House by taking over the consideration of all legal and commercial bills, and preparing them for merely a final third reading as it were in the House itself.

Both parties are agreed that the rules of debate are in want of considerable revision in order to render them effective, though the precise amendments requisite are a subject of controversy.

Reader, my task is ended. Future parliamentary historians will some day deliver to the world a fitting estimate of the men of the last decade—of Beaconsfield and Gladstone, Salisbury and Churchill, Hartington, Bright and Chamberlain; will find a niche for Parnell and Bradlaugh, perhaps even rise to the sublimest heights of prose in the apotheosis of Biggar. Now, it were a task at which impartiality itself might shudder. The mean between exaggerated admiration and equally exaggerated dispraise can never be strictly attained until the softening hand of time has smoothed down the angry passions which seem the inevitable concomitant of party differences.

INDEX.

Butler & Tanner, The Selwood Printing Works, Frome, and London.

1/7

M.H.

J.1 u · h